The Objectives of Islamic Law

The Objectives of Islamic Law

The Promises and Challenges of the *Maqāṣid al-Sharīʿa*

Edited by
Idris Nassery, Rumee Ahmed,
and Muna Tatari

Epilogue by
Anver Emon

LEXINGTON BOOKS
Lanham • Boulder • New York • London

Published by Lexington Books
An imprint of The Rowman & Littlefield Publishing Group, Inc.
4501 Forbes Boulevard, Suite 200, Lanham, Maryland 20706
www.rowman.com

Unit A, Whitacre Mews, 26-34 Stannary Street, London SE11 4AB

British Library Cataloguing in Publication Information Available

Library of Congress Cataloging-in-Publication Data

Names: Nassery, Idris, editor. | Ahmed, Rumee, editor. | Tatari, Muna, 1971-, editor.
Title: The objectives of Islamic law : the promises and challenges of the Maqāṣid al-Sharīʿa/ Edited by Idris Nassery, Rumee Ahmed, and Muna Tatari ; epilogue by Anver Emon.
Description: Lanham, Md. : Lexington Books, 2018. | Includes bibliographical references and index.
Identifiers: LCCN 2017052208 (print) | LCCN 2017055565 (ebook) | ISBN 9781498549943 (electronic) | ISBN 9781498549936 (cloth : alk. paper)
Subjects: LCSH: Maqāṣid (Islamic law) | Law reform. | Islamic law.
Classification: LCC KBP442 (ebook) | LCC KBP442 .O25 2018 (print) | DDC 340.5/911—dc23
LC record available at https://lccn.loc.gov/2017052208

∞™ The paper used in this publication meets the minimum requirements of American National Standard for Information Sciences—Permanence of Paper for Printed Library Materials, ANSI/NISO Z39.48-1992.

Printed in the United States of America

Contents

Editors' Introduction

The last century witnessed a meteoric rise in the popularity of the *maqāṣid al-sharīʿa*—loosely translated as "The Objectives of Islamic law"—among scholars of Islamic law. It is little wonder that the *maqāṣid* have received so much attention: in theory, they offer a way to derive and apply Islamic law in the contemporary world using an ancient methodology without being constrained by historical practice. By identifying core principles to which Islamic law must adhere, scholars can look at inherited Islamic laws with fresh eyes to see which continue to accord with those principles, and which do not. Following the work of medieval Muslim jurists like Abū Ḥāmid al-Ghazālī (d. 1111) and Abū Isḥāq al-Shāṭibī (d. 1388), modern scholars promoting the *maqāṣid* have identified five key objectives that Islamic law was designed to protect: life, intellect, lineage, and property. According to the *maqāṣid* theory, historical Islamic laws that continue to protect these objectives can be retained, and those that do not, no matter how entrenched in practice or embedded in religious texts, may be discarded or reformed.

All of this leads to the tantalizing prospect that the entire Islamic legal corpus may be subject to reexamination and reform. Indeed, we saw such a wholesale reexamination in the modern Islamic finance project, which has wholeheartedly embraced the *maqāṣid* approach to reshape Islamic monetary and investment law after the gold standard was dropped in the 1970s. The result has been a proliferation of Islamic financial products that vie for global prominence alongside, and sometimes within, the world's major financial institutions. Even though these financial innovations were necessary due to the introduction of floating currency, the *maqāṣid* played a central role both in justifying financial reforms and in describing how modern financial instruments can function Islamically. Many scholars now reason that if such reforms can be undertaken in the realm of Islamic finance, then other areas of law could similarly reform using the *maqāṣid* method.

No other legal device has received as much attention nor generated as much excitement inside and outside the Muslim world. Numerous institutions have been founded dedicated to the study and propagation of the *maqāṣid*, including the Centre for Islamic Legislation and Ethics at Qatar University, the Institute for Advanced Islamic Studies in Kuala Lumpur, and the Maqasid Research Centre, which has offices in the United Kingdom, Egypt, and Saudi Arabia. Several Muslim countries have provided state funding for further study, and prominent donors have endowed academic chairs, hosted conferences, and subvented publications about the potential and proper application of the *maqāṣid*.

Recently, however, several scholars have signaled caution when it comes to the *maqāṣid* method. They argue that the reforms it promises are limited and are predicated on presumptions about the role of Islamic law in state affairs, thus reinscribing legal boundaries rather than subverting them. They warn that the *maqāṣid* fully support notions of patriarchy, religious exceptionalism, and text fundamentalism that reformists are working against in the modern day. These scholars argue that adopting the *maqāṣid* wholesale would set the reform project back and ensure that inherited Islamic laws never fully reform to accord with more progressive values of gender egalitarianism and universal human rights.

Given the heated and oppositional nature of the debate, Professor Klaus von Stosch and Dr. Idris Nassery organized an international conference at the University of Paderborn in October 2014 titled, "*Maqaṣid al-Shari'ah*: The Objectives of Sharia and Contemporary Challenges." They invited proponents and opponents of the *maqāṣid al-sharīʿa* model to air and share their views on the subject. The resulting conversation was both pointed and productive, resulting in prospects for the future that might direct the *maqāṣid* in new and fruitful directions.

This volume aims to capture important contributions to that conversation, highlight some of the main voices engaged in the debate, and provide direction for the future. For clarity, the book is divided into two sections. The first gives voice to exponents and architects of the *maqāṣid* model who tout the potential for the *maqāṣid* to fashion Islamic law in the mold of justice and equality. In their articles, these scholars outline the contours of the *maqāṣid* as a legal tool (Auda and Kamali), discuss their immediate relevance to key Islamic concepts (Masud and Nassery), and explain how leading thinkers have theorized the *maqāṣid* to great effect (Duderija and Opwis).

The second section includes prominent and promising dissenting voices; these are scholars who argue that the *maqāṣid* have definitive limits that may well compromise their ability to realize their potential. These scholars question the taxonomy of the *maqāṣid* (Ademi Tatari), describe significant conceptual problems with particular objectives (Chaudhry and Khalfaoui), and discuss practical impediments that constrain the application of the *maqāṣid* (Habib Ahmed and Rumee Ahmed). A concluding essay from Anver Emon brings these critiques together under a helpful rubric, shining a light on the political work that the *maqāṣid* perform, the structures that they reinforce, and the social costs they incur.

Together, these articles demonstrate the immediate relevance of the *maqāṣid al-sharīʿa* to myriad social, political, and economic issues. Whether one agrees with the *maqāṣid* approach or not, examining the role of the *maqāṣid* in relation to these issues brings to the fore latent assumptions about justice, religion, and religious law that animate contemporary discussions about Islam and Islamic law in the modern world. It is our hope that this volume will encourage more intense discussion and debate on the scope of the *maqāṣid al-sharīʿa* as a legal tool, and that, in so doing, it will provide a framework for healthy and robust deliberations on the future of Islam and Islamic law in the world today.

We are grateful for the generous financial support provided by the Mercator Foundation, without which the conference in 2014 and this volume would not have been possible. We also want to thank our editor at Lexington Books, Sarah Craig, whose patient guidance and expert advice made the publication process a joy.

Part I

PROMISES

Chapter 1

Goals and Purposes *Maqāṣid al-Sharī'ah*

Methodological Perspectives

Mohammad Hashim Kamali

INTRODUCTION AND SUMMARY

The goals and purposes of Islamic law (*maqāṣid al-sharī'ah*) became the focus of renewed scholarly interest in the latter part of twentieth century and have remained in the forefront ever since. The *maqāṣid* were revived due mainly to their focus on real-life issues of concern to people's welfare. This is shown by the spate of doctoral dissertations, publication of books and conferences that are being held in their name. The methodology of *maqāṣid* has been a part of this renewed attention due to certain legacy issues and weaknesses that affect their utility and relevance to modern law making and governance. Whereas the traditional discourse of *maqāṣid* remained largely in the realm of theoretical jurisprudence, contemporary research on this subject has sought to underline the application of *maqāṣid* to particular themes, such as Islamic banking and finance, science and technology, family law, criminal law, and constitutional law, each representing a relatively new extension of the *maqāṣid* discourse in modern times.

A mere glance at the five essential (*ḍārūriyyāt*) *maqāṣid* that the *sharī'ah* seeks to safeguard and develop, namely of the respect for and promotion of life, protection and promotion of the values of religion and morality, promotion of rationality, knowledge and thoughtful conduct, promotion of property and wealth management, and protection of the family and progeny, all in all shows that the *maqāṣid* are concerned with vital human interests and values. In this regard, the *maqāṣid* offer a markedly different vision and approach to the protection of values compared to that of *uṣūl al-fiqh* (the science of the sources of law) that also upholds these values, but proposes certain methodologies of relevance only indirectly to their advancement.

The methodologies of *uṣūl al-fiqh* are, on the whole, retrospective and somewhat slow to relate effectively to modern legislative and decision-making processes. To speak, for instance, of *ijmā'* (general consensus), *qiyās* (analogical reasoning), and *istiḥsān* (juristic preference), one is likely to be involved in technicalities and methodological details. *Maqāṣid* are inherently dynamic by comparison and open to growth in tandem with changing conditions, just as they are also seen to strike a closer note with the contemporary human rights discourse. That said, it will be noted at the outset that this presentation is premised on a complementarity of values and objectives between the *uṣūl al-fiqh* and *maqāṣid*, visualizing them as two distinctive paths to the understanding of *sharī'ah* that can enrich and endorse one another.

For much of their history the *maqāṣid* remained relatively underdeveloped, due partly to a certain reluctance on the part of Muslim jurists to expatiate into the intents and purposes of the Lawgiver above and beyond what has been stated in the clear text. The onset of *taqlīd* (indiscriminate imitation), which advised unquestioning adherence to past authority and text, added to the problem. The *maqāṣid*-based approach and its methodology were consequently marginalized so much so that many a reputable text of *uṣūl al-fiqh* did not even assign a section or chapter to the study of *maqāṣid.*

The methodology of *maqāṣid* expounded in this presentation begins with the meaning and definition of *maqāṣid* and conditions of their validity, and proceeds to review briefly some of its allied expressions, such as *ḥikmah*, *'illah*, and *maṣlaḥah.* This will be followed by a review and appraisal of the ways in which the *maqāṣid* are known and identified and a review of the classification of *maqāṣid* into various types. We turn next to drawing a distinction between the purposes of *sharī'ah* and the means and accomplishers that are employed to secure them (i.e., *maqāṣid wa wasa'il*). The last segment of this presentation revisits the classification of *maqāṣid* into the category of *ḍārūriyyāt* and raises a question over opening its scope from a restrictive typology toward a more open and evolving aspect of the *maqāṣid.* A selection of the salient legal maxims (*qawā'id kulliyyah fiqhiyyah*) that are presented toward the end accentuate the importance of *maqāṣid* to *ijtihād* and a number of other more specific themes of the *sharī'ah*. The chapter ends with a conclusion and recommendations.[1]

MEANING AND DEFINITION OF *MAQĀṢID*

Maqāṣid (singular: *maqṣad*) signify the intents and purposes of the Lawgiver that the laws of *sharī'ah* seek to realize and protect. The renowned Andalusian scholar, Ibrahim al-Shāṭibī (d. 1388 CE), who developed the *maqāṣid* in the fourth volume of his *al-Muwāfaqāt*, quite surprisingly did not provide a definition for it. Abū Ḥāmid al-Ghazālī (d. 1111), as well as ʿIzz al-Dīn ʿAbd al-Salām al-Sulamī (d. 1262), who preceded al-Shāṭibī, wrote on the *maqāṣid* but they too did not attempt a definition, which did not exist until the Tunisian scholar ibn ʿĀshūr (d .1973) provided one. Ahmad al-Raysūnī, who wrote a book on al-Shāṭibī's work, noted that it was most likely due to the linguistic clarity of *maqṣad/maqāṣid* that such prominent contributors to the subject did not attempt a definition. He added that the renowned legal maxim, *al-umūr bi-maqṣidihā* (human affairs are judged by reference to their purposes), was commonplace and frequently cited from early times.[2]

Ibn ʿĀshūr defined the general objectives (*maqāṣid ʿāmmah*) of the *sharīʿah* as "the deeper meanings (*maʿānī*) and inner wisdom (*ḥikam*) that the Lawgiver has contemplated in respect of all or most of the *sharīʿah* ordinances."[3] Muḥammad al-Zuḥaylī provided a more detailed definition of *maqāṣid* as "the ultimate goals, aims, consequences and meanings which the *sharīʿah* has upheld and established through its laws, and consistently seeks to realise, materialise and achieve at all times and places."[4] Ibn ʿĀshūr also wrote that the overall purpose of *sharīʿah* (*maqṣad al-tashri' al-'am*) is "to preserve the order and prosperity of the *ummah* through educating and reforming the mental and behavioural self of the individual, [enabling him to] take care of the world around him and what has been placed under his custody and control."[5]

Al-Shāṭibī's contribution to the methodology of *maqāṣid* included induction (*al-istiqra'*) as a method of enquiry by which the *maqāṣid* can be known and identified. He is also noted for his contribution to two other aspects of the methodology of *maqāṣid*: the relationship of *maqāṣid* to *ijtihād*, and how the *maqāṣid al mukallaf*, that is the goals and purposes of the individual and those of the Lawgiver (*maqāṣid al- shariʿ*), relate to one another.[6]

ʿAllāl al-Fāsī (d. 1964) defined the *maqāṣid* as "the hidden meanings (*al-asrār*) and wisdom that the Lawgiver has considered in the enactment of all of the *sharīʿah* ordinances."[7] This definition differs only slightly from that of Ibn ʿAshur in that according to al-Fāsī none of the laws of the *sharīʿah* are without a purpose, whereas Ibn ʿĀshūr held that "all or most of *sharīʿah* ordinances" have their purposes. Al-Fāsī's usage of "hidden meanings—*al-asrār*" invites criticism, as it would fail to meet Ibn ʿĀshūr's four conditions that the general purposes of *sharīʿah* must qualify; they must be certain, evident, general, and exclusive (*thābit, ẓāhir, ʿāmm,* and *ṭard*, respectively).[8] A *maqṣad* is certain when it is protected by clear laws and its validity is not subject to disagreement and dispute; a *maqṣad* is evident if it can be proven, whenever needed, by admissible evidence; it is general when it is not focused on particular individuals, groups, or partisan interests; and it is exclusive when it applies to all its relevant applications while excluding that which is not of concern to it. The purpose of sale, for instance, is transfer of ownership for a price, and that of a gift is transfer of ownership without a price—clear laws establish the two, just as they are also evident, of general application, and mutually exclusive.

According to Yusuf al-Qaraḍāwī, "*maqāṣid al- sharīʿah* consists of the attraction of benefits (*al-maṣāliḥ*) to the people and repelling of harm and corruption (*al-maḍār wa'l-mafāsid*) from them."[9] *Maqāṣid*, according to al-Raysūnī, signify "the end-goals for which the *sharīʿah* has been promulgated in order to realise benefit for God's servants."[10] Even though the jurists have generally concurred that virtually all of the laws of *sharīʿah* have their purposes, it is uncertain however whether they are all known to us, since they are not always declared in the clear text.[11]

Technicalities apart, almost all the definitions of *maqāṣid* are focused on the realization of benefit for the individual and society, indeed for all people, regardless of status, color, and creed, both in this life and the hereafter. The benefits/interests can include a wide spectrum of the material, moral, and spiritual aspects of human life in this world and the next. Since the *maqāṣid* are concerned with human benefit and welfare, they can arguably subsume the contemporary human rights as are expounded in the Universal Declaration of Human Rights, albeit with some reservations.

Ḥikmah, 'Illah, and *Maṣlaḥah*—Are They Synonymous?

Ḥikmah (plural: *ḥikam*) in the sense of wisdom looks toward the positive end or purpose of conduct. It usually refers to the wisdom and end-result of legislation, a beneficial consequence of the *sharīʿah* as a whole, or of a particular ruling thereof. *Ḥikmah* is also used to signify the objective of legislation, in which case *ḥikmah* would be synonymous to *maqṣad.* It is unusual, however, to use *maqṣad* or *maqāṣid* in reference to God the Most High, such as *maqāṣid Allāh*, although *maqāṣid al-shariʿ* (objectives of the Law-Giver) is commonplace. The common expression *hikmat al-tashri'* signifies the philosophy of legislation, or of jurisprudence, in reference to Shariah. *Ḥikmah* and *maqṣad* can almost interchangeably be used in reference to the *sharīʿah.*[12]

The *uṣūlī* discourse on the identification of effective cause or *ʿillah* of a ruling draws a distinction between *ʿillah* and *ḥikmah*, while validating the former and disqualifying the latter; *ʿillah* must be constant and unchangeable (*munḍabiṭ*), but *ḥikmah* is changeable and therefore fails to provide a reliable basis of *ḥukm* and legislation. To illustrate, the *Qur'ān* grants a traveler during the fasting month a concession, which is not to fast. The *ʿillah* of this concession is deemed to be the fact of traveling itself, and not as it were the hardship that it involves, on the analysis that people vary in their tolerance of hardship. Hence, hardship, although the effective cause and *ḥikmah* of the concession, is disqualified and traveling itself is identified as the "correct"

ʿillah. To take a *maqāṣidī* approach to the identification of *ʿillah*, it is proposed that *ḥikmah* should in principle be accepted as a substitute to *ʿillah*. The purpose of the concession in question is evidently to prevent hardship, and traveling itself can sometimes become (as in our time of fast and comfortable means of transport) rather a juristic façade and less than satisfactory for it to be the only valid criterion to the exclusion of *ḥikmah*.

ʿIllah signifies two meanings, namely of cause, as in cause and effect, and in the context of legislation it refers to the effective cause of a ruling (*ḥukm*) of *sharīʿah* for which it was legislated in the first place. In their discussions of the *ʿillah* of analogy (*qiyās*), for instance, the *uṣūl* scholars have stated that *ʿillah* must be constant and unchangeable, (*munḍabiṭ*), whereas *ḥikmah* need not meet this qualification. For al-Āmidī (d. 1233 CE), *ʿillah* refers to the effective cause, or the *ḥikmah* and benefit the Lawgiver has considered in introducing a law.[13] This evidently brings *ʿillah* closer to *maqṣad*, as Muṣṭafā al-Zarqā' also wrote: "*ʿillah* could signify the *ḥikmah* of legislation in reference to the attraction of benefit or prevention of harm that may be sought through a legal command or prohibition." This would also equate *ʿillah* to *maqṣad* for the most part.[14] One may add, however, that *ʿillah* is normally tied to the existing text and status quo of the law, whereas *ḥikmah*, in the sense of end-result and purpose, looks to both the present and future and is also not so closely tied to the specificities of the text and therefore more versatile.[15]

It is often said that the mechanism for the identification of the *ʿillah* of a ruling (i.e., *taʿlīl*) is not very different to that of identifying the goal and purpose (*maqṣad*) of that ruling. However, when one looks into the juristic technicalities of *taʿlīl* and the restrictive approaches the *uṣūl* scholars have taken toward it, it would appear that both the rational and commonsense aspects of identifying the *ʿillah* of a ruling have become burdened by the heavy weight of literalism. Equating the *'illah* and *maqṣad* would therefore have the effect of compromising the versatility and openness of the *maqāṣid*.[16]

In a similar vein, *maqāṣid* are often equated with *maṣāliḥ* (interests, benefits) such that the two are used interchangeably. They do admittedly resemble in many ways but also differ in others. *Maqāṣid* are goals that suggest a degree of finality and permanence, which is not always the case with the *maṣāliḥ*. Abū Ḥāmid al-Ghazālī (d. 1111) and Fakhr al-Dīn al-Rāzī (d. 1198) validate *maṣlaḥah* only when it begets the purpose or *maqṣad* of the law. Al-Shāṭibī characterized the *maqāṣid* as "the fundamentals of religion, basic rules of the revealed law, and universals of belief."[17] Ibn ʿĀshūr similarly described the *maqāṣid* as either "certain, or uncertain close to certainty—*qaṭʿī aw ẓannī qarīb min al-qaṭʿī*."[18] *Maṣāliḥ* are, on the other hand, largely circumstantial and liable to change. Hence, the *maqāṣid* tend to be a rank above the *maṣāliḥ* and in many ways constitute the criteria of validity for them.[19] The *maqāṣid* would also appear to have a stronger base in the *Qur'ān* and *Sunnah*, whereas the *maṣāliḥ*, especially the *maṣāliḥ mursalah* (open or unregulated interests), are not so textually grounded. The *maṣlaḥah* may also be said to have a stronger utilitarian underpinning, whereas the *maqṣad* maintains a wider outlook that often rises above utilitarian concerns.

CLASSIFICATIONS OF *MAQĀṢID*

Maqāṣid have been classified into several types, depending on the viewpoint and purpose of classification. An understanding of the classification of *maqāṣid* into the following five types will also enable the researcher to best utilize the resources of *maqāṣid* and ascertain their application to particular cases and subjects.

From the viewpoint of their relative importance, the *maqāṣid* are classified into the three categories of essential *maqāṣid* (*ḍārūriyyāt*), complementary *maqāṣid* (*ḥājiyyāt*), and desirabilities (*taḥṣīniyyāt*). Only the first of these have been specified into the five headings of the protection, as earlier noted, of life, religion, intellect, family, and property. Briefly, the *ḍārūriyyāt* are essential to the survival of the individual and society, so much so that their destruction would precipitate chaos and collapse of the normal order. The *ḥājiyyāt* are defined as *maqāṣid* that seek to remove severity and hardship, which are, however, not essential to normal life. To illustrate, protection of life, which is an essential *maqṣad* in its own right, cannot be accomplished without attention to health-care facilities such as hospitals and clinics—hence providing them partakes in *ḍarūriyyāt*. This is because the means to a *daruri* also becomes *daruri*. Then if one hospital is not sufficient to provide the needed services for a locality, building a second one is likely to partake in complementary purposes, or *ḥājiyyāt*. *Taḥṣīniyyāt* are in the nature of desirabilities that seek refinement and perfection in people's lives at all levels, and they often complement the previous two classes of *maqāṣid*. For instance, having established a hospital equipped with basic facilities, it may then seem eminently desirable to acquire the more advanced and up-to-date diagnostic equipment, as and when they become available.[20]

From the viewpoint of their scope, *maqāṣid* have been further classified into the three categories of general purposes (*al- maqāṣid al- ʿammah*), particular purposes (*al-maqāṣid al-khāṣṣah*), and partial purposes (*al maqāṣid al-juz'iyyah*).[21]

The general purposes are those that extend to the whole of the *sharīʿah*, and they are altogether broad and comprehensive. Realization of benefit (*maṣlaḥah*), prevention of harm and corruption (*ḍarar, mafsadah*), building the earth (*iʿmār al-arḍ*), administration of justice, and removal of hardship (*rafʿ al-ḥaraj*) are examples of the general purposes of the *sharīʿah*. They differ from particular purposes, which are confined to specific areas and subjects, such as commercial transactions, crimes and punishments, matrimonial law, and so forth. The two are not totally separate in that the particular *maqāṣid* should comply with the broader objectives of the *sharīʿah* and should not go against the general *maqāṣid*.[22]

Partial purposes are those that signify the Lawgiver's intent and purpose regarding particular rulings of the *sharīʿah* in any area or topic. This bears close similarity to the effective cause (*ʿillah*) of a ruling, which the jurist needs to identify in the construction, for example, of analogy (*qiyās*).[23] One of the reasons why the *uṣūl al-fiqh* jurists have not expatiated on the *maqāṣid* is that, in their view, *ʿillah* is about the same as the *maqṣad* of a ruling.[24] That said, as already noted, the *ʿillah* of a ruling may or may not be the same as its purpose. For the *ʿillah* tends to be grounded in the status quo or existing order, whereas its end-goal and purpose may also be looking to the future and beyond status quo.

Maqāṣid have been further classified into the Lawgiver's purposes (*maqāṣid al-sharʿ*) and the human purposes (*maqāṣid al-mukallaf*). To illustrate, God's illustrious purposes of *ʿilm* is advancement of the knowledge of religion, and the rest of His creation whereas seeking employment or university qualifications may represent the human purpose of seeking knowledge. It is recommended that all competent persons should bring, as far as possible, their own purposes into conformity with the *maqāṣid* of the Lawgiver.[25]

Another classification of *maqāṣid* is its division into primary purposes (*al-maqāṣid al-aṣliyyah*), which the Lawgiver, or a human agent, has originally intended, whereas subsidiary purposes (*al-maqāṣid al-tabʿiyyah*) are those that support and complement the primary *maqāṣid*. For instance, the primary purpose of marriage is procreation of the human species, which may or may not materialize in a marriage among elderly persons contracted with the purpose mainly of companionship—which is a secondary purpose.[26]

Lastly, the *maqāṣid* may be either definitive (*qaṭʿī*) or speculative (*ẓannī*). The former signify purposes that are based in a clear text of the *Qur'ān*, *ḥadīth*, or general consensus (*ijmaʿ*), and even induction (*istiqra'*) according to al-Shāṭibī and Ibn ʿĀshūr, whereas the latter may be based on a speculative text, rationality, and *ijtihād*.[27] In the event of a conflict between them, the definitive takes priority over the speculative *maqāṣid*.

IDENTIFICATION OF *MAQĀṢID*

As already mentioned, the *maqāṣid* are either identified by the text (*nass*) or by *ijmaʿ*, failing which they may be identified through *ijtihād*. Al- Shāṭibī suggested that induction (*istiqra'*) is also a reliable method by which to identify the *maqāṣid*. To this, Ibn ʿĀshūr added in line with the writings of 'Izz al-Din 'Abd al-Salam and others that the human intellect (*ʿaql*) and unrestricted reasoning (*istidlāl*) could also identify the *maqāṣid*.[28]

The *Qur'ān* is often expressive of the rationale, benefit, and effective cause of its rulings, or else of the harm and corruption that may ensue their violation and neglect. Ibn Qayyim al-Jawziyyah (d. 1350 CE) has noted that the number of such references in the *Qur'ān* alone reaches not just one or two hundred, as some commentators had estimated, but that in over one thousand places the *Qur'ān* either directly or indirectly and in diverse manner of expressions identifies the rationale, purpose, benefits, and consequences of its rulings. All of these are then used as indicators toward identification of the *maqāṣid*.[29] For instance, when the *Qur'ān* characterizes itself as "guidance and mercy" (*hudan wa raḥmatan*) to the believers (Yunus, 10:57), and also describes Muhammad's prophethood (peace be upon him) as "a mercy to the worlds" (al-Anbiya,' 21:107), and where mercy and *raḥmah* also signify the most favorite of the ninety-nine Excellent Names of God (i.e., *al-Raḥmān* and *al-Raḥīm*), compassion (*raḥmah*) becomes a cardinal *maqṣad* of Islam. Similarly, when the *Qur'ān* describes the law of retaliation (*qiṣāṣ*) as a protector of life (al-Baqarah, 2:179), that of *jihād* as fighting aggression and injustice (al-Hajj, 22:39), and also that the purpose of prayer is to repel immorality and sin (al-'Ankabut, 29:45), the text in each case has identified the *maqṣad*/ purpose of its own ruling.

In a similar vein, the frequent Qur'anic invocations for people to think and exercise their intellect and reason (al-Nisa,'4:83) prompted the Prophet to speak in condemnation of those who "utter the *Qur'ān* without understanding its meaning and purpose."[30] The purpose so conveyed was that one should make an effort to understand the meaning and purpose of the *Qur'ān*.[31]

Whereas the clear text (*naṣṣ*) is the principal carrier of *maqāṣid* by general consensus, the question has arisen whether rationality (*ʿaql*) alone can also validate a *maqṣad* of *sharīʿah* without the authority of a scriptural proof, or *naql*. Some responses are given in the flowing paragraphs:

Clear Text

The Qur'ānic text, or *ḥadīth*, which validates/identifies a *maqṣad*, must be original (*ibtida'i*) and explicit (*tasrihi*), as al-Shāṭibī explained. A text is original if it is not attached to another text or ruling, to which it may be subsidiary or explanatory and therefore not original. A text is also explicit when it conveys its meaning without the aid of interpretation. In the absence of a clear text, one may recourse to what Imam al-Shāfiʿī and al-Ghazali's teacher, al-Juwaynī, have termed as "sound reasoning" (*istidlāl*) and which ʿIzz al-Dīn ʿAbd al-Salām has variously termed as the "intellect" (*al-ʿaql*), "experience" (*al-tajri bah*), and "sound human nature/natural insight" (*al-fiṭrah*). Each of these methods can be used as indicators of the *maqāṣid*, be it independently from one another or in combination, provided that:

a. In the event where a clear text validates a *maqṣad*, there is no other text that would introduce an element of uncertainty or doubt.
b. The *maqṣad* in question does not conflict with another *maqṣad* of equal standing.
c. The *maqṣad* concerned fulfils all four conditions: certainty over its existence (*thubūt*), clarity (*ẓuhūr*—it can be seen for what it is), generality (*'umum*—not limited in scope and obtains in all relevant situations), and exclusiveness (*iṭṭirād*—precluding confusion with its similitudes).

Plurality of methods by which a *maqṣad* is identified and known adds to credibility, while the use, in the meantime, of a single method does not diminish the value of the result arrived at.[32] In the event of a conflict arising between the evidential bases of two *maqāṣid*, recourse may be had to the rules of interpretation pertaining to conflict and preference (*al-ta'āruḍ wa'l-tarjīḥ*) as are explained in *uṣūl al-fiqh*.

Inductive Reasoning (*istiqrā'*)

Al-Shāṭibī proposed *istiqrā'* as a reliable identifier of *maqāṣid* next to the clear text. Here, induction consists of a general reading of the text. There may be a number of textual references to a subject, none of which amounts to a decisive declaration, yet when read together their collective meaning and weight leave little doubt as to the purpose on which they concur. A decisive conclusion may, in other words, be drawn from a plurality of speculative expressions. Al-Shāṭibī illustrates this by saying that nowhere in the *Qur'ān* is there a text to say that the Shariah has been revealed for the benefit of humankind. Yet, this is a definitive conclusion drawn from a general reading of the *Qur'ān*.[33] Similarly, the *Qur'ān* has nowhere enumerated the five essential *maqāṣid* (or *ḍarūriyyāt*) but they are so identified by way of induction and general reading thereof. The inductive method tends to provide insight into the source evidence on *maqāṣid* that can, in turn, reduce the prospects of error and doubt.

Human Intellect (*'aql*)

Can human intellect and judgment be a valid identifier of *maqāṣid* side by side with the text, or even in the absence of a text? Both the early and modern commentators have given different responses, and few would agree that *'aql* alone can validate the *maqāṣid* without any textual evidence. Most have agreed, on the other hand, that reason can evaluate human conduct of concern to temporal affairs, but that reason cannot provide a reliable basis of evaluation on devotional matters (*'ibādāt*).[34] Al-Ghazālī (d. 1111) wrote, "It is by means of ʿ*aql* that people know the benefits of this world."[35] Credibility is given, however, al-Ghazālī added, to the intellect of those with sound judgment and knowledge of the custom and culture of society. ʿIzz al-Dīn ʿAbd al-Salām (d. 1262 CE) observed:

> Temporal benefits and harms are mostly known and identified by ʿ*aql*, not only in the shariah of Islam, but in most other traditions. A person of sound judgment would know, even before the existence of a revealed text, that realisation of a pure benefit or prevention of a pure evil is praiseworthy. The learned in most legal traditions, and all the revealed laws, tend to be in agreement on the prohibition of murder, theft, adultery and the like. . . . As for the benefit/harm of concern to the hereafter, these can only be known by means of transmitted proof (*naql*).[36]

Ibn Taymiyyah's view on the authority of ʿ*aql* is similar but adds a reference to sound human nature (*al-fiṭrah*) that also plays a role in the identification of *maqāṣid*.[37] Al-Juwaynī (1085 CE) discussed the place of sound reasoning (*istidlāl*) in the categories of recognized proofs. The proponents of *istidlāl* were mainly from the Malikī, but also many from the Ḥanafī and Shāfiʿī, schools, all of whom accepted *istiṣlāḥ* (consideration of public interest) as a valid basis of law and judgment in the *shariah*. The Shāfiʿī school holds *istidlāl* to be a valid basis of judgment even if it cannot be traced back to a clear text, provided that it operates close to the meaning and spirit of the established proofs.[38] Imām al-Shāfiʿī referred to the precedent of Companions saying that leading figures among them exercised flexibility; whenever they could not find a textual ruling on a matter, they would resort to sound reasoning—*istidlāl*.[39] Human intellect is informed by the senses, but it has the capacity to go beyond the data of the senses, although it falls short of the wider reaches of revelation (*al-waḥy*). The intellect performs a number of functions. It perceives that which is unseen based on that which is seen, derives universals from concrete particulars, recognizes self-evident truth, and associates causes and effects. It is a criterion of responsibility, and the criterion by which God has honored human beings above the rest of His creation. It is also the only means by which human beings can know the *shariah* and the essence of responsibility and *taklīf*. Human reason is therefore a credible basis of judgment in the absence of revelation, provided that the judgment arrived at is in harmony with the general spirit and guidance of the revealed scripture.

There may be subtle differences between ʿ*aql* and wisdom (*ḥikmah*), yet ʿ*aql* should aim at inclusivity and merger with *ḥikmah*. This may, to some extent, be a question of the input ʿ*aql* can have from custom and culture that generate wisdom through the light of experience. The lessons drawn from past errors should inform one's perspective on formal logic, *istidlāl*, and syllogism that may or may not be endowed in cultural wisdom and the insight gained from experience.

Sound Human Nature (*al-fiṭrah*)

Fiṭrah is the natural disposition and order that God has instilled in every created being. Thus, the *fiṭrah* of human beings is the inward and outward condition of their creation, in intellect and body. "*Fiṭrah*" is a Qur'anic term denoting a human disposition that inheres in every person and thus is universal by the fact that it is common in all human beings. Islam calls its followers to safeguard the *fiṭrah* and preserve its characteristics in the building of a humane civilization.[40] The Qur'anic assignment of the vicegerency of humankind (*istikhlāf*—al-Baqarah, 2:30) makes everyone a carrier of a divine trust and mission to build the earth. *Fiṭrah* thus refers to the natural insight of God's trusted vicegerents, all of whom partake in a sparkle of the divine (Q 38:72), who excel in ranks above the rest of His creatures (Q al-Isra,' 17:70). This is also manifested in Islam's designation of itself as *dīn al-fiṭrah*, a religion that strikes harmony with enlightened human nature.

In his *Kitāb al-Najāt*, Ibn Sīnā (d. 1037 CE) equates *fiṭrah* with intellect (*ʿaql*) in a passage where he speaks of intuitive intellect (*fiṭrah*) endowed in someone who is brought into this world without even prior exposure to society, its realities, and its customs. Then he perceives and comprehends concrete realities and cases. Ibn Sīnā admits, however, that not everything affirmed by *fiṭrah* is true; what is true is the capacity of innate human nature to discern values, good and bad, in what is perceived by the senses.[41]

Ibn ʿĀshūr linked the *maqāṣid* to *al-fiṭrah*, quoting a Qur'ānic text, and concluded that both the *sharīʿah* and its *maqāṣid* bear harmony with *al-fiṭrah*:[42]

> And so, set thy face steadfast toward the one true faith, turning away from all that is false, in accordance with the natural disposition (*fiṭrah*) which God has endowed in humankind. Allow no change to alter (or corrupt) what God has endowed. (al-Rum, 30:30)

The human *fiṭrah* consists of both inward and outward manifestations. Walking on two feet is just as much an aspect of man's physical *fiṭrah* as is his intellect and reason. Similarly, relating effects to their causes and drawing conclusions from them is an intellectual *fiṭrah*. In a similar vein, protection of life and lineage, cooperation for the common good, building the earth, pursuit of knowledge, and intellectual creativity all correspond with the human *fiṭrah*.[43]

For Ibn ʿĀshūr, *fiṭrah* is an aspect of Islam's commitment to universality. He refers to the laws of Hammurabi, of ancient Egypt, Moses, Zoroaster, and ancient India, etc., but adds that none had the characteristics of universality that would transcend their geographic and sociocultural confines in which they appeared. Islam, on the other hand, emerged in an era and setting that had preserved its simplicity in isolation from major civilizational spheres of the ancient world. Islam emerged in an Arabian setting but never confined its outlook to that context and, as the *Qur'ān* proclaimed, brought a universal message for human guidance. Islam recognized the diversity of peoples and cultures, their laws and languages (Q 5:48; 30:22; 2:136), and encouraged recognition and friendship among them (Q 49:13). The Muslim community is described as the mid-most community (*ummatan wasaṭan*), committed to moderation and justice (Q 2:143). El-Messawi observed that through Ibn ʿĀshūr's understanding of *fiṭrah*, one can see how he conceived the universality of Islam and "the proposition that the *sharīʿah* objectives (*maqāṣid*) are grounded in man's *fiṭrah* . . . [signifying] a cardinal attribute of the *sharīʿah*."[44] The natural *fiṭrah* in our human make-up is not all of it known to us, but our intellect can learn much from our inner organisms and bodily architecture, genetic, cellular and intercellular communications, and interactions in and between organs. *Fiṭrah* is not sufficiently studied for us to know how it communicates with our intellect. One can assume, however, that when they go against one another, knowingly or otherwise, a corrective is called for. Whereas rationality is testable through closer scrutiny, *fiṭrah* is not so clearly testable due to our insufficient knowledge of it. Social custom, consultation, and consensus of people of sound nature may be said, however, to be reasonably reliable indicators of *fiṭrah*. The study of *fiṭrah* should enable one to identify what it is one must protect, how Islam protects it, and how does one restore the natural balance once disturbed. This may be illustrated as follows:

a. Many have urged preschooling facilities for children at the early age of two so as to help them become quickly intelligent. This may serve as good socialization, but it is premature and may even deprive children of their childhood. The *fiṭrah* of small children is that they learn by playing, not by studying. Excessive after-school tutoring also tends to rob children of their natural inclinations; they then grow up deprived and emotionally imbalanced.
b. The incessant drive for technological progress has taken industrial powers to an overutilization of earth's natural resources. The urge to gain a technological edge over a rival industry or country often results in indefensible sacrifices of human lives and values. The arms manufacturers stand out for their total disregard of natural human rights and values. Environmental degradation and the ever-increasing natural disasters are proof of these excesses and those of the oil-producing countries and companies in their

aggressive drive for commercial gain. The natural balance demanded by *fiṭrah* has been disturbed, and, in some cases, to the point of irreversibility.

c. Mainstream media and advertisements have turned women into sex symbols that denigrate their human dignity. One can advertise an elegant car for what it is without the addition of a half-naked woman to the picture. Yet the imbalances of greed and abusive advertising exceed natural *fiṭrah* and, worse still, put a car above the price of human dignity.
d. Similar tendencies of upsetting the natural balance of values could be seen in situations where the priorities of motherhood are neglected, and society bears the costs. Children are sometimes deprived of their mothers' time and attention.

PURPOSES AND MEANS (*MAQĀṢID WA WASĀ'IL/MUKAMMILĀT*)

The *sharīʿah*, in its entirety, consists of purposes (*maqāṣid*) and the means and accomplishers (*wasā'il* sing. *wasīlah*, also known as *mukammilāt*) toward attaining those purposes. A *wasā'il /mukammil* is the means that helps to achieve the intended result of the particular *maqṣad* it is attached to, be it an essential purpose (*ḍarūrī*), a complementary one (*ḥājī*), or a desirable (*taḥsīnī*). Means and accomplishers include the causes indicating the *sharīʿah* rules, the conditions necessary for their implementation, and the absence of impediments. Whereas the means are liable to change with the change of circumstances, the purposes/*maqāṣid* command greater stability and permanence.[45] The *maqāṣid* are also desired in themselves, whereas the *wasā'il/mukkammilāt* are not, as they are liable to substitution and change. The means are normally subsumed by their ends, depending on the strength or weakness of the relationship between them. If the means in question is indispensible to securing its relevant *maqṣad*, then according to the legal maxim, "That without which a *wājib* (obligatory command) cannot be accomplished also becomes a *wājib*." This maxim refers to means that is instrumental to its end but not to one that may be related only to a subsidiary or incidental aspect thereof.[46] The reverse of this is also true in that the means to a *haram* also partakes in *haram*. Unlawful means cannot therefore bring about lawful results—both the ends and means must be lawful. Confusing the means with its end can often result in the neglect of a *maqṣad* or exaggeration in the importance of means, and the subject, therefore, calls for a degree of jurisprudential insight.[47]

The means to a *maqṣad* may have been identified in the text of the *Qur'ān* or *ḥadīth,* failing which they are identified by rational enquiry and *ijtihād*. To illustrate the accomplisher of an essential *maqṣad*, the *Qur'ān* enjoins that a future obligation (*dayn*), or a mortgage (*rahn*) should be documented and reduced into writing (al-Baqarah, 2:283). This is to ensure preservation of property (*ḥifẓ al-māl*), which is one of the essential *maqāṣid*. Documentation in this case is not a goal in itself but a means toward the protection of an essential goal. Then, by way of analogy, the same requirement is extended to all contracts, pecuniary rights and obligations, which should also be documented in order to prevent future disputation and conflict over them.

To illustrate the accomplisher of a complementary purpose (*mukammil al-ḥājī*), a reference may be made to contractual options (*al-khiyārat*, sing. *khiyār*) that can be appended to a sale's contract. Upon concluding a sale, for instance, the purchaser may stipulate an option that he will ratify the deal in two or three days. The permissibility of sale, here, can be seen as a complementary purpose (*ḥājī*) in itself, if looked at independently, but it is also a means in relationship to an essential *maqṣad* (*ḍarūrī*), which is protection of property (*ḥifẓ al-māl*). Inserting an option into a sale contract merely serves as an accomplisher (*mukammil*) of the sale contract to ensure that it is validly concluded and free also of uncertainty and misrepresentation (*gharar*). To illustrate the accomplisher of a *taḥsīnī*, or a desirable *maqṣad*, in relationship to the permissibility of sale, one may refer to any legitimate means that keep the market place clean and clear of transactions over unclean, poisonous, and objectionable substances.[48]

It is a condition of the accomplisher (*mukammil*), however, that it does not exceed nor overrule the initial purpose that it seeks to accomplish. To take our previous example of sale and option again, the purpose of the option as a *mukammil* is to prevent uncertainty and ignorance (i.e., *gharar*) in a sale, but if one were to exaggerate the *mukammil* and demand total exclusion of *gharar* altogether, it would be difficult to achieve the purpose and may even obstruct the sale. For a slight *gharar* is unavoidable and usually tolerated in many transactions, including sale. To give another example, the existence of counter-values in an exchange contract is desirable as existence of the subject matter accomplishes the purpose of sale very well. Yet, if this were to be demanded in a contract of lease (*ijārah*), it would nullify the contract as only one of the two sides of the contract is usually present in *ijārah*, not both. Thus, to demand the accomplisher of sale in *ijārah*, on the assumption that *ijārah* is also a variety of sale, would exceed the characteristics of *ijārah* and may obstruct it altogether.[49]

When there are numerous means for the realization of one and the same purpose, the one that is most likely to secure the purpose in a complete, prompt, and direct manner must be selected. Should there be a situation, however, where several available means are equally good in order to realize a particular *maqṣad*, then any one or more may be selected for the purpose. The *sharī'ah*, thus, provides certain guidelines with regard to the selection of means, this being an area where flexibility and choice are granted and the individual trader, or scholar/judge, is expected to make appropriate decisions in the light of attendant circumstances.[50]

SCOPE OF *MAQĀṢID* REVISITED

The renowned Hanbali scholar, Ibn Taymiyyah (d. 1328 CE), who attempted to widen the scope of the *maqāṣid* so long ago, observed that anyone who reads the *Qur'ān* will find a variety of other values that also merit recognition, well beyond the scope of the five essentials. Thus, he added such other themes as fulfillment of contracts, trustworthiness (*amānah*), honoring one's neighbor, sincerity, and moral rectitude, reaching the conclusion that *maqāṣid* are open-ended and evolving.[51] Ibn Taymiyyah's approach has found common acceptance among leading twentieth-century jurists, including Ibn ʿĀshūr, Muḥammad al-Ghazālī (d. 1996), Yusuf al-Qaraḍāwī, Ahmad al-Raysūnī, Jamal al-Din Attia, Muḥammad Sirāj, and many others.[52]

Al-Qaraḍāwī added justice, human dignity, and human rights, especially the rights of the oppressed, freedom, and social welfare assistance, to the five leading *maqāṣid*, on the analysis that all of these find support in the *Qur'ān*.[53] Ghazālī, Attia, and Sirāj also made a strong case for the inclusion of equality and justice among the higher *maqāṣid*.[54] The present writer also proposes peace, economic development, science research, and fundamental constitutional rights to the list of the leading *maqāṣid*.[55]

Ibn ʿĀshūr noted that the conventional *maqāṣid* are, on the whole, premised on the well-being of individuals, thus leaving out well-being of the Muslim community as a *maqṣad*. Since the *ummah*'s well-being and international standing depend on its economic and scientific success, these should also be included in the *maqāṣid*. And then again, if the well-being of the *ummah* necessitates its unity, that too should be included.[56] Al-Qaraḍāwī similarly observed,

> I believe there is a category of *maqāṣid* which has not been duly recognised, namely those that concern the society at large. For if most of the *maqāṣid* are related to the individual, such as preservation of the individual's religion, life, faculty of reason, material wealth etc., then where do we stand with regard to such other goals as freedom, equality and justice, and how are they to be evaluated?[57]

Muḥammad al-Ghazālī posed the question: Are we not entitled to benefit from the fourteen centuries of Islamic history? Corrupt rule over the centuries led to baneful outcomes. Hence, we could add freedom and justice to the five essentials. Justice is a cardinal objective of Islam by the unequivocal testimony of the *Qur'ān* and *Sunnah*. Similarly, the affairs of community and state can hardly be regulated without the guarantee of freedom. Since the *Qur'ān* advocates freedom, it too should be recognized as a goal and *maqṣad* of the *sharīʿah*.[58] To this, al-Raysūnī added that the existing list of *ḍarūrīyyat* is based on *ijtihād* (in particular of Abu Hamid al-Ghazali) and so is the idea of raising their number beyond the initial five. There are other vital interests whose importance the religion has unequivocally affirmed, there remaining no reason why they too should not be added to the five recognized *maqāṣid*.[59]

Another aspect of the attempt to open the scope of *maqāṣid* is to facilitate their use as criteria of evaluation of *sharīʿah* rulings, *fatwā* and *ijtihād*. Traditional Islamic scholarship accorded this status to *uṣūl al-fiqh*. We now propose that the *maqāṣid* could also play this role while retaining, in the meantime, its nexus with the resources of *uṣūl al-fiqh*. The purpose is to strike a balance between the rules of *sharīʿah* and its higher goals and purposes, while ensuring also that our formulas and methods do not engage in burdensome technicalities. Methodological accuracy is undoubtedly important, yet it should not distance the modern reader of *sharīʿah* from the goals and purposes of *sharīʿah*—something that the *uṣūl al-fiqh* methodology has been unable to avoid. Human welfare remains as the mega-purpose of *sharīʿah*, an attempt or approach that facilitates human welfare should be encouraged, not otherwise. To quote al-Shāṭibī:

> Since it is established that the rules of *sharīʿah* aim to serve human interests, it follows that human action should be judged on its basis. . . . When an act is legitimate in both essence and appearance, no difficulty arises. However, if an act is consistent [with the law] in appearance yet contrary to human interest, it is invalid, and anyone who acts contrary to human welfare is engaged in an illegitimate exercise.[60]

Ibn Rushd al-Qurtubi (d .1198 CE) did not specifically write on *maqāṣid*. However, in the conclusion of his renowned book, *Bidāyat al-Mujtahid*, he identified moral and spiritual virtues such as gratitude, purity, truth, generosity, and justice as the ultimate objectives of all law. In an article on Ibn Rushd, Ahmad al-Raysūnī observed that Ibn Rushd's inclusion of the moral and spiritual aspects of conduct among the cardinal purposes of the *sharīʿah* (*al-maqāṣid al-ʿulyā li'l-sharīʿah*) was prompted by the fact that they are often overshadowed by legalities, yet so frequently emphasized in the *Qur'ān* side by side with faith, purity, and wisdom.[61] Ibn Qayyim al-Jawziyyah also emphasized the primacy of ethical norms to the whole structure of Islamic values:

> The *sharīʿah* is founded in wisdom and realisation of people's welfare in this life and the next. It is all about justice, mercy, and the common good. Thus any ruling that replaces justice with injustice, mercy with its opposite, common good with mischief, and wisdom with indiscretion does not belong to the *sharīʿah*, even if it is claimed to be so according to some interpretations.[62]

Ibn ʿĀshūr speaks of the greatest purpose (*al-maqṣad al-aʿẓam*) of the *sharīʿah*, as being "realisation of well-being, integrity, prevention of harm and corruption." The all-encompassing objective (*al-maqṣad al-ʿāmm*) of the *sharīʿah* is "prevention of normal order in the *ummah* and perpetuating its well-being and integrity through the well-being and integrity of . . . the whole of the human race."[63]

The *maqāṣid* can also be used to minimize the scope of disagreement in *ijtihād* and the differential conclusions that Muslim schools and scholars have often derived through *ijtihād, istidlāl* (open reasoning), and other *uṣūl al-fiqh* doctrines. One could expect wider levels of agreement if the *uṣūl* doctrines are read, not as independent tools and formulas, but in the light of their higher goals and purposes. It is not unusual, for instance, to see different juristic results from the application of analogy (*qiyās*) by different jurists that often stand in questionable relationship with their original objective and purpose. Had the leading *madhāhib* agreed over the primacy of *maqāṣid* and accorded them due prominence, greater uniformity in their rulings and interpretations could be expected.[64]

According to a survey report on the Sunnite and Shia applications of *maqāṣid*, it was found that their differences are minimal. Both tend to discuss

> the same topics: *ijtihād, qiyās, ḥuqūq, qiyam, akhlāq* and so on, they refer to the same jurists and books—al-Juwaynī's *Burhān*, Ibn Bābawayh's *ʿIlal al-Sharāʾiʿ*, al-Ghazālī's *Mustaṣfā*, al-Shāṭibī's *Muwāfaqāt*, and Ibn ʿĀshūr's *Maqāṣid*—and use the same theoretical classifications—*maṣāliḥ, ḍarūriyyāt, ḥājiyyāt, taḥsīniyyāt, maqāṣid ʿāmmah, maqāṣid khāṣṣah* and so on.[65]

The *ummah* of today is in greater need of consensus rather than *ikhtilāf* (disagreement). Our *ʿulamāʾ* and leaders are therefore reminded to nurture consensus and unity in their deliberations. This can be achieved by taking a more purposive/*maqāṣidi* approach to legal enquiry and research.

Based on the foregoing, the scope of *maqāṣidi* may be revised from its designated list of five toward an open-ended scale of values. The higher goals and purposes of the *sharīʿah* can logically not be limited to a particular number, simply because the *sharīʿah* itself is not limited in that order. Our understanding of the *sharīʿah* is one of its continuing relevance, development, and growth through independent reasoning (*ijtihād*), renewal, and reform (*tajdīd, iṣlāḥ*).[66] Hence, the goals and purposes of *sharīʿah* must also remain an evolving chapter of the juristic and civilizational edifice of Islam. We further propose to the institutions of research in Islamic law and major centres of higher learning in Muslim countries, consultative bodies and parliaments, to make unity and consensus-building over the *maqāṣid* a part of their collective endeavor and *ijtihad*.

LEGAL MAXIMS RELATING TO *MAQĀṢID*

Before concluding, we attach below a list of selected legal maxims that underline the importance of *maqāṣid* to *ijtihād* and various other themes of the *sharīʿah*. Most of these are self-explanatory, yet concise and expressive of the centrality of *maqāṣid* to the understanding of the *sharīʿah* and *sharīʿah*-based research.[67]

- "Acts are judged by their intentions". إنما الأعمال بالنيا ت (*ḥadīth*-cum-legal maxim)
- "[People's] affairs are determined by reference to their purposes"
الأمور بمقاصدها.
- "All dispositions that deviate from their [proper] purposes are null and void."
كل تصرف تقاعد عن تحصيل مقصوده فهو با طل.
- "Observance of purposes is always given priority over the observance of means."
مراعاة المقاصد مقد مة على رعا ية الوسـائل أبدا.
- "The whole of the *sharīʿah* is meant to subjugate whimsical desires of individuals to the purposes of the Lawgiver."
وضع الشريعة على أن تكون أهواء النفوس تابعة لمقاصد الشرعي.
- "Hindrances are not desired by the Lawgiver."
الموانع ليست بمقصودة للشار ع.
- "Facilitation is one of the objectives of *sharīʿah*."
من مقاصد الشريعة التيسير.
- "The means are subsumed by the value/ruling of their purposes."
الوسا ئل لها حكم المقاصد.
- "Building the earth and continuity of its benefits for the good of its inhabitants are a general objective of the *sharīʿah*."
المقاصد العا م للشريعة هو عمارة الأرض و إستمرار صلا حها بصلاح المستخلفين فيها.
- "A transaction that contradicts its [proper] purpose is invalid."
المعاملة بنقيض المقصود فاسد .
- "The purposes of *sharīʿah* are known by reference to the *Qur'ān*, the *sunnah*, and general consensus."
مقاصد الشرع تعرف بالكتا ب والسنة والإجماع.
- "Knowledge of the original context and occasions of revelation cast light on the purpose of the Lawgiver."
معرفة أسبا ب النزول والورود تكشف عن مقصود الشار ع.
- "The purposes of the *sharīʿah* and its benefits are known by reference to sound human nature."
مقاصد الشريعة ومصا لحها تعرف با لفطرة.
- "When there is no purpose to something it is invalid."
ما لا يترتب عليه مقصود فهو باطل.
- "The purpose of the *sharīʿah* behind legislation is validation/enactment and change."

مقصد الشريعة من تشريع تغير وتقرير.

- "Enactment of laws is to secure both the immediate and future benefits [of the people]."
  وضع الشرع إنما هو للمصا لح الأبد في الآجل والعا جل.
- "Looking into the consequences of acts is a valid purpose of the *sharīʿah*."
  النظر إلى مآلات الافعال معتبر مقصود شرعا.
- "The Lawgiver's purpose concerning the competent person is for the latter to align his action with the purpose of His law."
  قصد الشارع من المكلف أن يكون قصده في عمله موافقا لقصده في التشريع.
- "The Lawgiver's purposes can only be established through certainty or strong probability."
  مقاصد الشارع لا تثبت إلا با لقطع أو بالظن الراجح.
- "Credibility in words and acts is attached to their purposes and meanings."
  الاعتبا ر بالمقاصد والمعاني في الأقوال والأفعال.
- "The purposes of the *sharīʿah* provide permanent recourse for safeguarding the basics of legislation and adjudication in Islamic jurisprudence."
  مقاصد الشريعة هي المرجع الأبدي لاستقاء ما يتوقف عليه التشريع والقضاء في الفقه الإسلا مي.
- "The purposes of the *sharīʿah* are grounded in pristine human nature."
  إبتناء مقاصد الشريعة على الفطرة.
- "Primary and explicit prohibitions are indicative of the purposes of the Lawgiver."
  د لت النواهي الإبتدائية التصريحية على قصد الشرعي.
- "The general principles of *maqāṣid* can be established through inductive reasoning."
  كليا ت المقاصد إنما تثبت بالإستقراء.
- "All aspects of *ijtihād* require knowledge of the purposes [of the *sharīʿah*]."
  جميع وجوه الاجتها د تحتاج إلى معرفة المقاصد.
- "The valid purposes of contracts influence determination of their validity and vitiation."
  القصود.في العقود معتبرة تؤثر في صحة العقد وفسا ده.
- "Should the issue revolve around observance either of the literal meaning or the purpose of a word, the latter prevails."
  إذا دار ت المسألة بين مراعاة اللفظ ومراعا ت القصد فمراعاة القصد أولى.

"Forbearance and ease are among the higher purposes of religion."
السماحة واليسر من مقاصد الدين.

- "Protection of religion is a primary purpose of the *sharīʿah*."
  حفظ الد ين مقصد شرعي كلي.
- "Protection of life is a primary purpose of the *sharīʿah*."
  حفظ النفس مقصد شرعي كلي.
- "Protection of reason is a primary purpose of the *sharīʿah*."
  حفظ العقل مقصد شرعي كلي.
- "Protection of lineage is a primary purpose of the *sharīʿah*."

حفظ النسل مقصد شرعي كلي.

- "In the event of conflict among benefits/purposes, that which is certain takes priority over the uncertain and doubtful."
عند تعارض مصلحتين او مقصود ين يجب تقد يم الا قوى.

CONCLUSION AND RECOMMENDATIONS

The methodology of *maqāṣid* explored in this presentation has reviewed the current state of scholarship and contributions of prominent authors to the subject. It has also identified areas where further development and diversification can enrich the existing methodology of *maqāṣid*. An attempt has thus been made to explore additional indicators for the identification of *maqāṣid*, which was followed by a reappraisal of the conventional methodology over the classification and identification of *maqāṣid* and the avenues of their enhancement. The evidence presented thus far sustains the following conclusions:

- Methodological guidelines are needed to curb arbitrariness in the identification and employment of *maqāṣid*. A sound methodology inspires credibility and plays a key role in the proper understanding and future growth of *maqāṣid* as a distinctive discipline of the *sharīʿah*.
- The *uṣūl al-fiqh* methodology has historically provided the criteria of credibility and can still serve that purpose. Yet, the *uṣūl* methodology bears the vestiges of a different era and falls short of accommodating the demands of contemporary challenges facing the *ummah*. Compared to the *uṣūl* doctrines, the *maqāṣid* provide a more promising prospect and methodology to find valid *sharīʿah*-based responses to new issues.
- The *maqāṣid* provide an open and evolving chapter of the *sharīʿah* that can grow in tandem with the needs and aspirations of today's Muslims. The desire to rejuvenate the dynamism of Islamic thought can be better served through *maqāṣid*-oriented *ijtihād*.
- Equipped with a credible methodology to ensure the proximity and relevance of *maqāṣid* to the scriptural guidelines of Islam, the *maqāṣid* also provide a promising prospect for the advancement of values held in common between Islam and other civilizations.
- *Maqāṣid* should be given adequate coverage in the university teaching programmes of Islamic jurisprudence. This is beginning to be the case generally, yet greater attention to *maqāṣid* that would reflect the current state of scholarship on the subject is still wanting.
- It is submitted that Muslim leaders, parliamentarians, and judges should take the *maqāṣid* as a basis of justification for legislative and judicial

reform. This would make a meaningful contribution to stemming the hostile overtures of the so-called "clash of civilisations" in favour of peaceful coexistence and engagement.

- The specific applications of *maqāṣid* to new issues should naturally fulfill, in every case, all its conditions of validity and methodological postulates.
- Since the essential *maqāṣid* are all concerned with the protection and advancement of human welfare objectives, they can help unite the people in their common quest for improving the moral and material aspects of their lives across religious and ethnic divides.
- The methodology of *maqāṣid* is still a work in progress. This presentation has only addressed some aspects of that methodology. It is hoped that other researchers explore the prospects of how the maqasid can best be actualized and developed into pragmatic formulas for better ways of promoting accountability and good governance in Muslim countries.[68]

NOTES

1. Some of the subthemes of the methodology of *maqāṣid*, such as the ways in which the *maqāṣid* relate to *ijtihād* and to *uṣūl al-fiqh*, respectively, are not elaborated here as they are somewhat tangential to the methodology of *maqāṣid*, and the reader can in any case find a fuller treatment of these in Mohammad Hashim Kamali, *Shari'ah Law: An Introduction* (Oxford: Oneworld Publications, 2008), 123–141.

2. Aḥmad al-Raysūnī, *Naẓariyyāt al-Maqāṣid 'ind al-Imām al-Shāṭibī*, Engl. tr. as *Imam al-Shatibi's Theory of the Higher Objectives and Intents of Islamic Law* by Nancy Roberts (Herndon, VA: International Institute of Islamic Thought, 2006), 17.

3. Muḥammad al-Ṭāhir Ibn 'Āshūr, *Maqāṣid al-Sharī'at al-Islāmiyyah*, ed. Muḥammad al-Ṭāhir al-Missāwī (Amman: al-Basā'ir li'l-Intāj al-'Ilmī, 1998), 171. This book was first published in 1946, whereas 'Allāl al-Fāsī's book (see note below) was published in 1963.

4. Muḥammad al-Zuhaylī, *Maqāṣid al-Sharī'ah*: *Asās li-Huqūq al-Insān*, Kitab al-Ummah Series No. 87 (Doha: Ministry of *Awqāf* and Islamic Affairs of Qatar, 2003), 70.

5. Ibid., 63.

6. See for details on *al-istiqra'* and *al-Shāṭibī's* work on *Maqāṣid*, Mohammad Hashim Kamali, *Shari'ah Law*, 132f.

7. 'Allal al-Fāsī, *Maqāṣid al-Sharī'at al-Islāmiyyah wa Makārimuhā* (Casablanca: Maktabat al-Waḥdat al-'Arabiyyah, n.d.), 3.

8. Ibn 'Āshūr, *Maqāṣid*, 63. See also on the definition and conditions of *maqāṣid*, Mohammad Hashim Kamali, *Maqāṣid al-Shari'ah, Ijtihad and Civilisational Renewal*, Occasional Paper 20 (London: The International Institute of Islamic Thought, and Kuala Lumpur: the International Institute of Advanced Islamic Studies [IAIS] Malaysia, 2012), 6–7.

9. Yūsuf al-Qaraḍāwī, *Fiqh al-Zakāt* (Beirut: Mu'assasat al-Risālah, 2000), 1:31.

10. al-Raysūnī, *Naẓariyyāt*, 19. For a more detailed discussion of Raysūnī's definition and its critique, see Mohammad Hashim Kamali, "Law and Ethics in Islam: The Role of the *Maqāṣid*," in *New Directions in Islamic Thought: Exploring Reform and Muslim Tradition*, ed. Kari Vogt, Lena Larson, and Christian Moe (London: I. B. Tauris, 2009), 23–47.

11. Cf. ʿAbd al-Raḥmān Ibrāhim Zayd al-Kīlānī, *Qawāʿid al-Maqāṣid ʿind al-Imām al-Shāṭibī* (Damascus: Dār al-Fikr, 2000), 128.

12. Cf., Ẓaheer al-Dīn bin ʿAbd al-Raḥmān, *Maqāṣid al-sharīʿah fī aḥkām al-buyūʿ* (Kuala Lumpur: International Islamic University Malaysia [IIUM] Press, 2009), 16–17.

13. Sayf al-Dīn al-Āmidī, *al-Iḥkām fī Uṣūl al-Aḥkām*, ed. ʿAbd al-Razzāq ʿAfīfī, 4 vols (Beirut: al-Maktab al-Islāmī, 1982, 2nd ed.), 3:180.

14. Muṣṭafa Aḥmad al-Zarqā, *al-Madkhal al-Fiqhī al-ʿAmm* (Damascus: Dār al-Qalam, 1998), 1:392. Without engaging in technicalities, the *uṣūl* scholars define *ʿillah* as an attribute of the *ḥukm*, which is constant (*munḍabiṭ*) and evident (*ẓāhir*) and bears a proper (*munāsib*) relationship to the ruling (*ḥukm)* of the text.

15. See for details Mohammad Hashim Kamali, *Principles of Islamic Jurisprudence*, revised and enhanced edition (Cambridge: Islamic Texts Society, 2003), 274f.

16. See for details on *taʿlīl*, Kamali, *Principles*, 46f, and on the *uṣūlī* treatment of *maqāṣid*, Kamali, *Shari'ah Law*, 124f.

17. In the Arabic original: "*uṣūl al-dīn wa qawāʿid al-sharīʿah wa kulliyāt al-millah*," see Abū Isḥāq Ibrāhīm b. Mūsā al-Shāṭibī, *al-Muwāfaqāt fī uṣūl al-sharīʿah*, ed. ʿAbd-Allāh Darrāz, 4 vols. (Beirut: Dār al-Maʿrifah, 1975, 2nd ed.), 2:25.

18. Ibn ʿĀshūr, *Maqāṣid*, 225.

19. This is the view of Abū Ḥāmid al-Ghazālī, who validated *maṣlaḥah* only if it promoted the *maqāṣid*.

20. See for details and illustrations Mohammad Hashim Kamali, *Principles of Islamic Jurisprudence* (Kuala Lumpur: Ilmiyyah Publishers, 1998), 397–99.

21. This third class (i.e., *juz'iyyah*) has also its correlative, namely *al-maqāṣid al-kulliyyah*, or totalitarian purposes. However, the last category is almost identical with "general purposes"; hence, we combine the two classifications into one that consists of three varieties.

22. Cf., Muhammad Ibrahim Naqashi, "*Amaliyyāt al-Taṣkīk wa Dawruhā fi Taḥqīq Maqāṣid al-Sharīʿah al-Islāmiyyah,*" in IIUM Conference Proceedings, Vol. 2, Maqsid al-Shariah, 62.

23. Cf., Gamal Eldin Attia, *Towards Realisation of the Higher Intents of Islamic Law: Maqāṣid al-Shari'ah—A Functional Approach*, Eng. trans. by Nancy Roberts (London: The International Institute of Islamic Thought, 2007), 112.

24. Yet, the present writer has argued that this could also mean an attempt to subsume the *maqāṣid* under the *uṣūl* methodology and thus deny them independent recognition. See for further detail, Mohammad Hashim Kamali, "*Maqāṣid al-Sharīʿah* and *Ijtihad* as Instruments of Civilisational Renewal," *Islam and Civilisational Renewal*, Vol. 2, no. 2 (January 2011), 251f.

25. Abu Ishaq Ibrahim al-Shatibi, al-Muwāfaqāt fi-Usul al- *Sharī'ah*, ed. 'Abd Allah Diraz (Cairo: al-Maktabah al-Tijariyyah al-Kubra, n.d, Vol. II), 400. See also Attia, *Towards Realisation*, 113.

26. See for details on the classification of *Maqāṣid*, Kamali, *Shariah Law*, 134–37.

27. Ibid, 134.

28. See for details on *al-istiqra' and al-Shāṭibī's work on Maqāṣid*, Mohammad Hashim Kamali, *Shari'ah law*, 20f.

29. Ibn Qayyim al-Jawziyyah, *I'lām al-Muwaqqi'īn 'an Rabb al-'Alamīn*, ed. Ṭaha 'Abd al-Ra'ūf Sa'd (Beirut: Dār al-Jīl, 1973, Vol. 1), 169; see also Ahmad al-Raysuni, "al-Bahth fi maqāṣid al-shariah: Nish'atuh, Tatawwuruh wa Mustaqbaluh," in *Maqāṣid al-Shariah*, ed. El-Awa, 185.

30. Muḥammad b. Ismā'īl al-Bukhārī, *Ṣaḥīḥ al-Bukhārī* (Beirut: Dār al-Ma'rifah, 1961), *ḥadīth* no. 3344; *Ṣaḥīḥ Muslim*, ed. Muḥammad Fu'ād 'Abd al-Bāqī (Beirut: Dār Iḥyā' al-Turāth, 1980), *ḥadīth* no. 1064.

31. CF., Allal al-Fāsī, *Maqāṣid al-Shariat al-Islamiyyah wa Makarimuha* (Casablanca: Maktabat al-Wahdah al-'Arabiyyah, n.d.), 88.

32. Cf., Ibn 'Āshūr, *Maqāṣid*, 51; Gamal Eldin Attia, *Towards Realisation*, 16.

33. al-Shāṭibī, *al-Muwāfaqāt*, 1:243; see also Yūsuf al-Qaraḍāwī, *Madkhal li-Dirāsat al-Sharī'ah al-Islāmiyyah* (Cairo: Maktabah Wahbah, 1990), 64–65; Kamali, *Shari'ah Law*, 132.

34. This is the view of al-Juwaynī, al-Sarakhsī, al-Sulamī, and Ibn Taymiyyah. It is also noted that since Imam Mālik accepted *maṣlaḥah mursalah* as a basis of law and judgment, he can be assumed to have accepted *'aql* as a proof also of the *maqāṣid*. See for details Ẓaheer al-Dīn, *Maqāṣid*, 102f.

35. Abū Ḥāmid al-Ghazālī, *Iḥyā' 'Ulūm al-Dīn* (Cairo: al-Maktabat al-Tijāriyyat al-Kubrā, n.d.), 4:115.

36. 'Izz al-Dīn 'Abd al-Salām, *Qawā'id al-Aḥkām fī Masāliḥ al-Anām*, ed. 'Abd al-Laṭīf 'Abd al-Raḥmān (Beirut: Dār al-Kutub al-'Ilmiyyah, 1999), 1:8.

37. Cf., Ẓaheer al-Dīn, *Maqāṣid*, 104.

38. Imām al-Ḥaramayn al-Juwaynī, *al-Burhān fī Uṣūl al-Fiqh* (Doha: Dār al-Qalam, 1978), 2:114.

39. Ibid., 2:117.

40. Cf., Anas al-Shaikh-Ali & Shiraz Khan, eds., *Ibn Ashur Treatise on Maqasid al-Shari'ah* (London: International Institute of Islamic Thought, 2013), 7.

41. Abū 'Ali Ibn Sīnā, *Kitab al-Najāt fi' l-ḥikmah al-Manṭiqiyyah wa'l-Tabī'iyyah wa 'l-Ilāhiyyah*, ed. Majīd Fakhrī (Beirut: Dār al-Āfāq al-Jadīdah, 1985), 99.

42. Ibn 'Āshūr, *Maqāṣid*, 58.

43. Ibid., 266.

44. Mohamed El-Tahir El-Messawi, "Maqāṣid al-Shari'ah: An Usuli Doctrine or Independent Discipline: A Study Ibn Ashur's Project," in *Maqasid al-Shariah and its Realization in Contemporary Societies*, proceedings of the International Conference on Islamic Jurisprudence and the Challenges of the 21st Century, (International Islamic University Malaysia, IIUM, Kuala Lumpur, 8–10 August 2006), Vol. 3:84.

45. 'Abd Allah Bin Bayyah, *Maqāṣid al-sharī'ah fi'l-Muāmalāt,* Lecture series no. 6, al-Maqasid Research Centre in the Philosophy of Islamic Law, London, 2008, 52 and 54. See also al-Shaikh-Ali & Khan, eds., *Ibn Ashur Treatise*, 18.

46. Cf., Attia, *Towards Realisation*, 109. See also for a discussion of *maqāṣid* and *wasā'il*, Mohammad Hashim Kamali, "Goals and Purposes of Islamic Law," in *Defining Islamic Statehood*, ed., Imam Feisal Abdul Rauf (Basingstoke, UK: Palgrave Macmillan, 2015), 200–34, at 228–30.

47. Sayf al-Din 'Abd al-Fattah, "Nahw Taf'il al-Numuzij al- maqāṣidi fi'l-Majal al-Siyasi wa'l-Ijtima'i," in al- *Maqāṣid* Research Centre, *Maqāṣid al-Shari'ah wa Qadaya al-'Asr*, 187–88.

48. Cf., Riyad Mansur al-Khalifi, "al-maqāṣid al- *sharī'ah* wa atharuha fi'l-fiqh al-mu'amalt al-maliyyah," *Majallah Jami'ah al-Malik 'Abdulaziz al-Iqtisad al-Islami*, Vol. 17, no. 1 (1425/2004), 3–48, 14.

49. Al-Shatibi, *Muwāfaqāt*, II, 13–14; see also al-Khalifi in the previous note at p. 16.

50. See for details, Ibn 'Āshūr, *Maqāṣid al-Shari'ah*, 419–20.

51. Ibn Taymiyyah, *Majmū' al-Fatāwā*, 32:134. See for further details also Kamali, *Principles*, 402f.

52. See for a summary of their views Gamal Eldin Attia, *Towards Realisation*, 79–86. See also Kamali, *Principles*, 401–402.

53. al-Qaraḍāwī, *Madkhal li-Dirāsat*, 75.

54. As quoted in Attia, *Towards Realisation*, 84—excerpt from Siraj's seminar paper on "Islamic Legal Priorities."

55. Cf., Kamali, *Principles*, 402.

56. Ibn 'Āshūr, *Maqāṣid*, 39. See also Attia, *Towards Realisation*, 82.

57. Excerpt from al-Qaraḍāwī's seminar paper on the *Sunnah*, as quoted in Attia, *Towards Realisation*, 84.

58. Quoted from Attia's version of an excerpt from Muḥammad al-Ghazālī's seminar paper on the subject of Islamic legal priorities with minor linguistic adjustments by the present writer; Attia, *Towards Realisation*, 83.

59. Al-Raysūnī, *Naẓariyyāt*, 47f.

60. Al-Shatibi, *al-Muwāfaqāt*, 2:385.

61. Aḥmad al-Raysūnī, "al-Manhaj al-maqāṣidī fi fiqh Ibn Rushd," in: *Qaḍāyā Islāmiyyah Mu'āṣirah*, as quoted in Attia, *Towards Realisation*, 97–99.

62. Ibn Qayyim al-Jawziyyah, *I'lām al-Muwaqqi'īn*, 1:333.

63. Ibn'Āshūr, *Maqāṣid,* 64.

64. Cf., Aḥmad al-Raysūnī, *al-Fikr al-Maqāṣidī,* Rabat: Jarīdat al-Zaman, 1999, 129f.

65. Jasser Auda, *Maqāṣid al-Sharī'ah as Philosophy of Islamic Law: A System Approach* (London: International Institute of Islamic Thought, 2008), 244.

66. See for details on *tajdīd*, *islaḥ* and *ijtihād*, Mohammad Hashim Kamali "Tajdid, Islah and Civilisational Renewal in Islam," *Islam and Civilisational Renewal* 4 (2013): 484–511.

67. Almost all of the legal maxims quoted in this presentation are drawn from *Mu'allimah Zayid li'l-Qawa'id al-Fiqhiyyah wa'l-Usuliyyah,* Abu Dhabi: Mu'assasah Zayid b. Sultan Aal-Nahyan & Majma' al-Fiqh al-Islami al-Duwali, 41 vols.,

2013/1434. All entries are alphabetical in this extensive Arabic encyclopedia of legal maxims. I have also utilized Namr Ahmad al-Sayyid Mustafa, *Usul al-Nazar fi-Maqasid al-Tashri' al-Islami*, 2 vols. (Syria: Dar al-Nawadir, 2013/1434), and 'Ali Ahmad al-Nadwi, *al-Qawa'id al-Fiqhiyyah*, 10th ed. (Damascus: Dar al-Qalam, 2011/1432). All translations from Arabic into English are by the present writer.

68. The reader may be interested to know that the present writer's previous works engage in these and other relevant features of the *maqāṣid* methodology. There is a chapter entitled "Goals and Purposes (*Maqāṣid*) of *Sharī'ah*: History and Methodology" in Kamali, *Shari'ah Law: An Introduction* (Oxford: Oneworld Publications, 2008), 123–41; idem., *Maqāṣid al-Sharī'ah* Made Simple, Occasional Paper Series 13 (London: International Institute of Islamic Thought, 2008), 26ff.; idem., "Law and Ethics in Islam: the Role of the *Maqāṣid*," in *New Directions in Islamic Thought: Exploring Reform and Muslim Tradition*, eds., Kari Vogt et al. (London: I. B. Tauris, 2009), 23–47; and idem., *Maqāṣid al-Shari'ah, Ijtihad and Civilisational Renewal*, Occasional Paper Series 20, International Institute of Islamic Thought (London), and International Institute of Advanced Islamic Studies (Kuala Lumpur), 2012, 53ff. I have submitted two other articles, one to a book IAIS Malaysia has just sent for publication to MPH publications of Kuala Lumpur entitled "Maqasid al-Shariah in M'uamalat and Contracts," of which I am also the editor, and which carries a chapter by myself entitled "Shariah Purposes(Maqasid) of Transaction and Contracts." I have also submitted an article entitled "Actualisation (Taf'il) of the Higher Purposes (maqasid) of Shariah," appearing the IAIS quarterly journal, *Islamic and Civilisational Renewal,* Vol. 8, no. 3 (October 2017).

BIBLIOGRAPHY

'Abd al-Fattah, Sayf al-Din. "Nahw taf'il al-numuzij al- maqāṣidi fi'l-majal al-siyasi wa'l-ijtimai." In *Maqāṣid al-Shari'ah wa Qadaya al-'Asr*. London: Furqan Islamic Heritage Foundation, n.d.

'Abd al-Salām, 'Izz al-Dīn. *Qawā'id al-aḥkām fī masāliḥ al-anām*. Edited by 'Abd al-Laṭīf 'Abd al-Raḥmān. Beirut: Dār al-Kutub al-'Ilmiyyah, 1999.

Al-Āmidī, Sayf al-Dīn. *Al-Iḥkām fī uṣūl al-aḥkām*. Edited by 'Abd al-Razzāq 'Afīfī, 4 vols., 2nd edition. Beirut: al-Maktab al-Islāmī, 1982.

Al-Bukhārī, Muḥammad b. Ismā'īl. *Ṣaḥīḥ al-Bukhārī*. Beirut: Dār al-Ma'rifah, 1961.

Al-Fāsī, 'Allāl. *Maqāṣid al-sharī'ah al-islāmiyyah wa makārimuhā.* Casablanca: Maktabat al-Waḥdat al-'Arabiyyah, n.d.

Al-Ghazālī, Abū Ḥāmid. *Iḥyā' 'ulūm al-Dīn.* Cairo: al-Maktabat al-Tijāriyya al-Kubrā, n.d.

Al-Jawziyyah, Ibn Qayyim. *I'lām al-muwaqqi'īn 'an rabb al-'alamīn*. Edited by Ṭaha 'Abd al-Ra'ūf Sa'd, Beirut: Dār al-Jīl, 1973.

Al-Juwaynī, Imām al-Ḥaramayn. *Al-Burhān fī uṣūl al-fiqh*. Doha: Dār al-Qalam, 1978.

Al-Khalifi, Riyad Mansur. "Al-maqāṣid al-sharī'ah wa atharuha fi'l-fiqh al-mu'amalt al-maliyyah." *Majallah Jami'ah al-Malik 'Abdulaziz al-Iqtisad al-Islami*, vol. 17, no. 1 (1425/2004): 3–48.

Al-Kīlānī, ʿAbd al-Raḥmān Ibrāhim Zayd. *Qawāʿid al-maqāṣid ʿind al-imām al-shāṭībī.* Damascus: Dār al-Fikr, 2000.

Al-Nadwi, ʿAli Ahmad. *Al-Qawaʾid al-fiqhiyyah.* 10th edition. Damascus: Dār al-Qalam, 2011/1432.

Al-Qaraḍāwī, Yūsuf. *Fiqh al-zakāt.* Beirut: Mu'assasat al-Risālah, 2000.

———. *Madkhal li-dirāsat al-sharīʿah al-islāmiyyah.* Cairo: Maktabah Wahbah, 1990.

Al-Raysuni, Ahmad. "*Al-Bahth fi maqālīd al-shariah: nish'atuh, tatawwuruh wa mustaqbaluh.*" In *Maqāsid al-Shariah al-Islāmiyya : dirāsāt fī qaḍāyā al-manhağ wa-mağālāt al-taṭbīq*, edited by Mohamed Salim El-Awa. London: Furqan Islamic Heritage Foundation, 2006.

———. *Al-Fikr al-maqāṣidī.* Rabat: Jarīdat al-Zaman, 1999.

———. *Naẓariyyāt al-maqāṣid ʿind al-imām al-shāṭibī.* English translated as *Imam al-Shatibi's Theory of the Higher Objectives and Intents of Islamic Law* by Nancy Roberts. Herndon, VA: International Institute of Islamic Thought, 2006.

Al-Sayyid Mustafa, Namr Ahmad. *Usul al-nazar fi-maqasid al-tashriʿ al-islamī.* 2 vols. Syria: Dar al-Nawadir, 2013/1434.

Al-Shāṭibī, Abū Isḥāq Ibrāhīm bin Mūsā. *Al-Muwāfaqāt fī uṣūl al-sharīʿah.* Edited by ʿAbd-Allāh Darrāz, 4 vols., 2nd edition. Beirut: Dār al-Maʿrifah, 1975.

Al-Zarqā', Muṣṭafa Aḥmad. *Al-Madkhal al-fiqhī al-ʿamm.* Damascus: Dār al-Qalam, 1998.

Al-Zuhaylī, Muḥammad. *Maqāṣid al-sharīʿah: Asās li-huqūq al-insān.* Kitāb al-Ummah Series, no. 87. Doha: Ministry of Awqāf and Islamic Affairs of Qatar, 2003.

Anas al-Shaikh-Ali, and Shiraz Khan, eds. *Ibn Ashur Treatise on Maqasid al-Shari'ah* London: International Institute of Islamic Thought, 2013.

Attia, Gamal Eldin. *Towards Realisation of the Higher Intents of Islamic Law: Maqāṣid al-Shari'ah – A Functional Approach.* English translated by Nancy Roberts. London: The International Institute of Islamic Thought, 2007.

Bin ʿAbd al-Raḥmān, Ẓaheer al-Dīn. *Maqāṣid al-sharīʿah fī aḥkām al-buyūʿ.* Kuala Lumpur: International Islamic University Malaysia (IIUM) Press, 2009.

Bin Bayyah 'Abd Allah. *Maqāṣid al-sharīʿah fi'l-muāmalāt.* Lecture series no. 6, al-Maqasid Research Centre in the Philosophy of Islamic Law, London, 2008.

El-Messawi, Mohamed El-Tahir. "Maqāṣid al-Shari'ah: An Usuli Doctrine or Independent Discipline: A Study Ibn Ashur's Project." In *Maqasid al-Shariah and its Realization in Contemporary Societies*, proceedings of the International Conference on Islamic Jurisprudence and the Challenges of the 21st Century, International Islamic University Malaysia, IIUM, Kuala Lumpur, 8–10 August 2006.

Fu'ād, Muḥammad. *Ṣaḥīḥ Muslim.* Edited by ʿAbd al-Bāqī. Beirut: Dār Iḥyāʾ al-Turāth, 1980.

Ibn ʿĀshūr, Muḥammad al-Ṭāhir. *Maqāṣid al-sharīʿah al-islāmiyyah.* Edited by Muḥammad al-Ṭāhir al-Missāwī. Amman: al-Basā'ir li 'l-Intāj al-ʿIlmī, 1998.

Ibn Sīnā, Abū ʿAli. *Kitab al-najāt fi 'l-ḥikmah al-manṭiqiyyah wa'l-tabīʿiyyah wa 'l-ilāhiyyah.* Edited by Majīd Fakhrī. Beirut: Dār al-Āfāq al-Jadīdah, 1985.

Ibn Taymīyyah, Aḥmad ibn ʿAbd al-Ḥalīm. *Majmūʿ al-Fatāwā* lil-Imām Shaykh al-Islām Taqī al-Dīn ibn Taymīyyah. Beirut: Dār al-Kutub al-'Ilmīyah, 1995.

Kamali, Mohammad Hashim. "Actualisation (Taf'il) of the Higher Purposes (maqasid) of Shariah." in *Islamic and Civilisational Renewal,* vol. 8, no. 3 (October 2017).

———. *Principles of Islamic Jurisprudence.* Revised and enhanced edition. Cambridge: Islamic Texts Society, 2003.

———. "Goals and Purposes of Islamic Law." In *Defining Islamic Statehood*, edited by Imam Feisal Abdul Rauf, 200–34. Basingstoke, UK: Palgrave Macmillan, 2015.

———. "Law and Ethics in Islam: The Role of the Maqāṣid." In *New Directions in Islamic Thought: Exploring Reform and Muslim Tradition*, edited by Kari Vogt, Lena Larson, and Christian Moe, 23–47. London: I. B. Tauris, 2009.

———. "Maqāṣid al-Sharīʿah and Ijtihad as Instruments of Civilisational Renewal." *Islam and Civilisational Renewal*, vol. 2, no. 2 (January 2011): 245–271.

———. "Tajdid, Islah and Civilisational Renewal in Islam." *Islam and Civilisational Renewal*, vol. 4 (2013): 484–511.

———. *Maqāṣid al-Shari'ah, Ijtihad and Civilisational Renewal*, Occasional Paper 20. Herndon, VA: The International Institute of Islamic Thought, 2012.

———. *Shari'ah Law: An Introduction.* Oxford: Oneworld Publications, 2008.

———. "Law and Ethics in Islam: The Role of the Maqāṣid." In *New Directions in Islamic Thought: Exploring Reform and Muslim Tradition*, edited by Kari Vogt et al., 23–47. London: I. B. Tauris, 2009.

———. *Maqāṣid al-Shari'ah, Ijtihad and Civilisational Renewal*, Occasional Paper Series 20, International Institute of Islamic Thought (London), and International Institute of Advanced Islamic Studies (Kuala Lumpur), 2012, 53ff.

———. Maqāṣid al-Sharīʿah Made Simple. *Occasional Paper Series 13.* London: International Institute of Islamic Thought, 2008, 1–26.

Majma' al-Fiqh al-Islami al-Duwali. *Mu'allimah Zayid li'l-Qawa'id al-Fiqhiyyah wa'l-Usuliyyah.* Abu Dhabi: Mu'assasah Zayid b. Sultan Aal-Nahyan and Majma' al-Fiqh al-Islami al-Duwali, 41 vols., 2013/1434.

Mohammad Hashim Kamali. *Principles of Islamic Jurisprudence.* Kuala Lumpur: Ilmiyyah Publishers, 1998.

Chapter 2

Realizing *Maqāṣid* in the *Sharīʿah*

Jasser Auda

THE SCOPE OF *SHARĪʿAH*

Contemporary applications of the *sharīʿah* in any given Muslim society or juridical policy require a methodology that represents the universality and flexibility of the *sharīʿah* with changing circumstances. Without the components of the *sharīʿah* that are pertinent to accommodating various environments and cultures or, in other words, the dimensions of history and geography of the people, any application or policy would be counterproductive. This is due to the risk of jeopardizing the very well-known and absolute system of values and principles within the *sharīʿah* itself, the principles of justice, wisdom, mercy, and common good.

Shamsuddin Ibn al-Qayyim (d. 748 AH/1347 CE) summarized these principles with the following strong words:

> *Sharīʿah* is all about wisdom and achieving people's welfare in this life and the afterlife. It is all about justice, mercy, wisdom, and good. Thus, any ruling that replaces justice with injustice, mercy with its opposite, common good with mischief, or wisdom with nonsense, is a ruling that does not belong to the *sharīʿa*, even if it is claimed to be so according to some interpretation.[1]

Maqāṣid al-sharīʿah (the higher purposes and intents of Islamic law) is a system of values that could contribute to a desired and sound application of the *sharīʿah*. After introducing the system of values and the various theories of *maqāṣid*, this chapter suggests that it is necessary to analyze the following points of discussion:

1. Whether a proposed ruling of the *sharīʿah* is an absolute and fixed end in its own right, or otherwise, it is in itself a means to an end, and thus subject to change with changing circumstances. This method is expressed by differentiating between changing means and absolute ends, which is dealt with in the second section of this chapter.
2. Whether the verse or *ḥadīth* (authenticated tradition of the Prophet Muhammad, peace be upon him) under consideration should be understood with another verse(s) or *ḥadīth* (plural: *aḥadīth*), all in a unified context, or otherwise, there is no "opposing evidence" that exists and requires such consideration. This method is expressed within a multidimensional understanding of "opposing evidences," which is dealt with in the third section of this chapter.
3. Whether the ruling implied by the juridical evidence is subject to a specific tradition or custom, or not. This includes the traditions and customs of the original forms of some rulings, that is, the Arabian customs during the early Islamic era. This method is expressed within the *sharīʿah*'s universality across cultures, which is dealt with in the fourth section of this chapter.

The next section introduces *maqāṣid al-sharīʿah as* a system of values that has several theories and classifications.

MAQĀṢID AL-SHARĪʿAH AS A SYSTEM OF VALUES

Maqāṣid al-sharīʿah are the higher purposes and intents[2] behind Islamic rulings[3], which found expression in the Islamic philosophy of law[4] in various ways, such as public interests (*al-maṣāliḥ al-ʿāmmah*)[5], unrestricted interests (*al-maṣāliḥ al-mursalah*)[6], the avoidance of mischief (*mafsadah*)[7], the wisdom behind the scripts (*al-ḥikmah*)[8], the appropriateness of the juridical analogy (*munāsabat al-qiyas*)[9], the basis behind juridical preference (*asl al-istiḥsān*)[10], the basis behind the presumption of continuity principle (*asl al-istiṣḥāb*)[11], and a large number of other tools for juridical *ijtihād.* Recently, a large number of researchers from various backgrounds attempted to explore the theory and application of *maqāṣid al-sharīʿah* in various fields that belong not only to Islamic jurisprudence, but also to social sciences and humanities.[12] This expansion of the application of the theory opens up new channel for the development of Islamic thought and law.

The purposes or *maqāṣid* (singular: *maqṣid*) of Islamic law are classified in various ways, according to a number of dimensions. The following are some of these dimensions, based on an extensive survey of the topic:

1. Levels of necessity (traditional classification)
2. Scope of the rulings aiming to achieve purposes
3. Scope of people included in purposes
4. Level of universality of the purposes

Traditional classifications of *maqāṣid* divide them into the following three levels of necessity: necessities (*al-ḍarūrāt*), needs (*al-ḥājāt*), and luxuries (*al-taḥsīnāt*). Necessities are further classified into what preserves one's faith (*dīn*), soul (*nafs*), wealth (*māl*), mind (*'aql*), and offspring (*nasl*).[13] Some jurists added the preservation of honor to the above five widely popular necessities. These necessities were considered essential matters for human life itself. There is also a general agreement that the preservation of these necessities is the objective behind any revealed law, not just Islamic law.[14]

Purposes at the level of needs are less essential for human life. Examples are marriage, trade, and means of transportation. Islam encourages and regulates these needs. However, the lack of any of these needs is not a matter of life and death, especially on an individual basis. Purposes at the level of luxuries are "beautifying purposes," such as using perfume, stylish clothing, and beautiful homes. These are things that Islam encourages, but also asserts should take a lower priority in one's life. The levels in the hierarchy are overlapping and interrelated, and each level should serve the level(s) below. Furthermore, the general lack of one item from a certain level moves it to the level above. For example, the decline of trade on a global level, for example during the time of global economic crises, moves trade from a "need" into a "life necessity," and so on. That is why some jurists preferred to perceive necessities in terms of overlapping circles, rather than a strict hierarchy.[15]

Modern scholarship introduced new conceptions and classifications of *maqāṣid* by giving consideration to new dimensions. First, considering the scope of rulings they cover, contemporary classifications divide *maqāṣid* into three levels[16]:

1. General *maqāṣid*: These *maqāṣid* are observed throughout the entire body of Islamic law, such as the necessities and needs mentioned above and newly proposed *maqāṣid*, such as "justice" and "facilitation."
2. Specific *maqāṣid*: These *maqāṣid* are observed throughout a certain chapter of the Islamic law, such as the welfare of children in family law, preventing criminals in criminal law, and preventing monopoly in financial transactions law.
3. Partial *maqāṣid*: These *maqāṣid* are the intents behind specific scripts or rulings, such as the intent of discovering the truth in seeking a certain number of witnesses in certain court cases, the intent of alleviating

difficulty in allowing an ill and fasting person to break his/her fasting, and the intent of feeding the poor in banning Muslims from storing meat during Eid/festival days.

Moreover, the notion of *maqāṣid* has been expanded to include a wider scope of people—the community, nation, or humanity in general. Ibn ʿĀshūr, for example, gave *maqāṣid* that are concerned with the nation (*ummah*) priority over *maqāṣid* that are concerned with individuals, Rashid Rida included reform and women's rights in his theory of *maqāṣid* and Yusuf al-Qaradawi included human dignity and rights in his theory of *maqāṣid*.[17] The above expansions of the scope of *maqāṣid* allow the *sharīʿah* to respond to global issues and concerns, and to evolve from a wisdoms-behind-the-rulings system to a system of values and practical plans for reform and renewal. These extensions, in my view, reflect the values and principles that each of those scholars deemed primary from their perspective. None of the above scholars elaborated on the methodology through which they arrived at their new set of *maqāṣid*.

Contemporary scholarship has also introduced new, universal *maqāṣid* that are directly induced from the scripts, rather than from the body of *fiqh* (jurisprudence) literature in the schools of Islamic law. This approach, significantly, allowed *maqāṣid* to overcome the historicity of *fiqh* edicts and represent the scripts' higher values and principles. Detailed rulings would then stem from these universal principles. The following are examples of the new, universal *maqāṣid*:

1. Rashid Rida (d. 1354 AH/1935 CE) surveyed the *Qurʾān* to identify its *maqāṣid*, which included, "reform of the pillars of faith, and spreading awareness that Islam is the religion of pure natural disposition, reason, knowledge, wisdom, proof, freedom, independence, social, political, economic reform, and women rights."
2. Al-Ṭahir Ibn ʿĀshūr (d. 1325 AH/1907 CE)[18] proposed that the universal *maqṣid* of Islamic law is to maintain orderliness, equality, freedom, facilitation, and the preservation of pure natural disposition (*fiṭrah*).[19] It is to be noted that the purpose of "freedom" (*ḥurrīyah*), which was proposed by Ibn ʿĀshūr and several other contemporary scholars, is different from the purpose of "freedom" (*ʿitq*), which was mentioned by jurists such as al-Siwasi.[20] *Al-ʿitq* is freedom from slavery, not freedom in the contemporary sense. "Will" (*mashīʾah*), however, is a well-known Islamic term that bears a number of similarities with current conceptions of freedom and free will. For example, freedom of belief is expressed in the *Qurʾān* as the "will to believe or disbelieve" (Surat al-Kahf, 18:29). In terms of terminology, freedom is a newly coined purpose in the literature of Islamic

law. Ibn ʿĀshūr,[21] interestingly, accredited his usage of the term *ḥurrīyah* to "literature of the French revolution, which were translated from French to Arabic in the nineteenth century CE"[22] even though he elaborated on an Islamic perspective on freedom of thought, belief, expression, and action in the *mashīʾah* sense.[23]

3. Mohammad al-Ghazālī (d. 1416 AH/1996 CE) called for "learning lessons from the previous fourteen centuries of Islamic history" and, therefore, included "justice and freedom" in *maqāṣid* at the necessities level.[24] Al-Ghazālī's prime contribution to the knowledge of *maqāṣid* was his critique on the literalist tendencies that many of today's scholars have.[25] A careful look at the contributions of Mohammad al-Ghazālī shows that there were underlying *maqāṣid*, such as equality and justice, upon which he based all his famous new opinions, including those concerning women.
4. Yusuf al-Qaradawi (1345 AH/1926 CE—)[26] also surveyed the *Qurʾān* and concluded the following universal *maqāṣid:* preserving true faith, maintaining human dignity and rights, calling people to worship God, purifying the soul, restoring moral values, building good families, treating women fairly, building a strong Islamic nation, and calling for a cooperative world. However, al-Qaradawi explains that proposing a theory in universal *maqāṣid* should only happen after developing a level of experience with detailed scripts.
5. Ṭaha al-Alwani (1354 AH/1935 CE—)[27] also surveyed the *Qurʾān* to identify its "supreme and prevailing" *maqāṣid*, which are, according to him, "the oneness of God (*tawḥīd*), purification of the soul (*tazkīyah*), and developing civilisation on earth (ʿ*imrān*)."[28]

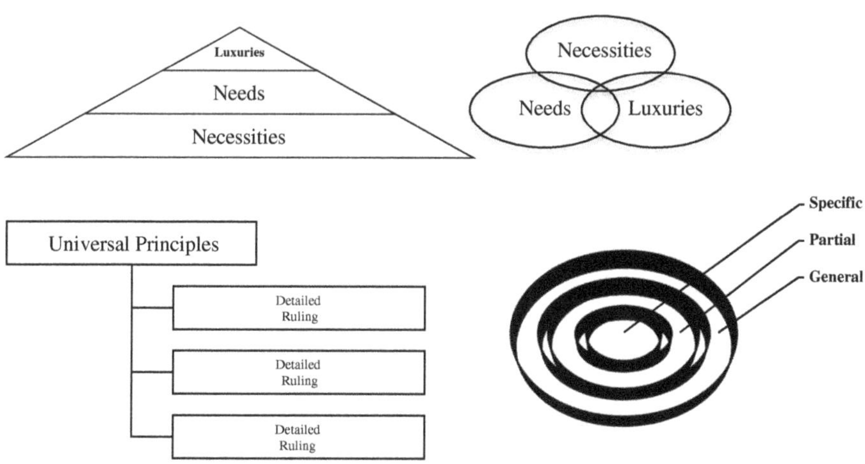

Figure 2.1 Graphic courtesy of the author.

All of the above *maqāṣid* were presented as they appeared in the minds and perceptions of the above jurists. Therefore, the *maqāṣid* structure is best described as a multidimensional structure, in which levels of necessity, scope of rulings, scope of people, and levels of universality are all valid dimensions that represent valid viewpoints and classifications (refer to Figure 2.1 for an illustration). As explained above, the next three sections explore different ways of utilizing *maqāsid* toward a much-needed, contemporary policy-making application of the *sharīʿah* in various circumstances.

DIFFERENTIATING BETWEEN CHANGING MEANS AND ABSOLUTE ENDS

Some scripts (verses or *ḥadīth*) are "scripts of means" (*nuṣuṣ wasāʾil*) and are not meant as ends in their own right; hence, they are not meant to be applied to the letter. A *maqāsidi* understanding of these scripts helps in identifying their true meaning and intent. For example, *Qurʾān* 8:60 states: "Hence, make ready against them whatever force and horse mounts you are able to muster, so that you might deter thereby the enemies of God, who are your enemies as well." "Horse mounts" are means and not ends in their own right that should literally be sought. In fact, moreover, the whole concept of "getting ready with force" is, in my view, a means to the ends of justice and peace, rather than an end in its own right. Mohammad al-Ghazālī extended this concept by differentiating between means (*al-wasāʾil*) and ends (*al-ahdāf*), whereas he argued for the possibility of what he called "expiry" (*intihāʾ*) of the former and not the latter. Al-Ghazālī mentioned the system of the distribution of the booty of war as one example, despite the fact that it is mentioned explicitly in the *Qurʾān*.[29] *Qurʾān* 8:41 states, "And know that whatever booty you acquire [in war], one-fifth thereof belongs to God and the Apostle, and the near of kin, and the orphans, and the needy, and the wayfarer. This you must observe if you believe in God and in what We bestowed from on high upon Our servant." The above understanding validates today's policies, where army personnel are compensated according to a scheme of salaries, ranks, and benefits, which are categorically separate from any economic gains they achieve via warfare. Recently, Yusuf al-Qaradawi and Faisal Mawlawi elaborated on the importance of the differentiation between means and ends during the deliberations of the European Council for Fatwa and Research. They both applied the same concept to the visual citation of the *hilāl* (Ramadan's new moon) being a mere means for knowing the start of the month, rather than an end in its own right. Hence, they concluded that pure calculations should be today's means of defining the start of the month. Thus, ministries of Islamic affairs, ministries of *awqāf*, and houses of *fatwa* in various countries could correctly base their calendar decisions on official astronomical reports and findings, instead of a costly contingency plan every month, especially during the seasons of fasting and pilgrimage. Al-Qaradawi has also applied the same concept to the Muslim women's garment (*jilbāb*), among other things, which he viewed as mere means for achieving the objective of modesty.[30]

In my view, differentiating between means and ends opens a whole lot of possibilities for new opinions in Islamic law. For example, al-Alwani[31] proposed a project for reform in his *Issues in Contemporary Islamic Thought*, in which he elaborated on his version of the method of differentiation between means and ends. The following illustrates how al-Alwani applied this approach to the issue of gender equality:

> The Qur'an transported the people of those times to the realm of faith in absolute gender equality. This single article of faith, perhaps more than any other, represented a revolution no less significant than Islam's condemnation of idolatry. . . . In the case of early Muslim society, given the long established customs, attitudes and mores of pre-Islamic Arabia, it was necessary to implement such changes in stages and to make allowances for society's capacity to adjust itself accordingly. . . . By establishing a role for a woman in the witnessing of transactions, even though at the time of revelation they had little to do with such matters, the Qur'an seeks to give concrete form to the idea of woman as participant. . . . The objective is to end the traditional perception of women by including them, "among such as are acceptable to you as witness" . . . the matter of witnessing served merely as a means to an end or as a practical way of establishing the concept of gender equality. In their interpretations of "mistake" and "remind," Qur'anic commentators have approached the issue from a perspective based on the assumption that the division of testimony for women into halves is somehow connected with women's inherent inequality to men. This idea has been shared by classical and modern commentators alike, so that generations of Muslims, guided only by *taqlid* (imitation), have continued to perpetuate this faulty understanding. Certainly, the attitudes engendered by such a misunderstanding have spread far beyond the legal sphere.[32]

This application of the suggested method of differentiating between changing means and fixed ends also spreads beyond the legal sphere, in the sense of making policies that aim at changing societies and cultures toward normalizing the value of equality between men and women, especially in their legal capacities before the judicial system. A similar expression can be found in Ayatollah Mahdi Shamsuddin's recommendation for today's jurists to take a "dynamic" approach to the scripts, and "not to look at every script as absolute and universal legislation, open their minds to the possibility of 'relative' legislation for specific circumstances, and not to judge narrations with missing contexts as absolute in the dimensions of time, space, situations, and people."[33] He further clarifies that he is "inclined to this understanding but would not base (any rulings) on it for the time being." Nevertheless, he stresses the need for this approach for rulings related to women, financial matters, and *jihad*.[34] In addition to this, Fathi Osman, for example, "considered the practical considerations" that rendered a woman's testimony to be less than a man's, as mentioned in *Qur'ān* 2:282. Thus, Osman reinterpreted the verse to be a function to these practical considerations, in a way similar to al-Alwani's method mentioned above.[35] Sheikh Hassan al-Turabi[36] holds the same view regarding many rulings related, again, to women and their daily-life practices and attires.[37]

Similarly, Abdul-Karim Soroush[38] suggested that the scripts should be "divided into two parts, essentials and accidentals, accidentals being functions of the cultural, social, and historical environment of the delivery of the main message."[39]

Some Mālikīs proposed "opening the means" (*fatḥ al-dharā'i*) in addition to "blocking" them (*sadd al-dharā'i*).[40] Imam al-Qarafi (1998) divided rulings into means *wasā'il* and ends/purposes *maqāṣid*. He suggested that means that lead to prohibited ends should be blocked, and means that lead to lawful ends should be opened.[41] Thus, al-Qarafi linked the ranking of means to the ranking of their ends and suggested three levels for ends: namely, "most repugnant" (*aqbaḥ*), best (*afḍal*), and "in between" (*mutawassitah*). Ibn Farhun (d. 769 AH)[42], also from the Mālikī school, applied al-Qarafi's "opening the means" to a number of rulings.[43] Thus, Mālikīs do not restrict themselves to the negative side of "consequentialist thinking," to borrow a term from moral philosophy. They expand this method of thinking to the positive side of it, which entails opening means to achieving good ends, even if these ends were not mentioned in specific scripts.

It is important to note here that some researchers and writers extend the above consideration of historical conditions into what is called the "historicization" of Islamic scripts, which is the abrogation or cancellation of their "authority" *in toto*. This historicist approach suggests that our ideas about texts, cultures, and events are totally a function of their position in their original historical context, as well as their later historical developments.[44] Applying this idea, borrowed from literature studies, to the *Qur'ān* entails that the Quranic script is a "cultural product" of the culture that produced it, as claimed by some writers.[45]

Therefore, it is claimed that the *Qur'ān* would become a "historic document" that is only helpful in learning about a specific historic community that existed in the prophetic era. Haideh Moghissi[46] further claims that "the *sharī'ah* is not compatible with the principle of equality of human beings."[47] For her, "no amount of twisting and bending can reconcile the Quranic injunctions and instructions about women's rights and obligations with the idea of gender equality" (140). Similarly, Ibn Warraq claims that the Islamic human rights scheme shows "inadequate support for the principle of freedom."[48] Thus, for Warraq, Islamic jurisprudence could not be evidence for an "ethical vision," in the contemporary sense.[49]

However, I think that rendering the *Qurʾān* "unfair" and "immoral" goes against the very belief in its divine source. Having said that, I also believe that historical events and specific juridical rulings detailed in the *Qurʾān* should be understood within the cultural, geographical, and historical context of the message of Islam. The key for this understanding is, again, to differentiate between changeable means and fixed principles and ends. Means could expire, as Sheikh Mohammad al-Ghazālī put it, while ends and principles are non-changeable. Based on such understanding, Quranic specifics could very well apply universally in every place and time and could very well present an ethical vision and value system for today's legislation and policy.

A MULTIDIMENSIONAL UNDERSTANDING OF OPPOSING EVIDENCES

In Islamic juridical theory, there is a differentiation between opposition or disagreement (*taʿāruḍ* or *ikhtilāf*) and contradiction (*tanāquḍ* or *taʿanud*) of scripts (verses or narrations). Contradiction is defined as "a clear and logical conclusion of truth and falsehood in the same aspect" (*taqāsum al-ṣidqi wa-l-kadhib*).[50] On the other hand, conflict or disagreement between evidences is defined as an "apparent contradiction between evidences in the mind of the scholar" (*taʿāruḍun fī dhihn al-mujtahid*).[51] This means that two seemingly disagreeing (*mutaʿāriḍ*) evidences are not necessarily in contradiction. It is in the perception of the jurist that they are in contradiction, which can occur as a result of some missing information or dimension regarding the evidence's timing, place, circumstances, or other conditions.[52] On the other hand, true contradiction takes the form of a single episode narrated in truly contradicting ways by the same or different narrators.[53] This kind of discrepancy is obviously due to errors in narration related to the memory and/or intentions of one or more of the narrators.[54] The "logical" conclusion in cases of contradiction is that one or more of the narrations is inaccurate and should be rejected. For example, Abu Hurairah narrated, according to Bukhari, "Bad omens are in women, animals, and houses." However, also according to Bukhari, ʿAisha narrated that the Prophet (peace be upon him) had said, "People during the days of ignorance (*jāhilīyah*) used to say that bad omens are in women, animals, and houses." These two "authentic" narrations are at odds and one of them should be rejected. It is telling that most commentators rejected Aisha's narration, even though other "authentic" narrations support it.[55] Ibn al-ʿArabi (d. 1149) for example, commented on ʿAisha's rejection of the above *ḥadīth* as follows, "This is nonsense (*qawlun sāqiṭ*). ʿAisha is rejecting a clear and authentic narration that is narrated through trusted narrators."[56]

According to various traditional and contemporary studies on the issue of *taʿāruḍ* in the above sense, is rare. Most cases of *taʿāruḍ* are disagreements between narrations because of an apparent missing context, not because of logically contradicting accounts of the same episode. There are six strategies that jurists defined to deal with these types of disagreements in traditional schools of law.[57]

1. Conciliation (*al-jamʿ*): This method is based on a fundamental rule that states that "applying the script is better than disregarding it (*iʿmāl al-naṣṣi awlā min ihmālih*)." Therefore, a jurist facing two disagreeing narrations should search for a missing condition or context, and attempt to interpret both narrations based on it.
2. Abrogation (*al-naskh*): This method suggests that the later evidence, chronologically speaking, should abrogate (juridically annul) the former. This means that when verses disagree, the verse that is (narrated to be) revealed last is considered to be an abrogating evidence (*nāsikh*) and others to be abrogated (*mansūkh*). Similarly, when prophetic narrations disagree, the narration that has a later date, if dates are known or could be concluded, should abrogate all other narrations. Most scholars do not accept that a *ḥadīth* abrogates a verse of the *Qurʾān*, even if the *ḥadīth* were to be chronologically subsequent. The concept of abrogation, in any of the above senses, does not have supporting evidence from the words attributed to the Prophet (peace be upon him) in traditional collections of *aḥadīth*. Etymologically, abrogation (*naskh*) is derived from the root *na sa kha*. I carried out a survey on this root and all its possible derivations in a large number of today's popular collections of *aḥadīth*, including, al-Bukhari, Muslim, al-Tirmidhi, al-Nasa'i, Abu Dawud, Ibn Majah, Ahmad, Malik, al-Darami, al-Mustadrak, Ibn Hibban, Ibn Khuzaimah, al-Bayhaqi, al-Darqutni, Ibn Abi Shaybah, and Abd al-Razzaq. I found no valid *ḥadīth* attributed to the Prophet (peace be upon him) that contains any of these derivations of the root *na sa kha*. I found about forty instances of abrogations mentioned in the above collections, which were all based on one of the narrators' opinions or commentaries, rather than any of the texts of the *ḥadīth*. I concluded that the concept of abrogation always appears within the commentaries given by companions or other narrators, commenting on what appears to be in disagreement with their own understanding of the related issues.[58] According to traditional exegeses, the principle of abrogation does have evidence from the *Qurʾān*, although the interpretations of the related verses are subject to a difference of opinion.[59]

3. Elimination (*al-tarjīh*): This method suggests endorsing the narration that is "most authentic" and dropping or eliminating other narrations. The "eliminating" narration is called *al-riwāyah al-rājiḥah*, which literally means the narration that is "heavier in the scale." According to scholars of *ḥadīth*, an eliminating (*rājiḥah*) narration must have, as compared to the other narration, one or more of the following characteristics: a larger number of other supporting narrations, a shorter chain of narrators, more knowledgeable narrators, narrators more capable of memorisation, more trustworthy narrators, first-hand account versus indirect accounts, shorter time between the narration and the narrated incident, narrators able to remember and mention the date of the incident versus others, less ambiguity, less rhetoric, and a number of other factors.
4. Waiting (*al-tawaqquf*): This method recommends that the scholar is not to make any decision until one of the above three methods are evident.
5. Cancellation (*al-tasaquṭ*): This method recommends that the scholar is to disregard both narrations because of the uncertainty in both.
6. Choice (*al-takhīr*): This method allows the scholar to choose whatever is rendered suitable for the situation at hand.

Hanafīs apply abrogation before any other method, followed by the method of elimination.[60] All other schools of law give priority, theoretically, to the method of conciliation (*al-jamʿ*). Although most schools of law agree that applying all scripts is better than disregarding any of them, most scholars do not seem to give priority, on a practical level, to the method of conciliation. The methods that are used in most cases of *taʿāruḍ* are abrogation and elimination.[61] Therefore, a large number of evidences are cancelled, one way or the other, for no good reason other than the jurists' failing to understand how they could fit them in a unified perceptual framework. Thus, invalidating these evidences is more or less arbitrary. For example, narrations are invalidated (outweighed) if narrators did not happen to mention the date of the incident, the wording related to the Prophet (peace be upon him) happened to be more metaphoric, or a narrator happened to be female—in which case the male's opposing narration takes precedence.[62] Therefore, *al-naskh* and *al-tarjīḥ* reflect the general feature of binary thinking in fundamental methodology. It is essential that the method of conciliation makes use of the concept of multi-dimensionality in overcoming this drawback and considers the dimension of *maqāṣid* in the understanding of the scripts.

One practical consequence of cancelling a large number of verses and prophetic narrations in the name of *naskh* and *tarjīḥ* is a great deal of "inflexibility" in Islamic law, that is, inability to address various situations adequately. Reflection upon pairs of *mutaʿāriḍ* or opposing narrations show that their disagreement could be due to a difference in surrounding circumstances, such as war and peace, poverty and wealth, urban and rural life, summer and winter, sickness and health, or young and old. Therefore, the Quranic instructions or the Prophet's actions and decisions (peace be upon him), as narrated by his observers, are supposed to have differed accordingly. Lack of contextualization limits flexibility. For example, eliminating the evidences that occurred in the context of peace for the sake of evidences that occurred in the context of war, combined with literal methods, limits the jurist's ability to address both contexts. When this is combined with a strict binary methodology, the outcomes result in specific rulings for specific circumstances that are made universal and eternal. One important example is *Qur'ān* 9:5: "But when the forbidden months are past, then slay the pagans wherever you find them, and seize them," which has come to be named "The Verse of the Sword" (*āyat al-saif*) and which has been claimed to have abrogated hundreds of verses and *aḥadīth*. One significant *ḥadīth* that was claimed to have been abrogated is "The Scroll of Medina" (*ṣaḥīfat al-madīnah*), in which the Prophet (peace be upon him) and the Jews of Medina wrote a "covenant" that defined the relationship between Muslims and Jews living in Medina. The scroll stated, "Muslims and Jews are one nation (*ummah*), with Muslims having their own religion and Jews having their own religion."[63] Classic and neo-traditional commentators on the *ṣaḥīfah* render it abrogated based on the Verse of the Sword and other similar verses.[64] Seeing all the above scripts and narrations in terms of the single dimension of peace versus war might imply a contradiction, in which the final truth has to belong to either peace or war. The result will have to be an unreasonable fixed choice between peace and war, for every place, time, and circumstance. This (mis)understanding eliminates the profession, ministry, and art of foreign policy altogether.

What added to the problem is that the number of cases of abrogation claimed by the students of the companions (*al-tābi'īn*) is higher than the cases claimed by the companions themselves, a fact concluded based on the survey mentioned earlier. After the first Islamic century, one could furthermore notice that jurists from the developing schools of thought began claiming many new cases of abrogation, which were never claimed by the *tābi'īn*. Thus, abrogation became a method of invalidating opinions or narrations endorsed by rival schools of law. Abu al-Hassan al-Karkhi (d. 951 CE), for one example, writes: "The fundamental rule is: every Quranic verse that is different from the opinion of the jurists in our school is either taken out of context or abrogated."[65] Therefore, it is not unusual in the *fiqhī* literature to find a certain ruling to be abrogating (*nāsikh*) according to one school and abrogated (*mansūkh*) according to another. This arbitrary use of the method of abrogation has exacerbated the problem of lack of multidimensional interpretations of the evidences.

Multidimensional thinking, introduced by the *maqāṣidī* approach, could offer a solution for the dilemmas of a large number of opposing evidences. Two evidences might be in opposition, in terms of this one attribute, such as war and peace, order and forbiddance, men and women, and so on. If we restrict our view to one dimension, we will find no way to reconcile the evidences. However, if we expand the one-dimensional space into two dimensions, the second of which is a *maqṣid* to which both evidences contribute, then we will be able to "resolve" the opposition and understand/interpret the evidences in a unified context, based on the purpose/*maqṣūd* of both evidences.

The following are typical examples from the classic literature on *ikhtilāf al-adillah* (opposition of evidences),[66] which also represent some traditionalist and modernist views today. However, it will be shown that the opposition claimed could be resolved via the multidimensional and purposeful method proposed above.

1. There is a large number of opposing evidences related to different ways of performing acts of worship (*ʿibādāt*), all attributed to the Prophet (peace be upon him). These opposing narrations have frequently caused heated debates and rifts within Muslim communities. However, understanding these narrations within a *maqṣid* of magnanimity (*taīsīr*) entails that the Prophet (peace be upon him) did carry out these rituals in various ways, suggesting flexibility in such matters.[67] Examples of these acts of worship are the different ways of standing and moving during prayers, concluding prayers (*tashahhud*), compensating prostration (*sujūd al-sahū*), reciting "God is Great" (*takbīr*) during *ʿeīd* prayers, making up for breaking one's fasting in Ramadan, details of pilgrimage, and so on.
2. There is a number of opposing narrations that address matters related to customs (*al-ʿurf*), which were also classified as in opposition. However, these narrations could all be interpreted through the *maqṣid* of "universality of the law," as Ibn ʿAshūr had suggested.[68] In other words, differences between these narrations should be understood as differences in the customs for which the various narrations attempted to show consideration, rather than "contradiction." One example is the two narrations, both attributed to ʿAisha, one of which forbids "any woman" from marriage without the consent of her guardian, while the other allows previously married women to make their own independent choices on marriage. It is also narrated that ʿAisha, the narrator of the two narrations herself, did not apply the condition of consent in some cases.[69] Hanafīs explained that, "the (Arabic) custom goes that a woman who marries without her guardian's consent is shameless."[70] Understanding both narrations in the context of considering customs based on the law's universality resolves the

contradiction and provides flexibility in carrying out marriage ceremonies according to different customs in different places and times.

The above method allows juridical policies related to family law, which accommodates the sociocultural norms that do not contradict with the fixed matters of Islam, even if they manifest in forms that are different from the forms they had during the early time of the message of Islam.

3. A number of narrations were classified under cases of abrogation, even though they were, according to some jurists, cases of gradual application of rulings. The purpose behind the gradual applications of rulings on a large scale is "facilitating the change that the law is bringing to society's deep-rooted habits."[71] Thus, opposing narrations regarding the prohibition of liquor and usury, and the performance of prayers and fasting, should be understood in terms of the prophetic tradition and policy of the gradual application of high ideals in any given society that is originally far from these ideals.
4. A number of opposing narrations are considered contradictory because their statements entail different rulings for similar cases. However, taking into account that these prophetic statements addressed different people (companions) could resolve the opposition. In these cases, the juridical *maqṣid* of "fulfilling the best interest of people" would be the key to interpreting these narrations based on the differences between these companions. For example, a few narrations reported that the Prophet (peace be upon him) told a divorcee that she loses her custody of her children if she gets married.[72] Yet, a number of other "opposing" narrations entail that divorcees could keep their children in their custody after they get married. The opposing narrations included Umm Salamah's case; Umm Salamah kept custody of her children after she married the Prophet (peace be upon him). Thus, relying on the first group of narrations, most schools of law concluded that custody is automatically transferred to the father if the mother gets married. They based their elimination of the second group of narrations on the fact that the first group was "more authentic," being narrated by Bukhari and Ibn Hanbal. Ibn Hazm, on the other hand, accepted the second group of narrations and rejected the first group based on his suspicion of one of the narrator's capability of memorisation. However, after citing both opinions, al-Sanaani commented, "The children should stay with the parent who fulfils their best interest. If the mother is the better caregiver and will follow up on the children diligently, then she should have priority over them. . . . The children have to be in the custody of the more capable parent, and the Law cannot possibly judge otherwise."[73] This very issue is a subject of repeated and strong complaints from legal reformers and women's right activists in various Muslim countries and communities. A *maqāsidi* approach to this matter, which is al-Sanaani's

approach mentioned above, puts first the welfare of children of divorce in this particular family policy. This is the policy that is closest to the Islamic system of values outlined before.

Multidimensionality also entails considering more than one *maqṣid*, if applicable. In this case, the way of resolving oppositions that fulfils these *maqāṣid* in the highest order should be given priority according to the hierarchies of *maqāṣid* that scholars had mentioned, for example necessities (*ḍarūrāt*), needs (*ḥājīyāt*), and luxuries (*taḥsīnīyāt*), in this order.

THE *SHARĪʿAH'S* UNIVERSALITY ACROSS CULTURES

Al-Ṭahir Ibn ʿAshūr (d. 1325 AH/1907 CE)[74] proposed a novel view of the fundamental of custom (*al-ʿurf*) based on the purposes of Islamic law. He wrote a chapter in his important book, "*Maqāṣid al-Sharīʿah*" on *al-ʿUrf,'* which was entitled with a *maqṣid* that he called, "The Universality of Islamic Law."[75] In that chapter, Ibn ʿAshūr did not consider the effect of custom on the application of narrations, as is the traditional view. Instead, he considered the effect of (Arabic) customs on narrations themselves. The following is a summary of Ibn ʿAshūr's argument.

Firstly, Ibn ʿAshūr explained that it is necessary for Islamic law to be a universal law, since it claims to be "applicable to all humankind everywhere on earth at all times," as per a number of Quranic verses and *aḥadīth* that he cited. Then, Ibn ʿAshūr elaborated on the wisdoms behind choosing the Prophet (peace be upon him) from among Arabs, such as the Arabs' isolation from civilization, which prepared them "to mix and associate openly with other nations with whom they had no hostilities, in contrast to Persians, Byzantines, and Copts." Yet, for Islamic law to be universal, "its rules and commands should apply equally to all human beings as much as possible," as Ibn ʿAshūr confirmed. That is why he wrote, "God has based Islamic law on wisdoms and reasons that can be perceived by the mind and which do not change according to nations and custom." Thus, Ibn ʿAshūr provided explanation as to why the Prophet (peace be upon him) forbade his companions to write down what he says, "lest particular cases be taken as universal rules." Ibn ʿAshūr then applied his ideas to a number of narrations, in an attempt to filter out Arabic customs from popular traditional rulings. He wrote:

> Therefore, Islamic law does not concern itself with determining what kind of dress, house, or mount people should use. . . . Accordingly, we can establish that the customs and mores of a particular people have no right, as such, to be imposed on other people as legislation, not even the people who originated them. . . .

> This method of interpretation has removed much confusion that faced scholars in understanding the reasons why the law prohibited certain practices . . . such as the prohibition for women to add hair extensions, to cleave their teeth, or to tattoo themselves. . . . The correct meaning of this, in my view . . . is that these practices mentioned in *ḥadīth* were, according to Arabs, signs of a woman's lack of chastity. Therefore, prohibiting these practices was actually aimed at certain evil motives. . . . Similarly, we read: . . . "believing women should draw over themselves some of their outer garments" *(Surat al-Aḥzāb)*. . . . This is a legislation that took into consideration an Arab tradition, and therefore does not necessarily apply to women who do not wear this style of dress.[76]

Therefore, based on the purpose of universality of Islamic law, Ibn ʿAshūr suggested a method of interpreting narrations through understanding their underlying Arabic cultural context, rather than treating them as absolute and unqualified rules. Thus, he read the above narrations in terms of their higher moral purposes, rather than norms in their own right.

CONCLUSION

Before calling for the application of the *sharīʿah* in Muslim societies or juridical systems, policy and methods have to be based on a new *ijtihād* based on understanding and applying the evidences contained in the verses of the *Qurʾān* or the *ḥadīth* of the Prophet (peace be upon him). In order for this *ijtihād* to meet the needs of Muslims with changing circumstances, this chapter suggested that it should be based on the following three criteria:

1. Differentiating between changing means and absolute ends: some verses or *aḥadīth* are "scripts of means" (*nuṣuṣ wasāʾil*) and are not meant as ends in their own right; hence, they are not meant to be applied to the letter. A *maqāsidī* understanding of these scripts helps in identifying their purposes.
2. A multidimensional understanding of opposing evidences: a *maqāṣidī* approach offers a solution for the dilemma of the large number of "opposing" evidences in our juridical heritage. If we restrict our view to one dimension, such as war and peace, order and forbiddance, men and women, and so on, we will find no way to reconcile the evidences. However, if we expand the one-dimensional space into two dimensions, the second of which is a *maqṣid* to which both evidences contribute, then we will be able to "resolve" the opposition and understand/interpret the evidences in a unified context based on the purpose/*maqṣūd* of both evidences.
3. Understanding the *sharīʿah's* universality across cultures: a *maqāṣidī* approach offers a method of interpreting the *ḥadīth* narrations themselves

through understanding their underlying Arabic cultural context, rather than treating them as unqualified rules.

Failing to include the above criteria in that *ijtihād* would create applications (or rather, misapplications) of the *sharīʿah* that are reductionist rather than holistic, literal rather than moral, and reductionist rather than multidimensional. Thus, the proposed *maqāṣidī* approach takes juridical decisions and policies to a higher philosophical ground and, hence, leads to a methodology that is holistic, moral, and multidimensional. This methodology achieves a much needed flexibility of the Islamic rulings with the change of time and circumstances, a flexibility that is essential for the universality of Islam and its way of life.

NOTES

1. Shamsuddin Ibn al-Qayyim, *Iʿlām al-Muwaqiʿīn*, annotated by Taha Saad, Vol. 1 (Beirut: Dar al-jīl, 1973), 333.
2. Also translated and understood as objectives, ends, or principles.
3. See al-Ṭahir Ibn ʿĀshūr, *maqāṣid al-sharīʿah al-islamiyah*, annotated by Mohamed al- Ṭahir al-Mesawi (Kuala Lumpur: al-Fajr 1997), 183.
4. Also deemed the theory or fundamentals of Islamic Law.
5. See Abdul-Malik al-Juwaini, *al-Burhān fī uṣūl al-fiqh*, annotated by Abdul-Azim al-Deeb (Qatar: Wazarat al-shu'un al-dīniyah, 1400 AH), 183.
6. See Abū Ḥāmid Muḥammad al-Ghazālī, *al-Mustasfā fīʿ ilm al- ʿuṣūl*, annotated by Mohammed Abdul-Salam Abdul Shafi, Vol. 1 (Beirut: Dar al-kutub al-ʿilmiya, 1413 AH), 172.
7. See Shihabuddin al-Qarafi, *al-Furūq (maʿa hawamishih)*, annotated by Khalil Mansour, Vol. 5 (Beirut: Dar al-kutub al-ʿilmiya, 1998), 478.
8. See Ali al-Amidi, *al-Iḥkam fī ʿuṣūl al-aḥkam*, Vol. 5 (Beirut: Dar al-kitāb al-ʿarabī, 1404 AH), 391.
9. See Abdullah Ibn Qudama, *Rawdat al-nazir wa-janat al-manazir*, annotated by Abdul Aziz Abdul Rahman al-Saeed, Vol. 3 (Riyadh: Mohammed ibn Saud University, 1399 AH), 42.
10. See Mohammed al-Sarakhsi, *ʿUṣūl al-Sarakhsi*, Vol. 9 (Beirut: Dar al-maʿrifa, n.d.), 205.
11. See Ibn Abdul-Salām, *Qawāʾid*, Vol. 1 (n.d.), 23.
12. See Mohammad Kamal Imam, *al-Daleel al-Irshadi Ila Maqasid al-Shari`ah al-Islamiyyah*, 6 vols (London: al-Maqasid Research Centre, 2010).
13. See al-Ghazālī, 2011, Vol. 1, 538.
14. See Abu Ishaq al-Shatibi, *al-Muwafaqat fī ʿuṣūl al-sharīʿah*, Vol. 2 (Beirut: Dar al-maʿrifa, n.d.), 5.
15. See Jamal Attiyah, *Nahwa taf'il maqāṣid al-sharīʿah* (Amman: al-Maʿhad al-ʿalami lil-fikr al-islami, 2001), 46.

16. See Numan Jughaim, *Turuq al-kashf ʿan maqāṣid al-sharia* (Malaysia: Dar al-nafaiss, 2002), 26–35.
17. See Jasser Auda, *Maqasid al-Shariah as Philosophy of the Islamic Law: A Systems Approach* (Herndon, VA: International Institute of Islamic Thought, 2008), 12–30.
18. See al-Ṭahir Ibn ʿĀshūr, *maqāṣid al-sharīʿah al-islamiyah*, annotated by Mohamed al- Ṭahir al-Mesawi (Kuala Lumpur: al-Fajr, 1997).
19. See ibid., 183.
20. Kamaluddin al-Siwasi, *Sharḥ fatḥ al-qadir*, Vol. 4 (Beirut: Dar al-fikr, n.d.), 513.
21. See al-Ṭahir Ibn ʿĀshūr, *Usul al-nizam al-ijtimaʿī fī-l islam*, annotated by Mohamed al-Ṭahir Mesawi (Amman: Dar al-Nafaʾis, 2001).
22. See ibid., 256, 268.
23. See ibid., 270–281.
24. See Jamal Attiyah, *Nahwa taf'il maqāṣid al-sharīʿah* (Amman: al-Maʿhad al-ʿalami lī-l-fikr al-islami, 2001), 49.
25. See Mawil Izzi Dien, *Islamic Law: From Historical Foundations to Contemporary Practice* (Edinburgh: Edinburgh University Press, 2004), 131–132.
26. See Yusuf al-Qaradawi, *Kayf nataʿamal maʿa al-qurʾā al-ʿazīm?* (Cairo: Dar al-shurūk, 1999).
27. Ṭaha Jabir al-Alwani, *Maqasid al-sharīʿah* (Beirut: IIIT and Dar al-hadī, 2001).
28. Ibid., 25.
29. See Mohammad al-Ghazālī, *al-Sunnah al-nabawiyah bayna ahl al-fiqh wa ahl al-hadīth* (Cairo: Dar al-shuruq, 1996), 161.
30. See Mohamed El-Awa, ed., *Maqasid al-sharīʿah al-islamiya: Dirasat fī qadaya al-manhaj wa qadaya al-tatbīq* (London: Al-Maqasid Research Centre, 2006), 85.
31. See Ṭaha Jabir al-Alwani, *Issues in Contemporary Islamic Thought* (London: International Institute of Islamic Thought [IIIT], 2005).
32. Ibid., 164–166.
33. Medhi Shamsuddin, *al-Ijtihad wal-tajdīd fī-l-fiqh al-islami* (Beirut: al-muʾassassah al-dawliyah, 1999), 128.
34. See ibid., 129.
35. See Abdelwahab El-Affendi, ed., *Rethinking Islam and Modernity: Essays in Honour of Fathi Osman* (London: Islamic Foundation, 2001), 45.
36. See Hassan al-Turabi, *Emancipation of Women: An Islamic Perspective* (London: Muslim Information Centre, 2000).
37. See ibid., 29.
38. See Abdul-Karim Soroush, "The Evolution and Devolution of Religious Knowledge," in *Liberal Islam: A Sourcebook*, ed. Charles Kurzman (Oxford: Oxford University Press, 1998).
39. See ibid., 250.
40. See Shihabuddin al-Qarafi, *al-Dhakhīrah*, Vol. 1 (Beirut: Dar al-arab., 1994), 153.

41. See ibid., Vol. 2, 60.
42. See Burhaneddin Ibn Farhoun, *Tabsirat al-ḥukkam fī 'uṣūl al-aqdiyah wa manahij al-aḥkām*, annotated by Jamal Mar'ashli (Beirut: Dar al-kutub al-'ilmiyah, 1995).
43. See ibid., Vol. 2, 270.
44. See Friedrich Meinecke, *Historicism: The Rise of a New Historical Outlook*, translated by J. E. Anderson (London: Herder and Herder, 1972); V. Taylor, and C. Winquist, ed., *Encyclopedia of Postmodernism* (New York: Routledge, 2001).
45. See Nasr Hamed Abu Zaid, "Divine Attributes in the Qur'an," in *Islam and Modernity: Muslim Intellectuals Respond*, ed. John Cooper, Ronald L. Nettler, and Mohamed Mahmoud (London: I. B.Tauris, 1998), 199; Mohamed Arkoun, "Rethinking Islam Today," in *Liberal Islam: A Sourcebook*, ed. by Charles Kurzman (Oxford: Oxford University Press, 1998), 211.
46. See Haideh Moghissi, *Feminism and Islamic Fundamentalism: The Limits of Postmodern Analysis* (New York: Zed Books, 1999).
47. Ibid., 141.
48. See Ibn Warraq, "Apostasy and Human Rights," *Free Inquiry* (February/March 2006): 53.
49. See ibid., 42.
50. See Abū Ḥāmid Muḥammad al-Ghazālī, *Maqāṣid al-falāsifah* (Cairo: Dar al-ma'arif, 1961), 62.
51. See Ahmad Ibn Taymiyah, *Kutub wa rasa'il wa fatwa*, ed. Abdur-Rahman al-Najdi (Riyadh: Maktabat Ibn Taymiyah, n.d.), 131.
52. See Abdul-Aziz al-Bukhari, *Kashf al-asrār*, Vol. 3 (Beirut: Dar al-kutub al-'ilmiyyah, 1997), 77.
53. See Jasser Auda, *Fiqh al-Maqāṣid: Inatat al-aḥkām al-shar'īya bi-maqāṣidiha* (Herndon, VA: al-Ma'had al-'alami lil-fikr al-islami, 2006), 65–68.
54. See Ali Al-Subki, *al-'Ibhaj fī sharḥ al-minhaj* (Beirut: Dar al-nashr 1983), 218.
55. See Jasser Auda, *Fiqh al-Maqāṣid: Inatat al-aḥkām al-shar'īya bi-maqāṣidiha* (Herndon, VA: al-Ma'had al-'alami lil-fikr al-islami, 2006), 106.
56. Abu Bakr Ibn al-Arabi, *'Aridat al-ahwadhi*, Vol. 10 (Cairo: Dar al-wahy al-muḥammadi, n.d.), 264.
57. See Badran Badran, *Adillat al-Tarjīh al-muta'aridah wa wujuh al-tarjīh baynaha* (Alexandria, VA: Mu'assasat shabab al-jami'ah, 1974), Ch. 4.
58. See Jasser Auda, *Naqd nazariyyat al-naskh* (Beirut: al-Shabakah al-arabiyyah 2012), 30–50.
59. See Mohammad Nada, *al-Naskh fī al-Qur'ān* (Cairo: al-Dar al-arabiyah li-l-kutub, 1996), 25.
60. See Ibn Amir al-Haj, *al-Taqrir wa-l-tahbir fī 'ilm 'uṣūl al-fiqh*, Vol. 3 (Beirut: Dar al-fikr, 1996), 4.
61. Auda 1996, 105–110.
62. See Abdul Majid al-Sousarah, *Manhaj al-tawfīq wa-l tarjīh bayn mukhtalaf al-hadīth wa atharuhu fī-l-fiqh al-islami* (Amman: Dar al-nafa'is, 1997), 395.
63. Burhan Zuraiq, *al-Sahifah: Mithaq al-rasūl* (Damascus: Dar al-numair & Dar ma'ād, 1996), 353.

64. See ibid., 216.
65. Ṭaha Jabir al-Alwani, *Maqasid al-sharī'ah* (Beirut: IIIT and Dar al-Hadi, 2001), 89.
66. See Abdullah Ibn Qutayba, *Ta'wil mukhtalaf al-hadīth* (Cairo: Dar al-fikr al-arabi, 1978).
67. See Jasser Auda, *Fiqh al-Maqāṣid: Inatat al-aḥkām al-shar'īya bi-maqāṣidiha* (Herndon, VA: al-Ma'had al-'alami lil-fikr al-islami, 2006), Ch. 3.
68. Al-Ṭahir Ibn 'Āshūr, *Maqasid al-Shari'ah al-Islamiyah*, annotated by Mohamed al- Ṭahir al-Mesawi (Kuala Lumpur: al-Fajr, 1997), 236.
69. See Kamaluddin al-Siwasi, *Sharh fath al-qadir*, Vol. 3 (Beirut: Dar al-fikr, n.d.), 258.
70. See Mohammad Amin Ibn Abedin, *Al-Hashiyah*, Vol. 3 (Beirut: Dar al-fikr, 2000), 55.
71. Mohammad Al-Ghazālī, *Nazarat fī al-Qur'ān* (Cairo: Nahdat misr, 2002), 194.
72. See al-Waleed Ibn Rushd, *Bidāyat al-mujtahid wa nihayat al-muqtasid*, Vol. 2 (Beirut: Dar al-fikr, n.d.), 42–44.
73. Mohammad Al-Sanaani, *Subul al-salam sharh bulugh al-maram min adilat al-aḥkam*, ed. Mohammad Abdul Aziz al-Khouli, Vol. 3 (Beirut: Dar ihya' al-turath al-'arabi, 1379 AH), 227.
74. Al-Ṭahir Ibn 'Āshūr, *maqāṣid al-sharī'ah al-islamiyah*, annotated by Mohamed al- Ṭahir al-Mesawi (Kuala Lumpur: al-Fajr, 1997).
75. See ibid., 234.
76. Ibid., 236.

BIBLIOGRAPHY

Abd al-Salām, 'Izz al-Dīn. *Qawā'id al-aḥkām fī masāliḥ al-anām*. Edited by 'Abd al-Laṭīf 'Abd al-Raḥmān. Beirut: Dār al-Kutub al-'Ilmiyyah, 1999.

Abu Zaid Nasr Hamed. "Divine Attributes in the Qur'an." In *Islam and Modernity: Muslim Intellectuals Respond*, edited by John Cooper, Ronald L. Nettler, and Mohamed Mahmoud. London: I. B. Tauris, 1998.

Al-Alwani, Ṭaha Jabir. *Issues in Contemporary Islamic Thought*. London: International Institute of Islamic Thought, 2005.

———. *Maqāṣid al-sharī'ah*. Beirut: International Institute of Islamic Thought and Dār al-Hadī, 2001.

Al-Āmidī, Sayf al-Dīn. *Al-Iḥkām fī uṣūl al-aḥkām*. Edited by 'Abd al-Razzāq 'Afīfī, 4 vols., 2nd edition. Beirut: Dar al-Kitāb al-'Arabī, 1983.

Al-Bukhārī, Abdul-'Azīz. *Kashf al-asrār*. Beirut: Dār al-Kutub al-'Ilmiyah, 1997.

Al-Ghazālī, Abū Ḥāmid Muḥammad. *Al-Mustasfā fī 'ilm al-uṣūl*. Annotated by Mohammed Abdul-Salām Abdul Shāfi. Beirut: Dār al-Kutub al-'Ilmiya, 1413 AH.

———. *Maqāṣid al-falāsifah*. Cairo: Dār al-Ma'ārif, 1961.

———. *Al-Sunnah al-nabawiyah bayna ahl al-fiqh wa ahl al-hadīth*. Cairo: Dār al-Shurūq, 1996.

———. *Nazarat fī al-qur'ān*. Cairo: Nahdat Misr, 2002.

Al-Haj, Ibn Amir. *Al-Taqrīr wa-l-tahbīr fī 'ilm uṣūl al-fiqh*. Beirut: Dār al-Fikr, 1996.
Al-Juwainī, Abdul-Mālik. *Al-Burhān fī uṣūl al-fiqh*. Annotated by Abdul 'Azim al-Dīb. Qatar: Wazarat al-Shu'un al-Dīniyah, 1400 AH.
Al-Qaradawi Yusuf. *Kayf nata'amal ma'a al-qur'ā al-'azīm*? Cairo: Dār al-Shurūk, 1999.
Al-Qarāfī, Shihabuddīn. *Al-Dhakhīrah*. Beirut: Dār al-Arab, 1994.
———. *Al-Furūq (ma'a hawamishih)*. Annotated by Khalil Mansour. Beirut: Dār al-Kutub al-'Ilmiya, 1998.
Al-Sanā'ī, Muḥammad. *Subul al-salām sharh bulūgh al-maram min adilat al-*aḥkām. Edited by Muḥammad Abdul 'Azīz al-Khūlī. Beirut: Dār Ihya' al-Turāth al-'Arabī, 1379 AH.
Al-Sarakhsī, Muḥammad. *Uṣūl al-Sarakhsī*. Beirut: Dar al-Ma'rifa, n.d.
Al-Shāṭibī, Abu Ishāq. *Al-Muwafaqāt fī uṣūl al-sharī'ah*. Beirut: Dār al-Ma'rifa, n. d.
Al-Siwāsī, Kamāluddīn. *Sharh fatḥ al-qadīr*. Beirut: Dār al-Fikr, n.d.
Al-Sousarah, Abdul Majid. *Manhaj al-tawfīq wa-l-tarjīh bayn mukhtalaf al-hadīth wa atharuhu fī-l-fiqh al-islāmī*. Amman: Dār al-Nafā'is, 1997.
Al-Subki 'Alī. *Al-'Ibhaj fī sharḥ al-minhaj*. Beirut: Dār al-Nashr, 1983.
Al-Turabi, Hassan. *Emancipation of Women: An Islamic Perspective*. London: Muslim Information Centre, 2000.
Arkoun, Mohamed. "Rethinking Islam Today." In *Liberal Islam: A Sourcebook*, edited by Charles Kurzman. Oxford: Oxford University Press, 1998.
Attiyah, Jamāl al-Dīn. *Nahwa taf'il maqāṣid al-sharī'ah*. Amman: al-Ma'had al-'Alamī lil-Fikr al-Islamī, 2001.
Auda, Jasser. *Fiqh al-maqāṣid: Inatāt al-aḥkām al-shar'īyah bi-maqāṣidiha*. Herndon, VA: al-Ma'had al-'Alamī li-l-Fikr al-Islāmī, 2006.
———. *Maqāṣid al-Shariah as Philosophy of the Islamic Law: A Systems Approach*. Herndon, VA: International Institute of Islamic Thought, 2008.
———. *Naqd nazariyyat al-naskh*. Beirut: al-Shabakah al-Arabiyyah, 2012.
Badran, Abū al-'Aynayn Badrān. *Adillat al-tarjīh al-muta'aridah wa wujūh al-tarjīh baynaha*. Alexandria, VA: Mu'assasat Shabāb al-Jāmi'ah, 1974.
El-Affendi, Abdelwahab, ed. *Rethinking Islam and Modernity: Essays in Honour of Fathi Osman*. London: Islamic Foundation, 2001.
El-Awa, Mohamed, ed. *Maqasid al-sharī'ah al-islamiyah: Dirasat fī qadaya al-manhaj wa qadaya al-tatbīq*. London: Maqasid Research Centre, 2006.
Ibn 'Ābidīn, Muḥammad Amīn. *Al-Hashiyah*. Beirut: Dār al-Fikr, 2000.
Ibn al-'Arabī, Abū Bakr. *'Aridat al-ahwadhī*. Cairo: Dār al-Wahy al-Muḥammadī, n.d.
Ibn al-Ashur, Tahir. *Maqasid al-shari'ah al-islamiyah*. Annotated by Mohamed al-Tahir al-Mesawi. Kuala Lumpur: al-Fajr 1997.
———. *Usūl al-niẓām al-ijtimā'ī fī-l-islām*. Annotated by Mohamed al-Tahir al-Mesawi. Amman: Dār al-Nafā'is, 2001.
Ibn al-Qayyim, Shamsuddīn. *I'lam al-muwaqi'īn*. Annotated by Taha Saad. Beirut: Dār al-Jīl, 1973.
Ibn Farhūn, Burhanuddīn. *Tabsirat al-ḥukkam fī uṣūl al-aqdiyah wa manāhij al-aḥkām*. Annotated by Jamal Mar'ashli. Beirut: Dār al-Kutub al-'Ilmiyah, 1995.

Ibn Qudāma, Abdullāh. *Rawdat al-nazīr wa-janat al-manāzir*. Annotated by Abdul Aziz Abdul Rahman al-Saeed. Riyadh: Mohammed ibn Saud University, 1978.
Ibn Qutayba, Abdullāh. *Ta'wīl mukhtalaf al-hadīth*. Cairo: Dār al-Fikr al-Arabi, 1978.
Ibn Rushd, al-Walīd. *Bidāyat al-mujtahid wa nihayat al-muqtasid*. Beirut: Dār al-Fikr, n.d.
Ibn Taymiyah, Aḥmad. *Kutub wa rasā'il wa fatwa*. Edited by Abdur-Rahman al-Najdi. Riyadh: Maktabat Ibn Taymiyah, n.d.
Ibn Warraq. "Apostasy and Human Rights." *Free Inquiry* (February/March 2006): 53–55.
Imām, Muḥammad Kamāl. *Al-Dalīl al-irshādī ilā maqāṣid al-sharī'ah al-islamiyah*. 6 vols., London: al-Maqasid Research Centre, 2010.
Izzi Dien, Mawil. *Islamic Law: From Historical Foundations to Contemporary Practice*. Edinburgh: Edinburgh University Press, 2004.
Jughaim, Nu'mān. *Turuq al-kashf 'an maqāṣid al-sharī'ah*. Malaysia: Dār al-Nafaiss, 2002.
Meinecke, Friedrich. *Historicism: The Rise of a New Historical Outlook*. Translated by J. E. Anderson. London: Herder and Herder, 1972.
Moghissi, Haideh. *Feminism and Islamic Fundamentalism: The Limits of Postmodern Analysis*. New York: Zed Books, 1999.
Nada, Mohammad. *Al-Naskh fī al-qur'ān*. Cairo: al-Dār al-Arabiyah li-l-Kutub.
Shamsuddīn, Medhi. *Al-Ijtihād wal-tajdīd fī-l-fiqh al-islamī*. Beirut: al-Mu'assassah al-Dawliyah, 1999.
Soroush, Abdul-Karim. "The Evolution and Devolution of Religious Knowledge." In *Liberal Islam: A Sourcebook*, edited by Charles Kurzman. Oxford: Oxford University Press, 1998.
Taylor, Victor E., and Charles E. Winquist, ed. *Encyclopedia of Postmodernism*. New York: Routledge, 2001.
Zuraiq, Burhan. *Al-Sahīfah: Mithāq al-rasūl*. Damascus: Dār al-Numair and Dār Ma'ād, 1996.

Chapter 3

Freedom of Religion in the Age of Multi-Religious Societies with Special Reference to *Maqāṣid al-Sharīʿah*

Muhammad Khalid Masud

DIVERSE APPROACHES TO THE CONCEPT OF *SHARI'AH*

Contemporary debates about freedom of religion are largely informed by perspectives on the possibility of diversity in religious thought. It is significant to note that *Fiqh*, often translated as Islamic law, is not the only Islamic way of life (*sharīʿah*) that Muslims developed. Like *adab* (literary tradition), *falsafa* (philosophy), *akhlāq* (ethics), *tasawwuf* (sufism), and *kalām* (theology), it is one of several approaches to law, ethics, and morality. These approaches differ in terms of authority, methods of interpretation, and emphasis in defining the way of life and boundaries of religion. Diversity, mentioned as *ikhtilāf* in the *Qurʾān* as a sign of divine creation and sustenance, includes references to the phenomena of change and continuity in nature, multiplicity in life forms, and differences of colors and languages and levels of understanding among humans. The *Qurʾān* invites the attention of scholars to deliberate on this diversity (Q 2:213, 3:22, 30:22, 5:48, 10:99, and 11:118).

Fiqh, as an effort to understand *sharīʿah*, produced more than nineteen schools, all of them recognizing each other's legal validity. Adherence to these different schools of law is still reflected in the diverse personal laws in Muslim societies. The method of legal reasoning (*ijtihād*) considers difference of opinion legitimate, even in the case of error. Most jurists in the formative period, like Abu Hanifa (d. 767) and Imam Malik (d. 795), supported this diversity, against the wishes of the Abbasid caliph Abu Jaʿfar al-Mansur (d. 775) and his secretary Ibn Muqaffa (d. 759), who were apprehensive of this legal diversity.[1] More significantly, Muslim jurists differed also in their methods of legal reasoning. A debate about the principles of interpretation among jurists continues, even today. The Hanafī and Mālikī jurists, for instance, employed principles like juristic preference (*istiḥsān*) and human good (*istislāḥ*). Imam al-Shafiʿī (d. 820) stressed that the *Qurʾān* and *sunnah* are the only primary sources and criticized reliance on principles like local practice, customs, and juristic preferences. He stressed on subjecting legal reasoning to the method of *qiyās*, a process of legal reasoning that regulated the deduction of rules by connecting the process to specific texts of the *Qurʾān* and *ḥadith* (sayings and practice of the Prophet Muhammad). He introduced the notion of *ijmāʿ* (scholarly consensus) to unify the laws. Diverse opinions, however, developed into numerous schools of law (*madhāhib*). All jurists recognized the legitimacy of adherence to a specific school (*taqlīd*), and thus validated legal and religious diversity. However, overemphasis on continuity and consensus in Islamic legal theory prevents an occasional visitor from seeing diversity in Islamic legal thought. Restricting *ijtihād* to the confines of the schools of law and limiting legal reasoning to textual precedence frequently exposed the limits of the method of *qiyās* in dealing with the social diversity. Al-Shāṭibī's doctrine of *maqāṣid al-sharīʿah* must be seen as a consequence of this progressive exposure that challenged the limits of religious freedom within the Islamic tradition.

MAQĀṢID AL-SHARĪʿAH ACCORDING TO AL-SHĀṬIBĪ

Al-Shāṭibī uses two terms, *maqāṣid*, plural of *maqṣid* (objective), and *qaṣd* (intent) to explain the objectives of Islamic law. Intent, used in its ordinary meaning, refers to the intent of the Lawgiver (God), as well as that of humans. Intent in the legal meaning refers to the objectives of law. From this perspective, al-Shāṭibī clarifies that there is no contradiction in the objectives of law and human interest because God also aims to protect human interest. He concludes by saying that as human and divine objectives both aim to protect human interests, they are the objectives of legal obedience, not only from human perspective but also from Divine.

Intent of the Lawgiver

Al-Shāṭibī elaborates the above point discussing the four levels of the intent of the Lawgiver (*qaṣd al-shāriʿ*) as summarized below.

Human Interests (maṣlaḥa)

According to al-Shāṭibī, the primary intent of the Lawgiver is to preserve collective, as well as individual, human interests in instituting the law. Muslim theologians, philosophers, and jurists before al-Shāṭibī questioned the role of *maṣlaḥa* as the intent of the Lawgiver. For instance, can cause or reason be attributed to the commands of God? Ash'arī theologians disallowed such attribution because it limits God's omnipotence and sovereignty. Similarly, God's intent cannot be separated from the action of creation; when He intends something it immediately comes into existence. If God intended *maslaḥa*, it would have immediately come into existence.

Al-Shāṭibī distinguished between will and intent, and between intent to create and intent to require or command to do or not to do something. In the latter case, human will, as agency to translate command into action, is required. He described that the Lawgiver intends *sharī'ah* to protect the five basic human interests: religion (*dīn*), life (*nafs*), progeny (*nasl*), intellect (*'aql*), and property (*māl*). He also describes the three zones of protection as the *ḍarūrīyyāt* (necessities), *ḥājīyyāt* (requirements), and *taḥsīnīyyāt* (supplements).[2] The first zone of necessities refers to the above-mentioned five values that Islamic law protects as basic universal human needs. The second zone protects the zone of basic needs by allowing required exceptions to rules in case of hardship and other contingencies. The third zone protects the first and second zones by taking care of local cultural aesthetics and supplementary needs to fulfill the overall objectives of law in a society. We will discuss this point later.

Communication (ifhām)

The second intent of the Lawgiver is communication, so that human beings can understand these laws. Here, al-Shāṭibī discusses the issues of communication related with language, human and social perception, hermeneutics, and semantics. Al-Shāṭibī explains two levels of communication: one relates to language referring to the ordinary meaning of the words (*al-dalāla al-aslīyya*) and the other relates to the social levels of understanding of the message. He clarifies that law must be understood to a common man at a general level (*ummīyya*) because otherwise it would be an impossible legal obligation. A command must be understandable to all of its subjects, not only in words and sentences but also in the linguistic and cultural meaning of understanding.[3]

Human Obligation (taklīf)

The third intent of the Lawgiver is obligation. Al-Shāṭibī discusses two aspects of legal obligation. First is the human physical capacity to undertake this obligation, particularly explaining the limits of human capacity in terms of physical ability (*qudra*) to carry out the obligation, and the second is the legal capacity (*ahlīyya*). He discusses physical capacity and its limits when it is considered a hardship (*mashaqqa*), which demands exception or exemption. Hardship is not the requirement of legal obligation. Similarly, legal capacity defines when a human is considered legally obliged.[4]

Human Agency (dukhūl al-mukallaf)

The fourth intent is human agency to legal obedience. Al-Shāṭibī explains why humans are required to abide by the law. Analyzing the notion of individual personal interests (*huzuz)*, al-Shāṯibī regards them inclusive with legal interests or rights (*huqūq*). He clarifies that individual human interests in legal obedience must not be regarded as analogous with arbitrary choices, pleasures, and desires (*hawā'*). He also explains that overexaggerated emphasis on religious obedience (*ta'abbud*) is not required for legal obedience.[5]

Intent of the Human Subject

The second level of the intent of the Lawgiver pertains to the intent of the human subjects (*mukallaf*). In this discussion, al-Shāṭibī distinguishes between legal intent and personal motives. Al-Shāṭibī is mainly concerned with the question of intention and issues related to law and psychology or personal behavior. Whereas he states that in obedience to law, humans must have the same objectives in mind as enunciated by the Lawgiver, in his analysis, al-Shāṭibī shows that the intent of the Lawgiver is not to seek mere obedience but rather what constitutes human interests.[6]

Al-Maṣlaḥa

Etymologically, the word *maṣlaḥa* is an infinitive noun of the root *ṣ-l-ḥ*. Its semantic field covers the meanings of good, uncorrupted, right, just, virtuous, and honest. *Maṣlaḥa* indicates the state of possessing these virtues. In English, *maṣlaḥa* has been translated as good, common good, human or public interest, human welfare, and so on. Al-Shāṭibī's doctrine of *maqāṣid al-sharī'ah* is an attempt to establish *maṣlaḥa* as the foundational principle of the objectives of law. He clarifies the assumption of the relativity of *maṣlaḥa*, its relationship with the notions of legal obligation (*taklīf*) and personal interest (*huzuz*). Al-Shāṭibī defines *maṣlaḥa* as 'that which concerns the subsistence of human life, the completion of man's livelihood, and the acquisition of what his emotional and intellectual qualities require of him, in an absolute sense.'[7]

The terms "subsistence," "completion," and "acquisition" in the above definition point to three zones of *maṣlaḥa*: *ḍarūrī*, *ḥājī*, and *taḥsīnī*. Arguably, these zones resemble al-Ghazālī's three categories of *maṣlaḥa* mentioned above but, according to al-Ghazālī, *taḥsīnī* is not supported by the *Qur'ān* and *sunnah*; hence, this category of *maṣlaḥa* is not acceptable to him.[8] On the other hand, al-Shāṭibī considers these three zones of *maṣlaḥa* as mutually protective. As *maṣlaḥa*, in the first zone, consists of the following five human needs (*ḍārūriyyāt* or basics)[9], and the principal objective of the *sharīʿah* is to preserve human subsistence, he calls first zone of *maṣlaḥa ḍarūrīyya*. *Sharīʿah* preserves the five needs by providing rules that one should abide by and prescribes punishments for those who violate these rules.[10] Al-Shāṭibī observes that these basic needs are universally recognized in all religious and legal systems.

The *sharīʿah* creates obligations and penalties to preserve *maṣlaḥa* in three ways: religious obligations (*ʿibādāt*), legal obligations (*muʿāmalāt*), and penalties (*jīnayāt*). The first two provide preservation in an affirmative sense; the third constitutes preventive measures to preserve them. Religious and legal obligations are intertwined; *ʿibādāt* include pure religious rituals like prayer, fasting, and pilgrimage but also the obligation of *zakah* that is paid annually on savings, and it is called "purification of wealth." *ʿIbādāt* pertains to relations between God and humans and preserves the basic needs of religion. *Muʿāmalāt* category covers matters relating to personal safety, protecting life and intellect, marriage, divorce and inheritance, protecting the progeny, and business transactions and property. In addition to legal obligations, basic needs in *muʿāmalāt* are also determined by social practices (*ʿadat*) defined by culture, habits, and customs.[11]

Al-Shāṭibī clarifies that *maṣlaḥa* in the second zone of *ḥājiyyāt* (needs) provides respite (*tawsiʿa*) by removing strictness of the literal application of law, which may lead to impediments and hardships and eventually to the disruption of law. He illustrates this respite in *ʿibādāt* with examples of the laws of concessions in prayer and in fasting on account of sickness or journey; these concessions preserve a person from hardship. Similarly, allowing partnership in trade with capital (*qirād*) and agrarian association (*musaqāt*) removes hardship in commercial life.[12] Al-Shāṭibī describes *taḥṣīniyāt*, the third zone of *maṣlaḥa*, as adopting the best practices (*ʿādat*) and avoiding manners that are disliked by wiser people. He illustrates this zone with the examples of cleanliness and decency in covering the private parts of the body, etiquette, and table manners.[13]

Al-Shāṭibī regards the above three zones of *maṣlaḥa* as a system connected to one another. His detailed analysis reveals two aspects of their relationships with one another. First, each zone requires additional elements to supplement and complement *maṣlaḥa* at this zone. Secondly, every zone is protective of the other.[14]

Al-Maṣlaḥa al-Mursala

Some scholars, like Hussain Hamid Hassan (1981), read al-Shāṭibī's doctrine of *maṣlaḥa* as a concept of *al-maṣlaḥa al-mursala*, not supported by a specific text. This perception overlooks not only the context of the doctrine, namely human interest as the intent of the Lawgiver, but also al-Shāṭibī's distinction between *al-maṣlaḥa al-mursala* and *maslaḥa.* Whereas Hassan confuses al-maslaḥa with *al-maslaḥa al-mursala* and questions its validity because it is not founded on a particular text of the Qur'an, for al-Shāṭibī the criterion is not the particular text but the overall intent of the Lawgiver. Hassan's criticism relocates *maṣlaḥa* in the framework of four-source theory. Al-Shāṭibī clarifies that evidence contrary to the specific text of the *Qur'ān* and *sunnah,* even a solitary *ḥadith (khabar al-waḥīd*), is not definitive evidence.[15] He questions even the claim indirect affinity (*al-munāsib al-gharīb*) for *al-maṣlaḥa al-mursala* if it is contrary to the overall objective of the text. According to al-Shāṭibī, *al-maṣlaḥa al-mursala* may not be based on a specific text but it is not contrary to the overall teachings of the Qur'an.[16]

To appreciate how al-Shāṭibī's approach to *al-maṣlaḥa al-mursala* differs from other jurists, one needs to keep in mind that two different definitions of *uṣūl* in the history of Islamic legal theory: some jurists defined *uṣūl* as basic rules on which the opinions of a group of jurists were founded; al-Shafi'ī defined them as sources of law. After al-Shafi'ī a general consensus developed to treat *uṣūl al-fiqh* as four sources, namely the *Qur'ān*, *sunnah*, *qiyās*, and *ijmā'*. The other principles were accommodated as secondary sources and were subjected to the rules of *qiyās*, especially to the rules of *ta'līl* (discovering the reason or cause behind a particular rule in the text) and *masālik al- 'illa* (methods of discovering the cause in the texts of the Qur'an and Hadith). It was from this perspective that al-Ghazālī challenged the validity of the principle of *istiṣlāḥ* and classified the notion of *maṣlaḥa* into three categories: one, supported by the scriptures (*maṣlaḥa mu'tabara*), the other dismissed by the scriptures (*maṣlaḥa mulgha*), and another which is neither supported nor prohibited *al-maṣlaḥa al-mursala*. The third was then subjected to the rules of *ta'lil*, applying the conditions and classifications of conformity (*mula'ima*) and affinity (*munāsaba*) to the texts.[17]

As explained above, rather than employing the deductive method of *qiyās* and *ta'līl* to examine specific evidence, al-Shāṭibī used the method of induction (*istiqrā'*) to examine all the commands and prohibitions, as well as the general teachings in the *Qur'ān* and *sunnah.* He discovered that *maṣlaḥa* was the general and universal intent of the Lawgiver. Al-Shāṭibī examined the principles of *istiṣlāḥ* (Maliki principle of inference on the basis of *public interest*), *istidlāl* (Shafi'i principle of logical inference), *al-istidlāl al-mursal* (logical inference in the absence of the four sources of Islamic law), *istiḥsān* (Hanafi principle of inference by juristic preference between analogy and logical inference), and al-*maṣlaḥa al-mursala* (principle of indirect inference from the text) from the perspective of *maqaṣid* (objectives *of sharī'a*). Strictly speaking, *uṣūl al-fiqh*, in al-Shāṭibī's discussion, means to discover the universals in the textual sources by the method of induction.[18]

Al-Shāṭibī treated only the *Qurʾān* and *sunnah* as sources (*adilla*), and excluded *qiyās* and *ijmāʿ* in his discussion. Defining *uṣūl al-fiqh* as principles rather than sources, al-Shāṭibī argued that, based on an inductive reading of all the Qur'anic verses, one finds that *maṣlaḥa* is the universal (*kulli*) and definitive (*qatʿī*) principle of the *sharīʿah*. Reconstructing al-Ghazālī's three categories of *maṣlaḥa* as mutually protective zones (*ḥimā*), al-Shāṭibī distinguished *maṣlaḥa* as the *maqṣid* of *sharīʿah* from *al-maṣlaḥa al-mursala,* which may be discussed as categories of neutral (*mubaḥ*), exception (*ʿafw*) or silence (*maskut ʿanhu*) of the Lawgiver, where there is no supporting explicit text.

Method of Reasoning

The *maqāṣid* are universal principles that are known by inductive analysis of the injunctions in the *Qurʾān* and *sunnah.* As far as linguistic and semantic aspects of determining the legal cause or reason are concerned, one must conform to the Arab usage. Also, in the process of legal reasoning, distinction is maintained between rational proof and legal proof; only the latter creates legal obligations. Al-Shāṭibī discusses only the *Qurʾān* and *sunnah* as sources, not *ijmāʿ* (consensus) and *qiyās*, which he usually terms as *raʾy* (opinion).

Regarding the *Qurʾān*, al-Shāṭibī analyzed the issues relating to language, like words and meanings that are essential to understanding the text and its interpretation. He discusses, for instance, how to decide what is clear or ambiguous (*iḥkām/tashabuh*), what are the modes of expression for commands and prohibitions (*awāmir/nawāhī*), how to distinguish between general and particular statements (*ʿumūm/khūṣuṣ*), and how to distinguish between the modes of exposition and concision (*bayān/ijmāl*) in the *Qurʾān.* He clarifies that sciences like *ʿilm al-kalām* (Muslim scholastic theology) are not directly related to the deduction of laws. He also stresses that the Qur'anic verses revealed in Mecca provide fundamentals and should be taken as guiding principles to understand and interpret the injunctions revealed in Medina, which are details of the Meccan principles. Al-Shāṭibī defines *sunnah* primarily to mean the statements, actions, and approvals of actions by the Prophet himself; the term thus also pertains to the practice of the companions of the Prophet. However, the *sunnah* is probably definitive (*maẓnūna*), and the *Qurʾān* is absolutely definitive (*maqṭūʿ bihi*). Since *sunnah* explains and provides details for the Qur'anic injunctions, it stands next to the *Qurʾān.*[19]

As for legal reasoning (*ijtihād),* al-Shāṭibī argues that, except for laws like *ʿibādāt* that cannot be extended further, need for *ijtihād* continues in other areas like *mu ʿāmalāt*. This type of *ijtihād* follows three processes: the first process pertains to clarifying, distinguishing, and sifting legal evidence and textual sources and is called *tanqīḥ al-manāṭ*; the second consists of deducing and locating the precedents and textual evidence and is called *takhrīj al-manāṭ*; and the third process identifies and applies the criteria for reasoning to the given cases and is called *taḥqīq al-manāṭ*. Al-Shāṭibī recognizes *fatwa* as a product of *ijtihād*. A *fatwa* must conform to a Mufti's own practice and deeds. The authority of a *fatwa* rests in its infallibility that is either based on revelation, as in case of the Prophet, or on consensus, as in case of companions of the Prophet, or on the official position of the Mufti. A *fatwā* by an unauthorized Mufti does not create legal obligation.

Al-Shāṭibī's doctrine of *maqāṣid al-sharīʿah* gained popularity in the modern period when the reformers and modern jurists found its application quite relevant to modern unprecedented problems for which *qiyās*, as a method of legal reasoning, was insufficient. Most Muslim thinkers like Muhammad Abduh (d. 1905), Muhammad al-Khudri (d. 1927), Muhammad Hasan al-Hajjawi (d. 1931), Muhammad Iqbal (d. 1938), Musa Jarullah (d. 1942), Abdullah Diraz (d. 1958), Abu Zuhra (d. 1946), Fadil b. Ashur (d. 1970), Abu'l Aʿla Mawdudi (d. 1979), Fazlur Rahman (d. 1988), and many others relied on this doctrine to respond to modern challenges. Rashid Rida (d. 1935) and others were influenced by al-Shāṭibī's definition of religion in his discussion of *bidʿa.*[20]

Among the contemporary intellectuals, Tunisian reformer Rashid al-Ghannushi found al-Shāṭibī's doctrine very helpful to reconstruct the concept of freedom as a basic right in his discussion of public law in Islam (*al-hurriyat al-'amma* 1993). Before proceeding to this debate on freedom of religion, let us first analyze al-Shāṭibī's concepts of religion and religious freedom.

Maqāṣid and Freedom of Religion

The *Qurʾān* uses the word *al-dīn* at least ninety-four times in at least the following four different meanings: the Day of Judgment (1:4, 107:1), faith (2:43, 217, 9:11), way (109: 6), and religion (2: 256, 3:19, 3:83, 85, 5: 3, 77, 9:33, and 22: 78). It would complicate the understanding of the message of the *Qurʾān* if one insists on only one single meaning of the term in all the verses.

Al-Shāṭibī defines the objective of religion as *islām* (submission to God), *īmān* (belief), and *iḥsān* (doing good). *Al-dīn* in the zone of *ḍārūriyyāt* consists of belief in one God and in Muhammad as his messenger, and his practices of praying (*ṣalah*), alms-giving (*zakah*), fasting (*ṣawm*), and pilgrimage (*hajj*) to Mecca.[21] These practices, called *ʿibādāt,* are aimed to fulfill the objectives of religion. This definition is derived inductively from the frequent usage of this word *dīn* in the *Qur'ān*: the phrase *farraqū dīnahum* ("those who divide their religion and break up into sects" 6: 159) refers to creed. According to him, *al-dīn* also refers to the teachings God first revealed in Mecca.[22] Teaching of its principles was completed before the death of the Prophet.[23] This perfection and completion (*kamāl*) means that there is no need for further universal rules for dealing with new infinite problems.[24]

Al-Shāṭibī distinguishes between the objectives (*maqāṣid*) of *al-dīn* in the three zones. Religion (al-Din) belongs to the first zone (*ḍārūriyāt*), which *sharī'ah* aims to protect. It means that the protection of the freedom of religion is among the first principles of Islamic law. In the second zone (*ḥājiyyāt*), *al-dīn* refers to the objectives of extension (*tawsi'a)*, convenience (*taysīr*), removal of impediments (*raf' ḥaraj*), and relaxation (*rifq*) that are necessary to preserve the principles in the first zone. He illustrates this necessity with the following examples: allowing dry ablution (*tayammum*) in the absence of water, shortening the prayer during journey, and exemption from fasting during illness and journey. Examples of *al-dīn* in the third zone (*taḥṣīniyyāt*) are requirement of purity, proper dress, using perfume, and giving the best as charity.[25]

Preservation of Religion (*Hifẓ al-Dīn*)

Preservation of religion means the protection of the principles of *al-dīn*; they are fulfilled by *'ibādāt, da'wā*, and *jihād* and by making up for gaps.[26] In case of conflict between religion and other rights in the first zone, religion gets priority. Even preservation of life is not prior to religion; it is prior to other rights like property and so on.[27] *Hifdh* is often translated as protection but it does not fully convey the sense of *hifdh* in the *Qur'ān*. The *Qur'ān* does not allow force in religious matters ["There is no compulsion in religion: The right direction is henceforth distinct from error" (Q2: 256), "Say: (It is) the truth from the Lord of you (all). Then whosoever will, let him believe and whosoever will, let him disbelieve" (Q18:29)]. Compulsion negates freedom and choice in the preservation of religion. This point is discussed later.

Ta'abbud

Ta'abbud, derived from the same root as *'ibadat*, means obedience. In al-Shāṭibī's discussion of religion, *ta'abbud* is used in two meanings: surrender and restriction. The first meaning refers to 'absolute obedience' without question. In other words, it is an obligation to surrender willingly to God and not to follow one's own desires; "serve God willingly as you do that without choice."[28] *Ta'abbud*, in this first meaning, refers to *'ibādāt* that one performs by choice and contrary to habits (*'adat*), which are acts that humans perform instinctively or habitually. The other meaning refers to a sense of finality; you cannot add to or subtract from religion because it is complete. Al-Shāṭibī refers to this meaning in his definition of *bid'a*, which is discussed next.

Bid'a

Bid'a is usually conceived as innovation, meaning something new, unprecedented, and not existing in early Islam. In that meaning, it is frequently contrasted with the *sunnah* or *ijmā'* in order to define it as deviation from the practice of the Prophet or from the agreed views of the Muslim jurists. This view gradually came to equate consensus with *sunnah* in the meaning of authenticity. Al-Shāṭibī distinguishes between religious and nonreligious innovations and excludes nonreligious innovations from the category of bid'a. He includes in this category such nonreligious practices also that are introduced as religious obligations. Because, he explains, the innovator knows that the people would not follow this practice if it were introduced as a nonreligious matter. This discussion leads al-Shāṯibī to delimit the meaning and scope of religion in Islamic law.

Al-Shāṭibī defines *bid'a* as "an innovated way [norm] (*ṭarīqa*) in religion that is meant to resemble legal (*sharī'ah)* [norms] and the act is performed with the sole intention of obedience (*ta'abbud*) to God, may He be exalted."[29] According to al-Shāṭibī, the definition of *bid'a* cannot be applied to every innovation and all unprecedented practices. He clarifies that *bid'a* and *sunnah* are not inversely related, that is, not mutually exclusive or antonym. In other words, every new thing is not deviation from *sunnah* and *ijmā'*. According to al-Shatibi, an innovation or new practice in religious matters that is performed with the intention of religious obligation or is believed to be analogous to it is regarded as Bid'a, even if it is suggested as a way of seeking God's pleasure.

Al-Shāṭibī does not regard innovations and practices that are outside the boundary of religion as *bid'a*. He illustrates this with the examples of built-up houses in place of huts and the use of sieves to sift or to strain unwanted elements from food; they are innovations in the sense that they were not common practices in early Islam, but they are not *bid'a* as they are not associated with belief and religion.[30] Al-Shāṭibī also distinguishes *'ibādāt* from *mu'āmalāt*. He argues that human reason and experience have a certain role in deciding good and bad *mu'āmalāt*, but not *'ibādāt*. He gives a very interesting example: "If a person travels to perform the obligation of *hajj* flying in the air or walking on the water he will not be counted as heretic. The purpose is to reach Mecca to perform the obligation and he achieved that purpose in its fullest sense."[31]

Explaining the implication of *ta'abbud* in the definition of *bid'a*, al-Shāṭibī argues that *bid'a* falls in the domain of *'ibādāt* because of this element. *Ta'abbud,* in the context of *'ibādāt*, refers to two meanings: seeking God's pleasure and absolute obedience. Absolute obedience refers to not exploring the reason and not extending this reason further to other than the prescribed practices. Likening *bid'a* with *'ibādāt*, one denies the boundaries between the religious and the nonreligious, namely between *'ibādāt* and *'adat* and *mu'āmalāt.* It does not mean that *'adat* are not meant to please God; in fact, even those commands and prohibitions in the *Qur'ān* and *sunnah* that are rationally understood accord with God's pleasure.[32] Al-Shāṭibī qualifies *'ibādāt* as *ta'abbud* because they cannot be amended or extended.

This clarification defines the boundaries of the meaning of *al-dīn*; it helps distinguish between *al-dīn* and *dunya* (worldly affairs), and changeable and unchangeable matters. Maintaining that distinction in his *fatāwā*, al-Shāṭibī justified taxes in his time for building a safety wall around Granada. He rejected the practice of collective invocation led by mosque leaders after the regular prayers as *bid'a*, first because it was considered a part of the religious obligation of *ṣalah*, and secondly, it was meant to enhance the religious authority of the prayer leader.[33] His contemporary jurists condemned the tax as *bid'a* and justified the collective invocation as approved practice. They accused al-Shāṭibī of *bid'a* and dismissed him from the positions he held. He wrote *'al-i'tiṣām'* to clarify the concept of *bid'a*.[34]

Some jurists divided *bid'a* into various categories and approved what they called *al-bid'a al-mustaḥsana* (good innovation) by attributing it to the companions and successors and made innovation in *'ibādāt*. Al-Shāṭibī argued that these jurists contradicted themselves when they disapproved *al-maṣlaḥa al-mursala* on the same grounds.[35] Al-Ghazālī, for instance, admitted that *al-maṣlaḥa al-mursala* was suitable (*munāsib*) but not acceptable (*gharīb*) because it was not directly derived from a specific text.[36]

Apparently, the above argument suggested similarity between *bid'a* and *al-maṣlaḥa al-mursala*, as they claimed suitability with the text, even though indirectly. Al-Shāṭibī explained the meaning of suitability (*munāsaba*) in detail and argued that a rule is not accepted or rejected solely based upon whether it is supported or rejected by explicit and specific textual evidence. One must take textual evidence as a whole into consideration; one specific text may support it but it is not acceptable if other texts reject it. *Al-maṣlaḥa* methods, including *istidlāl* (reasoning without reference to specific text), conform to the evidence of law in general and as a whole. It is not endorsed or rejected by a specific legal text, but is based on affinity to a large number of laws to the extent that one may regard it as a genus on which the Lawgiver relies as a whole, though not as a specific evidence.[37] Al-Shatibi differs with al-Ghazālī in defining suitability on the basis of induction, and not relying on specific textual evidence.

FREEDOM OF RELIGION

Freedom of religion and freedom of expression are discussed in contemporary Muslim societies as issues of *kufr* (disbelief) and heresy. According to a *ḥadīth* (reports of the Prophet Muhammad's words and deeds), Muslims will be divided into several sects and one of these sects will be saved.[38] Al-Shāṭibī clarified that the *Qur'ān* and *ḥadīth* condemn the schism that leads to hatred and violence, not due to difference of opinions.[39] He argued that it is impossible to identify the saved sect conclusively; it is only an individual opinion (*ijtihād*). It does not necessarily mean that this identification is definitive.[40] As for apostasy, al-Shāṭibī clarified that one should be declared an apostate only if he himself affirms it without duress, not if he refutes this attribution.[41] Al-Shāṭibī suggests the following rule: the issue does not relate to the principle of particularization of the general, and the particulars and details are in fact mentioned to point the general direction (*jiha umūm*).[42]

Freedom of religion includes the freedom not to believe, practice, and abide by the religious obligations. Al-Shāṭibī explained that the prophetic *ḥadīth*, "Whoever changes his religion kill him," refers to introducing changes in religion; it does not refer to changing religion. To illustrate, he referred to the debate among the companions of the Prophet about the tribes who refused paying *zakah*. Abu Bakr argued that by distinguishing *zakah* from *ṣalah*, those tribes were changing and dividing the religion. ʿUmar and others disagreed, but after long debates the companions came to agree with Abu Bakr.[43]

Kufr

In the *Qur'ān*, the general word for the religious other is *kāfir* (plural: *kuffār*), and in its semantic field it is used as opposite to both belief (*imān*) and gratefulness (*shukr*) (Q 2: 53, 27: 40, and 31: 12). A *kāfir* is not an infidel but is essentially one who is ungrateful (Q. 26: 19) (Izutsu 1959:115). The semantic field of the word *kufr* used in the *Qur'ān* also includes violence, tumult, and oppression (Q 2:117). The Prophet Muhammad was asked to fight against this aggressive unbelief. A believer should not indulge in violence but must also not tolerate oppression and violence (Q 8: 38). *Kāfir* in the *Qur'ān* usually refers to those who had not accepted Muhammad as Prophet. The *Qur'ān* further distinguishes the People of the Book from other non-Muslims. It mentions that Christians were closer to the Muslims. Muslims are advised to dialogue with the People of the Book in the best possible manner (Q 29: 46).

Debates about Freedom of Religion

Rāshid al-Ghannūshi found in al-Shāṭibī's doctrine of *maqāṣid* the theoretical framework to deal with basic human rights. He defined freedom of religion as the foremost to achieve these objectives. This general framework, in which religion is one of the five basic evident rights that should be protected by law, is quite relevant for an Islamic legal framework for human rights. The basic needs in al-Shatibi's doctrine may then be interpreted to include other basic rights, for instance protection of intellect relates with matters such as education, freedom of thought and expression. Implementation of these rights requires a social order and public law that ensures political freedom.[44] He mentions that several Muslim thinkers, for example 'Allal al-Fasi 1979, Abd al-Hakim Hasan al-'Ili 1983, and Fathi Uthman 1984, relied on al-Shāṭibī's doctrine to discuss the concept of civil and public liberties in Islam.[45]

Al-Ghannūshi defines freedom as antonym of duress (*ikrāh*), which the *Qur'ān* forbids explicitly with reference to religion (Qur'an 2:256) and, instead, allows the freedom to choose between the truth and falsehood and to believe or disbelieve what is evident. He disagrees with those who claim that the *jīhād* verses abrogated the above Quranic verses allowing this freedom. He argues that such claims are not based on research.[46] He also argues that apostasy was a political offence and one cannot be subjected to the fixed (*ḥadd*) punishment of death. Historically and legally, only lesser punishment (*ta'zir*) was applicable. As for religious apostasy, Mālikī and Hanafī jurists suggested respite of repentance.[47] Al-Ghannūshi argued that Islam teaches equal rights for men and women. No exception could be made to this general principle.

Referring to the famous *ḥadīth* cited to bar women from leadership, al-Ghannūshi cited al-Shāṭibī's rule, "a word is interpreted in its general meaning not in a particular conditional context," and concluded that "there is nothing in this text of this *ḥadīth* that definitively forbids a woman from public office of a judge or a ruler."[48] Al-Ghannūshi concluded his book *Al-Hurriyat Al-'Amma* by stating that freedom to believe is a basic human right. He examined the impediments to this right, including the law of apostasy, clarifying that it is not in conflict with the principle of freedom. Religious freedom includes freedom to interpret and to criticize, freedom to practice religion, and freedom to think.[49]

Shaykh Mashhur b. Ḥassan al-Salman, a student of Nāsir al-Dīn Albani, edited *al-Muwafaqāt* (1997), criticized, in his introduction as an editor, Abid al-Jabiri, Ḥasan Hanafi, and Rāshid al-Ghannūshi for misunderstanding al-Shāṭibī. He particularly censured al-Ghannūshi's above-mentioned book as an attempt to reconcile Islam with Western views about freedom and women.[50] Al-Salman explained that al-Shāṭibī did not assign any role to human reason in *sharīʿah* and that *maṣlaḥa* was not a rational principle. Referring to several other contemporary writings[51] that denounced such interpretations of al-Shāṭibī, he argued that contemporary Muslim thinkers refer to al-Shāṭibī to justify Western notions: "According to al-Shāṭibī, such assumptions have no basis and that affirms their falsehood."[52]

Al-Salman faulted al-Ghannūshi for including freedom of religion, freedom of expression, and freedom of ownership under the concept of public liberties. He explained that *hifẓ al-dīn,* in al-Shāṭibī's book, refers to the punishment of death for the apostate. He concludes, "Ghannūshī's claim that protection of religion means religious freedom is a lie."[53] Al-Salman also rejects al-Ghannūshi's argument that punishment for apostasy is political, not a religious sentence. According to him, there is no Islamic legal ground for such claims; these are only attempts to justify Western values in Islam.[54]

It is necessary to take al-Salman's concerns into account as they reflect the critique of the selective use of *maqāṣid* by the modernists. It is, however, important to keep in mind that al-Salman's view of al-Shāṭibī is also selective and essentialist. His neoconservative discourse makes absolute claims and rejects others as heretics and liars because they disagree with his view. It is a hegemonic technique that disallows open discussion and self-criticism. As discussed in detail above, his interpretation does not translate al-Shatibi's doctrine of Maqasid faithfully.

CONCLUSION

To conclude, contemporary scholarship has shown that during its encounters with modernity the concept of religion has also gone into semantic expansion and contraction like modernity.[55] The *maqāṣid* approach to *sharīʿah* suggests that we can construct an effective method of reasoning to deal with universal legal issues. The traditional method of insisting on a deductive method of *qiyās*, with its restriction to specific texts for evidence, has actually pushed Islamic legal reasoning to an arbitrarily selective approach to the scriptures that it originally aimed to redress. This chapter shows that Al-Shāṭibī's analysis of the legal doctrines of *bidʿa, kufr*, and apostasy meant to define boundaries between the religious and the nonreligious. New conservatives, like al-Salman, present more comprehensive definition of religion than the traditional Muslim jurists did. Generalizing the views of modernity, tradition, religion, democracy, and secularism in ideological terms as absolute and unchanging terms, the new conservative, both Muslim and Western, has generated dichotomous narratives of Islam and modernity. It has prevented us from observing the dynamism in present Muslim societies and compelled us to ignore the voices and tendencies for reform and change in the history of Islam.

NOTES

1. See Muhammad Khalid Masud, "Ikhtilāf al-Fuqahā: Diversity in Fiqh as a Social Construction," in *Wanted Equality and Justice in the Muslim Family*, ed. Zainah Anwar, 65–91. (Selangor: Musawah, 2009).
2. See Abū Isḥaq al-Shāṭibī, *al-Muwāfaqāt fī uṣūl al-sharī'ah*. Abū 'Ubayda Mashhūr b. Ḥassān Āl Salmān (Cairo: Dār Ibn 'Affān, 1997), 2: 17–100.
3. See ibid., 2: 101–67.
4. See ibid., 2: 171–287.
5. See ibid., 2: 289–547.
6. See ibid., 3: 7–164.
7. See ibid., 2: 44.
8. See Abū Ḥāmid al-Ghazālī, *al-Mustaṣfā min 'ilm al-uṣūl* (Baghdad: Maktaba al-Muthannā, 1970), 1: 284.
9. See Abū Isḥaq al-Shāṭibī, *al-Muwāfaqāt fī uṣūl al-sharī'ah*. Abū 'Ubayda Mashhūr b. Ḥassān Āl Salmān (Cairo: Dār Ibn 'Affān, 1997), 2: 20.
10. See ibid., 2: 20.
11. See ibid., 2: 19–20.
12. See ibid., 2: 22.
13. See ibid., 2: 22–23.
14. See ibid., 2: 44.
15. See Abū Isḥāq al-Shāṭibī, *al-I'tiṣām*. Edited by Muḥammad b. 'Abd al-Raḥmān al-Shaqīr, Sa'd b. 'Abd Allāh Āl-Ḥamīd, and Hishām b. Ismā'īl al-Sīnī (Riyadh: Dār Ibn al-Jawzī, 2008), 2: 238.
16. See ibid, 3: 5–87.
17. See Abū Ḥāmid al-Ghazālī, *al-Mustaṣfā min 'ilm al-uṣūl* (Baghdad: Maktaba al-Muthannā, 1970), 2: 295.
18. See Abū Isḥaq al-Shāṭibī, *al-Muwāfaqāt fī uṣūl al-sharī'ah*. Abū 'Ubayda Mashhūr b. Ḥassān Āl Salmān (Cairo: Dār Ibn 'Affān, 1997), 1: 19.
19. See ibid., 4: 294.
20. See Masud, 1976.
21. See Abū Isḥaq al-Shāṭibī, *al-Muwāfaqāt fī uṣūl al-sharī'ah*. Abū 'Ubayda Mashhūr b. Ḥassān Āl Salmān (Cairo: Dār Ibn 'Affān, 1997), 4: 346–47.
22. See ibid., 3: 236.
23. See ibid., 3: 312.
24. See Abū Isḥāq al-Shāṭibī, *al-I'tiṣām*. Edited by Muḥammad b. 'Abd al-Raḥmān al-Shaqīr, Sa'd b. 'Abd Allāh Āl-Ḥamīd, and Hishām b. Ismā'īl al-Sīnī (Riyadh: Dār Ibn al-Jawzī, 2008), 3: 266.
25. See Abū Isḥaq al-Shāṭibī, *al-Muwāfaqāt fī uṣūl al-sharī'ah*. Abū 'Ubayda Mashhūr b. Ḥassān Āl Salmān (Cairo: Dār Ibn 'Affān, 1997), 4: 350.
26. See ibid., 2:18–9; 4: 347.
27. See Abū Isḥāq al-Shāṭibī, *al-I'tiṣām*. Edited by Muḥammad b. 'Abd al-Raḥmān al-Shaqīr, Sa'd b. 'Abd Allāh Āl-Ḥamīd, and Hishām b. Ismā'īl al-Sīnī (Riyadh: Dār Ibn al-Jawzī, 2008), 2: 351.
28. See ibid., 3: 363.

29. See ibid., 1: 47.
30. See ibid., 1: 54.
31. See ibid., 1: 337.
32. See ibid., 2: 429–30.
33. See ibid., 2: 268.
34. See Muhammad Khalid Masud, *Shatibi's Philosophy of Islamic Law* (Islamabad: Islamic Research Institute, 1995), 73.
35. See Abū Isḥāq al-Shāṭibī, *al-I'tiṣām*. Edited by Muḥammad b. 'Abd al-Raḥmān al-Shaqīr, Sa'd b. 'Abd Allāh Āl-Ḥamīd, and Hishām b. Ismā'īl al-Sīnī (Riyadh: Dār Ibn al-Jawzī, 2008), 3: 5.
36. See Abū Ḥāmid al-Ghazālī, *al-Mustaṣfā min 'ilm al-uṣūl* (Baghdad: Maktaba al-Muthannā, 1970), 1: 284–315.
37. See Abū Isḥāq al-Shāṭibī, *al-I'tiṣām*. Edited by Muḥammad b. 'Abd al-Raḥmān al-Shaqīr, Sa'd b. 'Abd Allāh Āl-Ḥamīd, and Hishām b. Ismā'īl al-Sīnī (Riyadh: Dār Ibn al-Jawzī, 2008), 3: 5.
38. See Jāmi' al-Tirmidhī, in *Mawsū'at al-ḥadīth al-sharīf, al-kutub al-sitta* (Riyadh: Dār al-Salām, 2000), 1918.
39. See Abū Isḥāq al-Shāṭibī, *al-I'tiṣām*. Edited by Muḥammad b. 'Abd al-Raḥmān al-Shaqīr, Sa'd b. 'Abd Allāh Āl-Ḥamīd, and Hishām b. Ismā'īl al-Sīnī (Riyadh: Dār Ibn al-Jawzī, 2008), 3: 125.
40. See ibid., 3: 251.
41. See ibid., 3: 143.
42. See Abū Isḥaq al-Shāṭibī, *al-Muwāfaqāt fī uṣūl al-sharī'ah*. Abū 'Ubayda Mashhūr b. Ḥassān Āl Salmān (Cairo: Dār Ibn 'Affān, 1997), 4: 350, 2: 276.
43. See Abū Isḥāq al-Shāṭibī, *al-I'tiṣām*. Edited by Muḥammad b. 'Abd al-Raḥmān al-Shaqīr, Sa'd b. 'Abd Allāh Āl-Ḥamīd, and Hishām b. Ismā'īl al-Sīnī (Riyadh: Dār Ibn al-Jawzī, 2008), 3: 336.
44. See Rāshid al-Ghannūshī, *al-Ḥurriyāt al-'āmma fi al-dawlat al-islāmiyya* (Beirut: Markaz Dirāsāt al-Waḥdah al-'Arabīyah, 1993), 39.
45. See ibid., 43.
46. See ibid., 44.
47. See ibid., 48.
48. See ibid., 130.
49. See ibid., 320.
50. See Abū 'Ubayda Mashhūr b. Ḥassān Āl Salmān, ed., "Introduction." *Al-Muwāfaqāt* (Cairo: Dār Ibn 'Affān, 1997), 39.
51. See, for example: 'Abd al-Karīm Ḥasan, Maḥmūd, "Radd iftirā'āt 'alā al-imām al-Shāṭibī," Al-Wa'ī. 1415 H [1994], 8, 88:21ff.
52. See Abū 'Ubayda Mashhūr b. Ḥassān Āl Salmān, ed., "Introduction." *Al-Muwāfaqāt* (Cairo: Dār Ibn 'Affān, 1997), 39.
53. See ibid., 45.
54. See Abū 'Ubayda Mashhūr b. Ḥassān Āl Salmān, ed., "Introduction." *Al-Muwāfaqāt* (Cairo: Dār Ibn 'Affān, 1997), 45.
55. See, for example: Abdulkader Ismail Tayob, "Reading Religion and the Religious in Islam," inaugural lecture (Nijmegen: Redboud University, 2004).

BIBLIOGRAPHY

Abū Zuhra, Muḥammad. *Mālik*. Cairo: Maṭba'a Ahmad 'Ali, 1946.

Al-Fāsi, 'Allāl. *Maqāṣid al-Sharī'a wa makārimihā*. Rabāṭ: Matb'a al-Risāla, 1979.

Al-Ghazālī, Abū Ḥāmid. *Al-Mustaṣfā min 'Ilm al-Uṣūl*. Baghdad: Maktaba al-Muthannā, 1970.

Al-Ḥajjawī, Muḥammad b. Ḥasan. *Al-Fikr al-sāmī fī tārīkh al-fiqh al-Islāmī*. Fās: Jadida, 1931.

Al-'Īlī, 'Abd al-Ḥakīm Ḥasan. *Al-Ḥurriyāt al-'Āmma*. Kuwait: Dār al-fikr al-'arabī, 1983.

Al-Khuḍrī, Muḥammad. *Uṣūl al-Fiqh*. Cairo: Muṣṭafā Muḥammad, 1933.

Āl Salmān, Abū 'Ubayda Mashhūr b. Ḥassān, ed. "Introduction." *Al-Muwāfaqāt*. Cairo: Dār Ibn 'Affān, 1997.

Al-Shāṭibī, Abū Isḥaq. *Al-Muwāfaqāt*. Āl Salmān, Abū 'Ubayda Mashhūr b. Ḥassān. Cairo: Dār Ibn 'Affān, 1997.

———. *Al-I'tiṣām*. Edited by Muḥammad bin 'Abd al-Raḥmān al-Shaqīr, Sa'd b. 'Abd Allāh Āl-Ḥamīd, and Hishām b. Ismā'īl al-ṣīnī. Riyadh: Dār Ibn al-Jawzī, 2008.

———. *Al-I'tiṣām*. Edited by Rashīd Riḍā. Cairo: Muṣṭafā Muḥammad, 1915.

Al-Tirmidhī. *Jāmi'*in *Mawsū'at al-ḥadīth al-sharīf, al-kutub al-sitta*. Riyadh: Dār al-Salām, 2000.

Ghannūshī, Rāshid. *Al-Ḥurriyāt al-'Āmma fi al-dawlat al-Islāmiyya*. Beirut: Markaz Dirāsāt al-Waḥdah al-'Arabīyah, 1993.

Ḥasan, Maḥmūd 'Abd al-Karīm. "Radd iftirā'āt 'alā al-imām al-Shāṭibī." In *Al-Wa'ī* 8 (1994).

Ḥassān, Ḥusain Ḥāmid. *Naẓariyyat al-masṣlaḥa fī'l fiqh al-Islāmī*. Cairo: Maktaba al-Mutanabbī, 1981.

Iqbal, Muhammad. *Reconstruction of Religious Thought in Islam*. Lahore: Ashraf, 1965 [1930].

Jābirī, Muḥammad. "Ābid. "Rushdiyya 'Arabiyya am lātiniyya." *al-'Arabī* 33 (1986): 25–29.

Mabrūk, Muḥammad Ibrāhīm. *Tazyīf al-Islām wa akdhūbat al-fikr al-islāmi al-mustanīr*. Cairo: Dār Thābit, n.d.

Masud, Muhammad Khalid. *Shatibi's Philosophy of Islamic Law*. Islamabad: Islamic Research Institute, 1995.

———. "*Ikhtilāf al-Fuqahā*: Diversity in Fiqh as a Social Construction." In *Wanted Equality and Justice in the Muslim Family*, edited by Zainah Anwar, 65–91. Selangor: Musawah, 2009.

———. "Cosmopolitanism and Authenticity: The Doctrine of *tashabbuh bi'l kuffār* ('imitating the infidel') in Modern South Asian Fatwas." In *Cosmopolitanism in Muslim Contexts, Perspectives from the Past*, edited by Derryl N. MacLean and Sikeena Karmali Ahmed, 156–75. Edinburgh: Edinburgh University Press, 2013.

Mawdūdī, Abū'l A'lā. *The Islamic Law and Constitution*. Lahore: Islamic Publications, 1960.

Qur'an. English translation by Muhammad Marmaduke Pickthall. Islamabad: Islamic Research Institute, 1988.

Rahman, Fazlur. *Islamic Methodology in History*. Karachi: Central Institute of Islamic Research, 1965.

Tayob, Abdulkader Ismail. *Reading Religion and the Religious in Islam*. Inaugural lecture. Nijmegen: Redboud University, 2004.

ʿUthmān, Fatḥī. *Uṣūl al-fikr al-siyāsī al-Islami*. Beirut: Mu'assasat al-Risāla, 1984.

Chapter 4

The Inviolability of Human Dignity

A Maqṣidī Perspective

Idris Nassery

These days, human dignity is in fashion. It features prominently in the abortion debate and rarely do we hear topics such as in vitro fertilization, sperm donation, the cultivation of embryos, surrogate parenting or euthanasia discussed without someone, at some point, alluding to human dignity; the concept is treated at conferences, in publications, and in research papers. Yet many of the questions raised in connection with human dignity are not new and can be traced all the way back to antiquity.[1] However, unlike the philosophical discourse of ancient times, modern debate focuses more on legal aspects and on how legislation can help safeguard human dignity. In Europe, this discourse often refers back to the United Nations 1948 Universal Declaration of Human Rights and the way in which the protection of human dignity was enshrined in various constitutions throughout the twentieth century.[2]

Raising the subject of human dignity with legal experts in a German context will inevitably produce a host of considerations and definitions. When confronted with the subject of human dignity, representatives of the legal professions in Germany feel almost compelled, first and foremost, to refer to the fundamental rights listed in the Basic Law of Germany, the first of which is the protection of human dignity: "Human dignity shall be inviolable. To respect and protect it shall be the duty of all state authority" (Art. 1 sec. 1 of the Basic Law of Germany). In the same breath, they will point out the importance and evident nature of human rights against the backdrop of the barbarism that reigned in Germany during the Nazi era. You can be sure to expect a lecture on how human dignity is inalienable, how no one can forfeit or lose their dignity and how human dignity is not decreed by the legislator but inherently laid down and stipulated *to* the legislator, safely outside its grasp and exempt from any revision or revocation ("Eternity Clause"—Art. 79 sec. 3 of the Basic Law of Germany). Among the more internationally minded, you will hear about the Preamble to the International Covenant on Civil and Political Rights of December 19, 1966, and the corresponding economic, social, and cultural rights. Yet others will cite relevant decisions by the Federal Constitutional Court of Germany to illustrate the matter at hand.

Arguments such as the above clearly show just how singular human dignity is as a subject of constitutional law. And yet, in stark contrast to the high esteem in which it is held, there appears to be a curious hesitation when it comes to clearly defining human dignity, and no one seems to really dare speculate on the question of where it is derived and what underpins it. The search for a more detailed theoretical analysis of human dignity in the literature relating to legal doctrines principally reveals two distinct approaches. On one hand, we can find attempts to explain human dignity as a specific quality or trait of each individual being, endowed by their creator or deemed inherent in human nature. Chiefly inspired by the deliberations of Immanuel Kant, this approach argues that human dignity stems from the fact that human beings are subjects. Human beings are human by virtue of their intellect, which distinguishes them from their impersonal environment and gives rise to self-awareness and self-determination and empowers people to actively shape their environment—all out of free choice. Based on these premises, human dignity can be considered violated wherever a human being is relegated to the status of an object, a means, or a replaceable entity.[3]

Conversely, a second approach defines human dignity as a person's own creation, as an achievement of human subjectivity; human beings generate dignity through their own, self-determined behavior by successfully developing their own identity.[4] This approach calls for active engagement; human beings need to do something to attain dignity. That said, this is but a brief summary of the two opposing schools of thought. In reality, the complex discussion also sees some entirely negating any universal meaning of human dignity and advocating the deliberation of each individual case or of each perceived violation in order to establish the meaning of human dignity.[5] Among legal experts, this rather cursory overview of the discourse on human dignity nevertheless suffices to highlight that regardless of the complexity of the term "human dignity" as debated in legal circles in Germany, we are faced with an irrevocable judicial stipulation that remains to be fully untangled.

Moving on to the issue of human dignity as discussed in the context of Islamic law, it becomes evident that most modern Muslim scholars approached the subject in reaction to, or as a commentary on, the Universal Declaration of Human Rights.[6] In the early 1980s, in particular, discussing human dignity and human rights in Islam was limited to highlighting that in the Islamic tradition human dignity and human rights had been established and respected for centuries predating the Human Rights Declaration or any constitutions, in turn seemingly stripping the Universal Declaration of

Human Rights of its importance for Islam.[7] In 1981, the Islamic debate gave rise to the first Islamic Human Rights Declaration, which refers to human dignity as early as in the first few lines of the Preamble. The controversial Cairo Declaration on Human Rights in Islam (*Iʿlān al-Qāhira ḥaula ḥuqūq al-insān fī l-Islām*) followed this in 1990, which also refers to the protection of human dignity early on in Art. 1 sec. (a) before pointing out that "[t]he true religion is the guarantee for enhancing such dignity along the path to human integrity." However, we cannot witness a comprehensive debate on what human dignity actually constitutes and how it could be justified in a dogmatic sense based on Islamic legal tradition. This is despite the fact that studies have shown that a basic discussion of human dignity and freedom can be traced as far back as the legal discourse of the classical period.[8] Yet it is not until 1999 that we can see a comprehensive discussion and critical analysis of human dignity with the major oeuvre, *The Dignity of Man: An Islamic Perspective* by the Afghan legal scholar and professor of law Mohammad Hashim Kamali.[9] Referencing other important Muslim scholars, he illustrates that, based on primary Islamic sources, human dignity can be considered the product of divine mercy. It follows that a specifically Islamic justification of human dignity necessarily requires a theological underpinning.

This chapter aims to elaborate on Kamali's deliberations on human dignity and the objectives (*maqāṣid*) of the *sharīʿah* and take them as a basis to sketch out a more in-depth account. It goes without saying that such a brief analysis will not provide a conclusive answer as to the nature of human dignity in an Islamic-legal context. Rather, this represents a humble attempt to approach the highly complex concept of human dignity and its justification from a *maqṣidī* perspective. In doing so, the first part of this analysis will look at if and how human dignity can be derived from the objectives of the *sharīʿah*. Subsequently, it will take a closer look at some specific aspects of what human dignity entails, viewed in the context of the Islamic-legal debate. Finally, it will outline potential angles for further research.

PROTECTING HUMAN DIGNITY: FOUNDATION OR CULMINATION OF *MAQĀṢID*?

Any attempt to establish if and how human dignity can be justified based on the objectives of the *sharīʿah* necessarily involves revisiting the core elements of the *maqāṣid* theory. Let us start by pointing out that the "forefather" of the *maqāṣid* theory, Imam al-Juwainī (d. 478/1085), did not explicitly mention the protection of human dignity or other objects of protection. Rather, it was the methodology of Islamic law that governed the fundamental premises of his *maqāṣid* theory, and he first and foremost expressed his opposition to Abū l-Qāsim al-Balkhī (d.319/931) in reference to the category of actions labeled "permitted" (*mubāḥ*).[10] On the other hand, al-Juwainī's disciple, Imam al-Ghazālī (d. 505/1111), went beyond the legal-methodological level of the *maqāṣid* theory and early on established specific purposes for the objectives of the *sharīʿah*. In his *shifā al-ghalīl* texts, he states that "[t]he consideration of the objectives of the *sharīʿah* is fundamentally expressed in the preservation of life (*nafs*), the elimination of obstacles for life and in living life as such."[11] This is an early indication that al-Ghazālī considered the protection of life the very foundation of the objectives of the *sharīʿah*. It follows that in an *a fortiori* argument (i.e., drawing upon existing confidence in another proposition) we could argue that the protection of life is a necessary and sufficient condition for the protection of human dignity and that the latter is held implicit in the former. As a counterargument, you could put forward that the killing of human life, whether extracorporeal, prenatal, or postnatal, does not necessarily violate human dignity. A very vivid example of this would be turning off life support for a terminally ill person aimed at allowing this person to die "with dignity." At the same time, you could easily reverse the argument by saying that human dignity could well be violated without any threat to human life. This can be very well illustrated by the controversial issue of embryonic stem cell research. Despite the difficulties in clearly distinguishing the protection of life and the protection of human dignity, we can state that the protection of life, as highlighted by al-Ghazālī, can be considered the imperative foundation of all objectives of the *sharīʿah*.

However, al-Ghazālī does not limit the objectives of the *sharīʿah* to the protection of life; as early as in his *shifā al-ghalīl* text, he also lists the protection of reason (*ʿaql*), property (*māl*) and lineage (*buḍ*).[12] Later on, he replaces the rather unspecific term *buḍ* with *nasl* (progeny) and adds the protection of religion (*dīn*) to his concept of *maqāṣid*.[13] This construct of five objects of protection in the *sharīʿah* first proposed by al-Ghazālī, the "architect" of the *maqāṣid* theory, has remained the chief source of reference up until modern times. It does not, however, explicitly mention the protection of human dignity. That said, al-Ghazālī's framework of the *maqāṣid* theory can in turn serve as a basis for taking Kamali's thoughts and combining both to the proposition that the very protection of the aforementioned five objectives of the *sharīʿah* automatically entails the protection of human dignity: "The five essential values of the *sharīʿah* on which the '*ulamā*' are in agreement, namely, religion, life, intellect, property and lineage, are all premised on the dignity of the human person, which must be protected as a matter of priority."[14] What follows according to Kamali is "[a] firm commitment to protect these values [. . .] tantamount to the protection of human dignity."[15] So, while Kamali considers the protection of human dignity the *norma normantes* of the five essential values of the *sharīʿah* (*al-ḍarruiyyāt al-khamsah*), he sees no need for an explicit designation of the protection of human dignity as a value of the *sharīʿah*. Based on this, "human dignity" should not necessarily be treated as a legal term in the context of *sharīʿah* but rather as a term open to interpretation, subject to change over the course of time, and considered within the framework of the interpretation of the established objectives of the *sharīʿah*. Taking Kamali's approach even further, we could argue that the protection of human dignity would not necessarily require *expressis verbis* mention in the normative systems of modern constitutional states in order to ensure that human dignity is in fact protected in the respective state. Conversely, any codified normative texts in such a state would have to be based on the protection of human dignity as one of the foundations of legal order, which is not explicitly mentioned.

Yet, such a nonexplicitly codified determination of the protection of human dignity leaves the door open to an arbitrary interpretation of the legal order by individual governments and their legal bodies abusing their power, something that is clearly evident from European history and that can still be witnessed in a number of mainly Muslim countries. As a potential safeguard against this danger, which cannot entirely be avoided, it appears wise to explicitly include the protection of human dignity as a legal "bulwark" incorporated in the respective legal order. Explicitly stating the protection of human dignity as part of establishing a legal order also has the effect of being able to put the concept of dignity into concrete terms when it comes to the relationship between human beings and their individual rights. While Kamali starts out by saying that "[r]ights and obligations are a manifestation of human dignity in all major legal traditions and the Shari'ah is no exception,"[16] he fails to point out how the protection of human dignity as an explicit part of a legal order is a prerequisite for specifying individual rights. So in order to prevent any disregard of human dignity within the framework of the interpretation of the five essential values of the *sharīʿah* and at the same time create a basis for putting individual rights into concrete terms, it appears necessary to establish the protection of human dignity as an objective in its own right, within the framework of the objectives of the *sharīʿah*.

It seems that a number of other scholars also identified the necessity for the protection of human dignity in relation to the other values of the *sharīʿah* early on. The scholar Ibn at-Tilimsānī (d. 644/1246), for example, added the protection of honor (*ʿirḍ*) to the five essential values of the *sharīʿah* as established by al-Ghazālī.[17] In this context, Ibn at-Tilimsānī derives the protection of honor as an objective of the *sharīʿah* in its own right from the punishment for slanderous accusation (*qadhf*) stated in the *Qur'ān*. In terms of legal methodology and argumentation, he emulates al-Ghazālī, who in turn developed the five essential values of the *sharīʿah* from the respective *ḥudud* punishments (prescribed penalties). Building on the original five essential values of the *sharīʿah* by adding the protection of honor, as done by Ibn at-Tilimsānī, was later also advocated by other renowned scholars, such as Shihāb al-Dīn al-Qarāfī (d. 684/1285) and Taqi al-Din as-Subkī (d. 771/1370). Al-Qarāfī alone questioned whether the protection of honor should be considered an independent objective of the *sharīʿah* or rather a subcategory of the five essential values of the *sharīʿah*, already implicit in them.[18] This in turn raises the question of whether the protection of honor as an objective of the *sharīʿah*, as put forward by Ibn at-Tilimsānī, also refers to the protection of human dignity. It needs to be acknowledged that, semantically speaking, human dignity and honor are often very close in meaning. In Arabic, they are frequently rendered synonymously with the term *al-karamā* or *al-ʿirḍ*. This is particularly evident if we understand dignity as an expression of honor. For example, honor could refer to the distinct social status of a person of high social standing, that is, others are to honor this person. Nevertheless, dignity and honor are not identical. Rather, honor constitutes an individual's social entitlement to be respected by others, resulting from human dignity but not incorporating all the different facets of human dignity as a whole. Such an interpretation of the protection of honor is equally compatible with the message of the *Qur'ān* with regard to punishment for slanderous accusation (*qadhf*). It follows that you cannot automatically derive the protection of human dignity from the protection of honor; rather, the protection of honor must be considered a product of the protection of human dignity.

Khaled Abou El Fadl, professor of law, proposes a very elegant compromise that represents middle ground when it comes to the relationship between the protection of honor and the protection of human dignity. Talking about the relationship between *fiqh* and *sharīʿah*, he mentions, almost in passing, a reordered hierarchy of the five essential values of the *sharīʿah*: "(1) life; (2) intellect; (3) reputation or dignity; (4) lineage or family; and (5) property."[19] However, he does not explain in any detail how specifically he came to this new order for the five essential values of the *sharīʿah*, neither do we learn why his list does not explicitly include the protection of religion. Consequently, Abou El Fadl's order is open to several different interpretations. One possible interpretation of Abou El Fadl's approach would be that he does not consider it necessary to explicitly list the protection of religion, as he considers any propositions in the context of the *maqāṣid* theory to be based on religious sources. Along the same lines, we could deduce that Abou El Fadl considers the protection of religion to chiefly refer to the preservation of religiousness; that is, not only do the protection of life, intellect, and human dignity take priority over individual piety, these values of the *sharīʿah*, ranked on the first three levels, are the necessary condition for there being religiousness in the first place. This interpretation is mainly backed up by the fact that the protection of life is a vital prerequisite of any human action, and that it is their intellect that allows human beings to become cognizant of honor.[20] On the other hand, you could also interpret Abou El Fadl's decision by saying that he sees the protection of human dignity as a direct manifestation of the protection of religion, meaning he does not render the term *dīn* with religion or salvation[21] but as the protection of human dignity. In favor of this interpretation, it can be argued that human beings were first bestowed with dignity as an act of God's mercy: "We have bestowed dignity on the children of Adam [. . .] and conferred upon them special favours above the greater part of Our creation" (al-Isrā,' 17:70). Only once bestowed with dignity does religion become characterizing for a human being and complements it.[22] It would follow that religion or religiousness would primarily serve the function of preserving human dignity.

Without doubt, Abou El Fadl's order of the objectives of the *sharīʿah* is also open to other possible interpretations, but what we have said so far allows us to postulate that Abou El Fadl's approach enables us to justify the protection of human dignity with a direct link to the *maqāṣid* theory. While Abou El Fadl ranks the protection of human dignity third among of the objectives of the *sharīʿah*, the implicit meaning behind his approach does allow for a modification that would actually see the protection of human dignity be listed top. The notion of a hierarchy among the individual objectives of the *sharīʿah* as such is also not new but could, for example, be justified based on the teachings of the Shāfiʿī scholar al-Āmidī. Just as al-Āmidī considers religion to be the foundation and the culmination of *maqāṣid*,[23] we can transfer this notion to Abou El Fadl's approach and designate the protection of human dignity to be the culmination and the foundation of the objectives of the *sharīʿah*.

CRITERIA FOR DEFINING HUMAN DIGNITY

If we accept human dignity as a value of the *sharīʿah* in its own right, whether following Abou El Fadl or by taking the basic rationale proposed by al-Ghazālī or at-Tilimsānī into the equation, then this raises the question of how we can define human dignity in the context of the *maqāṣid* theory. When it comes to such a definition of human dignity, it was Kamali who aptly pointed out at the very beginning of his writings that any such attempt must be based on the *Qur'ān* and the Prophetic Tradition.[24] Not only do these sources allow us to deduce that human dignity can be understood as honor (al-Isrā,' 17:70), as an expression of might (al-Aʿrāf, 5:3) or as perfection (al-Tīn, 95:4), they also present multiple other specifications that help define the term "dignity."[25] Despite this, the following section is not aimed at defining human dignity based on the *Qur'ān* and the Prophetic Tradition in a comprehensive and substantial manner. Rather, the propositions put forward here represent merely a precursor to attaining such a definition of human dignity. The aim is to determine criteria that would need to be considered within the framework of any attempt to define what human dignity entails in the context of the *sharīʿah*. Only by taking these criteria into consideration can we hope to achieve any sort of consensus when it comes to defining human dignity as the foundation and the culmination of the *sharīʿah*, at the same time keeping up the connection to the specific objectives of the *sharīʿah* (*al-maqāṣid al-khāṣṣa*). The most crucial criterion, which was put forward early on by legal scholars in theoretical discussions regarding a definition of human dignity and other objectives of protection within the context of the *sharīʿah*, is universality. In saying this, these legal debates did not focus mainly on determining the universality of human dignity and the other objects of protection, rather, universality was a key point of contention when it came to the fundamental issue of the inviolability of human dignity (*ʿismah al-karamā*) and of humanity's other objects of protection, as well as humanity itself (*adamiyyah*) on Muslim (*dār al-Islām*) and non-Muslim (*dār al-harb*) territory. The conflict centered less on the question of whether or not human dignity and other objects of protection warrant protection, but more on the issue of whether this protection should only be extended to the rights of Muslims and to Muslim regions, or if it should apply to all of humankind.[26]

This legal debate between Ḥanafī and Shāfiʿī legal scholars gave rise to two main approaches in connection with the distinction and definition of the concept of inviolability (*ʿismah*) and humanity (*adamiyyah*), both of which in turn directly refer to the inviolability of human dignity and other objects of protection of humanity.[27] On one side, we have the followers of the Ḥanafī school of thought who, in line with their teacher Abū Ḥanīfa (d. 150/767), purported an indivisible union of the concepts of inviolability and humanity. On the other side, we have the followers of Shāfiʿī and a few other schools of thought for whom inviolability was directly linked to peace settlements (*amān*) and the declaration of the Islamic faith (*imān*). Based on their methodological approach of unifying the concepts of inviolability and humanity, the Hanafites saw the protection of the inviolability of human dignity and of other objects of protection as unconditional and applicable to all of humanity, allowing us to classify their point of view as a universalist.[28] In doing so, the followers of this universalist approach did not only put forward arguments that can merely be seen in the context of a concrete differentiation between Muslim and non-Muslim territory; they also, in particular, refer to the spirit of equality and freedom of humanity that can be derived from the *Qur'ān* and the Prophetic Tradition, as well as the sanctity of human life.[29] At the same time, they make it clear that even someone who has committed a crime can only have his dignity curtailed as part of a sentence pronounced by a judge (*mahall al-jaza*), never beyond that.[30]

On the other hand, the Shāfiʿī followers and some followers of other schools of thought, whose deliberations mainly focused on linking specific aspects of the Islamic faith (*imān*) with the concept of inviolability, see the inviolability of human dignity and other values of the *sharīʿah* as only applicable to Muslims. This point of view, anchored in particularism, assumes a territorially limited space, mainly reserved to Muslims and to be considered a religious and socio-cultural unit diametrically opposed to non-Muslims. In their arguments, they refer back not only to the terms "believer" (*mu'min*) and "disbeliever" (*kāfir*) but also to Qur'anic passages dealing with a conflict between Muslims and non-Muslims in order to make this territorially vague dividing line more poignant from a religious point of view.[31] At the same time, the followers of this approach conceded the inviolability of the dignity of non-Muslims and other objects of protection as long as the latter had entered into a peace treaty with Muslims.

Early on, it was not just Hanafite scholars who spoke up against this particularistic point of view, but also renowned representatives of other schools of thought, such as the above-mentioned al-Ghazālī.[32] They mainly did so by pointing to the occasions of revelation (*asbāb an-nuzūl*) for the Qur'anic verses quoted by the Shāfiʿī school, as well as by stating that the inviolability of human dignity is above all linked to human beings by virtue of their humanness and not to be seen as an aspect granted to humanity by way of legislation.[33] At the same time, critics of a particularistic view allude to the very practical concern that their isolation as a society prevents non-Muslims from learning about Islam, essentially stripping them of the potential opportunity to commit themselves to Islam.

This overview of the reality of the complex legal discourse involving opposing advocates of universalism and particularism is enough to show that the premises on which particularists based their arguments were mainly driven by historical developments, meaning that they can today be considered obsolete. Consequently, we must take the universalist approach to determine an explicit meaning of the term "human dignity" that, in light of this rich and pluralistic tradition of Islam and independent of cultural context, ideological conviction, societal traditions, or personal considerations for living one's life, can be understood and accepted by more or less every human being on this planet. If we do that, we can also achieve a definition of human dignity that can permeate all the different legal disciplines. Following this, we need to name another crucial criterion for defining human dignity in a specifically legal context: justiciability. This is then upheld when we are able to make an unambiguous decision as to whether an empirically given fact can be subsumed under this term or not. Admittedly, we are under no obligation to be more or less precise than for other legal interpretations of terms taken from everyday language. It is permissible to concede a certain vagueness as long as it is possible to name facts that clearly fall under this term, as well as facts that clearly do not. It follows that it must be possible to determine a clear link between human dignity and the rights and obligations of human beings.

Certainly, universalism and justiciability both undoubtedly represent a tall order for defining human dignity in the context of the *sharīʿah*. That said, it would be surprising if such a fundamental concept such as human dignity were not subject to complex considerations when analyzed in conjunction with Islamic sources. This is why overcoming this conceptual obstacle necessarily requires an interdisciplinary and open-minded approach to defining human dignity.

CONCLUDING REMARKS

With this brief analysis, I set out to outline a constructive concept of the protection of human dignity based on the *maqāṣid* theory and to determine two main criteria for defining human dignity. In doing so, my main ambition is to provide impetus for further deliberations on the fundamental questions that should be considered when developing a sustainable concept of human dignity. Particularly in need of explanation and justification is the universal claim to human dignity, its meaning, its beneficiaries and its relationship to modern constitutional concepts and other treaties under international law. While the important question of who has a claim to human dignity could only be touched upon in this chapter, we could nevertheless demonstrate that early confrontations between legal scholars with regard to the relationship between inviolability and humanness represent a profound basis for today's discourse. I definitely consider it feasible to develop a more detailed conception of a universalist view of human dignity as a basis of *maqāṣid* theory, and I believe that we have come some way in working toward this.[34] I am convinced that this is the only way for us to grasp the different objectives of the *sharīʿah,* whilepaying heed to the particularities inherent in their meaning and infrastructure, as components of a joint objective that links them all: preserving the dignity of the children of Adam.

Moreover, building on this universalist understanding of human dignity, which applies to all human beings without exception and without condition, would be a productive and critical way of referencing the Islamic tradition and translating these considerations to topical issues in connection with human rights or other challenges that arise from technological advancement. We have some way to go toward achieving this. So let's get started.

NOTES

1. For example, Plato and Cicero, cf. Dietmar von der Pfordten, *Menschenwürde (Human Dignity)* (Munich: C. H. Beck, 2016), 11–20.

2. For a comparative analysis of human dignity in European constitutions, cf. Hans Jörg Sandkühler, *Menschenwürde und Menschenrechte: Über die Verletzbarkeit und den Schutz der Menschen (Human Dignity and Human Rights: On the Vulnerability and Protection of Human Beings)* (Freiburg: Verlag Karl Alber, 2015), 177–90.

3. Cf. Günter Dürig, "Der Grundrechtssatz von der Menschenwürde. Entwurf eines praktikablen Wertsystems der Grundrechte aus Art. 1 Abs. I in Verbindung mit Art. 19 Abs. II des Grundgesetzes (The Basic Law Proposition of Human Dignity. An Outline of a Practicable Value System for the Fundamental Rights Set Out in Art. 1 Sec. 1 in Conjunction with Art. 19 Sec. II of the Basic Law of Germany)," in *AöR* 81 (1956): 127.

4. Cf. Ernst-Joachim Lampe, "Gleichheitssatz und Menschenwürde" (The Stipulation of Equality and Human Dignity), in *Rechtsstaat und Menschenwürde: Festschrift für Werner Maihofer (Constitutional State and Human Dignity: Commemorative Publication for Werner Maihofer)* (Frankfurt am Main: Klostermann Vittorio 1988), 253.

5. Cf. Klaus Berto von Doemming/Rudolf Werner Füsslein/Werner Matz, "Entstehungsgeschichte der Artikel des Grundgesetzes (The Story Behind the Articles of the Basic Law)," in *Jahrbuch des Öffentlichen Rechts der Gegenwart (Almanac of Public Law and Contemporary Times)* (Tübingen: Mohr Siebeck, 1951), 49.

6. Cf. Shahin Aawani, "Menschenwürde als ethisches Prinzip der Kodifikation von Menschenrechten (Human Dignity as an Ethical Principle for the Codification of Human Rights)," (Bonn: n.p., 2013), 110–33.

7. "Islam was the first to recognize basic human rights, and almost fourteen centuries ago it set up guarantees and safeguards that have only recently been incorporated in universal declarations of human rights." Cf. Human Rights in Islam. Report of a seminar held in Kuwait, Dec. 1980. Organized by the International Commission of Jurists, University of Kuwait and Union of Arab Lawyers, in *International Commission of Jurists* (Geneva: n.p., 1982), 9.

8. Muhammad Abu Zahra, *Tarikh al-Madhahib al-Islamiyya* (Cairo: n.p., 1977), 308–13.

9. Cf. Mohammad Hashim Kamali, *The Dignity of Man: An Islamic Perspective* (Cambridge: Islamic Text Society, 2002).

10. Cf. Abū l-Maʿālī ʿAbd al-Malik ibn ʿAbdallāh al-Ǧuwainī, *al-Burhān fī uṣūl al-fiqh*, Vol. 1 (Doha: n.p., 1978), 295–97.

11. Cf. Abū Ḥāmid al-Ghazālī, *shifā al-ghalīl* (Baghdad: n.p., 1971), 159.

12. Cf. idem, 160.

13. Cf. Abū Ḥāmid al-Ghazālī, *al-Mustaṣfā fī ʿilm uṣūl al-fiqh* (Beirut: Dār al- Fikr al-Lubānī, 1993), 174.

14. Kamali, *The Dignity of Man*, 90.

15. Idem.

16. Mohammad Hashim Kamali, *Human Dignity in Islam* 2, in http://www.iais.org.my/e/index.php/publications-sp-1447159098/articles/item/36-human-dignity-in-islam.html. (March 12, 2015).

17. Cf. Aḥmad al-Raysūnī, *Naẓariyyat al-maqāṣid ʿinda l-imām as-Shāṭibī* (Beirut: Al-mu'assasa al-ğāmi'iyya, 1992), 62–70.

18. Cf. Shihāb al-Dīn al-Qarāfī, *Sharḥ tanqīḥ al-fuṣūl fī ikhtiṣār al-Maḥṣūl fī l-uṣūl* (Beirut: Dār al-Kutub al-'Ilmīyah, 2004), 304–306.

19. Cf. Khaled Abou El Fadl, *Reasoning with God—Reclaiming Shariʿah in the Modern Age* (Lanham, MD: Rowman & Littlefield, 2014), xliii.

20. Cf. Jamāluddīn ʿAtīya, *Naḥwa tafʿīl maqāṣid as-Sharīʿah* (Damascus: Dār al-Fikr, 2001), 145.

21. Cf. Ebrahim Moosa, Abū Ḥāmid al-Ghazālī, in *Islamic Legal Thought—A Compendium of Muslim Jurists*, ed. Oussama Arabi, David S. Powers, and Susan A. Spectorsky (Leiden: Brill, 2013), 277.

22. Cf. for example, al-Ma'ida, 5:3 or al ʿImrān, 3:19.

23. Cf. ʿAlī b. Muḥammad al-Āmidī, *Iḥkām al-ḥukkām fī uṣūl al-aḥkām*, Vol. 4 (Riyadh: al- Maktaba al-'Aṣrīya, 2003), 337–40.

24. Cf. Kamali, *The Dignity of Man*, xvi.

25. Cf. Ayatollah Javadi Amoli, *Karamat dar Quran* (Tehran: Markaz-i Nashr-i Farhangī-i Rajā', 1993).

26. Khaled Abou El Fadl, "Islamic Law and Muslim Minorities: The Juristic Discourse in Muslim Minorities from the Second/Eighth to the Eleventh/Seventeenth Centuries," in *Islamic Law and Society* Vol. 1, no. 2 (1994): 141–87.

27. Cf. Baber Johansen, "Der 'isma-Begriff im hanafitischen Recht" (The Term 'isma in Ḥanafite Legal Doctrine), in idem, *Contingency in a Sacred Law: Legal and Ethical Norms in the Muslim Fiqh* (Leiden: Brill, 1999), 238–62.

28. Cf. Recep Senturk, "Sociology of Rights: 'I Am Therefore I Have Rights': Human Rights in Islam between Universalistic and Communalistic Perspectives," *Muslim World Journal of Human Rights* Vol. 2, no. 1 (2005): 11.

29. Cf. Badr al-Dīn al-ʿAynī, *al-Binaya Sharh al-Hidāyah*, vol. 5 (Beirut: Dar Al-Kotob Al-Ilmiyah, 1980), 830–31.

30. Cf. Burhān al-Dīn al-Marghīnānī, *al-Hidāyah fī Sharḥ Bidāyat al-Mubtadī*, Vol. 2 (Cairo: Dār al-Tanweer, 2000), 852; Johansen, *Der ʿisma-Begriff im hanafitischen Recht* (The Term 'isma in Ḥanafite Legal Doctrine), 250–55; Mouez Khalfaoui, "Human Dignity and the Creativeness of Muslim Fiqh: Reflections on Classical and Contemporary Muslim Approaches to the Challenges of Equality between Human Beings," in *New Approaches to Human Dignity in the Context of Qur'ānic Anthropology—The Quest for Humanity*, ed. Rüdiger Braun and Hüseyin I. Çiçek (Cambridge: Cambridge Scholars Publishing, 2017), 268.

31. Senturk, Sociology of Rights, 16.

32. Abū Ḥāmid al-Ghazālī, *Fayasl al-tafriqa bayn al-Islam wa-l-zandaqa* (Damascus: n.p., 1993).

33. al-Marghīnānī, *al-Hidāyah*, Vol. 2, 852.
34. Cf. Kamali, *The Dignity of Man*.

BIBLIOGRAPHY

Aawani, Shahin. *Menschenwürde als ethisches Prinzip der Kodifikation von Menschenrechten*. Bonn: Universität Bonn, 2013.

Abou El Fadl, Khaled. "Islamic Law and Muslim Minorities: The Juristic Discourse in Muslim Minorities from the Second/Eighth to the Eleventh/Seventeenth Centuries," *Islamic Law and Society* Vol. 1, no. 2 (1994): 141–87.

———. *Reasoning with God—Reclaiming Shari'ah in the Modern Age*. Lanham, MD: Rowman & Littlefield, 2014.

Abu Zahra, Muhammad. *Tarikh al-Madhahib al-Islamiyya*. Cairo: n.p., 1977.

al-Āmidī, 'Alī b. Muḥammad. *Iḥkām al-ḥukkām fī uṣūl al-aḥkām*, Vol. 4. Riyadh: al-Maktaba al-'Aṣrīya, 2003.

al-Ghazālī, Abū Ḥāmid. *Al-Mustaṣfā fī 'ilm uṣūl al-fiqh*. Beirut: Dār al-Kutub al-'Ilmīyah, 1993.

———. *Fayasl al-tafriqa bayn al-Islam wa-l-zandaqa*. Edited by Salim Dughayn. Beirut: Dār al- Fikr al-Lubānī, 1993.

———. *Shifā al-ghalīl*. Edited by Hamd al-Kabisi. Baghdad: n.p., 1971.

al-Ǧuwainī, Abū l-Ma'ālī 'Abd al-Malik ibn 'Abdallāh. *Al-Burhān fī uṣūl al-fiqh*. Beirut: Dār al-Gharb al-Islāmī, 1978.

al-Marghīnānī, Burhān al-Dīn. *Al-Hidāyah fī Sharḥ Bidāyat al-Mubtadī*. Cairo: Dār al-Tanweer, 2000.

al-'Aynī, Badr al-Dīn. *Al-Binaya Sharh al-Hidāyah*. Edited by Ayman Saleh Shaban, Vol. 13. Beirut: Dar Al-Kotob Al-Ilmiyah, 1980.

al-Raysūnī, Aḥmad. *Naẓariyyat al-maqāṣid 'inda l-imām as-Shāṭibī*. Beirut: Al-mu'assasa al-ğāmi'iyya, 1992.

al-Qarāfī, Shihāb al-Dīn. *Sharḥ tanqīḥ al-fuṣūl fī ikhtiṣār al-Maḥṣūl fī l-uṣūl*. Beirut: Dār al-Kutub al-'Ilmīyah, 2004.

Amoli, Ayatollah Javadi. *Karamat dar Quran*. Tehran: Markaz-i Nashr-i Farhangī-i Rajā', 1993.

'Atīya, Jamāluddīn. *Naḥwa taf'īl maqāṣid as-Sharī'ah*. Damascus: Dār al-Fikr, 2001.

Berto von Doemming, Klaus, Rudolf Werner Füsslein, and Werner Matz. "Entstehungsgeschichte der Artikel des Grundgesetzes." In *Jahrbuch des Öffentlichen Rechts der Gegenwart*. Tübingen: Mohr Siebeck, 1951.

Dürig, Günter. "Der Grundrechtssatz von der Menschenwürde. Entwurf eines praktikablen Wertsystems der Grundrechte aus Art. 1 Abs. I in Verbindung mit Art. 19 Abs. II des Grundgesetzes." *AöR*, Vol. 81 (1956): 117–127.

Johansen, Baber. "Der 'isma-Begriff im hanafitischen Recht." In *Contingency in a Sacred Law: Legal and Ethical Norms in the Muslim Fiqh*. Leiden: Brill, 1999.

Kamali, Mohammad Hashim. *The Dignity of Man: An Islamic Perspective*. Cambridge: Islamic Text Society, 2002.

———. *Human Dignity in Islam*. http://www.iais.org.my/e/index.php/publications-sp-1447159098/articles/item/36-human-dignity-in-islam.html.

Khalfaoui, Mouez. "Human Dignity and the Creativness of Muslim Fiqh: Reflections on Classical and Contemporary Muslim Approaches to the Challenges of Equality between Human Beings." In *New Approaches to Human Dignity in the Context of Qur'ānic Anthropology—The Quest for Humanity*. Cambridge: Cambridge Scholars Publishing, 2017.

Lampe, Ernst-Joachim. "Gleichheitssatz und Menschenwürde." In *Rechtsstaat und Menschenwürde: Festschrift für Werner Maihofer*. Frankfurt: Klostermann Vittorio, 1988.

Moosa, Ebrahim. "Abū Ḥāmid al-Ghazālī." In *Islamic Legal Thought – A Compendium of Muslim Jurists*. Leiden: Brill, 2013.

Sandkühler, Hans Jörg. *Menschenwürde und Menschenrechte: Über die Verletzbarkeit und den Schutz der Menschen*. Freiburg: Verlag Karl Alber, 2015.

Senturk, Recep. "Sociology of Rights: 'I Am Therefore I Have Rights': Human Rights in Islam between Universalistic and Communalistic Perspectives." *Muslim World Journal of Human Rights* Vol. 2, no. 1 (2005): 1–31.

von der Pfordten, Dietmar. *Menschenwürde*. Munich: C. H. Beck, 2016.

Chapter 5

Qur'ān, Sunnah, Maqāṣid, and the Religious Other

The Ideas of Muḥammad Shaḥrūr

Adis Duderija

In this chapter, I examine Muḥammad Shaḥrūr's *tartīl* method as an example of a *maqāṣid* (objectives) allied, thematic approach to *Qur'ān-sunnah* hermeneutics in relation to the question of Islam's relationship with the Religious Other. I argue that this *tartīl method* is akin to the inductive and thematic elements associated with the *maqāṣid* driven hermeneutics and that it should be considered as methodology that has strong affinity with and is in actual fact constitutive of *maqāṣid*.

After a brief overview of relevant literature and a discussion of factors which have normatively and historically influenced the nature of this relationship, I describe Shaḥrūr's views regarding the nature of the concepts of *al-islām* and *al-īmān*, their interrelationship and two systems of ethics that are associated with them. In the case of the former, Shaḥrūr talks about the universalist ethics (*al-furqān al-ʿāmm*) and in the case of the latter particularistic ethics or *al-furqān al-khāss*. I continue by deriving or identifying a number of *maqāṣid* that proceed or stem from these systems of ethics and assess their sociopolitical significance, especially in the context of Muslim majority societies.

MAQĀṢID-DRIVEN *QUR'ĀN-SUNNAH* HERMENEUTICS AND ITS LINKS WITH THE THEMATIC APPROACH TO INTERPRETATION

According to Auda, "*maqāṣid al-sharīʿa* is a system of values that could contribute to a desired and sound application of the *sharīʿa*."[1] The concept of *maqāṣid al-sharīʿa* is present and has been employed as a legal hermeneutical tool in premodern Islamic law (or legal theory, *uṣūl al-fiqh*) since the third-century *Hijrī* at least.[2] It is based on the idea that Islamic law is purposive in nature, that Islamic law serves particular purposes (e.g., promoting people's benefit and welfare and protecting them from harm), which are either explicitly present in, or can be derived from, the fountainheads of the sources of Islamic law, namely the *Qur'ān* and the *sunnah*. One major element of a *maqāṣid*-driven *Qur'ān-sunnah* hermeneutics is a thematic and corroborative-inductive approach to the interpretation of religious texts.[3]

A number of Muslim scholars, past and present, have demonstrated that one important element of a *maqāṣid*-oriented *Qur'ān-sunnah* hermeneutic is a thematic approach to interpretation of textual indicants (*adilla*). In the context of the *Qur'ān*, this thematic approach is known as the *mawḍū'ī* method of interpretation (*tafsīr mawḍū'ī*), which collects all of the related verses from all of the Qur'anic *suwur* (sing. sūrah, chapters) and analyses their interconnectivity before reaching a conclusion.[4] Kamali, for example, has recognized the organic, complementary link between thematic-based *tafsīr* and that of *maqāṣid*-based *tafsīr* because the former aims to uncover unity of theme and content in the *Qur'ān*. Reflecting this unity of theme and content in the legislative sphere of the *Qur'ān* would be also a task of the *maqāṣid* based *tafsīr*.[5] Similarly, Auda also conceptualizes a symbiotic and organic link between a thematic approach and a *maqāṣid* approach because they both approach the *Qur'ān* as well as *ḥadīth* as a unified whole.[6]

A thematic approach is based on the principle of corroborative induction, known in the classical Islamic period as *istiqrā'*. The *istiqrā'* dimension of the thematic approach refers to the actual methodology that underlies *maqāṣid*-driven *Qur'ān-sunnah* hermeneutics, according to which a correct understanding of a Qur'anic concept is gained only if all[7] the relevant verses dealing with that concept are analyzed and subsequently synthesized into a larger framework of its interpretation by means of a corroborative induction.[8] According to this view, the text is conceived as being weblike, within which ideas are interwoven and the task of reading is to uncover, what Mabrook terms, the comprehensive constant or reoccurring variable (*thabitan kulliyan*) through thematic and corroborative inductive approaches. The eventual uncovering of the *thabitan kulliyan* would, in turn, be the aim or the objective of the reading/interpreting process.[9] In other words, according to this thematic approach, the Qur'anic textual indicants (*dalīl*) do not function as a self-contained entity but are to be understood within their contexts, which must always be placed within the setting of the whole. As such, the Qur'anic text is to be studied in its textual unity, and this unity can only be arrived at through a thematic approach to the *Qur'ān*.

The aim of this chapter is to examine one example of a thematic approach exemplified in Muḥammad Shaḥrūr's *tartīl* method as a very important component of a *maqāṣid*-driven hermeneutics when exploring the question of the relationship between Islamic teachings and the Religious Other and its socio-ethical implications in a context of a multireligious society. Prior to doing so, we need to make note of existing scholarship that has attempted to apply the *maqāṣid*-driven *Qur'ān-sunnah* hermeneutic to the question of Islamic teaching's normative stance on the Religious Other; and, in the subsequent section, I make a few general remarks regarding the context behind this dynamic.

MAQĀṢID AL-SHARĪʿA AND THE RELIGIOUS OTHER

Traditionally, five major *maqāṣid* have been identified as those that Islamic societies, and Islamic law in particular, aim to preserve. For example, al-Ghazālī has identified five such objectives, namely preservation of life, religion, reason, progeny, and property.[10] Modern and contemporary scholars have broadened the scope of the five traditional *maqāṣid.* For example, Rashid Rida (d. 1935) included reform and women's rights in his theory of *maqāṣid*,[11] Muḥammad al-Ghazālī (d. 1996) added justice and freedom to the premodern five *maqāṣid*,[12] Yusuf al-Qaradawi included human dignity and rights in his theory of *maqāṣid* and Ibn ʿĀshūr included values such as equality, freedom, and orderliness, among others, as part of the universal *maqāṣid* of Islamic law.[13] In addition to this, Taha al-Alwani[14] added his concept of developing civilization on earth (*al-ʿimrān*), and Attia identified twenty-four essential *maqāṣid* (in contrast to the classical five as per al-Ghazālī) falling into four levels or realms (individual, family, *ummah* (Muslim nation), and all humanity).[15]

It is interesting to note that few of these efforts have *specifically* and *directly* identified *maqāṣid* that would be relevant to the relationship between Muslims and non-Muslims, beyond those inherited from the classical Islamic legal tradition,[16] apart from the above rather general ones, such as justice or human dignity. The only exception this author is aware of is that of Attia and Auda. Attia, one of the leading contemporary theoreticians of the *maqāṣid al-sharīʿa* approach to Islamic law, in the context of discussing the *maqāṣid* as they pertain to all of humanity, identifies mutual understanding, cooperation, international protection of human rights,[17] achievement of world peace based on justice and conditions, and the manner under which dissemination of the Islamic message is achieved as constitutive of *maqāṣid* at the level of humanity. Importantly, Attia, on the basis of citing *Qur'ān* 88:21–22, 10:99, and 2:256, argues that unbelief should never be used as a means of enmity and warfare against non-Muslims, contrary to a good number of traditional juristic writings.[18] Moreover, peace, and just peace in particular, is identified as the principle that governs the fundamental relationship between Muslims and non-Muslims as per, among others, *Qur'ān* 8:61 and 57:25.[19]As part of the dissemination of the objective (*qāṣd*) of the Islamic message, Attia writes that this is to be done through wisdom, gentle exhortation, and reasoned dialogue, and not by means of the coercion of others.[20] In this context, he also asserts that given the fact that the divinely revealed message is common among all God's messengers, Islam has given Christians and Jews, as people of the Book, a special status. He goes on to assert that despite the fact that some messages may have been eroded by forgetfulness or distortion, these religions share with Islam a single essence embodied in a faith in God, the Last Day and righteous action.[21]

Auda, in his systematic exploration of the theory of the *maqāṣid*, briefly explores how useful this concept is as a common basis for interfaith dialogue.[22] In this regard, he considers that his systems-based *maqāṣid* theory has great affinity, methodologically speaking, with that of systematic theology in Christianity because both are concerned with a holistic approach to interpretation that is concerned with the discovery of a philosophical *Weltanschauung* of a particular faith/religion on the basis of an inductive method. In Auda's words:

> A holistic (maqāṣidī) view allows theologians to place specific religious teachings and commands within a general framework of their underlying principles and governing objectives, rather than focusing on a piece-by-piece understanding and, therefore, a literal application of these teachings and commands. Thus, moral values intended by various commands will not be different across the religious spectrum, despite the fact that they take different forms in their specific practical environments. Hence, I believe that the above purpose-based approach to theology could play a significant role in inter-faith dialogue and understanding. It reveals commonalities that are necessary for such dialogue and understanding.[23]

Having briefly referred to the most relevant existing literature that employs a *maqāṣid*-driven hermeneutics in relation to the question of Islam's normative relationship with the Religious Other, in the next section I now wish to examine the importance of contextualization in understanding this relationship.

CONTEXTUALIZING THE RELATIONSHIP BETWEEN THE RELIGIOUS SELF AND THE RELIGIOUS OTHER

Apart from an emphasis on the thematic and inductive aspects of a *maqāṣid*-driven hermeneutics, an additional important element of a *maqāṣid*-oriented *manhaj* (methodology) is contextualization.[24] In relation to the *Qur'ān* and *sunnah*, put simply, it means investigating, in a methodical manner, the role of context in shaping the very content of the *Qur'ān* and its worldview.[25] In concrete terms, with the respect to the question of the relationship between the Islamic tradition and the Religious Other, it means paying close attention to a number of factors that will assist us in gaining a holistic understanding of the topic as outlined below.

In order to gain an accurate understanding of how the normative fountainheads of Islam approach the relationship between the Islamic tradition and the Religious Other, more needs to be said about the revelatory environment in which the revelation and Prophet's embodiment of it took place as it relates to the question of the formation of Muslim self-identity and that of the Religious Other, especially in the Medinian period. This is so, because not only was it primarily in Medina that Muhammad's message, and therefore the Muslim identity, became more self-conscious, but also because the Medinian model of the Prophetic and early Muslim community is considered, by many Muslims, as one to be emulated in as many aspects as possible, including that of the relationship with the Religious Other. This approach, furthermore, is warranted by the fact that even a cursory examination of Qur'anic content (and therefore the Prophet's legacy) was organically linked to this context, especially its dimension, which relates to the relationship between Muslims and the Religious Other.

Donner (2003), a leading scholar of early Islam, describes the context and the dynamics behind the relationship between Muslims, their normative tradition, and non-Muslims (in particular the People of the Book), in the following manner:

> Islam's relationship with the People of the Book has had its ups and downs. The growing familiarity of the inhabitants of the Arabian Peninsula with the ideas, institutions and the communities of the surrounding monotheisms followed by the initial and increasingly intense encounters of the nascent Muslim umma with the same, bred the complex mixture of attitudes to Judaism, Christianity and Zoroastrianism discernable through the classical literature of the faith. The seminal texts and genres-Qur'ān, Hadith, Tafsir, Sharh and fiqh-evince a multifaceted and pendulating posture vis-à-vis the religio-cultural—other that partakes more of dialectic than dogma.[26]

Based on this analysis of Donner, as well as Waardenburg[27] and Friedmann,[28] there are several general points that can de delineated or deduced when trying to understand the concept of the Religious Self and Other during the time of the Prophet, as depicted in the *Qur'ān* and the Prophet's embodiment of it.

First, the context behind the emergence of Prophet Muhammad's message in seventh-century Hijaz was such that it took place alongside other already well-established religious communities, most important of which were, apart from Arabian pre-Qur'anic beliefs, Judaism, Hanifiyya,[29] and Christianity. The very fabric and nature of the message embodied in the *Qur'ān* clearly depicts many of the events and attitudes of the Muslim community[30] toward non-Muslim others[31] and vice versa.

Secondly, it is essential to point out that the Qur'anic attitude (and Muhammad's praxis) toward the non-Muslim other is highly contextual in nature and therefore ambivalent or context dependent.[32]Additionally, for the large part of the formative period of the Muslim community in Medina, a climate of conflict, friction, and hostility between Muslims, polytheists (*mushrikūn*), large Jewish tribes, Christians,[33] and religious hypocrites (*munafiqūn*)[34] prevailed under which Muslims were constantly concerned about the sheer survival of their community, often expressing itself in a reactionary, antagonistic type of identity toward the Religious Other. Watt describes the circumstances and the motives behind the relationship between Muslims and non-Muslims, especially between the Prophet of Islam and Jews in Medina as follows:

> In Muhammad's first two years at Medina the Jews were the most dangerous critics of his claim to be a prophet, and the religious fervour of his followers, on which so much depended, was liable to be greatly reduced unless Jewish criticisms could be silenced or rendered impotent. . . . In so far as the Jews changed their attitude and ceased to be actively hostile, they were unmolested.[35]

This is well attested by the Qur'anic content itself. This context dependency of the scriptures toward the view of the Religious Other (and therefore by implication, the Religious Self) leads Waardenburg to assert that, "Looking back at the interaction of the new Islamic religious movement with the existing religious communities, we are struck by the importance of socio-political factors."[36]

Apart from the sociopolitical factors, religious ideas were also significant since Qur'anic gradual consolidation of Islamic religious identity is inextricably linked with the religious identity of others, notably Jews and Christians.[37] Indeed, it is clearly evident that in the *Qur'ān* itself aspects of religious identity, continuity, and commonality with other faiths[38] are intertwined with those of the emergence and emphasis on the Muslim identity's originality and distinctiveness.[39] Thus, the various religious aspects of, and interactions between, different religious communities in the Qur'anic *milieu* lead to the genesis of the construction of the religious identity of Muslims and played a very important role in it. For example, in his study of the question, to what extent did Prophet Muhammad and Qur'anic scripture emphasize confessional distinctiveness, Donner demonstrated that scripturally (i.e., based upon Qur'anic evidence) and in early Islam the community of believers was originally conceptualized independent of confessional identities and that it was only later, apparently during the third quarter of the first century A.H., a full generation or more after the founding of Muhammad's community, that membership in the community of believers came to be seen as confessional identity in itself, when, to use a somewhat later formulation of religious terminology, being a believer and Muslim meant that one could not also be a Christian or a Jew.[40] In other words, Donner adduces such a substantial amount of evidence that it could be argued that, Qur'anically, some Jews and Christians qualify as *mu'minūn* (believers) as well as *muslimūn* (those who submit to God).[41]

Friedman detects a similar "ancient layer" in the Islamic tradition during which the boundaries of the Muslim community had not been precisely delineated and according to which the Jews and the Christians belonged to the community of Muhammad.[42] This ancient layer of tradition, according to Friedman, was in general more considerate toward the people of the Book than that which eventually became the established law.[43] Thus, another trend significant in the historicity of the development of the Muslim Religious Self was the gradual, ever-growing religious self-consciousness of the Prophet of Islam and his early community. In this context, it is important to note that while attempts to find common ground and syncretism featured more frequently during the earlier periods of Muhammad's life,[44] later periods stressed "features constituting specific identity and what distinguished one [i.e. Muslims] fundamentally from others."[45]

An additional point to be considered in relation to the question under examination is the Qur'anic concept of a *ḥanīf/millat Ibrahīm* (monotheism/religion of Abraham).[46] Qur'anically, this belief system is presented as a primordial, monotheistic *urreligion* based on the belief in One, True God as embodied by Abraham's Message (Arabic: *Ibrahīm*) considered as the universal belief system and as *potentially* the final evolution in Muhammad's attitude toward the Religious Self and Other.[47] It is, however, unclear, whether the Prophet of Islam himself identified what we today describe as historical Islam as the *only* or merely one possible realization of the primordial religion, the *ḥanifiyyah*, on earth.[48] Moreover, the latter formulated what we could term a "classical Islamo-centric view" of Muslim perceptions of the Religious Other as stemming from a certain interpretation of the nature of the *Qur'ān* as revelation. This view is based upon the premise that the *Qur'ān* is a source of empirical knowledge of the Religious Other that is to be applied universally, ahistorically, and decontextually and which insisted on a clear demarcation of the Muslim Religious Self from the Religious Other.

In the post-revelatory times, the major delineating feature that marked the relationship between the Muslim Religious Self and the Religious Other was the fact that Islam became an imperial faith and Muslims belonged to the ruling elite. Hence, Muslims were in a position to determine the nature of their relationship with the Other in conformity with the classical Islamo-centric worldview alluded to above.[49]

So, in summary it would be fair to conclude that the relationship between the Muslim Religious Self and the Religious Other was contextual and underwent a number of shifts and developments which are evident both in the *Qur'ān* and early Muslim history.[50] Given the nature of the historical sources, the exact dating of these shifts cannot be ascertained definitely. However, I find myself in agreement with the following statement by Friedman on how we can approach the question of the relationship between the Muslim Religious Self and the Religious Other:

> Creating a personal system of values by choosing appropriate elements from one's religious tradition is legitimate for a believer and desirable for all, especially in view of the fact that the building blocks for a tolerant version of Islam are indeed available in the Muslim tradition if interpreted with this purpose in mind.[51]

This will become evident in our exploration of Shaḥrūr's approach to the issue.

SHAḤRŪR'S *TARTĪL* METHOD: THE CONCEPTS OF *AL-ISLĀM WA AL-ĪMĀN* AND UNIVERSAL VS. PARTICULAR ETHICS

As noted in the introductory section of this chapter, it is my contention that Muḥammad Shaḥrūr's (b. 1938) *tartīl* method (described in more detail below) is an example of a *maqāṣid* driven hermeneutic that incorporates the inductive (*istiqrā'*) and thematic (*mawḍū'ī*) elements and employs them in advocating for a particular understanding of a normative relationship between the Muslim Self and the Religious Other. Shaḥrūr has been described as one of "the most interesting and innovative thinkers in the contemporary Arab-Muslim world."[52] The success of his first book on Islam, *Al-kitāb wa'l Qur'ān: qira'a mu'asira (The Book and the Qur'ān: A contemporary Reading*, 1990.), which has sold vast number of copies, has been described as an extraordinary book that "challenges a millennium of Islamic tradition."[53] It propelled Shaḥrūr into being one of the most controversial and talked about figures among intellectuals, students, and scholars of the entire Middle East during the 1990s.

Without considering himself to be shackled by the classical Islamic disciplines and their methodologies, Shaḥrūr's sole concern in the work was to develop absolute consistency between what he considered to be the Qur'anic *Weltanschauung* and his own modern and rational experiences. Unlike the case of many reformist-minded Muslim intellectuals from the Muslim majority world,[54] the furore around Shaḥrūr's case was a relatively "restrained and civilized affair," and the credits for this should not in a small part be given to the Syrian bureaucracy at that time. For example, Shaḥrūr has never been accused of apostasy or blasphemy. He was never subjected to a public hearing, nor was there ever any attempt to arrest him. His writings were never officially banned in Syria. His *The Book and the Qur'ān* was officially banned in Egypt and temporarily forbidden in Saudi Arabia and Kuwait. Today, Shaḥrūr is considered as a major proponent of a reformist interpretation of Islam.[55]

Before we examine his views on the relationship between the Religious Self and the Religious Other in the *Qur'ān*, more needs to be said about his *Qur'ān-sunnah* hermeneutics in general and his thematic (*tartīl*) approach to the *Qur'ān* in particular. Shaḥrūr's hermeneutic has two general elements: philosophical and linguistic-hermeneutical. For the purposes of this chapter, our focus is mainly on the linguistic-hermeneutical. Some of Shaḥrūr's most important linguistic-hermeneutical tools relevant to our discussion are as follows:

a. The argument of the utmost perfection with which the *Qur'ān's*[56] structure, composition and meaning is defined and employed.
b. The premise that every single word in *al-Kitāb* deliberately has its own specific function and meaning. This implies that no Qur'anically employed word can be considered as an exact synonym of another.
c. The idea that the explicit meaning of the word can be derived from its implicit meaning which, in turn, is derived from the composition and the grammatical structure of a certain piece of text.
d. The notion that *al-Kitāb* has nothing redundant or superfluous in it.
e. *Al-Kitāb's* ontological and hermeneutical self-sufficiency.

Furthermore, applying his tripartite concept of the existence model, which is part of his philosophical hermeneutics whose details need not detain us here, Shaḥrūr argues that only the *al-Kitāb* possess the ontological quality of "being in and for itself" and not the *sunnah*. He defines *sunnah* as the Prophet's own human-bound, nonabsolute *ijtīhad* (independent reasoning/interpretation/understanding of the *al-Kitāb*). After critiquing the traditional concept of *sunnah*, Shaḥrūr argues for a specific and circumstantial nature of this concept based on five principles including the following:

1. The idea that the Prophet's decisions were conditioned by his historical context.
2. His *ijtīhad* in restricting "the allowed" did not need divine revelation.
3. His restrictions of the "unrestricted permissions" (*ḥalal mutlāq*) were subject to constant corrections as a result of a change in circumstances in his own life.

4. His *ijtīhad*, unlike revelations, were not infallible.
5. His *ijtīhad*, regardless if they are of prophetic or nonprophetic nature, do not constitute Islamic legislation.[57]

Based on the above hermeneutical and philosophical principles, Shaḥrūr has developed a new understanding of the concepts of *al-islām* and *al-īmān*, their pillars and the systems of ethics they give rise to, which have important sociopolitical implications and which will be discussed in some details in this chapter. Shaḥrūr applies a distinctly thematic approach to interpretation, or what he refers to as the *tartīl* method (which is traditionally described as the *Qur'ān's* self-referenciality), in order to discover a logical order or meaningful sequence, which would enable a proper interpretation of a specific theme or topic.[58] As such, I argue that this *tartīl* is akin to the inductive and thematic elements associated with the *maqāṣid*-driven hermeneutics as alluded to in the introductory section of this chapter.

The Concept of *al-Islām*, its Pillars and its Universalist Ethics (*al-Furqān al-ʿĀmm*)

Shaḥrūr, as based upon his above-outlined linguistic hermeneutics, is adamant in making a conceptual distinction between *al-īmān* and *al-islām* to argue against their traditionally assumed synonymity and conceptual conflation as being incompatible with their Qur'anic usage and meaning. In this context, he argues that the concepts *al-islām* and *al-muslimūn* refer to those "who assent to God," that *al-islām* is a religion that is shared by all the life forms in the entire universe and not just those on planet earth, that *al-islām*, as a religion, cannot, for reasons explained below, be "identified with Muhammad's messenger hood nor with any other prophetical message,"[59] and, finally, that no other heavenly religion has been known to humanity apart from *al-islām*. Hence, for Shaḥrūr, *al-islām* can be defined as being based on "an axiomatic truth" whose lowest common denominator is belief in God's existence and in the Hereafter. *Al-islām* is also linked with righteous action (*al-ʿamal al-ṣaliḥ*).

Hence, Shaḥrūr identifies, in contrast to the Islamic tradition, three pillars of *al-islām*:

1. Belief in the existence of God
2. Belief in the Hereafter
3. Doing what is righteous (*al-ʿamal al-ṣaliḥ*)

Anyone who subscribes to these beliefs can rightly be considered as *al-muslim* in the Qur'anic sense of the term.[60] Importantly, the third pillar of *al-islām* also implies the existence of universal ethics, which is derived from it. According to Shaḥrūr, *al-ʿamal al-ṣaliḥ* refers to "the entire body of teachings, instructions, moral commandments and ethical ideals that all religions have issued throughout human history."[61] Shaḥrūr delineates ten such commandments on which universal ethics are based. These commandments are derived from his reading of *Qur'ān* 6:151–53.[62] Significantly, nine out of these ten commandments are moral and only one is creedal. They include:

1. "Join not anything as equal with Him"
2. "Be good to your parents"
3. "Kill not your children on a plea of want"
4. "Come not nigh to shameful deeds, whether open or secret"
5. "Take not life, which God has made sacred, except by way of justice and law"
6. "And come not nigh to the orphan's property, except to improve it"
7. "Give measure and weight with (full) justice"
8. "Whenever you speak, speak justly, even if a near relative is concerned"
9. "Fulfil the covenant of God"[63]
10. "Verily, this is My way, leading straight, follow it; follow not (other) paths"

In Shaḥrūr's view, this final set of commandments appeals to humanity to:

> Follow the path of God and to fulfil the divine commandments unharmed by friction, animosity, and sectarian strife. It implies that unity, agreement, and concord between religions and denominations is a law of human nature and that it is a great offence to violate this law by stirring up animosity and hatred between religious communities. As the tenth commandment it comprises all other nine commandments as it urges the muslimun to fulfil them all and not to be content with only adhering to a few of them.[64]

These commandments form the "universal moral laws of *al-islām*," which Shaḥrūr also refers to as general ethics (*al-furqān al-ʿāmm*). For Shaḥrūr, they were revealed prior to the *Qur'ān* but were further elaborated and fully perfected in the form of Muhammad's messengerhood.[65]

The Concept of *al-Īmān,* its Pillars and its Particularistic Ethics (*al-furqān al-Khāss*)

Now we turn to Shaḥrūr's understanding of the concept of *al-īmān and al-mu'minūn* as based on his thematic Qur'anic hermeneutic. Shaḥrūr has identified a number of principles that govern the relationship between *al-īmān* and *al-islām*. The first one is that *al-islām* always takes precedence over *al-īmān*. By this, Shaḥrūr means that *al-īmān*, both historically and conceptually, proceeds from and precedes *al-islām*. The second one is that "*al-islām* and *al-īmān* mean two different types of faith." As explained above, for Shaḥrūr, *al-islām* is based on its three pillars of belief, namely the belief in God's existence, in the Hereafter and on subscription to universalist ethics. *Al-islām* is therefore universalist in nature and encompasses all other kinds of faiths, including *al-īmān*, which is a particular manifestation or subspecies of *al-islām*. The third principle is "*al-islām* and *al-īmān* combined receive a double portion of God's mercy." Shaḥrūr explains this relationship by asserting that those who assent to God (the first type of faith, *al-islām*) are entitled to the first share of God's mercy and that those who believe in His Apostle Muhammad (the second type of faith, *al-īmān*) also benefit from the second share of God's mercy.[66] The fourth principle that stems directly from the previous one entails an argument that God does not deprive Divine reward for any of the two types of believers. In this context, Shaḥrūr argues that the *al-muslimūn* will receive God's reward and that *al-mu'minūn* will get double of the same reward. The fifth principle is tied to the idea that "the term *al-īmān* is always linked to a relationship with a specific messenger." Shaḥrūr explains that, Qur'anically, the verb *āmana* (to believe), from which the word *al-īmān* is derived, is indicative of a person following and believing in a particular messenger, either as an individual or as a member of a specific religious community. Another aspect of this conceptual relationship between *al-islām* and *al-īmān* is that the latter signifies a particular type of *piety*. In relation to this point, Shaḥrūr forms the view that there exist three types of piety in the *Qur'ān*: *al-islām, al-īmān* and *al-ihsān*. The first refers to all theists. The second manifests itself in the belief in each of the specific messengers throughout history and their respective revelations. The third is a combination of the first two types of piety that can be practiced through *al-iḥsān* or particularistic ethics (*al-akhlāq al-khāss*).

Shaḥrūr, as in the case of *al-islām*, also identifies the pillars of *al-īmān*, which are, in moral or ethical terms, a higher form of *al-islām*. He defines *al-īmān* as faith in Muhammad and his messengerhood, whose pillars include the following:

1. To witness (*al-shahada*) that Muhammad is Allah's apostle
2. The prayer "at stated times"
3. The giving of alms tax (spending)-zakat
4. The fast in the month of Ramadan
5. The *ḥajj*
6. Consultation (*al-shūra*)
7. The fight in God's way for freedom, justice, and equality[67]

Needless to say, such a definition of *al-īmān*, of course, is/has been identified with the historical Islam itself. Based on the above, Shaḥrūr summarizes the variance between *al-islām* and *al-īmān* as follows:

> So the difference between al-islām and al-īmān is that al-islām means faith that entails belief in Allah, the Hereafter, and doing what is righteous; al-īmān, in contrast, pertains to faith in the truth of messengerhoods, that is, divine revelations put down in heavenly scriptures and transmitted by God's apostles, and finally in doing what is fair and just.[68]

Shaḥrūr also discusses the concept of *kufr* (disbelief) since it is linked to the concept of *al-islām*. Here, Shaḥrūr maintains that we need to distinguish between two types of kufr: *al-kufr bi-llah*, which pertains to atheists only as it rejects the pillars of al-islām. The second *kufr*, *al-kufr bi-nubuwatihi* or *al-kufr bi-l risalatihi*, rejects belief in Muhammad's prophethood and messengerhood and his book. However, for Shaḥrūr, before one can label anyone a *kafir* (disbeliever) of any kind, certain conditions must be met. In the words of Shaḥrūr:

> Both kinds of disbelief must be expressed in deliberate, fully articulated, and publicly stated views by which the disbelievers antipathetically oppose either kind of faith. Only those who have declared their disbelief in such an open and antagonistic manner, like for example Abu Lahab who became a *kafir* because he was openly hostile towards Muhammad (s), shall be declared infidels. Others who did not openly contradict Muhammad's message even though they did not believe in it, were—quite rightly so—not regarded as *kafirs*.[69]

Just like in the case of *al-islām* and its universalist ethics, Shaḥrūr associates with *al-īmān* a particularistic ethics or *al-furqān al-khāss*. This system of ethics of *al-īmān* is described as a "consistent model of ethical behaviour" and referred to as the straight path of God (*al-siraṭ al-mustaqīm*). Shaḥrūr identifies the call to spread peace (*al-salām*) and speaking in a mild-mannered way as the two most important elements of *al-furqān al-khāss* in terms of their social impact. Importantly, Shaḥrūr argues that *as-salām* Qur'anically means much more than just a form of greeting, as it refers to all efforts that aim at the avoidance of war and conflict. Other elements of the particular ethics of *al-īmān* include prohibition of scornful behavior toward others, prohibition of slander, prohibition of all forms of spying and espionage, prohibition of accusing other people without clear evidence and hard (empirical) facts, peace-building, duty to respect the property and privacy of individuals, doing what is fair and just (*al-iḥsān*) to everyone, especially those in need, moral obligation to fulfill all our contracts and written agreements, and prudence in spending both in private and public.[70] Importantly, Shaḥrūr opines that all moral guidelines or ethical teachings that existed before Muhammad's messengerhood and which might contradict them are to be considered as repealed or abrogated for the reasons that ethical rules of *al-islām* were subject to abrogation and which Prophet Muhammad came to confirm or/and complete.

Shaḥrūr also explains the nature of the relationship between the universalist ethics of *al-islām* and that of the particular ethics of *al-īmān*. In this context, Shaḥrūr argues that a number of principles of *al-islām* are shared, but not exclusively embodied, by *al-īmān*, including the idea that all humans possess an inner conscience (*al-ḍamīr*) which comes about through the process of education, innate moral values that exist in the inner conscience such as sincerity and honesty that *al-islām* seeks to establish, the idea that behind these ethical guidelines additional ethical truths reside that might not be explicitly referred to in the *Qur'ān* but which human beings can discover by means of an accumulated "wisdom" of their cultural past, the idea that the moral guidelines of *al-islām* are tightly interrelated and form an indivisible whole, and, finally, the idea that holding onto these moral guidelines is in accordance with the human innate nature.[71]

Importantly, Shaḥrūr also forms the view that *al-islām's* system of morality is a "socio-spiritual law" that lays the foundation of the relationship between the members of the human race, irrespective of the economic structure in a society. It is universal and has universal validity because this system of morality is "the common (human) denominator which unites cultures, political systems, race, class, and gender."[72] In this sense, these universalist ethics for Shaḥrūr are first and foremost moral, rather than religious or political in nature. He justifies his view on the basis that in the *Qur'ān* this *morality* differs from references to custom and tradition which can also be found in the Qur'ān. This is so because *Qur'ānic* references to customs and traditions, unlike those pertaining to morality, were never specified explicitly either in form of specific rules or in form of specific norms.[73]

Shaḥrūr concludes his discussion on the conceptual distinction between *al-islām* and *al-īmān* by arguing that the top priority for Muslims today ought to be to uphold the imperatives of universal ethics associated with *al-islām* as "a shared platform upon which we [i.e. Muslims] cooperate and interact with the rest of the world." This is because, for Shaḥrūr, most of the world comprises of the *al-muslimūn* in the sense that they naturally accept *al-islām's* beliefs and ethical values, despite these beliefs and ethics taking a different form and articulation in different states and societies. Interestingly, Shaḥrūr opines that the particular beliefs and ethics associated with *al-īmān* are ethically neither self-sufficient nor self-explanatory and their authentication depends on upholding, what he calls, the moral ethos of *al-islām*.[74] In Shaḥrūr's words:

> It is our responsibility [as Muslims] to advise people of the importance of "doing what is righteous" and "doing what is fair and just" and to tell them that these are fundamental pillars of *al-islām* and *al-īmān* . Every Muslim on this earth is called upon to fulfil this duty. It is the only criterion in judging a person's righteousness. The gates and avenues of "doing what is good" are many and they will be kept open until the Day of Resurrection. Innovation and diversity in "doing what is good" is of high priority and will be rewarded by God because everything that is of benefit to His creation is registered with Him for all eternity.[75]

So, what kind of *maqāṣid* can be derived from Shaḥrūr's discussion of the universalist ethics of *al-islām* and particularistic ethics of *al-īmān*?

DERIVING *MAQĀṢID* FROM THE *AL-ISLĀM* AND *AL-ĪMĀN* SYSTEMS OF ETHICS

At the level of *al-islām*, which regulates the relationship between Muslims and non-Muslims in the conventional sense of these words, the major *maqāṣid* that can be derived from the universalist ethics with the largest sociopolitical impact are as follows:

a. The upholding of religious harmony and concord between religions
b. The upholding of justice and the rule of law
c. The protection and empowerment of the marginalized and the impoverished segments of society regardless of their faith, gender, race, or ethnicity

In relation to ethical responsibilities of conventional Muslims (or Muslims as political entities including in the position of governance) at the level of *al-īmān* referred to by Shaḥrūr as *al-mu'minūn*, the major *maqāṣid* that could be derived in addition to those associated with *al-islām* include the following:

1. Peace building strategies, including avoidance of war and conflict
2. Doing what is fair and just (*al-iḥsān*)
3. Respecting the privacy of individuals
4. Moral obligation to fulfil contracts and written agreements
5. Being judicious in spending at the level of governments as well as individuals

CONCLUSION

In this chapter, I argued that Shaḥrūr's *tartīl* method is one example of a thematic approach to the interpretation of the *Qur'ān* and *sunnah* that is closely linked to a *maqāṣid*-driven *Qur'ān-sunnah* hermeneutics. Furthermore, I examined how Shaḥrūr employs this approach with reference to the question of Islam's relationship with the Religious Other. I described the delineating features of Shaḥrūr's understanding of the concepts of *al-islām* and *al-īmān* and the types of ethics associated with them. We also attempted to derive a number of major *maqāṣid*, which proceed from these types of ethics and which aim to regulate the relationship between the adherents of the Islamic tradition and those which do not, especially in relation to the Muslim majority society. In this regard, the most significant one's include promotion of religious harmony, justice, fairness and peace, commitment to the rule of law that does not discriminate on the basis of gender, race, religion or ethnicity, protection of privacy of individuals, judicious use of resources and spending which protects and seeks to improve the conditions of the most marginalized and poor segments of society, and the honoring of contracts and agreements, to name but a few.

NOTES

1. Jasser Auda, "A *Maqasidi* Approach to Contemporary Application of the *Shariah*," *Intellectual Discourse* 19 (2011): 193–217.
2. See Imran Nyazee, *The Outlines of Islamic Jurisprudence* (Islamabad: Advanced Legal Studies institute, 2000), 162–75.
3. A. Duderija, "Maqāsid Al Shari'a, Non-patriarchal Qur'ānic Hermeneutics and the Reformation of Muslim Family Law," in *Maqasid Al-Shari'a and Contemporary Muslim Reformist Thought: An Examination*, ed. A. Duderija (London: Palgrave Macmillan, 2014), 193–219.
4. Al-Shadr, *Al-Madrasa Al-Qur'āniyya:al-Tafsīr al-maudu'ī wa al-tafsīr al-tajzi fi al-Qur'ān al-Karīm* (Beirut: Dar al-Ta'arruf li al-Matba'a, n.d.).
5. A. Duderija, "Islamic Law Reform and Maqāṣid al-sharīʿa in the Thought of Mohammad Hashim Kamali," in *Maqasid Al Shari'ah and Contemporary Muslim Reformist Thought*, ed. A. Duderija (London: Palgrave Macmillan, 2014), 13–39.
6. Y. Auda, *Maqasid Al-Shariah A Beginner's Guide* (Google eBook). Front Cover Jasser Auda (Washington, DC: IIIT, 2008), 35.
7. For the purposes of Islamic law derivation, these indicants do not necessarily need to be restricted to the *Qur'ān* only. Here I refer to Prof. Jackson's principles of juristic induction defined as the aggregate of a number of texts, *literally* interpreted, that point to a meaning that transcends each text individually but implicitly inheres in the group, the whole equaling more than the sum of its parts. Sh. Jackson, "Literalism, Empiricism, and Induction: Apprehending and Concretizing Islamic Law's Maqāsid al-Sharī," *Mitch.St.L.Rev.* (2006): 1469–86.
8. S. al-Awa, *Textual relations in the Qur'an: Relevance, Coherence and Structure* (London: Routledge, 2006).
9. A. Mabrook, "A New Historical Discussion in Islam," in *The Blackwell Companion to Contemporary Islamic Thought*, ed. I. M. Abu Rabi (Hoboken, NJ: Blackwell Publishing, 2006), 271–83.

10. See al-Ghazālī, *Al-Mustasfa fi 'ilm al-Uṣūl* (Cairo: Makba'at Dar al-Kutub al-Misriyya, 1997).

11. Rida, Rashid, *Al-Wahi al Mohammadi: Thubut al-Nubuwwah bi al-Qur'ān* (Cairo: Muʿasasah ʿizz al-din, n.d.).

12. Muhammad al-Ghazālī, *Nazart fi al-Qur'ān* (Cairo: Nahdat Misr, 2002).

13. Ibn ʿAshūr, Tahir. *Maqāṣid al-Sharīʿa al-Islamiyyah*, ed. El-tahir el-Mesnawi (Kuala Lumpur: Al-fajr, 1999).

14. Taha al-Alwani, *Issues in Contemporary Islamic Thought* (Washington, DC: IIIT, 2005).

15. Gamal Eddin Attia, *Toward Realization of the Higher Intent of Islamic Law (Maqāṣid al-Sharīʿa): A Functional Approach*, trans. Nancy Roberts (Kuala Lumpur: IIIT, 2010), 116–51.

16. Y. Friedmann, *Tolerance and Coercion in Islam: Interfaith Relations in the Muslim Tradition* (Cambridge: Cambridge University Press, 2003).

17. This includes freedom of thought and religious belief.

18. Ibid., 145. Attia, as well as Auda, do not agree with the view that the *Qur'ān*'s sword verse (9:5) abrogated some 200 verses, which legitimize the use of aggression against non-Muslims only on the basis of self-defence.

19. Ibid., 146.

20. Ibid., 147.

21. Ibid.

22. Auda, *Maqasid Al Shari'a—Beginner's Guide*, 46–48.

23. Ibid., 53.

24. Adis Duderija, "The Hermeneutical Importance of Qur'anic Assumptions in the Development of a Values Based and Purposive Oriented Qur'an-Sunna Hermeneutic: Case Study of Patriarchy and Slavery," *HAWWA-Journal of Women in the Middle East and the Muslim World* Vol. 11, no. 1 (2013): 58–88.

25. Ibid.

26. F. M. Donner, "From Believers to Muslims: Confessional Self-Identity in the Early Islamic Community," *al-Abhath* Vols. 50–51 (2002–2003): 267–68.

27. J. Waardenburg, *Muslims and Others: Relations in Context* (Berlin: De Gruyter, 2003).

28. Y. Friedmann, *Tolerance and Coercion in Islam: Interfaith Relations in the Muslim Tradition* (Cambridge: Cambridge University Press, 2003); Cf Z. Maghen, "The Interaction between Islamic Law and Non-Muslims," *Islamic Law and Society* Vol. 10, no. 2 (2003): 267–75.

29. Explained in a subsequent part of this section.

30. That is, the *mu'minūn* (believers).

31. That is, *mushrikūn* (polytheists), *munafiqūn* (hypocrites), *al-ins* (humankind), and *ahl-Kitāb* (People of the Book or recipients of previous revelations, primarily Jews and Christians).

32. This ambivalence and contextuality is also found in non-Qur'anic elements of tradition as embodied in various *aḥadīth* corpuses. On Qur'anic ambivalence in relation to the other, see Maghen, "The Interaction between Islamic Law," 268.

33. The presence of Christians in Medina was much less numerically. Additionally, Christians had much less economic influence. Thus, the *Qur'ān*'s "complaint" about Christians pertains primarily to the domain of dogma. For more, see J. D. McAuliffe,

Qur'anic Christians. An Analysis of Classical and Modern Exegesis (Cambridge: Cambridge University Press, 1991).

34. A group of people in Medina who only superficially and for their own self-interest became Muslims but in reality were on the side of enemies of the Muslim community. They were termed the *munafiqūn*, or the religious hypocrites.

35. W. M. Watt, *Muhammad at Medina* (Oxford: Oxford University Press, 1956), 217.

36. Waardenburg, *Muslims and Others*, 99; cf. J. Waardenburg, "World Religions as Seen in the Light of Islam," in *Islam: Past Influence and Present Challenge*, ed. A. T. Welch and P. Cachia (Edinburgh: Edinburgh University Press, 1979), 245–76.

37. K. Zebiri, *Muslims and Christians-Face to Face* (Oxford: Oneworld, 1997). Also, Donner, "From Believers to Muslims."

38. Such as belief in Allah (One, True God), previous Prophets, belief in the Hereafter, and Day of Judgment.

39. The latter trend being more prominent in the context of Muslim Medinian community.

40. Donner, "From Believers to Muslims," 12; cf. Maghen, "The Interaction Between," 268–69.

41. Donner, "From Believers to Muslims," 17–24; 28–34.

42. Friedmann, *Tolerance and Coercion in Islam*, 194–95.

43. Ibid., 194, 32.

44. Such as, for example, the importance of Jerusalem and the praxis of Muslims to turn to it in prayer.

45. Waardenburg, *Muslims and Others*, 44. A case in point being the change of direction in prayer from Jerusalem to Makkah. Traditions reportedly going back to the Prophet, such as those found in Saḥiḥ Bukhāri, for example, are largely stressing the distinctiveness and uniqueness in Islamic religious identity.

46. For more on this refer to E. Beck. "Die Gestalt des Abraham am Wendepunkt der Entwicklung Muhammads: Analyse von S.2.118 (124)–135(141)," *Le Museon* Vol. 65 (1952): 73–94.

47. Waardenburg, *Muslims and Others*, 87–94.

48. Ibid., 106–107, also Qur'anic verses such as 5:48 seem to see the existence of religious plurality as a manifestation of God's will.

49. Friedmann, *Tolerance and Coercion in Islam*, 1.

50. Friedmann summarizes it as follows: Islam formulated a particular attitude toward each community that it faced, which was shaped by the historical circumstances in which the encounter took place, and was influenced to a certain extent by the nature of the respective non-Muslim religious tradition. Ibid., 1.

51. Ibid., 5.

52. M. Shaḥrūr, *The Qur'an, Morality, and Critical Reason: The Essential Muhammad Shahrur*. Trans., ed., and intro. Anderas Christmann (Leiden: Brill, 2009), xvii.

53. P. Clarke, "The Shahrur Phenomenon: A Liberal Islamic Voice from Syria," *Islam and Christian-Muslim Relations* Vol. 7, no. 3, (1996): 337–41, at 337.

54. The most famous case being that of the Egyptian scholar H. N. Abu Zayd (d. 2010).

55. Shaḥrūr, *The Qur'an, Morality, and Critical Reason*, Introduction.

56. Shaḥrūr, as part of his broader linguistic-hermeneutical methodology, does not consider the words *al-Kitāb* to mean the same as al-*Qur'ān*. By *al-Kitāb*, he actually means the fixed text of the *musḥaf*. To reflect this, I will retain the word *al-Kitāb* instead of the al-*Qur'ān* when making reference to Shaḥrūr's ideas.

57. Ibid., 101–102.

58. Ibid., 28.

59. Ibid., 28–29.

60. Ibid., 30–35.

61. Ibid., 35.

62. Say: Come, I will rehearse what God has (really) prohibited you from. Join not anything as equal with Him; be good to your parents; kill not your children on a plea of want. We provide sustenance for you and for them. Come not nigh to shameful deeds, whether open or secret; take not life, which God hath made sacred, except by way of justice and law: thus does He command you, that you may learn wisdom. And come not nigh to the orphan's property, except to improve it, until he attains the age of full strength, give measure and weight with (full) justice. No burden do We place on any soul, but that which it can bear. Whenever you speak, speak justly, even if a near relative is concerned; and fulfil the covenant of God: thus does He command you, that you may remember. Verily, this is My way, leading straight, follow it. Follow not (other) paths, they will scatter you about from His (great) path. Thus does He command you that you may be righteous.

63. Shaḥrūr argues that this covenant refers to the covenant of *al-islām* but is inclusive of others too, for example the covenant of faith (*al-imān*), a marriage contract, the covenant of a nation state (the oath of citizenship), and others.

64. Ibid., 41.

65. Ibid., 41–42.

66. Ibid., 52.

67. But Shaḥrūr points out not for purposes of religious compulsion as "there is no compulsion in religion," al-Baqara 2:256.

68. Ibid., 55.

69. Ibid., 55.

70. Ibid., 44–45.

71. Ibid., 46–48.

72. Ibid., 48.

73. Ibid.

74. Ibid., 65–66.

75. Ibid., 66.

BIBLIOGRAPHY

al-Alwani, Taha. *Issues in Contemporary Islamic Thought*. Washington, DC: IIIT, 2005.

al-Awa, Salwa. *Textual Relations in the Qur'an: Relevance, Coherence and Structure*. London: Routledge, 2006.

Al-Sadr, Ayatullah Sayyid Muhammad Baqir. *Al-Madrasa Al-Qur'āniyya:al-Tafsīr al-maudu'ī wa al-tafsīr al-tajzi fi al-Qur'ān al-Karīm*. Beirut: Dar al-Ta'arruf li al-Matba'a, n.d.

Attia, Gamal Eddin. *Toward Realization of the Higher Intent of Islamic Law (Maqāṣid al-Sharī'a): A Functional Approach*. Translated by Nancy Roberts. Kuala Lumpur: IIIT, 2010.

Auda, Jasser. "A Maqasidi Approach to Contemporary Application of the Shariah." *Intellectual Discourse* 19 (2011): 193–217.

———. *Maqasid Al-Shariah A Beginner's Guide*. London: IIIT, 2008.

Beck, Edmund. "Die Gestalt des Abraham am Wendepunkt der Entwicklung Muhammads." In *Der Koran: Wissenschaftliche Buchgesellschaft*. Darmstadt: Kohlhammer Verlag.

Clarke, Peter. "The Shahrur Phenomenon: A Liberal Islamic Voice from Syria." *Islam and Christian-Muslim Relations* Vol. 7, no. 3 (1996): 337–41.

Donner, Fred. "From Believers to Muslims: Confessional Self-Identity in the Early Islamic Community." *al-Abhath*, Vols. 50–51 (2002–2003): 9–53.

Duderija, Adis. "Maqāsid Al Shari'a, non-patriarchal Qur'ānic Hermeneutics and the Reformation of Muslim Family Law." In *Maqasid Al-Shari'a and Contemporary Muslim Reformist Thought: An Examination*, edited by Adis Duderija, 193–219. Basingstoke, UK: Palgrave Macmillan, 2014.

———. "Islamic Law Reform and Maqāṣid al-sharī'a in the Thought of Mohammad Hashim Kamali." In *Maqasid Al Shari'ah and Contemporary Muslim Reformist Thought: An Examination*, edited by Adis Duderija, 13–39. Basingstoke, UK: Palgrave Macmillan, 2014.

———. "The Hermeneutical Importance of Qur'anic Assumptions in the Development of a Values Based and Purposive Oriented Qur'an-Sunna Hermeneutic: Case Study of Patriarchy and Slavery." *HAWWA-Journal of Women in the Middle East and the Muslim World* Vol. 11, no. 1 (2013): 58–88.

Friedmann, Yohanan. *Tolerance and Coercion in Islam: Interfaith Relations in the Muslim Tradition*. Cambridge: Cambridge University Press, 2003.

Ibn 'Ashūr, Tahir. *Maqāṣid al-Sharī'a al-Islamiyyah*. Edited by El-tahir el-Mesnawi. Kuala Lumpur: Al-fajr, 1999.

Jackson, Sherman. "Literalism, Empiricism, and Induction: Apprehending and Concretizing Islamic Law's Maqāsid al-Sharī." *Michigan State Law Review* (2006): 1469–86.

Mabrook, Ali. "A New Historical Discussion in Islam." In *The Blackwell Companion to Contemporary Islamic Thought*, edited by I. M. Abu Rabi', 271–83. Hoboken, NJ: Blackwell Publishing, 2006.

Maghen, Ze'ev. "The Interaction between Islamic Law and Non-Muslims." *Islamic Law and Society* Vol. 10, no. 2 (2003): 267–75.

McAuliffe, Jane Dammen. *Qur'anic Christians. An Analysis of Classical and Modern Exegesis*. Cambridge: Cambridge University Press, 1991.

Nyazee, Imran. *The Outlines of Islamic Jurisprudence*. Islamabad: Advanced Legal Studies Institute, 2000.

Shaḥrur, Muhammad. *The Qur'an, Morality, and Critical Reason: The Essential Muhammad Shahrur*. Translated, edited, and introduction by Anderas Christmann. Leiden: Brill, 2009.

Waardenburg, Jacques. *Muslims and Others: Relations in Context*. Berlin: De Gruyter, 2003.
———. "World Religions as Seen in the Light of Islam." In *Islam: Past Influence and Present Challenge*, edited by A. T. Welch and P. Cachia, 245–76. Edinburgh: Edinburgh University Press, 1979.
Watt, William. *Muhammad at Medina*. Oxford: Oxford University Press, 1956.
Zebiri, Kate. *Muslims and Christians Face to Face*. Oxford: Oneworld, 1997.

Chapter 6

Ibn ʿĀshūr's Interpretation of the Purposes of the Law (*Maqāṣid al-Sharīʿa*)

An Islamic Modernist Approach to Legal Change

Felicitas Opwis

INTRODUCTION

Changing circumstances continuously challenge a legal system like Islamic law that is based on finite textual sources (*Qurʾān* and *ḥadīth*). Novel situations that require legal solutions have to be addressed and regulated within the confines of the texts. In the same way that every US law and judicial ruling is subject to the provisions of the US Constitution, every Islamic law has to be in consonance with the scriptural basis of Islam, the *Qurʾān* and the *ḥadīth*,[1] and be derived from the accepted sources of law: *Qurʾān, sunna*, consensus (*ijmāʿ*), and legal analogy (*qiyās*).[2] In the absence of continuous revelation or a legislating prophet-*imām* who determines the legal status of unprecedented incidents, Islamic jurists[3] integrate new and changed rulings[4] into Islamic law by justifying and legitimizing them within the realm of what H. L. A. Hart calls the "secondary rules" of law. By this term, Hart refers to the "rule of recognition," "rule of change," and "rule of adjudication," which determine how "primary rules" (the do's and don'ts) are ascertained and by which criteria a ruling is recognized as valid and legitimate (rule of recognition), how to alter it (rule of change), as well as who determines infractions and their judgment (rule of adjudication).[5] These secondary rules of law are usually not explicitly articulated but are reflected in the way particular rulings are identified. In order to incorporate and legitimize novel legal situations into the existing framework of law, legal experts alter the parameters of textual application,[6] interpret legal principles in novel ways or develop new methodologies of law-finding.

Reinterpreting existing and widely accepted legal procedures and principles has always been the primary means by which Islamic jurisprudents have addressed and accommodated legal change.[7] In the modern period, with its rapidly changing social, economic, political, and technological environments, Islamic legal experts increasingly rely on manipulating the rules of recognition in their efforts at justifying the introduction of new rules or altering existing ones. Of particular importance in this process is the concept of *maqāṣid al-sharīʿa*, often translated as the purposes, intentions, or objectives of the divine law. Though not novel,[8] their relevance in legal discourse has grown to the point that they often dominate writings on legal theory (*uṣūl al-fiqh*) and are repeatedly referenced by *muftī*s when issuing legal opinions (*fatāwā*). In contemporary Islamic legal writings recourse to the purposes of the law is a primary tool for legitimizing legal change and is seen as a way to reform, adapt, and modernize Islamic law.

The fast-paced scientific and societal change associated with the modern period is, however, not the only reason that accommodating legal change has been at the forefront of Islamic juristic thought. Just as important is the continuous encroachment of the state and its offices into the sphere of law. Since the onset of modernity,[9] Islamic law, its practitioners, teachers, interpreters, and institutions were increasingly drawn into the control of the state.[10] Matters governed by Islamic law, which once were largely outside the realm of state legislation, slowly but surely came to be under state control.[11] This process had started prior to the Napoleonic invasion of Egypt in 1798 and culminated in subsuming all legal and legislative matters under state institutions with the establishment of nation-states in the Middle East in the first half of the twentieth century; separate *sharīʿa* courts were abolished in many secular-leaning countries in the 1950s.[12] More importantly, for Islamic law, the modern nation-state's legal system is based on constitutions, legal codes, and statutes, thereby altering or departing fundamentally from the interpretive process of law-finding of the premodern period.[13] The concept of what "law" constitutes also changed. Law was no longer necessarily the all-encompassing system that guides all aspects of a believer's life, that is, *sharīʿa* in the larger sense, as espoused by Ashʿarī theology. Law became mostly limited to regulating the relationship of the state to its citizens as well as the citizens' relations among each other as far as their rights and duties are concerned; quasi-legal matters that pertain to issues of performance of rituals, to theological doctrine, as well as to ethics were increasingly understood to lie outside the realm of law.

The reaction of the *ʿulamāʾ*, who in the premodern period held the prerogative of interpreting the divine scripture and who were the agents of law-finding, varied. Some withdrew, others wholeheartedly engaged in modernizing their country's legal system, and still others sought to preserve the traditional function of *sharīʿa* law as much as possible. Others still tried to straddle or combine both aspects of the law; the modernist understanding of law as deriving from state legislative bodies which regulate matters of "law" in the narrow sense and the Ashʿarī approach to *sharīʿa* law as an all-encompassing guide for the believer's conduct. In what follows, I present a key example of a twentieth-century Muslim intellectual struggling to sustain Islamic legal traditions within the framework of a modern nation-state by reinterpretation of the secondary rules of law.

IBN ʿĀSHŪR: TRADITION, MODERNITY, AND LEGAL CHANGE

The career and intellectual project[14] of the Tunisian scholar Muḥammad al-Ṭāhir Ibn ʿĀshūr (1296–1394/1879–1973) combines commitment to the Islamic tradition with embracing modernity. From his upbringing and education, he squarely belonged to the traditional scholars, the *ʿulamāʾ*. Scion to a revered family of scholars, he received the traditional *madrasa* (Islamic school) education and graduated from the Zaytūna, the foremost religious institution in Tunisia, at which he later taught.[15] At the same time, Ibn ʿĀshūr was "modern" and "reformist" in the aims he pursued.[16] He actively engaged with the modernizing state authorities, be that the French or nationalist government of Bourguiba, serving in the administration of Tunisia's religious schools and the judiciary, holding posts such as Grand Mufti and Dean of Zaytūna.[17] In his official positions he worked at reforming the education of the Zaytūna and other such institutions, where he added modern sciences to the curriculum and reduced the study of those religious sciences that he deemed unnecessary for the modern world.[18] Ibn ʿĀshūr belongs to the fluid group of "Islamic modernists," who, in the words of William Shepard, "are 'modern' in that they take with utmost seriousness the changes that constitute 'modernity'" and see "Islam, properly understood, adequately suited to modern needs."[19]

The modern streak in Ibn ʿĀshūr's ideas is also evident in his emphasis on concepts such as freedom and equality.[20] His *magnum opus*, a *Qurʾān* exegesis, is tellingly entitled *al-Taḥrīr wa-l-tanwīr*, Liberation and Enlightenment.[21] While Ibn ʿĀshūr's qurʾanic exegesis has not yet gained the popularity and wide study it deserves,[22] his legal thought has received much attention. The last two decades, in particular, saw a revival of interest in Ibn ʿĀshūr's writings on law,[23] and one may even say that his book *Maqāṣid al-Sharīʿa al-Islāmiyya* (The Purposes of the Islamic Sharīʿa), first published in 1946–1947,[24] has spurred several commentaries, thus continuing a popular genre of legal writing.[25]

Ibn ʿĀshūr utilizes the concept of the purposes of the law (*maqāṣid al-sharīʿa*) to incorporate mechanisms of legal change in a fashion that bridges tradition and modernity. He explicitly states that knowledge of the purposes of the law is "the guarantor of perpetuating rulings of Islamic law over the centuries and generations."[26] By turning to established principles of the Islamic legal tradition, Ibn ʿĀshūr also achieves the necessary component of fruitful legal change, namely authenticity. As Horowitz's research demonstrates, authenticity is an important aspect to explain legal change and its mechanisms.[27] To be successful, any changes in the law need to be deemed authentic and morally appropriate to those pronouncing and acting upon the law.[28] Given the heritage of Western imperialism and the importation of legal codes and statutes from the West, legal change in Islam is only acceptable and effective when it is also perceived as being authentically Islamic, as opposed to an alien law derived from outside the legal system, irrespective of whether such perception is a fiction or not.

Ibn ʿĀshūr's interpretation of the purposes of the *sharīʿa* is part of the contemporary trend toward managing legal change by recourse to principles that are, on the one hand, derived from the revealed texts but are, on the other hand, abstract enough to subsume under them newly encountered legal questions. The new hermeneutical approach that Ibn ʿĀshūr brings to law-finding makes Islamic law compatible to the legislative system of a nation-state. Yet, as will be shown below, he consciously turns away from understanding Islamic legislation to encompass all of the believer's conduct. It is this vision of a restricted sense of Islamic law, compatible and competent to meet the challenges of modern life that differentiates Ibn ʿĀshūr from many contemporary religious figures, such as Yūsuf al-Qaraḍāwī, Saʿīd Ramaḍān al-Būṭī, or Jamāl al-Dīn ʿAṭiyya. These scholars also employ the *maqāṣid al-sharīʿa*, yet in a manner that enlarges the regulatory function of the state, making state officials the judge of what is "Islamic law." The following presents Ibn ʿĀshūr's articulation of the purposes of the law as a means of legal change,[29] paying particular attention to his understanding of the guidelines and procedures to accommodate the changing environment into the realm of Islamic law.

IBN ʿĀSHŪR'S INTERPRETATION OF THE PURPOSES OF THE LAW (*MAQĀṢID AL-SHARĪʿA*)

Uṣūl al-Fiqh Vs. *Maqāṣid al-Sharīʿa*

A striking feature of Ibn ʿĀshūr's interpretation of the purposes of the law is that he expressly distinguishes them from the discipline of legal theory (*ʿilm uṣūl al-fiqh*). Different from most other jurists, who discuss the purposes of the law within works on and according to the categories of legal theory, Ibn ʿĀshūr exclaims that these are two separate sciences that discuss different topics, use different methodologies, and have distinct epistemologies. The subject matter of legal theory (*uṣūl al-fiqh*), he states, is the articulation of methods of law-finding and identification of legal indicants (*al-adilla al-fiqhiyya*). Furthermore, he argues that the principles (*uṣūl*) arrived at by legal theorists are, contrary to most jurisprudents' claims, only probable (*ẓannī*) in nature.[30] Ibn ʿĀshūr rejects postulations by eminent scholars of the past, ranging from the Shāfiʿī al-Juwaynī (d. 478/1085) to the Mālikī al-Shāṭibī (d. 790/1388), that the principles arrived at in legal theory are certain (*qaṭʿī*), pointing out that there is too much disagreement on almost all aspects of this science to speak of certainty in any of the fundamentals of the law. Those claiming certainty, he states, do so because they want to give legal principles the same status as that of the fundamentals of religion (*uṣūl al-dīn*).[31] In contrast to legal theory, the science of the purposes of the law aims at articulating "definite principles" (*uṣūl qaṭʿiyya*) in order to understand the religion of Islam.[32]

Ibn ʿĀshūr asserts that the science of the purposes of the law is building upon the insights and findings of the principles of jurisprudence,[33] yet he clearly subordinates the latter to the former with respect to their epistemology. From induction (*istiqrāʾ*) of the *Qurʾān* and the sound *sunna*, he says, it is known with certainty (*yaqīn*) that the rulings of the Islamic *sharīʿa* all encompass the intentions of the Lawgiver, namely wisdoms (*ḥikam*), well-being (singular: *maṣlaḥa*; plural: *maṣāliḥ)* and benefits (*manāfiʿ*) that aim to achieve the general well-being of society and the individual and avert *mafsada* (harm) from them.[34] Ibn ʿĀshūr admits that not all *maqāṣid* are known with certainty; nevertheless, it is important to have some definite purposes in order to take them as foundation for law-finding.[35] In other words, we know with certainty that the divine law is purposeful, though our knowledge about the individual purposes themselves may fall short of certainty.

The level of probability of a particular purpose of the law depends on the source text of induction and the strength of the indication. For Ibn ʿĀshūr, the *Qurʾān* as a whole enjoys certainty based on its mode of literal and widespread transmission (*mutawātir al-lafẓ*).[36] The verses of the *Qurʾān* that are clear (*bayyin*) in their indication lead to the highest level of probability.[37] For example, Ibn ʿĀshūr states that there is hardly any disagreement that the qurʾanic verses mentioning grape wine (*khamr*)[38] indicate with high probability that the Lawgiver intends to prohibit its consumption. However, scholars disagree over the legal status of drinking date wine (*nabīdh*) and drinking a small amount of an inebriant (*muskir*); neither case is clearly indicated in the authoritative sources to be prohibited, and thus the intention of the law regarding them is known with only a lower degree of probability.[39]

Irrespective of the lack of certainty about particular objectives of the law, Ibn ʿĀshūr asserts as universal rule (*qāʿida kulliyya*) known with certainty that the *sharīʿa* seeks to attain humankind's *maṣlaḥa* and avert *mafsada* from them. This, he says, is the greatest purpose of the *sharīʿa*.[40]

Ibn ʿĀshūr's assertion that the purposes of the law are certain, at least with regard to our knowledge of the general objective of attaining *maṣlaḥa* and averting *mafsada*, establishes the *maqāṣid* as a more sound form of law-finding over the methods expounded in legal theory. Within the secondary rules of law, Ibn ʿĀshūr thus ascertains the validity of considering the purposes of the law in legislation by postulating that epistemologically they are of higher probability than methods of *uṣūl al-fiqh*, such as analogical reasoning (*qiyās*). Before turning to the application of the *maqāṣid* in law-finding, I want to lay out Ibn ʿĀshūr's understanding of what they are and where they apply.

What are the Purposes of the Law?

A corollary of Ibn ʿĀshūr's differentiation between legal theory and the purposes of the law is his understanding of "Islamic legislation" (*tashrīʿ islāmī*). The general purpose of legislation, Ibn ʿĀshūr states, is to preserve the order (*niẓām*) of the Islamic community (*umma*), to perpetuate its well-being (*ṣalāḥ*) and the well-being of humankind on an individual level.[41] He emphasizes that attaining *maṣlaḥa* and averting *mafsada* is a universal rule in legislation.[42] Although not rejecting outright the well-established definition of *maṣlaḥa* in terms of preserving the five essential necessities listed by al-Ghazālī,[43] namely religion, life, intellect, progeny, and property, Ibn ʿĀshūr steers away from narrow definitions, following rather the thought of al-ʿIzz b. ʿAbd al-Salām (d. 660/1263) and al-Shāṭibī. Hence, he defines *maṣlaḥa* broadly as a characteristic of an act that leads to good (*ṣalāḥ*) in that benefit always, or predominantly, obtains for the whole of society or for the individual. *Mafsada*, in contrast, is characterized as an act that leads to corruption (*fasād*) in that harm (*ḍarar*) always, or predominantly, obtains from it for society or the individual.[44] Such *maṣlaḥa* and *mafsada* may be general (*ʿāmma*), that is, affecting primarily all people, or may be specific (*khāṣṣa*), affecting primarily one individual and only secondarily affecting all of society as part of the whole. For example, protecting the property of a mentally insane person from being spent irresponsibly, Ibn ʿĀshūr says, is primarily a benefit for the insane individual but secondarily also for the whole of society.[45]

Ibn ʿĀshūr argues for broadening the definition of the purposes of the law beyond the preservation of necessities that pertain to the individual human being (i.e., religion, life, intellect, progeny, and property) because, he says, qualities such as equality (*musāwat*) and freedom (*ḥurriyya*) belong just as much to the fundamental purposes (*maqāṣid aṣliyya*) of the *sharīʿa* as do the preservation of the five necessities.[46] Similarly, he says that the preservation of life (*nafs*) means to protect lives from ruin on the level of the individual and society in general, which includes, for example, protecting against contagious diseases. Understanding the preservation of the essential of life only in terms of retaliation (*qiṣāṣ*)[47] is, according to him, the weakest form because it takes effect after a life is lost.[48] Such an interpretation of the preservation of life could justify, and even demand, the establishment of public health policies aimed at preventing the occurrence of epidemics as well as, say, AIDS.

In order to capture various levels of the purposes of the law, Ibn ʿĀshūr distinguishes between immediate (*qarība*) and higher (*ʿāliya*) purposes of the Lawgiver. An immediate purpose is characterized by being universal, for example preserving the intellect, on the level of the individual, and a higher purpose relates to a higher universal, namely attaining *maṣlaḥa* and averting *mafsada* on the level of the community.[49] Although Ibn ʿĀshūr does not always specify what he exactly means by "higher purposes," often simply saying they are *maṣlaḥa* and *mafsada*, from his book as a whole it becomes clear that higher purposes capture more abstract values that aim at preserving order in society, and are thus akin to what he calls the general purpose of Islamic legislation.

When to Apply the Purposes of the Law?

Jurists take recourse to the purposes of the law when no authoritative text applies to the situation at hand, that is, when no ruling for a legal incident is apparent from the indicants of the textual sources of the law and no similar case exists to which to analogize the situation.[50] The pressing and unprecedented incidents faced in this day and age, says Ibn ʿĀshūr, cannot always be solved by looking at textual rulings but legislators need to look at the purposes of the law and the various types of *maṣāliḥ* to have a model and guide to follow.[51]

In order to avert accusations of innovation and deviation from the established procedures of Islamic law, Ibn ʿĀshūr reassures the reader that his interpretation is not new. He provides authenticity to his interpretation by claiming that past jurists also took recourse to the purposes of the law, though not necessarily calling it by that name. Mālik b. Anas (d. 179/795), the eponym of the Mālikī school of law, he argues, held that it is valid to resolve issues not addressed in the authoritative texts of the law by drawing on *maṣlaḥa mursala*, that is, basing such decisions on a *maṣlaḥa* that does not find concrete attestation in the texts. Other eminent jurists, he says, called this "safeguarding necessary legal universals" (*murāʿāt al-kulliyyāt al-sharʿiyya al-ḍarūriyya*), linking to them categories of need (*ḥājiyya*) and improvement (*taḥsīniyya*) and calling all such rulings "suitable" (*munāsib*) in the sense that they are deemed compatible with the purpose of the law.[52]

With this brief reference to other scholars' solutions for coping with legislative voids in the textual sources of the law, Ibn ʿĀshūr puts himself squarely within the Mālikī school tradition as well as following the line of jurisprudents who defined the purposes of the law in connection with the concept of *maṣlaḥa* and categories of necessities, needs, and matters of improvement, a tradition going back to at least the eleventh century CE. Yet, distinguishing between the science of legal theory and the purposes of the law, he points toward his own interpretation being not simply regurgitation, but more overarching than previous efforts at accommodating legal change.

In contrast to past legal scholars, Ibn ʿĀshūr wants to build a framework for law-finding guided by the underlying reasons and objectives of the Lawgiver. This approach to legislation has the advantage of circumventing disputed legal principles and methodologies, for example analogical reasoning, juristic preference (*istiḥsān*), or averting means to illegal ends (*sadd al-dharāʾiʿ*). Ibn ʿĀshūr even warns jurists against blindly taking characteristics of textual rulings as *ratio legis* (*ʿilla*) when applying analogy (*qiyās*) instead of looking at the purposes of the law.[53] Whereas other scholars[54] subsume legal arguments based on the purpose of the law under the methods of law-finding developed in legal theory (*uṣūl al-fiqh*), in particular the identification of the *ratio legis*, he understands those methods to be subsumable under the purposes of the law. In order to identify the *ratio legis* in legal analogy, Ibn ʿĀshūr asserts, one needs to be cognizant of the purposes of the law.[55] One may say that his theory of law-finding looks at the authoritative texts together with the purposes of the law and thus strengthens individual, probable rulings through the certainty of the *maqāṣid* to arrive at rulings of highest Islamic validity. In short, when the textual sources and the conventional methods of law-finding developed in legal theory are insufficient, Ibn ʿĀshūr advocates turning to God's objectives with revealing His law to humankind to find legal solutions.

How to Apply the Purposes of the Law?

Despite differentiating between legal theory and the purposes of the *sharīʿa* as two sciences, Ibn ʿĀshūr combines them when it comes to actual law-finding, which for him appears to be primarily done through the procedure of analogy (*qiyās*). The certainty with which it is known that the rulings of the *sharīʿa* encompass the intentions of the Lawgiver means, according to Ibn ʿĀshūr, that the *ʿulamāʾ* need to know the *rationes legis* (*ʿilal*) of divine legislation as well as their purposes, be they apparent or hidden.[56] He expands the practice of analogy by including in it two types. One type is based on characteristics that are occasions (*asbāb*) for the pinpoint or linchpin (*manāṭ*) of the ruling.[57] The other type is based on characteristics that are the intentions of the Lawgiver. Here, the characteristics upon which an analogy is based are either those commonly referred to as *ratio legis*, like inebriation (*iskār*) for prohibiting alcoholic beverages which Ibn ʿĀshūr calls derivative (*farʿiyya*) characteristics, or universal purposes of the law. The universal purposes are twofold, they belong either to an immediate (*qarīb*) purpose (e.g., preserving the intellect) or to the higher objectives (i.e., attaining *maṣlaḥa* and averting *mafsada*). Ibn ʿĀshūr bemoans that jurists all too often hasten to analogize based on similarities and particulars instead of turning in support of their law-finding to the immediate universal meanings or establishing the existence of higher universals. They do that because, he claims, they view the indication of a similar to its similar to be more directly leading to the meaning God expressed to be considered in the law.[58] Contrary thereto, he argues that taking an inductively arrived at *maṣlaḥa* as the basis (*aṣl*) in analogy is more appropriate and adequate for the procedure of analogy than using a particular characteristic. This type of analogy, Ibn ʿĀshūr asserts, not only constitutes legal proof, but "we can rest assured that [rulings arrived at this way] are 'Islamic legal rulings' (*aḥkām sharʿiyya islāmiyya*)."[59]

This statement makes it obvious that Ibn ʿĀshūr understands the *maqāṣid* as a way to incorporate new legal instances, and especially those that lack direct precedent in the authoritative texts, into the fold of Islamic law. Ibn ʿĀshūr expands *qiyās* from understanding it as a deductive method of reasoning by analogy, which moves from one particular instance to another particular, to include the inductive reasoning process of the purposes of the law. By looking at the immediate, higher, or universal objectives of the law, jurists are able to find legal solutions for cases that were not addressed during the time of the Prophet, that is, in all those cases when analogy to concrete or particular characteristics is not possible.[60] Moreover, in Ibn ʿĀshūr's interpretation of *qiyās* rulings based on *maṣlaḥa* and known through inductive reasoning actually have epistemologically higher status than rulings arrived at in analogy to a particular textual statement. Such manipulation of the secondary rules of law, those that validate the correctness of procedures of law-finding, enables Ibn ʿĀshūr to accommodate the rapid legal change of the modern period. He thereby avoids, on the one hand, the theologically problematic conclusion that the need to add to the rulings expressed in the revealed law implies deficiency on God's part. On the other hand, basing the validity of "new" rulings on the purposes of the law, he averts charges that these are man-made laws. Rather, such rulings are "Islamic," even though they are not based directly on scriptural evidence and are of highest epistemological value. Differentiating between the sources of law (*Qurʾān, sunna*, consensus, and analogy) and Islamic legislation, which is based on the purposes of the divinely revealed law, means that a nation-state can have Islamic legislation that is not bound by the literal wording of the texts of the *Qur'ān* and *ḥadīth*, but based on abstract principles like equality, liberty, and justice, which receive their legal validity by being objectives intended by the Lawgiver.

What is Subject to Islamic Legislation?

How much Ibn ʿĀshūr subscribes to the reformist-modernist attitude is clearly displayed when he discusses which areas of human conduct should be subject to Islamic legislation. He diverges from the Ashʿarī approach to law that deems the revealed law to encompass all of human affairs.[61] In contrast, he limits the reach of Islamic law by defining legislation (*tashrīʿ*) in more narrow terms. Instead of applying to all things laid down by the Lawgiver (*muṭlaq al-shay' al-mashrūʿ*), Ibn ʿĀshūr understands legislation to refer to the laws (*qawānīn*) of civil transactions (*muʿāmalāt*) and customs (*ādāt*) of the Muslim community (*umma*), and, more importantly, only to those matters that fall within the categories of prohibited (*ḥarām*) and obligatory (*wājib*), excluding the recommended (*mandūb*) and reprehensible (*makrūh*).[62] Likewise, issues of ritual worship (*ʿibādāt*) are outside the arena of law-finding, although they, according to Ibn ʿĀshūr, nevertheless point to the general intentions of the divine law.[63]

Differentiating in such a manner between the types of issues that are subject to Islamic legislation means that Islamic jurists speak to matters of civil transactions and customary acts that are enforceable in this world (hard laws), while those that guide the behavior of Muslims and the performing or omitting of which are judged in the afterlife (soft laws) are beyond the reach of legislation. Furthermore, focusing on the two extreme evaluations of legal acts (prohibited and obligatory), in a sense, divides the legal from the moral. Some types of acts may be reprehensible but fall outside the arena of the legislative power of the state and are left to the conscience of the individual and God's judgment. Such an approach accords the individual more liberty of action in all those matters that are not obligatory or prohibited to perform, and thereby reduces the sphere of law that is subject to regulation by the state. Ibn ʿĀshūr, thus, creates a "private sphere" for Islamic law. It is this distinction between *sharīʿa* as an all-encompassing system of divine guidance for human life and Islamic legislation as a set of rules and laws practiced and enforceable within the confines of the nation-state which shows Ibn ʿĀshūr's modernist outlook. Although acknowledging that ultimately all law derives from God, Ibn ʿĀshūr's interpretation of Islamic legislation approaches Western positivist legal philosophy in which questions of morality are, in the legal sphere, separated from laws legislated and enforced by the political sovereign nation-state. Furthermore, the abstract nature of the purposes of the law allows Ibn ʿĀshūr to incorporate general public policies pronounced by the state, such as fighting contagious diseases, and the individual regulations arising from such policy considerations into the fold of Islamic legislation because they are based on the general purposes of God's law. Ibn ʿĀshūr thereby is able to embrace the modern nation-state without compromising the Islamic character of its laws and policies. His thought lends authentically Islamic solutions to the legal concerns of the modern world.

CONCLUSIONS

The above presentation of Ibn ʿĀshūr's interpretation of the purposes of the law shows how this influential scholar navigates the secondary rules of law to devise a method for legal change suited to the modern nation-state. He ascertains recourse to the purposes of the law as a valid procedure of law-finding by providing a novel interpretation of their relationship with other principles of law-finding developed in the discipline of legal theory (*uṣūl al-fiqh*). By differentiating between the methodologies of legal theory and the objectives of the law, Ibn ʿĀshūr asserts that the latter, while building on the former, are of higher epistemological status than the former. Being known with a higher level of probability close to certainty, the purposes of the law not only are more valid to use in legislation but also provide an overarching framework within which the methodologies of law-finding expounded in legal theory function.

Furthermore, subsuming the methodologies of law-finding under the purposes of the law enables Ibn ʿĀshūr to reinterpret the procedure of analogical reasoning (*qiyās*), one of the sources of Islamic law. In addition to the deductive reasoning process that takes a textually attested ruling (*ḥukm al-aṣl*) to transfer it to an unprecedented but similar situation (*farʿ*) on account of the two instances sharing a common occasion (*sabab*) or legal rationale (*ʿilla*), Ibn ʿĀshūr includes under analogy also inductive reasoning that takes as its basis for analogy not a textual statement but the purposes of the law more generally. In a way, this intellectual move expands the sources of the law from concrete, limited texts to include abstract concepts, the interpretation of which are less determined by the specific wording of the text than the interpretation of these concepts in a particular context. The legal interpreter moves away from philological analysis of scripture to the inner or deeper meaning of the revealed texts and their implications.

Such an approach to legal texts, on the one hand, provides jurists with more flexibility and possibilities to interpret the law and allows accommodating legal change within an Islamic legal framework. On the other hand, without concrete definitions of the purposes of the law and what constitutes *maṣlaḥa* and *mafsada*, it has the potential for extensive abuse on part of the state legal apparatus of what scripture requires the believer to do and not to do. Ibn ʿĀshūr seems to be acutely aware of that danger. His explicit restriction of Islamic legislation to matters of obligation and prohibition ensures that Islamic law has its place in society without stifling plurality of opinions in those matters that are open to interpretation and without making all of human conduct subject to the enforcement of the state. Islamic legislation, in Ibn ʿĀshūr's conception, draws near to a Western positivist understanding of law, in which matters of morality are largely left outside the legal sphere. Restricting Islamic legislation based on *maṣlaḥa* and the purposes of the law to obligatory and prohibited matters is rather unusual. Yūsuf al-Qaraḍāwī, for example, proposes applying considerations of *maṣlaḥa* and the purposes of the law in all areas of modern society. As Zaman pointedly remarks about al-Qaraḍāwī's expansive application of the purposes of the law, "the distinction between sin and crime, and between moral and legal infractions, collapses."[64] Similarly, the Syrian scholar al-Būṭī employs the purposes of the law to give the state more control over the behavior of citizens by, for example, justifying the permissibility of state censorship with preserving the intellect (*ḥifẓ al-ʿaql*).[65] Ibn ʿĀshūr, in contrast, envisions Islamic law as a legal system on par with that of modern nation-states (in particular Western conceptions of law), without denying it an active role in the legislative activities of the state.

Understanding the purposes of the law as the universal underpinning of Islamic legislation is coupled in Ibn ʿĀshūr's thought with an emphasis on the probability of particular laws. His approach to law-finding thus provides the Islamic legal system with a standard by which to evaluate from a religious vantage point the ever-changing environment and at the same time it allows for polyvalent interpretations, even of the scriptural foundations of the law. When Ibn ʿĀshūr discusses how to determine cases to which multiple *maṣāliḥ* or *mafāsid* (plural of *mafsada*) apply, he proposes that one should rule in a fashion that the most preponderant *maṣlaḥa* prevails, though he admits that people often disagree over which one attains the greater *maṣlaḥa*. What is considered to constitute *maṣlaḥa* is decided according to custom.[66] Ibn ʿĀshūr's approach to Islamic law thereby accommodates legal change, as well as recognizes and respects the reality of legal pluralism existing among the community of believers (*umma*).

Unresolved in Ibn ʿĀshūr's articulation are questions of hierarchy and priority among the *maqāṣid* as well as vis-à-vis rulings derived from the authoritative texts or analogy. The hierarchy of immediate (*qarība*) and higher (*ʿāliya*) purposes is largely void of express acknowledgment of when and why one has priority over the other. For example, when the purpose of "equality" is understood as "equality of rights," then the divine intention can only be achieved by every individual having equal rights (i.e., an immediate purpose). When one member of society has unequal rights, the purpose is not achieved on the collective level of society (i.e., higher purpose). The hierarchical terminology of Ibn ʿĀshūr suggests that the higher purpose has priority, allowing for unequal rights on the individual level. Following Ibn ʿĀshūr's articulation of epistemological values of rulings and purposes, a ruling or purpose known with certainty should receive priority over one of high probability. Thus, the qurʾanic injunction of unequal inheritance shares for sons and daughters[67] (i.e., a clear verse of high probability) is in conflict with the divine purpose of equality. Postulating the purposes of the law as certain implies that attaining equality is the aim that ought to be achieved, thereby allowing, in theory, for the qurʾanic verse to be superseded. Such practical applications of the purposes of the law are, however, rarely addressed by Ibn ʿĀshūr.[68]

Irrespective of such shortcomings, Ibn ʿĀshūr's thought provides an Islamic modernist approach to legal change, one that embraces modernity yet conveys authenticity. His ideas are not new or foreign to the Islamic legal discourse but derived from the intellectual heritage going back to the founding fathers of Islamic law. He links the existing framework of the sources of the law with the purposes of the law through expanding the application of analogical reasoning beyond the scope of the deductive to include as basis or *ratio legis* of analogy attaining *maṣlaḥa* and averting *mafsada*. Thereby, he successfully provides Islamic scholars, jurists, and politicians with an outline of how a legal system, the history of which spans almost a millennium and a half, can be carried on in the age of modernity and applied within the legal framework of a modern nation state. *Sharīʿa*, as once practiced, may irretrievably be gone,[69] but the purposes of the *sharīʿa* retain their relevance even today.

NOTES

1. Although the *ḥadīth* is not a closed body of text like the *Qurʾān*, it approaches the *Qurʾān* in its authoritativeness as a source of law, notwithstanding debates over the validity of individual *aḥadīth*.
2. Islamic law allows for nontextual laws to enter the legal system, for example in the form of rulings based on consensus (*ijmāʿ*) as well as customary laws. However, such laws ought not to be contrary to the *Qurʾān* and *sunna*.
3. I use the term "Islamic" jurist to indicate that the person is a scholar-practitioner of Islamic law, in contrast to a "Muslim" jurist who is Muslim by faith yet practices US law.
4. With "new" ruling I mean that the incident ruled upon has no precedent in the textual basis of the law or legal tradition and constitutes an addition to the existing legal rulings (e.g., rulings pertaining to embryonic stem cell research); a "changed" ruling is one that finds precedent in the legal tradition but is changed in its details

(e.g., setting the minimum marriage age for women to 21 years, when previously it has been 16 years).

5. Cf. H. L. A. Hart, *The Concept of Law* (London: Oxford University Press, 1961), 92–108; see also Reinhart's summary and application of Hart's categories to Islamic law (A. Kevin Reinhart, "Law," in *Key Themes for the Study of Islam*, ed. Jamal J. Elias [Oxford: Oneworld, 2010], 220–43, at 222–33).

6. Reinterpreting the meaning of a legal text is a common feature in all textually based legal systems. An example from a constitutional system is the US Supreme Court ruling of 2010 that reinterpreted the First Amendment prohibiting the government from restricting independent political expenditures by a nonprofit corporation to apply also to for-profit corporations, thereby substantially altering the parameters of election campaign finance law (cf. *Citizens United v. Federal Election Commission*, 558 U.S. 310, S. Ct. 876 [2010]). An example of modernists' reinterpretation of Islamic family law is the late Pakistani scholar Fazlur Rahman's view that the qurʾanic injunction (Q 4: 34), which states that a husband provides for the maintenance of his wife, is a descriptive rather than prescriptive statement. Consequently, he argued for equal responsibility of spouses regarding maintenance of the marital household since in today's age women can be economically independent (Fazlur Rahman, "Modernization of Muslim Family Law," *International Journal of Middle East Studies* 11 [1980]: 451–65, at 453).

7. For example, al-Qarāfī (d. 684/1285) rethought the principle of *sadd al-dharāʾiʿ*, blocking means to illegal ends, arguing that it also needs to apply to permit illegal means when it leads to legal ends. Drawing on this novel interpretation, he justified the legality of paying ransom for Muslim prisoners of war, a practice deemed prohibited since it aids the enemy (Aḥmad b. Idrīs al-Qarāfī, *al-Dhakhīra*, 2 vols. [Cairo: Maṭbaʿa Kulliyyat al-Sharīfa, 1381/1961], 1: 145–6).

8. For a detailed account on the historical development of the purposes of the law as a legal concept, see Felicitas Opwis, *Maṣlaḥa and the Purposes of the Law: Islamic Discourse on Legal Change from the 4th/10th to 8th/14th Century* (Leiden: Brill, 2010); for a short summary cf. idem, "Islamic Law and Legal Change: The Concept of *Maṣlaḥa* in Classical and Contemporary Legal Theory," in *Shari'a: Islamic Law in the Contemporary Context*, ed. Abbas Amanat and Frank Griffel (Palo Alto, CA: Stanford University Press, 2007), 62–82, at 66–71.

9. For a discussion of dating the start of the modern period in the Middle East with a wide array of positions and research reviewed, see Dror Ze'evi, "Back to Napoleon? Thoughts on the Beginning of the Modern Era in the Middle East," *Mediterranean Historical Review* 19, no. 1 (2004): 73–94.

10. This transformation leads Hallaq to argue that *sharīʿa* law, as it existed in the premodern period, is irretrievably lost (Wael B. Hallaq, "Can the Sharīʿa be Restored?" in *Islamic Law and the Challenges of Modernity*, ed. Barbara Stowasser and Yvonne Haddad [Walnut Creek, CA: Altamira Press, 2004], 21–53).

11. For an example of the competing claims of Islamic and state law on deciding criminal cases see Rudolph Peters, "Islamic and Secular Criminal Law in Nineteenth Century Egypt: the Role and Function of the Qadi," *Islamic Law and Society* 4 (1997): 70–90.

12. For a good overview of the relationship between *sharīʿa* and the state since the nineteenth century, see Nathan J. Brown, "Shariʿa and State in the Modern Muslim Middle East," *International Journal of Middle East Studies* 29 (1997): 359–76, in particular 359–68.

13. For a discussion of how the introduction of legal codes and statutes affected Islamic law, see Aharon Layish, "The Transformation of the *Sharīʿa* from Jurists' Law to Statutory Law in the Contemporary Muslim World," *Die Welt des Islams* 44 (2004): 85–113.

14. For a detailed and insightful biography of Ibn ʿĀshūr see Basheer M. Nafi, "Ṭāhir ibn ʿĀshūr: The Career and Thought of a Modern Reformist *ʿālim*, with Special Reference to His Work of *tafsīr*," *Journal of Qurʾanic Studies* 7 (2005): 1–32.

15. Nafi, "Ṭāhir ibn ʿĀshūr," 10–12.

16. A succinct overview of the ideas and sociopolitical context of modernist/reformist thought presents Basheer M. Nafi, "The Rise of Islamic Reformist Thought and its Challenge to Traditional Islam," in *Islamic Thought in the Twentieth Century*, ed. Suha Taji-Farouki and Basheer M. Nafi (London: Tauris, 2004), 28–60.

17. See Nafi, "Ṭāhir ibn ʿĀshūr," 1–13.

18. Nafi, "Ṭāhir ibn ʿĀshūr," 12.

19. William Shepard, "The Diversity of Islamic Thought: Towards a Typology," in *Islamic Thought in the Twentieth Century*, ed. Suha Taji-Farouki and Basheer M. Nafi (London: Tauris, 2004), 61–103, at 63 and 70.

20. Equality and freedom are values that Ibn ʿĀshūr also expounds as goals of an Islamic sociopolitical system (Nafi, "Ṭāhir ibn ʿĀshūr," 15).

21. Nafi translates the title of the *tafsīr* as "Verification and Enlightenment" (Nafi, "Ṭāhir ibn ʿĀshūr," 17). The term verification for *taḥrīr*, might be defendable in light of the original longer title of the work, which is *Taḥrīr al-maʿnā al-sadīd wa-tanwīr al-ʿaql al-jadīd min tafsīr al-kitāb al-majīd*, translated by Nafi as *Verification of the Sound Meaning and Enlightenment of the New Mind in the Exegesis of the Glorious Book* (ibid., 29). I opt for "liberation" which stays closer to the literal meaning and reflects the parallel theme of "enlightenment."

22. Saleh comments that Ibn ʿĀshūr's *Qurʾān tafsīr*, although "one of the most important works of the reform movement of the twentieth century in the Islamic world, has gone totally unnoticed" (Walid Saleh, "Marginalia and Peripheries: A Tunisian Historian and the History of Qur'anic Exegesis," *Numen* 58 [2011]: 284–313, at 288). Recently, a PhD dissertation on gender questions in modern Sunni *tafsīr* literature accords much attention to Ibn ʿĀshūr's interpretations (see Hadia Mubarak, *Intersection: Modernity, Gender, and Qurʾanic Exegesis*, PhD thesis, Georgetown University, 2014).

23. A vast literature exists on the topic of the purposes of the *sharīʿa*, most of which discuss and compare the views of many Islamic jurisprudents of the premodern and contemporary periods; notable for its breadth and depth is Gamal Eldin Attia's study *Towards Realization of the Higher Intents of Islamic Law: Maqāṣid al-Sharīʿah, A Functional Approach* (London: International Institute of Islamic Thought, 2007).

24. The work has been translated into English as *Ibn Ashur: Treatise on Maqāṣid al-Shariʿah*, translated from the Arabic and Annotated by Mohamed El-Tahir

El-Mesawi (London: The International Institute of Islamic Thought, 1427/2006). This paper refers to the Arabic edition: Muḥammad al-Ṭāhir Ibn ʿĀshūr, *Maqāṣid al-sharīʿa al-islāmiyya* (Tunis: al-Sharika al-Tūnisiyya li-l-Tawzīʿ, 1978).

25. See Ismāʿīl al-Ḥasanī, *Naẓariyyāt al-maqāṣid ʿind al-imām Muḥammad al-Ṭāhir b. ʿĀshūr* (London: International Institute of Islamic Thought, 1995). The work was deemed important enough to be translated into Persian with the title *Maqāṣid al-sharīʿa az nigah-i Ibn ʿĀshūr* (Qom: Saḥīfah-i Khirad, 2004). Al-Ḥasanī is sometimes identified as the "commentator of Ibn ʿĀshūr" (cf., e.g., Attia, *Towards Realization*, 68; and Nafi, "Ṭāhir ibn ʿĀshūr," 29). Other popular commentaries are by Muḥammad al-Ḥabīb Ibn Khūja, *Muḥammad al-Ṭāhir b. ʿĀshūr wa-kitābih Maqāṣid al-Sharīʿa al-Islāmiyya* ([one of several editions was published in] Qatar: Wizārat al-Awqāf wal-l-Shuʾūn al-Islāmiyya, 2004); and by al-Ṣuḥbī ʿAtīq, *Tafsīr wa-l-Maqāṣid ʿind al-Shaykh Muḥammad al-Ṭāhir b. ʿĀshūr* (Tunis: Dār al-Sanābil lil-Thaqāfa wa-l-ʿUlūm, 1989).

26. Ibn ʿĀshūr, *Maqāṣid al-sharīʿa*, 15.

27. Donald L. Horowitz, "The Qurʾan and the Common Law: Islamic Law Reform and the Theory of Legal Change," *The American Journal of Comparative Law* 42 (1994): 233–93 and 543–80, at 244–54.

28. Horowitz, "The Qurʾan and the Common Law," 569–72 and 578.

29. The Egyptian legal scholar ʿAbd al-Razzāq al-Sanhūrī (d. 1971), in contrast, sees in Consensus (*ijmāʿ*) the tool of attaining legal change (David Johnston, "A Turn in the Epistemology and Hermeneutics of Twentieth Century *Uṣūl al-Fiqh*," *Islamic Law and Society* 11, 2 [2004]: 233–82, at 268).

30. Ibn ʿĀshūr, *Maqāṣid al-sharīʿa*, 7–8.

31. Ibid., 8, and 41–42. Ibn ʿĀshūr follows in this aspect Fakhr al-Dīn al-Rāzī (d. 606/1210), who permitted probable knowledge in matters of *uṣūl al-fiqh* but demanded that the fundamentals of religion, *uṣūl al-dīn*, are known with certainty (Roger Arnaldez, "L'Oevre de Fakhr al-Dīn al-Rāzī, Commentateur du Coran et Philosophe," *Cahiers de Civilisation Medievale* 3 [1960]: 307–27, at 315).

32. Ibn ʿĀshūr, *Maqāṣid al-sharīʿa*, 8.

33. Ibid.

34. Ibid., 14, 17, 48, and 64.

35. Ibid., 40.

36. Ibid., 21.

37. Ibn ʿĀshūr frequently uses the term *al-ẓann qarīb min al-qaṭʿ*, "probability close to certainty" to express that there is little disagreement as to the (legal) validity of the indicated; this category is the highest level of probability (see, e.g., Ibn ʿĀshūr, *Maqāṣid al-sharīʿa*, 14, 19, 41, and 52).

38. See Qurʾān 2: 219; and 5: 90–91.

39. Ibn ʿĀshūr considers the rulings to prohibit drinking *nabīdh* as well as a small inebriating quantity to be derived from the principle of blocking the means to illegal ends (*sadd al-dharāʾiʿ*) (Ibn ʿĀshūr, *Maqāṣid al-sharīʿa*, 43). It deserves notice that most jurists deem the prohibition of small quantities of inebriants to be based on analogical reasoning, namely as *a fortiori* argument (*qiyās al-awlā*).

40. Ibn ʿĀshūr, *Maqāṣid al-sharīʿa*, 17 note 1, and 64.

41. Ibid., 14 and 63.

42. Ibid., 63–64.

43. Al-Ghazālī (d. 505/1111) was probably the first jurisprudent to define the purposes of the Lawgiver as attaining *maṣlaḥa* for humankind by preserving for them their religion (*dīn*), life (*nafs*), intellect (*ʿaql*), offspring (*nasl*), and property (*māl*) (Abū Ḥāmid al-Ghazālī, *al-Mustaṣfā min ʿilm al-uṣūl*, ed. Ḥamza b. Zuhayr Ḥāfiẓ, 4 vols. [Jedda: Sharikat al-Madīna al-Munawwara lil-Ṭibāʿ wa-l-Nashr, 1993], 2: 481–82). Although these so-called five necessities (*ḍarūrāt* or *ḍarūriyyāt*) have been contested, al-Ghazālī's definition of the purposes of the law has become widely accepted over the centuries until very recently when Islamic jurisprudents revisited the definition and categories of the purposes of the law and of *maṣlaḥa* (see, e.g., the discussion in Attia, *Towards Realization*, 77–90; Felicitas Opwis, "New Trends in Islamic Legal Theory: *Maqāṣid al-Sharīʿa* as a New Source of Law?" *Die Welt des Islams* 57 [2017]: 7–32).

44. Ibn ʿĀshūr, *Maqāṣid al-sharīʿa*, 65.

45. Ibid., 65–66.

46. Ibid., 95–99, and 130–35.

47. Al-Ghazālī justifies the importance of the preservation of life (*nafs*) with reference to the divine injunctions on retaliation (al-Ghazālī, *al-Mustaṣfā*, 2: 482).

48. Ibn ʿĀshūr, *Maqāṣid al-sharīʿa*, 80.

49. Ibid., 108.

50. Ibid., 15 and 48.

51. Ibid., 77–78.

52. Ibid., 15–16, and 17 note 1. While Ibn ʿĀshūr does not mention any names beside Mālik, he obviously refers to scholars like al-Ghazālī, Fakhr al-Dīn al-Rāzī, al-Qarāfī, al-Shāṭibī, and others, who articulated and developed *maṣlaḥa* as a legal concept to address legal change.

53. Ibn ʿĀshūr, *Maqāṣid al-sharīʿa*, 45 and 108–109.

54. For example, al-Ghazālī, al-Rāzī, but also contemporary scholars such as al-Būṭī, ʿAbd al-Wahhāb Khallāf, and ʿAllāl al-Fāsī (cf. Felicitas Opwis, "*Maṣlaḥa* in Contemporary Islamic Legal Theory," *Islamic Law and Society* 12, no. 2 [2005]: 182–223).

55. Ibn ʿĀshūr, *Maqāṣid al-sharīʿa*, 17.

56. Ibid., 48.

57. For example, in sale transactions acceptance of the offer is the occasion for the sale to be deemed contracted.

58. Ibn ʿĀshūr, *Maqāṣid al-sharīʿa*, 108.

59. Ibid., 83–84.

60. This type of analogical reasoning is frequently called "unattested" *maṣlaḥa* (*maṣlaḥa mursala*) and was largely accepted by premodern jurisprudents.

61. The Ashʿarī view that the revealed law speaks to all aspects of human behavior contributed, as this author argues elsewhere, to Ashʿarī jurisprudents being at the forefront of developing the concept of *maṣlaḥa* as a vehicle for legal change. It allows to address the contingencies in law and enables to incorporate unprecedented cases within the fold of Islamic law (Opwis, "Islamic Law and Legal Change," 63–65;

Opwis, Maṣlaḥa *and the Purpose of the Law*, 27–32). Many modernist jurists display a tendency to turn away from some of the Ashʿarī principles without however necessarily fully embracing Muʿtazilī theological thought (cf. Nafi, "The Rise of Reformist Thought," 40–43).

62. Ibn ʿĀshūr, *Maqāṣid al-sharīʿa*, 9.

63. Ibid. Ibn ʿĀshūr authored a book dealing primarily with the acts of devotion as fundamentals of the social order in Islam, entitled *Uṣūl niẓām al-mujtamaʿ fī-l-islām*, ed. Muḥammad al-Ṭāhir Maysāwī (Amman: Dār al-Nafāʾis, 2001).

64. Muhammad Qasim Zaman, "The ʿUlama of Contemporary Islam and the Conceptions of the Common Good," in *Public Islam and the Common Good*, eds. Armando Salvatore and Dale F. Eickelmann (Leiden: Brill, 2004), 129–55, at 134–35.

65. Muḥammad Saʿīd Ramaḍān al-Būṭī, *Ḍawābiṭ al-maṣlaḥa fī-l-sharīʿa al-islāmiyya* (Beirut: Muʾassasat al-Risāla, 4th ed. 1402/1982), 252–53.

66. Ibn ʿĀshūr, *Maqāṣid al-sharīʿa*, 67 and 75–76.

67. See Qurʾān 4: 11.

68. Jackson similarly criticizes the current discourse of the universalism of the *maqāṣid al-sharīʿa* as empty unless coupled with the admission that in concrete applications, the purposes of the law differ according to time, place, and peoples (Sherman Jackson, "Literalism, Empiricism, and Induction: Apprehending and Concretizing Islamic Law's *Maqâṣid al-Sharīʿah* in the Modern World," *Michigan State Law Review* [2006]: 1469–86, at 1479–80 and 1486).

69. Hallaq argues that the *sharīʿa*, as we know it, is irretrievably gone (Hallaq, "Can the Sharīʿa be Restored?"). I agree with his findings that the institutionalization of the teaching and practice of Islamic law have been altered to an extent that cannot be restored to the way it was in the premodern period. Yet, I see this process to be similar to the changes that the practice and societal integration of *sharīʿa* underwent in previous times, such as during the consolidation of the schools of law in the third/fourth and tenth/eleventh centuries, and the rise of institutionalized study of *fiqh* in the following centuries.

BIBLIOGRAPHY

al-Būṭī, Muḥammad Saʿīd Ramaḍān. *Ḍawābiṭ al-maṣlaḥa fī-l-sharīʿa al-islāmiyya*, 4th edition. Beirut: Muʾassasat al-Risāla, 1982 [1402].

al-Ghazālī, Abū Ḥāmid. *al-Mustaṣfā min ʿilm al-uṣūl*. Edited by Ḥamza b. Zuhayr Ḥāfiẓ, 4 vols. Jedda: Sharikat al-Madīna al-Munawwara lil-Ṭibāʿ wa-l-Nashr, 1993.

al-Ḥabīb Ibn Khūja, Muḥammad. *Muḥammad al-Ṭāhir b. ʿĀshūr wa-kitābih Maqāṣid al-Sharīʿa al-Islāmiyya*. Qatar: Wizārat al-Awqāf wal-l-Shuʾūn al-Islāmiyya, 2004.

al-Ḥasanī, Ismāʿīl. *Naẓariyyāt al-maqāṣid ʿind al-imām Muḥammad al-Ṭāhir b. ʿĀshūr*. London: International Institute of Islamic Thought, 1995.

al-Qarāfī, Aḥmad b. Idrīs. *al-Dhakhīra*, 2 vols. Cairo: Maṭbaʿa Kulliyyat al-Sharīfa, 1961 [1381].

al-Ṣuḥbī, ʿAtīq. *Tafsīr wa-l-Maqāṣid ʿind al-Shaykh Muḥammad al-Ṭāhir b. ʿĀshūr*. Tunis: Dār al-Sanābil lil-Thaqāfa wa-l-ʿUlūm, 1989.

al-Ṭāhir Ibn ʿĀshūr, Muhammad. *Maqāṣid al-sharīʿa al-islāmiyya*. Tunis: al-Sharika al-Tūnisiyya li-l-Tawzīʿ, 1978.

Arnaldez, Roger. "L'Oevre de Fakhr al-Dīn al-Rāzī, Commentateur du Coran et Philosophe." *Cahiers de Civilisation Medievale* 3 (1960): 307–27.

Brown, Nathan J. "Shariʿa and State in the Modern Muslim Middle East." *International Journal of Middle East Studies* 29 (1997): 359–76.

Eldin Attia, Gamal. *Towards Realization of the Higher Intents of Islamic Law: Maqāṣid al-Sharīʿah, A Functional Approach*. London: International Institute of Islamic Thought, 2007.

Hallaq, Wael B. "Can the Sharīʿa be Restored?" In *Islamic Law and the Challenges of Modernity*, edited by Barbara Stowasser and Yvonne Haddad, 21–53. Walnut Creek, CA: Altamira Press, 2004.

Hart, H. L. A. *The Concept of Law*. London: Oxford University Press, 1961.

Horowitz, Donald L. "The Qur'an and the Common Law: Islamic Law Reform and the Theory of Legal Change." *The American Journal of Comparative Law* 42 (1994): 233–93 and 543–80.

Ibn ʿĀshūr, Muḥammad al-Ṭāhir. *Uṣūl niẓām al-mujtamaʿ fī-l-islām*. Edited by Muḥammad al-Ṭāhir Maysāwī. Amman: Dār al-Nafāʾis, 2001.

Jackson, Sherman. "Literalism, Empiricism, and Induction: Apprehending and Concretizing Islamic Law's *Maqâṣid al-Sharīʿah* in the Modern World." *Michigan State Law Review* (2006): 1469–86.

Johnston, David. "A Turn in the Epistemology and Hermeneutics of Twentieth Century *Uṣūl al-Fiqh*." *Islamic Law and Society* Vol. 11, no. 2 (2004): 233–82.

Layish, Aharon. "The Transformation of the *Sharīʿa* from Jurists' Law to Statutory Law in the Contemporary Muslim World." *Die Welt des Islams* 44 (2004): 85–113.

Mubarak, Hadia. *Intersection: Modernity, Gender, and Qurʾanic Exegesis*. PhD thesis, Georgetown University, 2014. https://repository.library.georgetown.edu/bitstream/handle/10822/712424/Mubarak_georgetown_0076D_12739.pdf?sequence=1&isAllowed=y.

Nafi, Basheer M. "Ṭāhir ibn ʿĀshūr: The Career and Thought of a Modern Reformist *ʿālim*, with Special Reference to His Work of *tafsīr*." *Journal of Qurʾanic Studies* 7 (2005): 1–32.

———. "The Rise of Islamic Reformist Thought and its Challenge to Traditional Islam." In *Islamic Thought in the Twentieth Century*, edited by Suha Taji-Farouki and Basheer M. Nafi, 28–60. London: Tauris, 2004.

Opwis, Felicitas. "Islamic Law and Legal Change: The Concept of *Maṣlaḥa* in Classical and Contemporary Legal Theory." In *Shariʾa: Islamic Law in the Contemporary Context*, edited by Abbas Amanat and Frank Griffel, 62–82. Palo Alto, CA: Stanford University Press, 2007.

———. *Maṣlaḥa and the Purposes of the Law: Islamic Discourse on Legal Change from the 4th/10th to 8th/14th Century*. Leiden: Brill, 2010.

———."*Maṣlaḥa* in Contemporary Islamic Legal Theory." *Islamic Law and Society* Vol. 12, no. 2 (2005): 182–223.

———. "New Trends in Islamic Legal Theory: *Maqāṣid al-Sharīʿa* as a New Source of Law?" *Die Welt des Islams* 57 (2017): 7–32.

Peters, Rudolph. “Islamic and Secular Criminal Law in Nineteenth Century Egypt: the Role and Function of the Qadi.” *Islamic Law and Society* 4 (1997): 70–90.
Rahman, Fazlur. “Modernization of Muslim Family Law.” *International Journal of Middle East Studies* 11 (1980): 451–65.
Reinhart, A. Kevin. “Law.” In *Key Themes for the Study of Islam*, edited by Jamal J. Elias, 220–43. Oxford: Oneworld, 2010.
Saleh, Walid. “Marginalia and Peripheries: A Tunisian Historian and the History of Qur᾽anic Exegesis.” *Numen* 58 (2011): 284–313.
Shepard, William. “The Diversity of Islamic Thought: Towards a Typology.” In *Islamic Thought in the Twentieth Century*, edited by Suha Taji-Farouki and Basheer M. Nafi, 61–103. London: Tauris, 2004.
Zaman, Muhammad Qasim. “The ʿUlama of Contemporary Islam and the Conceptions of the Common Good.” In *Public Islam and the Common Good*, edited by Armando Salvatore and Dale F. Eickelmann, 129–55. Leiden: Brill, 2004.
Ze’evi, Dror. “Back to Napoleon? Thoughts on the Beginning of the Modern Era in the Middle East.” *Mediterranean Historical Review* Vol. 19, no. 1 (2004): 73–94.

Chapter 7

Maqāṣid al-Sharīʿah in Islamic Contracts

A Study of Current Practices of Islamic Finance in Light of Islamic Legal Maxims

Younes Soualhi

INTRODUCTION

Islamic finance has attracted enough attention to justify its introduction as a robust financial system with a unique value proposition. Aiming to establish a real economy, Islamic finance endeavored to trade in real assets and have returns that commensurate with risks. Not only does Islamic finance prohibit usury, gambling, uncertainty, and trading in unlawful goods, but it also aims at establishing a financial system that enhances justice and welfare for all stakeholders at macro and micro levels. This value proposition hinges upon many requirements, namely the observance of a *maqāṣid al-sharīʿah* (objectives of Islamic law) that is inherently pervading and permeating the very essence of Islamic finance. Since the latter is entirely based on *sharīʿah* contracts, this research aims to unveil the *maqāṣid* dimension underlying them, as well as evaluating the extent to which *sharīʿah* contracts hold on to their objectives when applied in contemporary Islamic finance. Equally important in this research is an evaluation of current Islamic finance in light of Islamic legal maxims.

MAQĀṢID AL-SHARĪʿAH IN ISLAMIC FINANCE AND THE THRUST OF *IJTIHĀD*

Islamic finance is a system that adheres to the Islamic principles in fund mobilization, provision of finance, and investment. The *maqāṣid* underlying this system are of two categories: explicit *maqāṣid* that are stated in the revealed texts and formulated ones that are traced from a number of particular rulings and jurisprudential principles through the process of induction (*istiqra'*). Both must be observed when establishing a new Islamic legal ruling (*fatwa*). Ibn ʿAshūr emphasizes on the necessity of observing *maqāṣid al-sharīʿah* in *ijtihād*:

> In sum, we can say that we are certain that all the shariah commands embody the lawgiver's purposes, which consists of underlying reasons, benefits, and interests. It is, therefore the duty of the scholars of the shariah to search for the reasons and objectives of legislation, both the overt and the covert.[1]

The knowledge of *maqāṣid* is an important condition of *ijtihād*, as maintained by al-Shāṭibī.[2] In the field of contemporary Islamic finance, *ijtihād* has adopted two approaches: adaptive (*takyyif fiqhi*) and innovative (*ibtikar*). The former would adapt existing conventional financial products and instruments to relevant Islamic principles, hence a simulative approach, and the latter would innovate new instruments that combine nominated contracts (*ʿuqud musamah*), which are embedded with instruments of surety (*daman*) and agency to achieve the objectives of financing and investment. Both approaches employ *maqāṣid al-sharīʿah*, and both thrust to maintain *sharīʿah* compliance and economic viability.

SHARĪʿAH CONTRACTS AND THE REALIZATION OF THE *MAQĀṢID AL- SHARĪʿAH* OF WEALTH

A contract, in its specific sense, is a voluntary and binding agreement between two or more persons to create enforceable rights and duties. Al-Jurjani (d. 1078 AD) defines it as an agreement that "binds the contracting parties with offer and acceptance."[3] The Ḥanafī's define it as "the correspondence of the offer of any of the contracting parties with the acceptance of the other."[4] The Shāfiʿī's would define a contract as a forceful link between the offer and acceptance.[5] As for the Ḥanbalī's, they emphasize on the specific meaning of a contract as an agreement between two or more promises to initiate or transfer obligations.[6] These definitions have not explicitly highlighted the objectives of a contract as they emphasized on contracts initiating obligations and rights. Imam al-Qarāfī (d. 684 H) from the Mālikī school shed some light on what is deemed to be the *maqāṣid al-sharīʿah* of contracts. In his seminal work '*al-Furūq*,' he reiterated that a contract, in principle, is binding as it is promulgated to achieve the legitimate objective of the contracting party and to remove hardship. The binding feature, according to Qarāfī, is suitable to remove hardship and to achieve the objectives of a bilateral contract, whereas the objectives of unilateral contracts are achieved without any binding element.[7] To emphasize the legal effects of a contract, Majella (2005) defines a contract as "the legitimate link between the offer and acceptance in such a way the legal effects of a contract are realized."[8] Qarāfī's view on the removal of hardship and Majella's referral to the legal effect sum up to a great extent the objectives of a *sharīʿah* contract, which is generally the realization of *maṣlaḥa* (benefit) and the removal of *mafsadah* (harm). The latter is the ultimate goal of all *sharīʿah* rulings, including those of Islamic commercial law.

Maqāṣid al-sharīʿah in contracts are traceable in three areas in Islamic jurisprudence: specific objectives of wealth, the principle of intention in contracts, and the pillars and conditions of contracts. The specific objectives of wealth, according to Ibn ʿAshūr (d. 1973 AD), are five:

> "circulation (*rawaj*), clarity (*wuduh*), protection (*ḥifd*), firmness (*thabat*) and justice (*ʿadl*)."[9] We shall analyze the relationship between these *maqāṣid al-sharīʿah* on the one hand, and contracts and principles in their capacity as means (*wasa'il*) on the other. This is addressed on the premise that the means hold the same ruling as the *maqāṣid* (*li-l wasa'il aḥkam al-maqāṣid*) as maintained by Qarāfī[10] and many Muslim scholars. Abu Ghuddah highlighted the general *maqāṣid* of contracts as being "justice for exchange contracts, intactness for options (*khiyarat*), fairness and integration for partnership contracts (*muharakat*), *benevolence* (*iḥsan*) for donation contracts, and *security* for surety instruments.[11]

The principle of intention in contracts is manifested in the formidable integration of the *maqāṣid al-sharīʿah* of wealth with the intention of the contracting parties. In the course of engaging in any financial activity, the contracting parties must align their intention with the *maqāṣid al-sharīʿah.* Al-Shāṭibī ascertains that "the objective of the lawgiver is to make the intentions of the person (*mukallaf*) in full conformity with the objectives of *sharīʿah* . . . the person [thus] should not aim [something] not intended by *sharīʿah.*"[12] Muslim jurists have long emphasized the importance of linking *sharīʿah* contracts to their legitimate objectives. Their debates revolved around the principle of form versus substance when concluding a contract. The issue is well summed up in the Islamic legal maxim "contracts are judged by the intention and meanings and not by the word and forms," which will be further explained in the latter part of this research. As for the third area, namely the pillars of a *sharīʿah* contract, it will be highlighted in the next point which will analyze more extensively the relationship between *maqāṣid al-sharīʿah* and *sharīʿah* contracts and evaluate their level of convergence or divergence in contemporary Islamic banking and finance.

As for the conditions (*shurūt*) of a contract, the *sharīʿah* upholds any condition that does not contravene the established rulings and principles of Islamic commercial law. Imam al-Shāṭibī (d. 790 H) links between *shurūt* and *maqāṣid al-sharīʿah*. He is of the view that a condition vis-à-vis the contracts has three scenarios: first, a condition that complements the objective of the contract, such as stipulating collaterals in loans, thus such a condition is permissible; secondly, a condition that contravenes the objective of a contract, such as stipulating that the buyer of an asset should not make use of it, such a condition is void; and thirdly, a condition that is vague as to its conformity with the objectives of a contract.[13] However, Abu Zahra accentuated the fact that schools of jurisprudence have disagreed when it come to the application of these general principles.[14]

The Objective of Justice (*ʿadalah*)

Justice in Islamic finance is of paramount importance. It will not be achieved without the provision of financing itself, which "refers to money that makes it possible to acquire existing wealth for consumption and/or as inputs in the production process."[15] It entails the equal preservation of the right of the contracting parties, the realization of the legal effect of the contract, such as the transfer of a property after a payment is fully or partially made, and the prohibition of usury, gambling, and uncertainty. Ibn ʿAshūr held that justice in wealth entails "its acquisition by way of labor, exchange, donation, or inheritance."[16] To achieve justice in Islamic contracts, the *sharīʿah* looks at contracts from two perspectives: structure and type.

Structure

The structure emphasizes on the validity of the contract's pillars, terms, and conditions, as well as the validity of supporting contracts, such as guarantee and pledge. As for the pillars, the unequivocal nature of the offer and acceptance, the legal capacity of the contracting parties, as well as the validity of the subject matter would have ensured *sharīʿah* compliance of the contract with both parties' rights protected and not infringed. The pillars and conditions of a contract are reflective of many objectives that conform to *maqāṣid al-sharīʿah*. Muslim jurists had two approaches in tackling this topic: the literal and the contextual. As for the offer and acceptance, the majority of scholars are more literal in considering the offer to come only from the seller or the lessor while the acceptance is to come from the buyer or the lessee.[17] The Ḥanafī's held rather a different approach, considering the offer initiated by either party, be it the seller or the buyer, while the acceptance must come only from the second party.[18] The thrust of the offer and acceptance is to attain a level of satisfaction for the contracting parties[19] precluding any possibility of dispute over the price, type of goods, service offered, or mode of delivery. Satisfaction (*rida*) is thus an objective of a *sharīʿah* contract.

While pursuing justice in *sharīʿah* contracts, contemporary Islamic finance has reinvented the classical debate on "form versus substance" in financial transactions. The debate is triggered by the offer and acceptance vis-à-vis the underlying intention. In the classical theory of *sharīʿah* contracts, the Ḥanafī's adhered strictly to the principle of "substance over the form" when the offer and acceptance are exchanged, considering the *wafa'*[20] contract, for example a guarantee rather than a sale. The Mālikīs reiterated the significance of the meaning of a contract as a parameter of its validity allowing, for example, *bay' al-mu'atat* (sale by conduct) and any business activity deemed by people as a sale.[21] Although the Shāfiʿī's are more inclined to consider the form over the intention of the contracting parties when such intention is not obvious,[22] they don't subscribe to the ultimate supremacy of intention over form in the absence of a signifier (*qarinah*).[23] Imam al-Nawawi (d. 1277 AD) held that "the principle consideration of contracts, according to us, is their forms, not the intention of the contracting parties. As such, '*inah* transaction . . . is valid."[24] Thus, a *hibah* (gift) with a condition of exchange (*hibah al-thawab*) is deemed as a sale, given its meaning, but is deemed as an actual gift, given its form. Similarly, a guarantee with the right of recourse is deemed as a loan, given its meaning, but is deemed as an actual *kafalah* (guarantee), given its form. The '*inah* transaction is valid according to Shāfiʿī, given the form that precludes any prior agreement to circumvent the prohibition of *riba*, but Shāfiʿī himself would consider '*inah* "reprehensible if the contracting parties have an overt intention that invalidates the sale contract."[25] The majority of jurists would prohibit '*inah* as they consider it to be a usurious loan in disguise.[26] According to the Islamic Fiqh Academy and Accounting and Auditing Organization for Islamic Financial Institutions (AAOIFI), this transaction is prohibited as it is prohibited by clear texts, let alone its contradiction to *maqāṣid al-sharīʿah*. This applies to organized *tawarruq* as well.[27]

The Islamic banking industry does not generally practice '*inah*, except in Malaysia, relying heavily on the Shāfiʿī view on the issue. However, in 2012 the Shariah Council of the Malaysia Central Bank released a resolution in which it obliged all Islamic banks to remove the interconditionality clause binding the two legs of the '*inah* contract.[28] This has purified the practice of '*inah* to a great deal, a step which can be seen as a corrective measure rather than a new resolution. Contemporary scholars such as Rafiq al-Misri,[29] Nejatullah Siddiqui, Sami al-Suwailim, Taqi Umani, and many others have all called for a critical review of Islamic banking practices so that justice is upheld among the contracting parties. According to them, the current practices of Islamic finance are more about form rather than substance, given the way contracts are being amalgamated to serve the same purpose as conventional loans. The articulation of this debate is beyond the scope of this research.

The structure of a contract is also supported by contracts such as *kafalah* (guarantee) and *rahn* (pledge) to secure payment and reduce events of defaults that may impair capital. This is in line with the protection of wealth as a universal objective of the *sharīʿah*. Further, the removal of the element of *riba* in Islamic contracts aims at establishing justice by blocking the transfer of risks from the lender to the borrower. Besides, the lender would have earned unfairly since he neither acts as a partner nor as a trader, absolving himself from taking risks. In modern capital market products, the debt financial market create a liability on the part of the issuers, widening the gap between the real economy,[30] which is based on real assets, and the financial economy that raises the debt ratios through money lending and speculation, although regulated. The control of central banks may prove defective when securitization of debts goes viral and may create bubbles leading to acute financial crises similar to the 2008 subprime crisis in the United States.

We shall see later how the profit and loss sharing features in equity-based contracts are more just in terms of risk sharing and promotion of real economy.

The structure of *sharīʿah* contracts must also be free from *gharar* (uncertainty) to protect the right of the buyer. Selling a good without identifying its type, price, or mode of delivery would amount to *gharar* that affects either the buyer or the investor. Exchanging an insurance policy with a premium in order to cover a defined loss may run counter to the rights of the insured, as an insurance contract involves a *gharar*.[31] The cover will be provided in case the risk occurs, otherwise no cover is provided; hence the uncertainty.

In contemporary Islamic finance, contracts are used in combination (*uqud murakkabah*) to serve certain objectives, namely cash and liquidity management, risk management, reduction of cost and obligation, and an exit from prohibited transactions.[32] However, the AAOIFI has regulated the practice by stipulating some parameters, namely that the combination should not lead to a usurious activity, the combination should not be a trick to circumvent the prohibition of *riba* and two contradicting contracts should not be combined, such as lending the *murābaḥah* capital to the *mudarib*.[33]

Type

Monzir Kohf summarized the main principles upon which all *sharīʿah* contracts are built: satisfaction, equitable rights, ethical dimension, and transacting in real business activities.[34] All types of *sharīʿah* contracts guarantee the rights of the contracting parties to ensure the prevalence of justice. Apart from a typical sale contract, whereby the value and the counter value are exchanged on the spot, the other contracts, namely debt-based and equity-based, also promote justice. For example, the *murābaḥah* contract (cost plus profit), which was developed into *murābaḥah* to the purchase orderer (MPO), is structured in such a way that the *maqāṣid* of *murābaḥah* are achieved. In this transaction, justice is observed in many ways, namely the deferred payment facility, which benefits the purchase orderer, is compensated by the increment of the price, which would benefit the seller. The "time has value,[35]" a principle approved by the *sharīʿah*, is the basis for such increment. However, the opportunity cost should be discarded. The agency agreement in a *murābaḥah*, in which the Islamic financial institution appoints the purchase orderer to purchase the good from the supplier, is meant to facilitate the procedure of the whole transaction and insure a speedy and convenient financing mechanism. However, AAIOFI confined this agency only to situations where there is a pressing need and also to hold the Islamic bank fully responsible for the purchase of the good and ascertain the true acquisition of the asset.[36]

The binding nature of the *wa'd* in MPO ensures that the purchase orderer would not revoke his *wa'd* so that the Islamic financing institution would not incur losses after buying the asset from the supplier. Al-Misri[37] and others have categorically objected to the binding force of the *wa'd* declaring the structure as mere *hila* (legal stratagem) aiming to circumvent the prohibition of *riba*. Nazih Ḥammad would consider MPO as a *makhraj shariʿī* (legal exit from a hardship) rather than *hila* as the intention of the contracting parties is to get rid of hardship and prohibited elements.[38] Majma' Fiqhi and AAOIFI have ruled on the permissibility of an MPO structure with conditions, namely the prohibition of having reciprocal binding *wa'd* (*muwa'adah*) from both bank and client to rid the MPO from the exchange feature at the stage of *wa'd*.[39]

However, the overreliance on *murābaḥah* in Islamic banking has irked many scholars as they believe it has derailed Islamic finance from equity to debt, undermining the very objectives of the *sharīʿah* of wealth. Due to its low-risk profile to the Islamic bank,[40] MPO has become the norm of Islamic finance. According to Mehmet Asutay, this has developed as an approach[41] and a "pragmatic approach adopted by Islamic finance plays an important role in the internationalisation of 'capitalist' desires into Islamic finance." Siddiqui, on the other hand, noted that MPO has many negative aspects, such as its risk-free nature and the lack of flexibility.[42] Sami al-Suwailem, however, did not refer specifically to MPO, highlighting that the repercussion of debt, such as the borrowing syndrome, undermines the borrower's appetite for long-term investment and bearing risks to justify earnings.[43] The debate, as mentioned before, is beyond the scope of this research.

While the collateral is meant to compensate the bank in case of the customer's default, the security deposit (*hamīsh jidīyyah*) is meant to seize the commitment of the purchase orderer so that the bank's efforts to provide financing would not go in vain. Justice is also observed when *sharīʿah* stipulates that *hamīsh jiddīyyah* can be fortified in proportion to the actual expenses incurred as result of the revocation of the *wa'd* by the customer. Equally important is the fact that *murābaḥah* promotes "trust," as both cost and profit is disclosed to the contracting parties. The Fiqh Encyclopedia of Kuwait made a reference to the *ḥājah* (need) of people to know the cost and profit in *murābaḥah,* especially the inexperienced businessmen who may be fouled in the market.[44] Mustafa al-Zarqa reiterates that as far as *murābaḥah* is concerned "failure to disclose the capital or any information that impacts the price is an act of betrayal."[45]

Further, all debt-based contracts such as *murābaḥah*, *istisna,' ijārah*, and *salam* are structured in a risk transfer model of banking, thus they tend to be similar in the form, but not in the substance, to conventional loans. This arbitrary similarity may create confusion to many stakeholders who may ultimately revert to conventional banks as a result. The fact *is* that the *sharī'ah* is against risk transfer in 'loans with interest' but is not against risk transfer in trade. That marks the clear distinction between usury and trade emphasized by the Holy *Qur'ān* in 2:275.

Equity-based contracts such as *musharakah* and *muḍārabah* manifest a great deal of justice as an objective of the *sharī'ah*. In *musharakah*, whether capital is in cash or in kind, both partners share profits and losses in proportion to their capital. Both of them have an interest in the business and are both responsible for the success or failure of the venture. Thus, it is not permissible for one partner to stipulate a lump-sum payment at the end of the venture as it amounts to capital guarantee, a stipulation that defeats the profit and loss aspect of *musharakah*; hence justice. Guarantee, however, is applicable upon negligence of either party and is determined by the terms and conditions of the contract, as well as commercial custom. The same is applied to *muḍārabah* where profit is shared based on a preagreed ratio, but pecuniary losses are borne solely by the capital provider and the entrepreneur would have lost his efforts and time invested in the venture. However, the *muḍārabah* contract served a rather bigger objective, which is to fund mobilization. Muslim economist Salman Syed Ali held that "the resource mobilization was made possible by *muḍārabah* contracts in Muslim lands during 7th, 8th, and 9th centuries."[46]

The Objective of Wealth Circulation (*rawaj*)

Ibn 'Āshūr defines *rawaj* as "fair circulation of wealth in the hands of as many people as possible."[47] Wealth circulation is an important cycle in a society aiming to be economically stable. The means to achieve the *maqṣad* of *rawaj* are manifold; *sūrah al-baqarah* verses 275 and 282 clearly call for trade as a means of wealth creation, and *sūrah al-muzammil* verse 20 elevates traders to a higher position in the eyes of God. Omar ibn al-Khaṭṭāb urged guardians of orphans to invest their wealth so that it is not impaired as a result of the yearly *zakāt* payment. The *sharīʿah* in particular shuns wealth concentration and encourages distribution through a myriad of channels. *Sūrah al-Hashr* verse 7 states that wealth should not be concentrated in the hands of the rich. This provides an additional justification for the prohibition of *riba*, as it leads to the concentration of wealth in the hands of the lenders.

Rawaj is achieved via two sets of contracts: investments contracts and contracts of exchange. Investment contracts, that is, *muḍārabah* and *musharaka*, are typically the most important vehicles toward a productive society. In *muḍārabah*, funds are channeled toward the production of goods that create a balance between saving and investment.[48] It invites entrepreneurs with various risk appetites to grow their wealth so that it is not left idle. In venturing into *muḍārabah*, high returns are expected as a result of the rigor with which the entrepreneur runs the *muḍārabah* venture. This means a more sophisticated investment infrastructure is established that would employ sound business strategies, financial engineering, and hedging mechanisms that protect capital but should not in any way culminate in capital guarantee. As a result, more competent investors and fund managers are bred in the market that would eventually realize the level of trust capital providers are looking for, particularly in volatile markets that threaten the erosion of capital.

Musharakah has the same objectives as *muḍārabah* but its application is much wider and sophisticated. In retail banking, *musharakah* is applied in home financing using *musharakah mutaniqisah* (diminishing *musharakah*); however, its real objectives are well observed in the Islamic capital market where funds are moved from surplus units to deficit units. Whether the new public-listed companies aim to attract capital or to grow their share capital, the Islamic capital market facilitates the flow of liquidity needed. The equity market, which is based on *musharakah*, injects more capital every day. *Sharīʿah* compliant indices and unit trusts, such as Real Estate Investment Trusts (REITS) and Exchange-Traded Funds (ETFs), motivate investors to take more risks to justify high returns. This guarantees more wealth circulation.

Contracts of exchange are equally important in realizing *rawaj* in modern Islamic banking and finance. These contracts enhance the relationship between production and financing, as the latter is not possible without the former. A typical *murābaḥah* contract would stimulate production of finished goods to fulfill the needs of customers, which would make the *maqṣad* of the *mukallaf* (customer) in conformity with the *maqṣad* of *sharīʿah*, an important concomitant requirement stipulated by the decrees of *maqṣad*. An *istisna'* contract stimulates the manufacturing of goods and is particularly ideal for the construction of infrastructure facilities with Build, Operate, and Transfer Structures (BOTs). It encourages labor and takes into account the customers want to buy manufactured products according to certain specifications. The *salam* contract would provide working capital to producers so that production is not hindered by lack of capital. *Ijarah* recognizes the sale of usufruct with the retention of the legal title by the lessor. Its modern application is similar to "hire-purchase" whereby the lessee would own the leased asset at the end of the lease period by way of sale or automatic transfer of property, depending on the prevailing jurisdiction. All these contracts with their modern structures fulfill the short-, medium-, and-long term needs of customers who don't have enough capital to purchase goods or services needed. Conversely, some traders don't have enough working capital to start production. All these are forms of *maqāṣid* (objectives) of traders and are fully endorsed by *maqāṣid al-sharīʿah*. These contracts simply provide "convenience" by meeting the needs of customers; hence, convenience is a *maqṣad* of *sharīʿah* by itself.

In the same vein, the *sharīʿah* promulgated many contracts called *ʿuqud musammah* (nominated contracts) to facilitate the creation, accumulation, and circulation of wealth. New contracts are also formed but should adhere to the purport of the Lawgiver, which is enshrined in the revealed texts. The new contracts are generally a combination of two or more contracts supported by contracts embedded to realize the objectives of financing or investment.

To widen the scope of *rawaj*, *sharīʿah* allows the incorporation of *shurūt ja'liyah* (man-made conditions) to secure more rights to the contracting parties and hence provides more confidence and trust in markets marred by stiff competition and uncertainties, factors that sometimes drive away investors and cause capital to remain idle. Equally important in creating confidence in trade and finance are the legitimatization of a set of options (*khiyarāt*) that mainly protect the rights of the buyer in the asset purchased. The option of *shart* (grace period of normally three days), for instance, would grant the buyer the right to confirm the contract or rescind it within an agreed period,[49] with both value and countervalue returned.

There are issues on whether modern Islamic finance has helped achieve wealth circulation when it is actually involved in a risky debt creation via debt financing. On the one hand, Islamic finance operates on a risk transfer model as most of its products are based on deferred sales with higher prices compared to lower prices paid on the spot. On the other hand, debt-based contracts contribute to gross domestic product (GDP), stimulate production, and reduce unemployment rates.[50] This point is still controversial, as many researchers tend to hold that Islamic finance and conventional finance do converge rather than diverge and that all polemics on the unique value proposition of Islamic finance are merely a theoretical abstraction that lacks practicality and feasibility in an interest-based financial environment. An example of such convergence is the Islamic modes of financing such as *murābaḥah* and *ijarah*, which are structured to operate like conventional loans according to critics of Islamic banking,[51] especially on the benchmarking of the profit rate against the interest rate and the binding force of the *wa'd* (promise) that ultimately binds the customer to pay cost plus profit on a deferment basis and taking the time value of money into consideration. However, debt could be channeled to stimulate the economy via investment. Ibn ʿAshūr maintained that "credit is one of the modes of the expansion of Islamic financial transactions as the skillful investor may need to borrow capital to show his skills in business, manufacturing and agriculture."[52]

The Objective of Transparency (*wuduh*)

The renowned scholar Abdullah Bin Biyyah asserts in his seminal work on the *maqāṣid* of Islamic financial transactions that "*wuduh* in the contemporary context means transparency."[53] Accordingly, Islamic contracts are formed to reflect the utmost rights of the contracting parties. The terms and conditions of those contracts are supposed to be as transparent as possible to avoid disputes and prevent fraud, cheating, and misrepresentation. Offer and acceptance must use explicit expressions, whether written or verbal. The contracting parties must have full legal capacity of execution (*ahliyat al-ada' al-kamilah*) to conclude a contract so that they can clearly understand the legal effects of the concluded contract. The "subject matter" must be clearly identified, segregated, and delivered without any encumbrance. The price must be fixed and agreeable to the contracting parties during the contract session. However, issues pertaining to using conventional London Interbank Offered Rate (LIBOR) as a benchmark to determine profit rates in debt-based *sharīʿah* contracts such as *murābaḥah* should not cast any doubt on the legitimacy of such pricing, even though an Islamic benchmark is always sought and recommended. Linking the rental rate in *ijarah* to the performance of indices in subsequent lease periods has also been approved by *sharīʿah* authorities to consider the prevailing rate by the time the new lease contract is signed. Taqi Usmani held that "it is thus clear that the use of the rate of interest merely as a benchmark does not render the contract invalid as an interest-based transaction."[54] This is to provide the market price and market rental rate to ensure market stability, which is undoubtedly one of the *maqāṣid al-sharīʿah*.

Transparency is very much present in the terms and conditions of each *sharīʿah* contract. In *murābaḥah*, both cost and markup must be disclosed. In *salam* (forward sale), the price, quantity, and quality, as well as the mode and time of delivery of the produced good, must be clearly identified. In *istisna'*, the manufactured asset must be specified in advance and the mode of delivery must be free from any ambiguity. In modern Islamic finance, disclosure of financial statements of listed companies in the stock market is essential for investors to make the right investment decisions. The turbulences of financial crises have urged for the adoption of robust *sharīʿah* corporate governance that advocates transparency as a prerequisite of good governance. The Sharīʿah Audit that checks each and every aspect and activity of an Islamic financial institution provides an adequate scrutiny of what is going on behind the glaring walls of those institutions. Violation of processes and procedures, noncompliance to *sharīʿah* and local regulations, mismatch between assets and liabilities, the lack of check and balances, and money laundering, to mention but a few, can ensue if audit is not conducted in a transparent manner.

Further, transparency is quite apparent in the legal documentation of *sharīʿah* contracts so that the terms and conditions can be enforced in a court of law. According to *sūrah al-baqarah* verse 282, this is called *kitābah*. The verse urges both creditor and debtor to document the debt-based transaction in writing. Ibn ʿAshūr further noticed that the verse actually refers to both creditor and debtor, but is more relevant to the debtor who is urged to satisfy his creditor.[55]

Transparency, as one of the *maqāṣid al-sharīʿah* of wealth, is further enhanced by the principles of collateral (*rahn*) and *kafalah* (guarantee). Being a typical requirement in modern Islamic banking practices in deferred sales (*al-buyʿu al-ajilah*), the collateral is needed to safeguard the right of the seller in the payment in the event of defaults. The collateral is liquidated as per the terms and conditions of the *rahn* contract. *Kafalah* from a third party would only safeguard the right of the creditor in the payment, but also creates confidence in the market and encourages financiers to provide financing to customers with adequate guarantors.

The Objective Firmness (*thabāt*)

This *maqṣad* refers to the right of ownership of both value and counter value after a contract has been concluded. The seller's right in the price is permanently secured, and the buyer's right in the purchased asset is permanently secured. To that effect, both value and countervalue must be present, deliverable, and not legally encumbered. The purchaser should not be bankrupt, and the collateral must not be charged to another financing that would make it legally impossible to liquidate.

The firmness of the *sharīʿah* contract is realized through the binding nature (*luzum*) of contracts after they are concluded. According to the theory of Islamic law, a contract is deemed binding as soon as "offer and acceptance" are exchanged, which is the view of the Imām Mālik and Imām Abu Ḥanīfah who denied the "option of the contract session" (*khiyar al-majlis*).[56] A more flexible view was adopted by Imām Shafiʿī and Imam Aḥmad who maintained that a contract is not binding so long as the contracting parties have not separated.[57] Accordingly, the parties can exchange the offer and acceptance during the contract session and rescind it at their discretion, but once they make the offer and acceptance then separate, the contract becomes binding and the legal effect of the contract would ensue. This binding force of the contract, however, is not applicable in certain contracts such as *wakālah* (agency), *muḍārabah*, *musharakah* (partnership), *wadīʿah* (deposit taking), and *ju'alah* (promise of commission) as long as work has not commenced yet. This is because no liabilities have been created and the rescinding of the contract after work that has commenced would not lead to dispute or incur any financial loss.

One modern example would be the issuance of *sukūk musharakah*. The current practice is that capital is raised through *sukūk* issuance, which represents an undivided ownership of the capital raised after the closure of subscription. Once the venture has commenced and the raised capital has been injected, the *sukūk* program agreement becomes binding and thereafter *sukūk* could be traded in the secondary market at market value. In case the *sukūk* program is rescinded, the *sukūk* holders would redeem their capital at par and not at market value, as the *sukūk* have not been listed and traded.

In conclusion of the above research, it is now obvious that the theoretical underpinning of *sharīʿah* contracts is imbued with *maqāṣid al-sharīʿah*. However, the degree of realizing those *maqāṣid* in contemporary Islamic finance is still debatable and open for further research. In the next part, we shall address the current practices of Islamic finance in light of Islamic legal maxims.

CURRENT PRACTICES OF ISLAMIC FINANCE IN LIGHT OF ISLAMIC LEGAL MAXIMS

Islamic legal maxims (*al-qawā'id al-fiqhiyyah*) are "abridged constitutional universal juristic principles containing general Islamic legal rulings about issues (*furuʿ*) that can be subsumed thereunder."[58] Under each maxim, many *sharīʿah* issues (*furuʿ*) can be subsumed for easy recognition and reference. They have been formulated to facilitate the recognition of *fiqhī* rulings, which are, in the course of *ijtihād*, very difficult to remember. New emerging issues can be subsumed under these maxims and hold the same value of law governing the relevant maxim. There are five Islamic legal maxims around which all legal maxims revolve. We shall use these maxims to assess the practices of modern Islamic finance. It is imperative to mention that Islamic finance nowadays is institutionalized and is being practiced in three major sectors: Islamic banking, Takaful, and the Islamic capital market, an industry that has stretched in almost all corners of the globe, with a global asset of more than $3 trillion forecasted for 2018.[59] With over 500 Islamic financial institutions and new bold initiatives to grow and expand the industry globally, Islamic finance is set to present itself as a unique value proposition that could mobilize funds, provide global business opportunities, and champion ethical finance to avert financial crises. Critics of Islamic finance are not swayed by this horizontal expansion as they still see it plagued by the seeds of its failure.

We shall use the following Islamic legal maxims to evaluate the following current practices of Islamic finance: matters are determined by intentions, hardship begets facility, and harm is to be eliminated.

Matters are Determined by Intentions (*al-umuru bi-maqāṣidiha*)

From *Sharīʿah* perspective, the intention of the individual is the thrust of validity and acceptability of his actions and sayings. Ibn Qayyim says, "intention is the essence of every matter, its pillar and the foundation on which it is based."[60] Out of this major legal maxim, jurists have formulated the maxim, "what is considered in *sharīʿah* contracts are their objectives and meanings and not the forms and texts." Accordingly, current and saving accounts, which the Islamic bank is permitted to use, are deemed by jurists as loans, despite bearing the name *wadīʿah* (deposit), which basically connotes safekeeping; discounting of bills in conventional banking is deemed by jurists as a usurious loan.[61]

In modern Islamic finance, there are a few practices that triggered heated debates among scholars. Two transactions seem to have poured more ink as far as *maqāṣid al-sharīʿah* and Islamic finance is concerned: *bay' al-'inah* (sell and buy back) and *tawarruq* (commodity *murābaḥah*). As we have covered *'inah* in part one, we shall shed some light on the *tawarruq* contract.

Tawaruqq attracted a great deal of disputes until 2009 when Majma' Fiqh ruled that "organized *tawaruqq*" is prohibited. *Tawarruq* is also seen by the majority of scholars as a trick to circumvent the prohibition of *riba*. In the organized *tawarruq*, the outward intention of both customer and the Islamic bank tends to procure immediate cash for deferred cash via two legs of transactions. The first is when the bank sells an asset to the client on a *murābaḥah* basis and deferred payment, and the second ensues immediately with the client appointing the bank to sell the same asset to a third party with a lower price (the finance cash). The main contention of the opposing view is that the "arrangement feature" in *tawarruq* would render the whole structure fictitious, as the asset is just an intermediary to generate the cash flow, hence the "loan" applied for by the client. Neither the client nor the bank is interested in acquiring the asset, nor are they able to break the whole *tawarruq* arrangement. According to Nazih Ḥammad, this is permissible as long as the asset does not go back to the first seller.[62]

The Malaysian application of *tawarruq* has taken a turn with the introduction of Bursa Suq al-Sila', an international platform using *tawarruq* to provide liquidity to individuals and the corporate sector worldwide. It follows the same arrangement of *tawarruq* with two features: using a real asset in the form of Crude Palm Oil (CPO), plastic risen, and timber wood, and the client has the right to take delivery of the asset to effectuate the feature of true sale. Additionally, the parties involved (commodity trading suppliers-commodity trading participants (CTPs), Bursa Suq al-Sila') are not obliged to adhere to the prearrangement to demonstrate the true sale and possession of the asset. This has earned the platform enough credibility to attract big Islamic banks such as Rajhi, KFH, Inma', and others to become active CTPs. However, *tawarruq* seems to be the order of the day due to the increasing volume of *tawarruq* assets that behave like conventional loans (in form but not in substance). This may raise the debt ratios and encourage consumerism, which could have an adverse effect on the whole industry despite the economic value created as a result of its contribution to national GDPs.

On the services side of Islamic banking, some practices may cast doubts on the purity of the intention of Islamic banks. Saving accounts in some Islamic banks give away *hibah*, and, although discretionary, it is viewed by many as a replication of the conventional interest rate to attract or retain depositors. Indicative rates on *muḍārabah* accounts, although based on historical performance of the investment and not promised, are also seen by some as an attempt to guarantee capital.

In the *sukūk* market, particularly *sukūk ijarah*, an obligor would sell an asset to the trustee/Special Purpose Vehicle (SPV) who acts on behalf of *sukūk* holders and thereafter rents it from the same trustee/SPV on rental rates higher than the selling price. At maturity, the trustee is bound to sell the same asset to the obligor and the latter is bound to buy it (selling undertaking and purchase undertaking). This is coupled with the fact that the trustee/SPV only owns the beneficial ownership (not the legal ownership) when he purchased the asset. This is because these *sukūk* are structured as asset based (not asset backed), a structure that make these *sukūk* behave like a conventional bond in view of the fact that in case of default, the trustee has recourse to the obligor and not to the asset *per se*. Thus, critics of *sukūk* are of the view that the intention of the parties involved is not really to sell and buy the securitized asset but rather to raise funds in the capital market. Other views would attest to the purity of these *sukūk* as jurisdictions are different in defining beneficial ownership and the associated rights. AAOIFI in its review of the *sukūk*[63] standard reiterated the importance of *sukūk* being asset backed to reflect the true sale of the asset, and that equity-based *sukūk*, such as *muḍārabah* and *musharakah*, should be redeemed at market value, and that the obligor should not grant a loan to *sukūk* holders in case profits fall short of expected returns. Presently, still 90 percent of *sukūk* are asset based and have not made that radical move to asset backed.[64] The reason, in our view, is that *sukūk* still operate in a risk transfer environment that does not encourage risk sharing in the *sukūk* market.

Hardship Begets Facility *(al-mashaqqah tajlibu al-taysīr)*

This maxim aims at relieving and relaxing obligations, which in normal circumstances become stringent and even not achieving *maqāṣid al-sharīʿah*. The hardship need not be so pressing to trigger the *ḍarūrah* dispensation; it suffices to serve the *ḥājiyāt* (exigencies) class of *maqāṣid al-sharīʿah*.[65] This maxim is the basis of legal concessions (*rukhas*) in the whole spectrum of *sharīʿah*.[66] Islamic finance in particular is in dire need of this maxim due to the complexity of the modern financial system in which the Islamic law of finance operates. As a result, scholars become savvy of the fact that some *fiqhī* rulings must be applied in a dynamic way, taking the difficulties and challenges of modern finance into consideration. This is in line with the *maqāṣid al-sharīʿah* that urge scholars to consider *waqi'* (reality) as an important ingredient of the contemporary *ijtihād* process. In treasury products, for example, there is a need to hedge against the fluctuation of currency at the settlement day. FX forward product, being a typical treasury product, is structured on the basis of unilateral *wa'd* with actual exchange taking place two days before the settlement date (T+2) due to system constraints that pose a hardship to secure spot exchange as required by *sharīʿah*. Despite this fact, many *sharīʿah* scholars allowed this arrangement due to *mashaqah* (hardship),[67] whose removal is a *maṣlaḥa*. Another example would be the calculation of the administrative fee for each financing amount/free interest loan. A solution was provided by the Fiqh Academy that tends to propose that the

> Islamic bank determines the total actual cost incurred in administrating the aggregate of loans in a year. That could then be distributed across the total sums lent within that year. This would yield a cost ratio as a percentage of the loan amounts and then this percentage would be used for the administrative charges of each loan.[68]

In the Islamic capital market, it has been observed that pure *sharīʿah* compliant companies are quite rare since most of them are engaged in business activities that may be tainted with some *sharīʿah* noncompliant elements such as deposit placements in conventional banks that pay interest on saving accounts. It would cause a big hardship to ask those companies to fully purify their income before they are listed in the stock exchange. To elevate hardship, *sharīʿah* standard setters such as AAIOFI have come up with a benchmark for mixed companies (*ḥalāl*, permitted and *ḥarām*, forbidden), taking into account the ratio of revenues of *ḥarām* activities as a determinant of their *sharīʿah* compliance. Other benchmarks, such as Islamic Down Jones, FUTSI, and Malaysia Shariah screening methodology, would all focus on the nature of business activities and financial ratios of conventional debts/total assets and conventional placements/total assets. By virtue of these benchmarks, many companies have been listed as *sharīʿah* compliant companies despite having some *sharīʿah* noncompliant elements.

What is important in this respect is that all *sharīʿah* compliant products structured based on hardship must be subjected to regular review. Hardship is normally a situation that justifies the departure from an original ruling whose application, in its ordinary form, brings about such a hardship; therefore, if the reasons that necessitated the departure cease to exist, then it would be imperative to reestablish the original ruling.

Harm is to be Eliminated *(al-ḍarar yuzāl)*

Ibn Nujaym held that "many areas of Islamic jurisprudence are based on this maxim, such as returning defective goods [to the sellers], all legal options (*khiyarat*) . . . and the right of *shuf'ah*."[69] One of the ultimate goals of Islamic finance is the elimination of harm for both the Islamic financial institution and the customer. Harm is a broad concept referring to the present and future harms if the latter's anticipation is quite definitive. To eliminate Islamic bank's harms, it offers products that are developed, engineered, and marketed in such a way that their provision in the market would not face the risks envisaged. Like conventional banks, Islamic banks would not offer a product until its risks are identified, assessed, and mitigated.

Techniques of risk management are employed to address market, liquidity, credit, and profit rate risks. *Sharīʿah* risk in particular has become quite cogent as the whole thrust of Islamic finance is about adherence to the *sharīʿah*. The latter could bring about a substantial harm to the whole Islamic finance industry; similar to the kind of harm that the Goldman Sachs *sukūk* program has caused when its *sharīʿah* compliance was questioned. On the other hand, customer credit profiles are being assessed to minimize default cases. Issues of fidelity of the banks staff are being covered by *takāful* plans. House financing products such *musharakah mutanaqiasah* (diminishing *musharakah*) and *ijarah muntahiyah bi tamlīk* (hire-purchase) are generally secured by a family *takāful* cover that would not harm the heirs if the customer passes away. Further, since customer current and saving deposits are lent to the bank in the form of a guaranteed free interest loan, Islamic banks are continuously participating in "Deposit Guarantee Schemes" to guarantee customer deposits in case of the bankruptcy or liquidation of the Islamic bank. However, investment deposits, which are based on *muḍārabah* are not guaranteed by the "Deposit Guarantee Institutions," the absence of such an incentive could pose a challenge to Islamic banks to attract investment account holders.

The aforementioned measures taken by Islamic banks are merely examples of some practices to eliminate harm whenever possible. However, a few concerns have been recorded and may be classified as harmful activities that Islamic banks are inflicting upon their customers. The first one refers to financing houses under construction. Precedent cases happening in Malaysia at inception stages of Islamic banking showed how vulnerable Islamic finance practices are. This refers to the BBA cases in Malaysia that left many customers reeling behind huge debts after their financed houses had been abandoned by the developers and yet they continued to be indebted to their financiers, the Islamic banks. Upon the abandonment, customers have been obliged to pay both principle and profits, and without acquiring the houses at the end of the day. That was perceived as the most devastating harm befalling customers in the Malaysian Islamic finance experience. Stiff measures have been taken by the regulators to avoid the repetition of the problem.

The second harm would be the high prices of Islamic products offered by some Islamic banks compared to conventional ones. Customers are not able to understand the reason and often express their dismay on the matter. Some of the reasons suggest that Islamic banks are not able to apply the "economy of scale" rule when pricing their products. Their market share is very small and the cost is higher than conventional products due to additional expenses, namely in marketing and *sharīʿah* advisors' remunerations. This is happening in an environment controlled by conventional forces of supply and demand, to which Islamic banks are subservient. However, customers would also appreciate the Islamic banks procedure to grant them *ibra'* (discount on early payment) that commensurate with the period in which the whole payment has been settled.

CONCLUSION

The chapter has attempted to decipher *sharīʿah* business contracts and unlock the *maqāṣid al-sharīʿah* imbued therein. The emphasis was on the level of adaptation and variation needed to apply those contracts in contemporary finance. As for Islamic legal maxims, the chapter was selective of three, all of which were deemed very critical in evaluating the *maqāṣid* observance in structuring Islamic financial products. The chapter found that the *maqāṣid* are championed by all stakeholders and observed in most of the products by virtue of the contracts used, but some are marred by malpractices causing more harm to customers and creating a reputation risk that may hinder the development of Islamic finance. One of the main conclusions that we can emphasize is that Islamic finance is subservient to the dictates of globalization and the contemporary financial landscape, a situation necessitating the observance of reality that must be incorporated in the whole thrust of Islamic finance. Since Islamic finance is still in its infancy and has yet to reach economy of scale, let alone the level of independence that will allow it to operate freely, the pure realization of *maqāṣid al-sharīʿah* both at macro and micro levels, in a way that grounds itself as an alternative financial model, is a far-reaching objective. There is a need to discard the idea that only an Islamic commercial bank can realize *maqāṣid al-sharīʿah.* It is high time to confine debt-based products operating on a "risk transfer model" to Islamic commercial banks only, and move toward establishing Islamic investment banks that operate on a "profit and loss sharing model." On the whole, the gap between theory and practice in Islamic finance is being gradually narrowed down with more equity-based products introduced for both financing and investment.

NOTES

1. Ibn ʿAshūr, *Treaties on Maqasid al-Shariah*, trans. Mohammed El-Tahir El-Mesawi (London: IIIT, *al-Furqān*, Islamic Book Trust Year?), 64.
2. Shatibi, *Muwafaqat* (al-Khobor: Dar ibn 'Affan, 1997), 5/40.
3. Al-Jurjani, *al-Ta'rifāt* (n.p.: dar al-Kitab al-Arabi: n.d), 196.
4. Kamal al-Din bin Mohammad, *Sharh Fath al-Qadīr* (Beirut: Dar al-Fikr, n.d), 3/187.
5. Badrul Din al- Zarqashi, *al-Manthour fi al-Qawa'id al-Fiqhiyyah* (Kuwait: Wizarat al-Awqaf wa al-sh'un al-Islamiyyah, n.d), 2/397.
6. Zainuddin Abdurahman Ibn Rajab, *al-Qawa'id* (n.p.: Dar al-Kutub al-'Ilmiyyah, n.d), 1/78.
7. Shihab al-Din al-Qarafi, *al-Furuq* (n.p.: 'Alam al-Kutub, n.d), 4/31.
8. Majella, Articles 103-104 (n.p.: *al-Jami'ah al-Islamiyya*, 2005).
9. Mohammad al-Tahir bin ʿAshūr, *Maqāṣid al-Sharīʿah*, ed. Mohammad el-Tahir al-Miwasi (Amman: dar al-Nafa'is, 2001), 464.
10. Qarafi, *Furuq*, 2/42. See also al-'Izz bin 'Abdussalam, *Qawa'id al-Aḥkam fi Maṣāliḥ al-Anam* (Cairo: Maktabat al-Kulliyat al-Azhariyyah, 1991), 1/123.
11. Abu Ghuddah, *Awfu bil ʿuqud* (n.p.: Majmu'at Dellah al-Barakah, 1997), 5.
12. Muwafaqat (n.p.: Dar Ibn qayyim, dar idn 'Affan, 2003), 2/24.
13. Shatibi, *Muwafaqāt* (n.p.: Dar ibn 'Affan, 1997), 1/438.
14. Abu Zahra, *al-Milkiyyah wa Nazarayat al-ʿAqd Fi al-Sharīʿah al-Islamiyyah* (Cairo: Dar al-Fikr al-Arabi, 1996), 237–38.
15. Mohammad Nejatullah Siddiqi, *Riba, Bank Interest and the Rationale of its Prohibition* (Jeddah: IRTI, 2004), 30.
16. Ibn ʿAshūr, *Maqāṣid al-Sharīʿah*, 477.
17. Ibn Qudamah, *al-Mughni* (Cairo: Maktabat al-Qahirah, n.d), 3/480–81.
18. Al-Kamal ibn al-Humam, *Sharh Fath al-Qadīr ʿ ala al-Hidayah* (Bulaq: Matba'at Bulaq, n.d), 2/244.
19. *Mawsu'ah*, 198–201.

20. The *wafa'* contract binds the buyer to return the goods to the seller when the latter returns the price. Both parties must honor the terms of the contract, hence the term *wafa'* (honesty).

21. Qarafi, *al-Furuq*, 1/39.

22. *Mawsu'ah*, 30/205.

23. Ibid.

24. Yahya bin Sharaf al-Din al-Nawawi, *al-Majm'u Sharh al-Muhadhab*, ed. Mohammad Najib al-Mati'I (Jeddah: Maktabat al-Irshad, n.d.), 9/314.

25. Mohammad bin Idriss al-Shafi,' *Al-Umm* (Beirut: Dar al-Ma'rifah, 1990), 3/79.

26. *Al-Mawsu'ah al-Fiqhiyyah* (Kuwait: Wizarat al-Awqaf wa al-Shu'un al-Islamiyyah, 2007), 9/96–97.

27. See Majma' Fiqhi resolution on organized *tawarruq*, session 2009.

28. The resolution reads: "2. The sale and purchase agreements must not stipulate any terms and conditions or create an obligation for both transacting parties to repurchase or resell the subject matter of the sale. Failure to observe this shariah requirement may render the agreements void from the shariah perspective." Bank Negara Malaysia, SAC in its 128th meeting on September 25th, 2012.

29. Rafiq Yunus al-Misri, *Fiqh al-Mu'amalat al-Maliyyah* (Damascus: Dar al-Qalam, 2007); Sami al-Suwailem, *Qadaya fi al-Iqtisad wa al-tamwil al-Islami* (Riyadh: Dar Kunuz Ishbilya, 2009).

30. Only one-fourth of investment bank revenues come from real economy. See Owen Davis, How Does Wall Street Work? Only One-Quarter Of Investment Bank Revenue Comes From Activities In The Real Economy (online), March 13, 2015 (cited on March 24, 2015), http://www.ibtimes.com/how-does-wall-street-work-only-one-quarter-investment-bank-revenue-comes-activities-1845162.

31. Insurance is prohibited by the OIC Fiqh Academy (Resolution N.200, 2013) and AAOIFI (standard No.26) on the basis of *gharar*.

32. Shahrul Azman bin Abdul Razak, Combination of contracts in Islamic Commercial law and its application in Islamic financial services in Malaysia, Phd. Dissertation Year?, 87–99.

33. AAIOFI, 350.

34. Monzir Kohf, *Asasiyyat al-Tamwīl al-Islami* (Kuala Lumpur: International Shariah Research Academy for Islamic Finance, 2011), 20.

35. This is known in Islamic jurisprudence as *bay' al-Taqsīt* (sale by installment), which is approved by OIC Fiqh Academy, 1410 H.

36. AAOIFI, 95.

37. Rafiq al-Misri, al-Wa'd al-Mulzim fi Mu'amalat al-Masarif al-Islamiyyah, in *al-Iqtisad al-Islami*, 2003, 15, 119–23.

38. Nazih Hammad, *fi fiqh al-Mu'amalat al-Maliyyah wa al-Masrafiyyah al-Mu'asirah* (Damascus: Dar al-Qalam, 2007), 81.

39. AAOIFI, 93.

40. Sunil Kumar, "Risk structure of Islamic finance contracts" in *Euromoney Encyclopedia of Islamic Finance*, ed. Aly Khorshid (London: Euromoney institutional investor PLC, 2009), 222.

41. Mehmet Asutay. (2007). Conceptualization of the second best solution in overcoming the social failure of Islamic finance: Examining the overpowering of

Homoislamicus by Homoeconomicus. *IIUM Journal of Economics and Management 2007*, 15, 1–1.

42. Mohammad Nejatullah Siddiqui, Mushkilat al-Bunuk al-Islamiyyah fi al-Waqt al-Hadir, in *Qadaya Mu'asirah fi al-Nuqud wa al-Bunuk, wa al-Musahamah fi al-Sharikāt*, IRTI, 281–82.

43. Al-Suwailim, *Qadaya*, 22.

44. Mawsu'ah, 36/319.

45. Mustafa Ahmad al-Zarqa, *al-ʿUqud al-Musamah fi al-fiqh al-islami: 'Aqd al-bay,'* (Damascus: Dar al-Qalam, 1999), 89.

46. Salman Syed Ali, 'Islamic Finance and Economic Development: An Introduction and Overview' in *Islamic Finance and Economic Development*, ed. Salman Syed Ali (Jeddah: IRTI, 2014), 4. The other two key purposes of a financial sector are resource allocation and facilitating economic transactions.

47. Ibn ʿAshūr, *Maqāṣid al-Sharīʿah*, 279.

48. Ahcen Lahsasna, *Maqasid al-Shariah in Islamic Finance* (Kuala Lumpur: IBFIM, 2013), 155.

49. Mohammad bin Ahmad Ibn Rushd, *Bidayat al-Mujtahid wa Nihatat al-Muqtasid* (Beirut: Dar al-Kutub al-'Ilmiyyah, 1988), 2/209.

50. There are divergent views on how substantial debt-based products contribute to the GDP, bearing in mind the various repercussions on the economy. Undoubtedly, those products are quite dominant in Islamic finance due to many reasons, namely their low-risk profile, profitability, and easy structuring.

51. See Rafiq al-Misri, al-Wa'd al-Mulzim fi Mu'amalat al-Masarif al-Islamiyyah, in *al-Iqtisad al-Islami*, 2003, 15, 119–23.

52. Ibn ʿAshūr, *al-Tahrīr wa al-Tanwīr* (Tunis: al-Dar al-Tunisia lil al-Nashr, 1984), 3/98.

53. Abdullah bin Biyyah, *Maqāṣid al-Mu'malat wa Marasid al-Waqi'at* (London: Al-Furqan Islamic Heritage Foundation, 2010), 28.

54. Muhammad Taqi Usmani, *An Introduction of Islamic Finance* (Karachi: Maktaba Ma'ariful Qur'an, 2007), 170.

55. Ibn ʿAshūr *al-Tahrīr wa al-Tanwīr*, 3/98.

56. Qarafi, *al-Furuq*, 3/269.

57. Ibn Qudamah, *al-Mughni*, 4/6–7.

58. Mustapha Ahmad al-Zarqa,' *al-Madkhal al-Fiqhi al-'Amm* (Damascus: Dar al-Fikr, n.d), 2/947.

59. Ernst & Young, 2013.

60. Ibn Qayyim, *I'lam al-Muwaqqi'in* (Cairo: Matba'at al-Sa'adah, 1955), 3/123.

61. Ahmad Ali al-Nadwi, *Jamharat al-Qawa'id al-Fiqhiyyah Fi al-Mu'amalat al-Maliyyah* (Riyadh: Rajhi Bank, 2000), 560–61.

62. Nazih Hammad, 'al-Tawarruq' in *Fi Fiqh al-Mu'amalāt al-Masrafiyyah*, 187.

63. AAIOFI, *Sukuk Standard*, 235.

64. Securities Commission Malaysia, *The Islamic Securities (Sukuk) Market* (Kuala Lumpur: Lexis Nexis, 2009), 49.

65. Khalifah Babkar al-Hasan and Hasan Ahmad Mur'I, *al-Maqāṣid al-Sharīʿah wa al-Qawa'id al-Fiqhiyyah* (Cairo: Dar al-Tiba'ah la-Muhamadiyyah, 1998), 232.

66. Laldin and others, *Islamic Legal Maxims and their Application in Islamic Finance* (Kuala Lumpur: ISRA, 2013), 82.
67. Shariah Resolutions in Islamic Finance (Kuala Lumpur: Bank Negara Malaysia, 2007), 45.
68. Laldin and others, *Islamic Legal Maxims*, 87–88.
69. Ibn Nujaym, *al-Ashbah wa al-Naza'ir* (Beirut: Dar al-Kutub al-'Ilmiyyah, n.d), 85.

BIBLIOGRAPHY

'Abd al-Sattar Abu Ghuddah. *Awfu bil ʿ uqud*. N.p.: Majmu'at Dellah al-Barakah, 1997.

Abu Zahra, Mohammad. *al-milkiyyah wa nazarayāt al-ʿaqd fi al-sharīʿah al-islamiyyah*. Cairo: Dar al-Fikr al-Arabi, 1996.

al-'Abidin ibn Ibrahim Ibn Nujaym, Zain. *al-Ashbah wa al-Naza'ir*. Beirut: Dar al-Kutub al-'Ilmiyyah, n.d.

al-Dīn al-Qarāfi, Shihab. *al-Furūq*. N.p.: 'Alam al-Kutub, n.d.

al-Dīn bin Moḥammad, Kamāl. *Sharh Fath al-Qadīr*. Beirut: Dar al-Fikr, n.d.

al-Hasan, Khalifah Babkar/Mur'i, Hasan Ahmad. *al-Maqāṣid al-Sharīʿah wa al-Qawa'id al-Fiqhiyyah*. Cairo: Dar al-Tiba'ah la-Muhamadiyyah, 1998.

Al-'Izz bin 'Abdussalam, *Qawa'id al-Aḥkam fi Maṣāliḥ al-Anam*. Cairo: Maktabat al-Kulliyat al-Azhariyyah, 1991.

al-Jawziyyah, Ibn Qayyim. *I'lam al-Muwaqqi'in ann Rab al-ʿ Alamin*. Cairo: Matba'at al-Sa'adah, 1955.

Al-Kamal ibn al-Humam. *Sharh Fath al-Qadīr ʿ ala al-Hidayah*. Bulaq: Matba'at Bulaq, n.d.

al-Misri, Rafiq. "al-Wa'd al-Mulzim fi Mu'amalāt al-Masarif al-Islamiyyah." *al-Iqtisad al-Islami* 15 (2003): 119–123.

———. *Fiqh al-Mu'amalat al-Maliyyah*. Damascus: Dar al-Qalam, 2007.

al-Nadwi, Ahmad Ali. *Jamharat al-Qawa'id al-Fiqhiyyah Fi al-Mu'amalāt al-Maliyyah*. Riyadh: Rajhi Bank, 2000.

al-Shafi', Mohammad bin Idriss. *Al-Umm*. Beirut: Dar al-Ma'rifah, 1990.

al-Shạtibī, Abu Ishaq. *Muwafaqāt fi uṣūl al-sharīʿah*. al-Khobor: Dar ibn 'Affan, 1997.

al-Suwailem, Sami. *Qadaya fi al-Iqtisad wa al-tamwil al-Islami*. Riyadh: Dar Kunuz Ishbilya, 2009.

al-Tahir Ibn 'Ashur, Mohammad. *Maqāṣid al-Sharīʿah*. Edited by Mohammad el-Tahir al-Miwasi. Amman: Dar al-Nafa'is, 2001.

———. *Treaties on Maqasid al-shariah*. Translated by Mohammed El-Tahir El-Mesawi. London: IIIT, 2006.

al-Zarqa', Mustapha Ahmad. *al-Madkhal al-Fiqhi al-'Amm*. Damascus: Dar al-Fikr, n.d.

———. *al-ʿUqud al-Musamah fi al-fiqh al-islami: 'aqd al-bay,'*. Damascus: Dar al-Qalam, 1999.

al-Zarqashī, Badrul Dīn. *al-Manthour fī al-Qawaʿid al-Fiqhiyyah*. Kuwait: Wizarat al-Awqaf wa al-sh'un al-Islamiyyah, n.d.

al-Zin Al-Jurjani, 'Ali bin Moḥammad. *al-Ta'rifāt*. N.p.: Dar al-Kitab al-Arabi, n.d.
Ali, Salman Syed. "Islamic Finance and Economic Development: An Introduction and Overview." In *Islamic Finance and Economic Development*, edited by Salman Syed Ali. Jeddah: IRTI, 2014.
Asutay, Mehmet. "Conceptualisation of the second best solution in overcoming the social failure of Islamic finance: Examining the overpowering of Homoislamicus by Homo-economicus." *IIUM Journal of Economics and Management* 15 (2007): 167–195.
Bank Negara Malaysia. *Shariah Resolutions in Islamic Finance*. Kuala Lumpur: Bank Negara Malaysia, 2007.
bin Biyyah, Abdullah. *Maqāṣid al-Mu'malāt wa Marasid al-Waqi'at*. London: Al-Furqan Islamic Heritage Foundation, 2010.
bin Sharaf al-Din al-Nawawi, Yahya. *al-Majm'u Sharh al-Muhadhab*, edited by Mohammad Najib al-Mati'i. Jeddah: Maktabat al-Irshad, n.d.
Hammad, Nazih. *Fi Fiqh al-Mu'amalāt al-Maliyyah wa al-Masrafiyyah al-Mu'asirah*. Damascus: Dar al-Qalam, 2007.
Ibn 'Ashūr. *al-Taḥrīr wa al-Tanwīr*. Tunis: al-Dar al-Tunisia lil al-Nashr, 1984.
Ibn Qudamah, Muwafaq al-Din Mohammad. *Al-Mughni*. Cairo: Maktabat al-Qahirah, n.d.
Ibn Rajab, Zainuddin Abduraḥmān. *al-Qawa'id*. N.p.: Dar al-Kutub al-'Ilmiyyah, n.d.
Ibn Rushd, Mohammad bin Ahmad. *Bidayat al-Mujtahid wa Nihatat al-Muqtasid*. Beirut: Dar al-Kutub al-'Ilmiyyah, 1988.
Kahf, Monzir. *Asasiyyat al-Tamwīl al-Islami*. Kuala Lumpur: International Shariah Research Academy for Islamic Finance, 2011.
Kumar, Sunil. "Risk Structure of Islamic Finance Contracts." In *Euromoney Encyclopedia of Islamic Finance*, edited by Aly Khorshid. London: Euromoney institutional investor PLC, 2009.
Lahsasna, Ahcen. *Maqasid al-Shariah in Islamic Finance*. Kuala Lumpur: IBFIM, 2013.
Laldin et al. *Islamic Legal Maxims and their Application in Islamic Finance*. Kuala Lumpur: ISRA, 2013.
Majella. Articles 103-104. n.p.: *al-Jami'ah al-Islamiyya*, 2005.
Razak, Shahrul Azman bin Abdul. *Combination of Contracts in Islamic Commercial Law and its Application in Islamic Financial Services in Malaysia*, PhD Dissertation, 2014.
Securities Commission Malaysia. *The Islamic Securities (Sukuk) Market*. Kuala Lumpur: Lexis Nexis, 2009.
Shatibi, *Muwafaqāt*. N.p.: Dar Ibn Qayyim and Dar idn 'Affan, 2003.
Siddiqui, Mohammad Nejatullah. "Mushkilāt al-Bunuk al-Islamiyyah fi al-Waqt al-Hadir." In *Qadaya Mu'asirah fi al-Nuqud wa al-Bunuk, wa al-Musahamah fi al-Sharikāt*. Jeddah: IRTI, 2003.
———. *Riba, Bank Interest and the Rationale of it's Prohibition*. Jeddah: IRTI, 2004.
Usmani, Muhammad Taqi. *An Introduction of Islamic Finance*. Karachi: Maktaba Ma'ariful Qur'an, 2007.
Wizārat al-Awqāf wa-al-Shu'ūn al-Islāmīyah. *Al-Mawsu'ah al-Fiqhiyyah*. Kuwait: Wizarat al-Awqaf wa al-Shu'un al-Islamiyyah, 2007.

Part II

CHALLENGES

Chapter 8

Reason and Revelation

A Meaningful Contribution to Contemporary Ethical Debates in a Secular Context

Muna Tatari

Abū Ishāq al-Shāṭibī (d. 1388) is associated with the term *maqāṣid al-sharīʿah* (the higher objectives of Islamic law) like no other Muslim jurist. Although he was neither the first nor the last to work on this subject, he notably identified within the *maqāṣid* a universal perspective. He classified the protection of life, religion, reason, family, and property as universal values for which, in his regard, every religion provides an ethical framework to protect and preserve.[1] These five objectives of the *sharīʿah*, as they were called from a certain point on in the Islamic legal discourse, cannot be found as such in the *Qurʾān*. According to Anver Emon, they were the result of an interpretative engagement with the text and were intuitively induced from certain *Qurʾānic* prohibitions.[2] Due to this textual induction, scholars such as Abū Ḥāmid Muḥammad al-Ghazālī (d. 1111) and al-Shāṭibī argued that the prohibition of alcohol, for example, indirectly aims to protect reason.

As such, in favor of the view held by Wael Hallaq, concepts from which the *maqāṣid al-sharīʿah* were formulated in the past are not as rationalistic as is sometimes argued today. It is rather due to certain projections that were shaped by a concern to identify universal and timeless ethical and social-philosophical approaches as already negotiated at the time of the Prophet Muhammad that modulated the *maqāṣid* discourse.[3]

Due to the loose connection between the *maqāṣid* and the *Qurʾānic* text, which took place within the approach of a text-based argumentation, the approach of value-based assumptions should be taken into consideration because of the overlapping dynamics between both. In this regard, it can be noted that the objectives, as the—so-proclaimed—results of text-based assumptions, were often implemented as value-based assumptions. Value-based assumptions in Islamic legal philosophy (*uṣūl al-fiqh*) often served as hermeneutical keys for further legal discussions. In this context, Khaled Abou

El Fadl (2001) calls attention to the fact that this classical methodology can satisfy current requests only in a limited way because he qualifies the values themselves as underdetermined. It is obvious that those values were mainly defined by the prohibitions of their opposites. Hence, serious and ongoing debate surrounding their deeper content is often lacking. According to Abou El Fadl, the often unthematized confluence of textual and sociological dynamics, which led to the setup and definition of these values, may involve fruitful possibilities but constitute, in general, a risk of a *de facto* unnoticed shift in values that accompany changing times and contexts.[4] Being unaware of sociological dynamics that underpin the *maqāṣid* can lead to an attitude that Ebrahim Moosa calls "text fundamentalism." In his words, "[t]ext fundamentalism in part perpetuates the fiction that the text actually provides the norms, and we merely 'discover' the norms. The truth is that we 'make' the norms in conversation with the revelatory text.[5]" Therefore, a critical awareness of the interdependence between text and context should be part of any engagement with the text, its interpretation, and its application.

DEFINING VALUES THROUGH CONSCIOUS RECONSTRUCTION

In my chapter, I will focus on the objective of reason and its relation to revelation in the quest for ethical orientation as part of the *maqāṣid al-sharīʿah* debate. I will highlight crucial aspects of the debate in order to point out important challenges, which will need further and deeper elaboration but is a task beyond the scope of this chapter.

A surprisingly large number of papers on the subject of *maqāṣid al-sharīʿah* do not acknowledge that the concept of reason, whether in the *Qurʾānic* use or in the theological, philosophical, or legal perspectives of classical scholarship, must be distinguished from present-day concepts of reason. Navid Kermani, as an exemplary exception, has pointed to the gap between the *Qurʾānic* use of reason and late modern uses of the term.[6] Much more needs to be done on the subject, because the academic character of theology in general was, and is, contested in modern Western contexts in large part based on competing concepts of reason. Thus, in regard to Islamic theology there are good grounds for an approach of definitions of reason which derive on the one side from major texts in the Islamic tradition and are put in dialogue on the other side into contemporary nontheological academic debates on the same concern.[7] The motivations for such an approach are twofold: first, the ambition to be an equal member of current academic discourses, including to contribute to them in a meaningful manner; second, the acceptance of Islamic theology as an equal member in Western academic contexts provides grounds on which ethical and emancipatory potentials of Islamic theology can be offered to different communities of discourse in a comprehensible way.

THE RELATION BETWEEN REASON AND REVELATION IN THE ISLAMIC TRADITION

According to Kevin Reinhart, framing the relation between reason and revelation is a topic that the Muslim jurists and theologians have dealt with in a significant manner since the ninth century and has a surprisingly modern touch.[8] The issue of different provenances of knowledge either by revelation or by reason culminated at that time in the hypothetical question, how can an action be classified as good, *before revelation*, as if revelation would not have been be available.[9] The epistemic possibilities of human beings were elaborated, and the debate revolved around whether human efforts can attain knowledge of certainty, independent from revelation.

Before relating this approach to actual contemporary questions, some selected parts of the historical debate should be reconstructed, at least briefly. The followers of the rationalistic ethico-theological school of the Muʿtazila[10] are characterized in regard to theological and ethical truths by having a huge confidence in the epistemic ability of human beings. For instance, the Muʿtazilite theologian ʿAbd al-Ḥasan al-Qāḍī ʿAbd al-Jabbār (d. 1024/25) considered reason to prevail over revelation. To conceive an ultimate reality as God and to identify the *Qurʾān* as God's message requires, as a first step, the effort of reason, so his argument. In his view, all other theological and ethical truths could be generated by reason too, except for specific detailed regulations, such as the number of obligatory prayers.[11] The great Muʿtazlite confidence in the ability of human epistemic skills to find out what is good for himself/herself and what can cause his or her salvation in thought, belief, and action gives humans emancipatory potential. God, in this conception, is perceived as a reasonable being and humans are able, through their reason, to approach God.[12] However, one might critique this line of reasoning by questioning the limits of humans and their epistemic skills. Identifying these epistemic limitations was a preoccupation of al-Ghazālī, who adhered to the Ashʿarite theological school. Al-Ghazālī was deeply convinced that reason could give humans no assurance about what is religiously true and good. One of his great achievements was a critical examination of the epistemological foundation of the philosophies of his time. He analyzed the limitations of philosophical thought from a decidedly theological perspective and concluded that it was impossible to have rational knowledge of things as they are (e.g., good and bad).[13] As a consequence, al-Ghazālī focused on intrapersonal access to knowledge through mystical experience, which he put in relation to a stronger emphasis on the *Qur'ānic* text and the tradition of Prophet Muhammad in the search for normative truth.

In contrast to al-Ghazālī, a number of Muslim philosophers, such as Muḥammad ibn Aḥmad Ibn Rushd (d. 1198) or Muḥammad ibn ʿAbd al-Mālik ibn Tufayl (d. 1185), pointed out two ways to the "one truth": a philosophical route through means of reason and a theological route through means of revelation. Both philosophers refer to the fundamental compatibility and agreement between the contents of the two sources, but from a today's perspective they are subject to the same critique already directed at the approach of ʿAbd al-Jabbār: the limits of rational, conditional cognition to comprehend the unconditional (God). Ibn Rushd, as Frank Griffel has shown, is one of the last representatives of a certain type of Islamic philosophy (*falsafa*) and with him the end of Islamic philosophy was declared. However, this is only true in so far as this philosophical approach was not taken further in most parts of the Sunni world.[14] Within this *falsafa* approach it is assumed that, following the Aristotelian theory of science in the form of syllogisms, it would be, in principle, possible to gain knowledge of certainty in metaphysics and that this method is superior to the theological one, because philosophical reasoning is based on, and results in, apodictic arguments (*qiyās*), while theological arguments rely on premises which are not unequivocal (*burḥān*).[15]

Al-Ghazālī, critiquing that approach, doesn't doubt the results of syllogistic rationality in general, but rather the inviolability of the premises of philosophical arguments and thus the assumption that *falsafa* provides a means to come to knowledge with certainty[16]. Scholars such al-Shāṭibī also struggled to identify the locus of reason. He viewed reason as subordinate to revelation, since reason is always constrained by context and should thereby be limited and framed by revelation. Historical research on this point has now shown convincingly that one must not ascribe to al-Shāṭibī a fundamental distrust of reason because of his effort to set boundaries therein.[17] Rather, it seems plausible that by this methodological setting he was thinking of his civic responsibility. Al-Shāṭibī was vehemently opposed to those using reason to violate the spirit of the law and to justify ethically dubious practices through religiously inflected literature like, for example, *kutub al-ḥiyal* (books of legal strategems).[18] The inviolability of revelation in al-Shāṭibī's approach served thus as a kind of protection wall against political leaders, which made the possibilities of reason as a means to argue for their own political interests.

It is noteworthy, that by this, al-Shāṭibī diagnosed an abuse of reason, which corresponds to the dialectic of the Enlightenment. The concept of enlightenment implies that one never owns (all at once) the state of being enlightened, but a state of enlightenment is always in danger to be corrupted by heteronomies. Critique of reason can therefore be understood rudimentarily as an early theme of scholastic Islamic theology and contains thereby a reminder to examine in which contemporary discourses reason might be in danger to lose its reasonability.

MOTIVATION TO RECONSTRUCT

These contextual definitions of the role and task of reason should be understood in no case as the last word in this matter, and Islamic theology today must make an effort, especially in the face of important questions of Western philosophy, to define the relation of reason and revelation anew. Islamic theology should face this task with the aim, as mentioned earlier, to rebut the European *a priori* prejudice of the antiacademic character of theology per se, and in particular Islamic theology. Here, Islamic theology should envisage a decisive paradigm shift if it wants to gain full academic participation and social responsibility.

The *maqāṣid al-sharīʿah* discourse can provide fruitful insights and can contribute to contemporary general ethical debates that have the potential to be relevant beyond a specific inner-theological, inner-Islamic circle.[19] The common Islamic position that revelation can be understood by means of reason, which was also a position of al-Ghazālī, should therefore be extended to ensure discourse ability in the current academic context.

Secular framed societies and discourses in which Islamic theology should get rooted are characterized by multireligiousness and atheistic worldviews in which the meaningfulness of Islamic theology (and theology in general) is questioned from a philosophical perspective. In this context, the academic discourse of Islamic theology should not remain intra-theological. To meet contemporary academic requirements, the inner theological hermeneutic circle of revelation, faith, reason, and practice should also face the challenges of modern concepts of reason, such as those of the autonomous conceived reason (Immanuel Kant) and discourse-bound conceptions of reason (Jürgen Habermas, Alasdair McIntyre, and Charles Taylor). It is crucial for Islamic theology to provide a concept of reason that integrates the concept of reason of the scholastic time. In that period, reason was always understood to be geared by its inner nature to the ultimate reality, namely God. Reason was understood as being enlightened by God's presence, a presence that was usually not questioned.

Concretely, for this purpose, this means on the one hand that questions of philosophy, literature, science, or history should be taken up and, on the other hand, that the plausibility of the contents of Islamic theology should be unfolded by that means of reason conceived *independently* from theology. From this line of thought, it is obvious that Islamic theology would not do well to define itself as a kind of *sui generis* in regard to academic discourses but that it should, as a specific science with an internal perspective, also seek to exchange with other disciplines in a comparative perspective. If Islamic theology can prove that theologically formulated truths do not contradict an independently working reason, it gains in strength and significance. This can enrich the society and thus offer impulses by which a society can be shaped, not in the sense that a given secular structure would be called into question, but rather, with regard to questions of meaning and ethics, convincing arguments can be introduced in terms of social discourse in the Habermasian sense. Following this path, Islamic theology, through the additional means of autonomous conceptualized philosophical reason respectively a discourse framed reason, will be able to make its assumptions in a manner plausible enough to be understood beyond the intra-Islamic circle of addressees, and thereby specific contents can be meaningfully translated into secular speech.[20]

CORRESPONDING STRUCTURES AS A FIRST STEP FOR UNDERSTANDING

The approach of Jürgen Habermas in regard to discourse ethics provides interesting insight into modern concepts of reason and community, which correspond to traditional Islamic views in certain points. A reflection on both can offer a basis for constructive and trustful cooperation between members of different beliefs and conviction that must not neglect these backgrounds but deal with them in fruitful manners. It seems to me that discourse ethics (reasoning in community), as Habermas moulded, could reasonably uphold the method of *ijmāʿ* (consensus). The richness of results from the formative Islamic time, and later, can grow further and can get reshaped by the means of discourse.

Up until recent times, Habermas continued to figure out how values can be filled with meaningful content and how a society should function to enforce those defined values. He sees the best way to a set an ideal discussion to be a "free of domination discourse"[21]. In later works like *Truth and Justification*,[22] he critically reviewed his own theses and concluded that the truth-finding process—by reason—depends on ideal conditions, which are just not possible to implement; and therefore, trustworthy, valid results of such a discourse can't be granted. He, as a consequence, was not able to consider the "the unforced force of the better argument"[23] as the ultimate means. Truth, he says, incorporates more than discourse ethic can reach, and room for an unconditional moment must be given.[24] From a theological point of view, this is very interesting because this statement can function as an argument to give revelation, as an unconditioned moment, a constructive point of reference again from a nonreligious strand of argumentation. Based on this, the relationship between both can be reframed as a mutual one.[25]

As a consequence of those reframings, Habermas turned to a definition of reason that is based on intersubjective exchange, to give space to the corrective function of the other.

Aiming to define concepts, which can happen only within concrete contexts, the approach of a discourse ethics is, in my regard, understandable as an appropriate means to build bridges between itself and the classical Islamic source of consensus *(ijmāʿ)*. But, as already said, due to the insight of Habermas, ideal circumstances of a fruitful and meaningful discourse can by their very nature not be implemented fully, and due to the possibility that majorities can fail, there must be a place for a moment of objection and resistance, which, within Islamic tradition, was incorporated as a consent of being in dissent *(ikhtilāf)* in theory and practice if necessary.

Coming back in a stopover to the second part of the chapter, it can be concluded tentatively that with a concept of reason, which is defined separately from revelation, Islamic theology grapples in contemporary contexts with the hypothetically formulated question of the scholastic time: Can human come to insights and judgments *before revelation*? At the same time, I would advocate that Islamic theology should keep an openness to different concepts of reason and revelation because human insights remain contingent. While one could see at the peak of enlightenment almost a deification of reason, the postmodern is devoted in large parts to the deification of the other of reason: the narrative, the myth, the experience, and mystic.[26]

In this chapter, the aforementioned reconstructions of the past are not motivated by the position that everything is only "Islamic" if it is mentioned in the Qur'ān, the ḥadīth (sayings of the Prophet Muhammad), or the early traditions. But an analytic approach to tradition is useful because texts of the traditions can't be ignored due to the fact that they are always embedded in any attempt at interpretation. They constitute the preconceptions, the assumption with which an interpreter approaches a text.[27] Moreover, as Moosa (2006) points out, traditions are more than texts; they are a "state of mind and a set of embodied practices."[28] An awareness of them and their influences provides a basis for an emancipatory engagement with them, the ability to choose knowingly which discourses are meaningful for oneself and for framing theological debates in the future, and which are not. Especially in regard to the tradition-neglecting movements, like the neo-salafis and neo-wahabis, it is important to maintain a constructive dialogue with tradition that helps to root ones scientific efforts in the identity-establishing past.[29]

Precisely in regard to the convictions of the last-mentioned communities, the following reconstruction may provide surprising insights. The approach to come to meaningful insights apart from revelation can be also traced back to Taqī al-Dīn Aḥmad ibn Taimiyya (d. 1328).

Ibn Taimiyya commented to the already-mentioned discussion, which was shaped by the intention to somehow harmonize reason and revelation with each other, the motive of an ignorance or rejection of revelation, which can nevertheless provide ethical values.

> The affairs of men in this world can be kept in order with justice and a certain connivance in sin, better than with pious tyranny. This is why it has been said that God upholds the just state even if it is unbelieving, but does not uphold the unjust state even if it is Muslim. It is also said that the world can endure with justice and unbelief but not with injustice and Islam.[30]

Ibn Taimiyya said that a state that is not based on religion but provides justice is a better state supported by God than a Muslim, unjust state. It would of course be anachronistic to label Ibn Taimiyya a vanguard of a separation of religion and state in terms of a secular structure. He was deeply convinced that the revelation and the *sunnah* (tradition of the Prophet Muhammad) provide truth and orientation, and that politics should be shaped by both (*siyāsah shar'iyyah*).[31] But, at the same time, he made in his regard concrete disappointing experiences with politics and politicians and thereby gained an awareness of the problem: being part of a religious community does not automatically lead to good character and consequently just politics. In his remarks, he indirectly points to an acceptance of sources for ethical action beyond religion. But he nevertheless explicitly emphasizes that for the quest of salvation in the hereafter, action based on nonreligious sources do not have a salvific impact at all.[32]

Interesting for the concern of this chapter is Ibn Taimiyya's appreciation of the results of reason, which work independent from revelation.[33] From today's perspective, common engagement in ethical questions can thus not just be seen as a reasonable answer to complex challenges in a globalized world, but also as a contemporary expression of one's tradition.[34]

THE POSITIONING OF REASON AND ANTHROPOLOGICAL CONSEQUENCES

From the standpoint of theological convictions, the idea of an independent conceptualized reason is an important step toward the appreciation of the human being and human conditions. Common or corresponding points to figure out possible ways to argue that the idea of an anthropological turn, by which the human condition and perspective is the starting point, can be found in the Islamic tradition, as aspects of the discussion within Islamic legal philosophy show.

The *Qur'ānic* text is filled with expressions of human cognitive faculties. There is a constant appeal to think, expressed in different verbs like *faqiha, fahima, 'aqila*, and *tadabbara*. The widespread contemporary conviction that human's perspective in the end is the only possible one by which human knowledge is gained finds important forerunners in classical Islamic legal philosophy and was may be rooted in the following transmission:

> In one such report, members of the Khawārij accused 'Ali of accepting the judgment and dominion (*ḥākimiyya*) of human beings instead of abiding by the dominion of God's law. Upon hearing of this accusation, 'Ali called upon the people to gather around him and brought a large copy of the Qur'an. 'Ali touched the Qur'an while instructing it to speak to the people and inform them about God's law. Surprised, the people gathered around 'Ali exclaimed, "What are you doing? The Qur'an cannot speak, for it is not a human being!" Upon hearing this, 'Ali exclaimed that this was exactly his point. The Qur'an, 'Ali explained, is but ink and paper, and it does not speak for itself. Instead, it is human beings who give effect to it according to their limited personal judgments and opinions.[35]

If the human perspective of understanding is even true for revelation, how much more should that insight get applied as a condition of any knowledge? This does not mean a denial of the ontological reality, but states it as an epistemologically ambiguous object.

The question of epistemical possibilities and boundaries of humans shaped the Islamic legal philosophy discourse in history continuously. Thereby, two strands of positions came up. The school of Mukhaṭṭī'a assumed that there can only be one correct solution, for God had predicted that solution. It is up to human efforts to detect that solution. All results that didn't fit with that one solution were thus wrong (*khaṭa'*). Nevertheless, the initiators of wrong solutions, which will show up just at the end of time, were not labeled by the majority of jurists as sinners. Relying on the transmission of the Prophet which stated that every *mujtahid* [person qualified to exercise *ijtihād* (independent reasoning)] gets a reward which will be doubled if his/her solution matches with that of God, every honest solution was considered as meritorious, at least by God.[36]

On the other hand, the school of Muṣawwiba held the view that at least in the area of the nonfixed questions (*al-masā'il al-fiqhiyyah al-ẓanniyyah*) there exists no fixed solution from God. Therefore, every *mujtahid* who struggled hard, reaching his/her limits in the endeavor to find the right solution was right (*muṣīb*). For most of the followers of that school (who were in the majority, Ash'arites) that assessment didn't apply to the area of fixed rules and commands (*al-qaṭ'iyyāt*). To the *qaṭ'iyyāt* belong, for example, the determination of the sources of *uṣūl al-fiqh* and the five times of prayer in the area of *'ibādāt* (actions of worship). Here, the followers of the Muṣawwiba school also advocated the view of the Mukhaṭṭi'a that only one solution could be right. But there were, as exceptions, scholars who held the view that even in the case of theological questions, every honest effort was right even if that meant that in regard to the nature of God and his attributes, for example, different opinions emerged. The argument behind that position was that God couldn't punish for what a human being is not able to achieve.[37]

At this point, Anver Emon introduces remarkable theological consideration to both approaches. In regard to the Mukhaṭṭi'a and Muṣawwiba school, he admits, like Khaled Abou El Fadl, that in both the freedom of research is not limited due to the fact that nobody can claim to know the thoughts of God and hence nobody can have an authoritarian legitimation to shut the process of searching for the best answer to a problem. However, as Emon annotates critically, the creativity of human beings in the Mukhaṭṭi'a approach is limited to discover what God has already determined. In fact, that doesn't affect human freedom practically, but in regard to questions of anthropology it matters. There is a difference between the concepts of humans which are regarded to be able to detect what is (already) present but still hidden to a concept of humans that can create innovatively, as the school of the Muṣawwiba advocates. Consequently, Emon states that within the later approach more freedom for human efforts and therefore a higher appreciation of human beings themselves and their conditions.[38]

In both disciplines, the juristic and the theological, it is important to state that freedom is of course not whimsical. Maximal effort to come to the best solutions (*ijtihād* and *ghalabat al-ẓann*) is required in correspondence to the insight of one's own responsibility in front of God and human judgement. But, it is the freedom of human that is called into action.

THEOLOGICAL SETTING AND CONCLUSION

In my opinion, the aforementioned efforts to negotiate the relation between revelation and reason should be embedded in an approach that commits itself to tradition in a specific way, which was introduced by Ebrahim Moosa as *critical traditionalism* in the academic discourse.[39] To imprint the scientific discourses of the time and to be challenged by foreign ideas, methods, and contents is not just the order of the day. It has its precursor in the Islamic intellectual history and therefore must not be perceived as alien to Islam. The intellectual openness and curiosity with which, for example, al-Ghazālī argued that for his theological approach taking and creatively integrating foreign methods and contents of his contemporary environment is to be interpreted as an expression of the intellectual openness of Islamic theology as such and is instructive for dealing with other contemporary disciplines today.[40] With the expression of critical traditionalism, it can be programmatically noted that the academic development of Islamic theology on the one hand is committed to a 1,400-year-old tradition and, at the same time, takes efforts to express its contents in accordance with contemporary academic standards.

This chapter searched within the Islamic tradition for promising arguments and views in regard to contemporary questions of the definition of reason and its relationship with revelation. As part of the *maqāṣid al-sharīʿah* discussion, it tried to focus on ethical questions. Besides further in-depth researches, which this chapter could not provide, a reconstruction of the definition of revelation remains an urging need.

NOTES

1. See Abū Ishāq al-Shāṭibī. *Al-Muwāfaqāt fī uṣūl al-sharīʿah*. Edited by Ibrāhīm Ramaḍan, 4 vols. (Beirut: Dār al-Maʿrifa, 1994), here vol. 2, 326–32.

2. Anver M. Emon. *Islamic Natural Law Theories*. Oxford: Oxford University Press, 2010), 166.

3. See the position of Wael Hallaq as unfolded in Yasir S. Ibrahim. "Rashid Riḍā, and Maqāṣid al-Shariʿā." *Studia Islamica* 102/103 (2006): 157–98, here 161, 163.

4. See Khaled Abou El Fadl, *Speaking in God's Name: Islamic Law, Authority and Women*. Oxford: Oneworld, 2001, 154–61.

5. Ebrahim Moosa, "The Debts and Burdens of Critical Islam," in *Progressive Muslims. On Justice, Gender and Pluralism*, edited by. Omid Safi, 111–144. Oxford: Oneworld 2003, here 125.

6. See Navid Kermani, "Appelliert Gott an den Verstand? Eine Randbemerkung zum qur'ānischen Begriff ʿaql und seiner Paret'schen Übersetzung," in *Encounters of Words and Texts: Intercultural Studies in Honor of Stefan Wild on the Occasion of his Sixtieth Birthday, March 2, 1997*, edited by Edzard Lutz, Stefan Wild, and Christian Szyska, presented by his pupils in Bonn. 43–66. Hildesheim 1997 (Arabistische Texte und Studien; 10.

7. For example, Richard Rorty holds the view that due to secularization processes theology does not deserve the degree of an academic discipline anymore and belongs, therefore, only to the private and individual realm. See Richard Rorty/Gianni Vattimo, *Die Zukunft der Religion*, Übersetzt von Michael Adrian und Nora Fröder; Frankfurt a.M.: Suhrkamp, 2006. To unfold an Islamic derived definition of reason does not intend an uncritical adaption of already-existing definitions in the academic Western discourse, but calls for a comprehensible intellectual and critical involvement with them.

8. See A. Kevin Reinhart, *Before Revelation. The Boundaries of Muslim Moral Thought*. Albany: SUNY Press, 1995 [SUNY Series in Middle Eastern Studies], 11–28.

9. See ibid.

10. See Vasalou Sophia, *Moral Agents and Their Deserts. The Character of Mu'tazilite Ethics*. Princeton, NJ: Princeton University Press, 2008, 33–66.

11. See A. Kevin Reinhart, *Before Revelation. The Boundaries of Muslim Moral Thought*. Albany: SUNY Press, 1995 [SUNY Series in Middle Eastern Studies], 181.

12. As history has shown, an emphasis on reason and rationality doesn't necessarily prevent intolerant practices [refer to the *miḥna* (inquisition) in the reign of the Mu'tazilī influence caliphs from 833 to 849].

13. See Abū Ḥāmid Muḥammad al-Ghazālī. *Der Erretter aus dem Irrtum* [Al-Munqiḏ min aḍ-ḍalāl]. Aus dem Arabischen übersetzt, mit einer Einleitung, mit Anmerkungen und Indices herausgegeben von 'Abd-Elṣamad 'Abd-Elḥamīd Elschazilī, Hamburg 1988 (Philosophische Bibliothek; 389), 22 and see also: Frank Griffel, *Al-Ghazālī's Philosophical Theology*. New York: Oxford University Press, 2010, 98–109.

14. See Muḥammad ibn Aḥmad Ibn Rushd, *Maßgebliche Abhandlung. Faṣl al-Maqāl*, Aus dem Arabischen übersetzt und herausgegeben von Frank Griffel. Berlin: Verlag der Weltreligionen, 2010, 66–70.

15. See ibid., 107.

16. Since this approach of the philosophers is contested and critical inquiries are additionally supported by the epistemological insights since late modernity, the question arises whether the contemporary Moroccan philosopher Mohammed Abed Al-Jabiri, for example, is well advised to refer to Aristotelianism in its Ibn Rushd reception for an inner-Islamic renewal movement. See Mohammed Abed Al-Jabiri. *Kritik der arabischen Vernunft. Naqd al-'aql al-'arabī. Die Einführung*. Berlin: Perlenverlag, 2009. See also: Muḥammad 'Ābid al-Jābirī. *Naqd al-'aql al-'arabī; 1: Takwīn al-'aql al-'arabī*. Bairūt: Markaz dirāsāt al-waḥdah al-'arabiyyah, 1991; Muḥammad 'Ābid al Jābirī. *Naqd al-'aql al-'arabī; 2: Bunyat al-'aql al-'arabī*. Bairūt: Markaz dirāsāt al-waḥdah al-'arabiyyah, 1993; Muḥammad 'Ābid al-Jābirī. *Naqd al-'aql al-'arabī; 3: al-'Aql al-siyāsī al-'arabī*. Bairūt: Markaz dirāsāt al-waḥdah al-'arabiyyah, 1992. In modern times, it was Immanuel Kant who also negated the human capacity to perceive objective knowledge. It is to consider whether the basal truth in the approach of Wittgenstein could be regarded as a modern update of the Aristotelian approach, leaving the claim for objective truth but continuing the claim of certainty in knowledge. See Ludwig Wittgenstein. *Über Gewissheit*. Frankfurt a.M.: Suhrkamp Wissenschaft, 1984, § 96, 97.

17. See Abū Isḥāq al-Shāṭibī. *Al-Muwāfaqāt fī uṣūl al-sharī'ah*. Edited by Ibrāhīm Ramaḍan, 4 vols. (Bairūt: Dār al-Ma'rifa, 1994), here vol. 1, 35.

18. See Abū Isḥāq al-Shāṭibī. *Al-Muwāfaqāt fī uṣūl al-sharī'ah*. Edited by Ibrāhīm Ramaḍan, 4 vols. (Bairūt: Dār al-Ma'rifa, 1994), here vol. 1, 41. See also Ibrahim Yasir S., "Rashid Riḍā and Maqāṣid al-Sharī'ah." *Studia Islamica* 102/103 (2006): 157–98, here 163.

19. See for the concept of public theology: Robert Cummings Neville. *Religion in Late Modernity*. New York: SUNY Press, 2002 and Heinrich Bedford-Strohm. *Gemeinschaft aus kommunikativer Freiheit. Sozialer Zusammenhalt in der modernen Gesellschaft. Ein theologischer Beitrag*. Gütersloh: Chr. Kaiser/Gütersloher Verlagshaus: 1999 (zugl. Habilschr. Univer.-Heidelb. 1998).

20. At the same time, as Habermas is aware, in the translation process dimensions of meaning can get lost. The translation of man being the image of God, for example, to the

sacrosanct dignity of all people is not the same and the concept of salvation covers more dimensions than the term "liberation" contains. In this respect, theology according to Habermas also has the task of keeping a dimension open, the religious one, for those who want to follow this invitation. Insofar, the task of Islamic theology exceeds the function of a motivation resource for ethical action without, however, intending to diminish this effect. Parts of the chapter on Habermas are taken from Muna Tatari. *Gott und Mensch im Spannungsverhältnis von Gerechtigkeit und Barmherzigkeit. Versuch einer islamisch begründeten Positionsbestimmung.* (Graduiertenkolleg Islamische Theologie 4). Münster: Waxmann Verlag, 2016; zugleich: Paderborn University, Diss., 2013, 192–193.

21. Jürgen Habermas. "Wahrheitstheorien." In: Ders., *Rationalitäts- und Sprachtheorie. Philosophische Texte Studienausgabe in fünf Bänden.* Bd. 2, Frankfurt a.M.: Studienausgabe Suhrkamp, 2009, 214, zitiert nach Anne Weber. "Religion im postsäkularen Diskurs. Bemerkungen aus interreligiöser Perspektive." In: *Religion, Öffentlichkeit, Moderne. Transdisziplinäre Perspektiven.* Edited by Judith Könemann/Saskia Wendel, 257–88. Bielefeld: transcript-verlag, 2016, here 263.

22. Jürgen Habermas. *Wahrheit und Rechtfertigung.* Erw. Ausg., Frankfurt a.M.: Suhrkamp: 2004.

23. See Jürgen Habermas. Wahrheitstheorien. In: Ders., *Rationalitäts- und Sprachtheorie. Philosophische Texte Studienausgabe in fünf Bänden.* Bd. 2, Frankfurt a.M.: Studienausgabe Suhrkamp, 2009, 264–65.

24. See Jürgen Habermas. *Wahrheit und Rechtfertigung.* Erw. Ausg., Frankfurt am Main Suhrkamp, 2004, 260, 316–18, 342 and Jürgen Habermas. "Wahrheitstheorien." In *Wirklichkeit und Reflexion. Walter Schulz zum 60. Geburtstag.* Edited by Helmut Fahrenbach, 211–65. Pfullingen: Neske, 1973. See also: Walter Reese-Schäfer. *Jürgen Habermas.* 3. überarb. Aufl., Frankfurt a.M.: Campus, 2001, 22–23.

25. For defining the relation between revelation and reason as a mutual one, see Klaus von Stosch. "Offenbarung und Vernunft in Islam und Christentum." In *Herausforderung Islam.* Edited by Anja Bettenworth/Andreas Funke/Mirja Lecke/Klaus von Stosch, 100–130. Paderborn u.a.: Ferdinand Schönigh Verlag, 2011.

26. See Wladimir Alekseevitč Abaschmik. "Das Vernunftsverständnis im postmetaphysischen Zeitalter. Mit besonderer Berücksichtigung der Positionen von Karen Gloy und Wolfgang Welsch." In *Unser Zeitalter—ein postmetaphysisches*? Edited by Karen Gloy, 73–81. Würzburg : Königshausen & Neumann, 2004, here 74.

27. See Hans-Georg Gadamer, *Hermeneutik I. Wahrheit und Methode. Grundzüge einer Philosophischen Hermeneutik.* Tübingen: Mohr Siebeck, 1990, 301.

28. Ebrahim Moosa, "Transitions in the 'Progress' of Civilization: Theorizing History, Practice, and Tradition," In *Voices of Change*, edited by Omid Safi, 115–30. London: Praeger, 2006 (Voices of Islam; 5), here 124.

29. See Oliver Roy. *Der Islamische Weg nach Westen. Globalisierung, Entwurzelung und Radikalisierung.* Aus dem Englischen von Michael Bayer, Norbert Juraschitz und Ursel Schäfer. Bonn: Pantheon, 2006, 229–83.

30. Fatih Emriş, *A History of Ottoman Economic Thought: Developments Before the Nineteenth Century.* New York: Routledge, 2014 (Routledge History of Economic Thought), 32, based on Ibn Taymiyya. *Traité sur la Hisba- Al-hisba fi l-islâm.* Publié et traduit par Henri Laoust. n.p.: Librairie Orientaliste Paul Geuthner, 1984, 85.

31. See Baber Johanson, "A Perfect Law in an Imperfect Society: Ibn Taymiyya's Concept of 'Governance in the Name of the Sacred Law,'" In *The Law Applied:*

Contextualizing Islamic Sharia, edited by Peri Bearman, Wolfhart Heinrichs, and Bernard G. Weiss, 259–94. London: I. B. Tauris, 2008, here 173, 275.

32. See Baber Johanson, *Contingency in a Sacred Law: Legal and Ethical Norms in the Muslim Fiqh*. Boston: Brill, 1999, 270.

33. In the frame of his time, reason was considered as created by God and, therefore, naturally orientated toward God and toward the good. Modern concepts of reason try not to use the existence of God as a useful explanation for unexplainable or difficult situations. See Dietrich Bonheoffer. *Widerstand und Ergebung*. Herausgegeben von Christian Gremmels und Eberhard Bethge und Renate Bethge in Zusammenarbeit mit Ilse Töd, Band 8. Gütersloh: Gütersloher Verlagshaus, 1998, 454.

34. A theological appreciation of atheistic worldviews is sometimes claimed but not yet examined systematically for its pros and cons.

35. Khaled Abou El-Fadl. "Islam and the Challenge of Democratic Commitment." *Fordham International Law Journal* 27 (2003): 4–71, here 15–16, incl. the footnote [. . .] as reference: "[. . .] Ahmad ibn ʿAli ibn Hajar al-Asqalani. *Fath al-bari bi-sharh al-bukhari* 303 (Dar al-Fikr 1993) [. . .] [and] Muhammd ibn ʿAli Shawkani. *Nayl al-awtar: sharh muntaqa al-akhbar min ahadith sayyid al-akhyar* 166 (Dar al-Hadith 1993)."

36. See Muḥammad bin ʿAlī al-Shawkānī. *Al-Qawl al-mufīd fī adillat al-ijtihād wa al-taqlīd.* Cairo: Maktaba al-Qurʾān, 1988, 89–91.

37. In the summary of the approaches of the Mukhaṭṭiʾand Musawwiba schools I relied on: Abbas Poya, "Iǧtihād' und Glaubensfreiheit. Darstellung einer islamisch-glaubensfreiheitlichen Idee anhand sunnitisch-rechtsmethodologischer Diskussionen." *Der Islam* 75 (1998): 226–58, here 244–56. This chapter, in a slightly different version, is part of another paper of the author and in the publishing process: Muna Tatari. "Using Comparative Insights in Developing Kalām: A Personal Reflection on Being Trained in Comparative Theology," In *How We Do Comparative Theology: European and American Perspectives in Dialogue*, edited by Francis X. Clooney, SJ/Klaus von Stosch. Fordham: University Press, 2017.

38. See Anver M. Emon, *Religious Pluralism and Islamic Law. Dhimmīs and Others in the Empire of Law*. Oxford: Oxford University Press, 2012 (Oxford Islamic Legal Studies), 201–02.

39. See Ebrahim Moosa/A. A. Mian. Art. "Islam," In *Encyclopaedia of Applied Ethics*. Edited by Ruth Chadwick, 769–76. San Diego, CA: Academic Press, 2012, here 772.

40. See Ebrahim Moosa. *Ghazālī and the Poetics of Imagination.* Chapel Hill: North Carolina, 2005, 28, 57.

BIBLIOGRAPHY

Abaschmik, Wladimir Alekseevitč. "Das Vernunftverständnis im postmetaphysischen Zeitalter. Mit besonderer Berücksichtigung der Positionen von Karen Gloy und Wolfgang Welsch." In *Unser Zeitalter—ein postmetaphysisches*? edited by Karen Gloy, 73–81. Würzburg: Königshausen & Neumann, 2004.

Abou El Fadl, Khaled. "Islam and the Challenge of Democratic Commitment." *Fordham International Law Journal* 27 (2003): 4–71.

———. *Speaking in God's Name: Islamic Law, Authority and Women*. Oxford: Oneworld Publications, 2000.

Al-Asqalānī, Aḥmad ibn ʿAlī ibn Hajar. *Fatḥ al-bārī bi-sharh ṣaḥīḥ al-bukhārī*. Beirut: Dār al-Fikr, 1993.

Al-Ghazālī, Abū Ḥāmid Muḥammad. *Der Erretter aus dem Irrtum* [al-Munqiḏ min al-ḍalāl]. Aus dem Arabischen übersetzt, mit einer Einleitung, mit Anmerkungen und Indices herausgegeben von ʿAbd-Elṣamad ʿAbd-Elḥamīd Elschazilī. Hamburg: Felix Meiner Verlag, 1988 (Philosophische Bibliothek; 389).

Al-Jabiri, Abed. *Kritik der arabischen Vernunft. Naqd al-ʿaql al-ʿarabī. Die Einführung*. Berlin: Perlen Verlag, 2009.

Al-Shāṭibī, Abū Isḥāq. *Al-Muwāfaqāt fī uṣūl al-sharīʿah*. Edited by Ibrāhīm Ramaḍan, 4 vols. Beirut: Dār al-Maʿrifa, 1994.

Al-Shawkānī, Muḥammad ibn ʿAlī. *Al-Qawl al-mufīd fī adillat al-ijtihād wa-l-taqlīd*. Cairo: Maktaba al-Qurʾān, 1988.

———. *Nayl al-awṭār: sharh muntaqā al-akhbār min ahadīth sayyid al-akhyār*. Cairo: Dār al-Hadīth, 1993.

Bedford-Strohm, Heinrich. *Gemeinschaft aus kommunikativer Freiheit. Sozialer Zusammenhalt in der modernen Gesellschaft. Ein theologischer Beitrag*. Gütersloh: Christian Kaiser/Gütersloher Verlagshaus, 1999.

Bonheoffer, Dietrich. *Widerstand und Ergebung*. Herausgegeben von Christian Gremmels und Eberhard Bethge und Renate Bethge in Zusammenarbeit mit Ilse Töd, Band 8. Gütersloh: Gütersloher Verlagshaus, 1998.

Emon, Anver M. *Islamic Natural Law Theories*. Oxford: Oxford University Press, 2010.

———. *Religious Pluralism and Islamic Law. Dhimmīs and Others in the Empire of Law*. Oxford: Oxford University Press, 2012 (Oxford Islamic Legal Studies).

Emriş, Fatih. *A History of Ottoman Economic Thought: Developments Before the Nineteenth Century*. New York: Routledge, 2014 (Routledge History of Economic Thought).

Gadamer, Hans-Georg. *Hermeneutik I. Wahrheit und Methode. Grundzüge einer Philosophischen Hermeneutik*. Tübingen: Mohr Siebeck, 1990.

Griffel, Frank. *Al-Ghazālī's Philosophical Theology*. Second edition. New York: Oxford University Press, 2010.

Habermas, Jürgen. "Wahrheitstheorien." In *Rationalitäts- und Sprachtheorie*, 4. Auflage, herausgegeben von Ders. Frankfurt a.M.: Suhrkamp, 2014 (Philosophische Texte Studienausgabe in fünf Bänden).

———. *Wahrheit und Rechtfertigung. Philosophische Aufsätze*. Erw. Ausg. Frankfurt a.M.: Suhrkamp, 2004.

Ibn Rushd, Muḥammad ibn Aḥmad. *Maßgebliche Abhandlung. Faṣl al-Maqāl*. Aus dem Arabischen übersetzt und herausgegeben von Frank Griffel. Berlin: Verlag der Weltreligionen, 2010.

Ibn Taymiyya. *Traité sur la Hisba - Al-hisba fi l-islām*. Publié et traduit par Henri Laoust. n.p.: Librairie Orientaliste Paul Geuthner, 1984.

Ibrahim. Yasir S. "Rashid Riḍā and Maqāṣid al-Shariʿā." *Studia Islamica* 102, no. 103 (2006): 157–98.

Johanson, Baber. “A Perfect Law in an Imperfect Society: Ibn Taymiyya’s Concept of ‘Governance in the Name of the Sacred Law’.” In *The Law Applied. Contextualizing Islamic Sharia*, edited by Peri Bearman, Wolfhart Heinrichs, and Berhard G. Weiss, 259–94. London: I. B. Tauris, 2008.

———. *Contingency in a Sacred Law: Legal and Ethical Norms in the Muslim Fiqh*. Boston: Brill,1999.

Kermani, Navid. “Appelliert Gott an den Verstand? Eine Randbemerkung zum qur’ānischen Begriff ‘aql und seiner Paret’schen Übersetzung.” In *Encounters of words and Texts: Intercultural Studies in Honor of Stefan Wild on the Occasion of his 60th Birthday, March 2, 1997*, edited by Edzard Lutz, Stefan Wild, and Christian Szyska and presented by his pupils in Bonn, 43–66. Hildesheim: G. Olms, 1997 (Arabistische Texte und Studien; 10).

Moosa, Ebrahim. “The Debts and Burdens of Critical Islam.” In *Progressive Muslims: On Justice, Gender and Pluralism*, edited by Omid Safi, 111–27. Oxford: Oneworld, 2003.

———. “Transitions in the ‘Progress’ of Civilization: Theorizing History, Practice, and Tradition.” In *Voices of Change*, edited by Omid Safi, 115–30. London: Praeger, 2006 (Voices of Islam; 5).

———. *Ghazālī and the Poetics of Imagination*. Chapel Hill: University of North Carolina Press, 2005.

Moosa, Ebrahim, and A. A. Mian. “Islam.” In *Encyclopaedia of Applied Ethics*. Edited by Ruth Chadwick, 769–76. San Diego, CA: Academic Press, 2012.

Neville, Robert Cummings. *Religion in Late Modernity*. Albany: State University of New York Press, 2002.

Poya, Abbas. “‘Iǧtihād‘ und Glaubensfreiheit. Darstellung einer islamisch-glaubensfreiheitlichen Idee anhand sunnitisch-rechtsmethodologischer Diskussionen.” *Der Islam* 75 (1998): 226–58.

Reese-Schäfer, Walter. *Jürgen Habermas*. 3. überarb. Aufl. Frankfurt a.M.: Campus, 2001.

Reinhart, A. Kevin. *Before Revelation: The Boundaries of Muslim Moral Thought*. Albany: State University of New York Press, 1995 (SUNY Series in Middle Eastern Studies).

Rorty, Richard, and Gianni Vattimo. *Die Zukunft der Religion*. Übersetzt von Michael Adrian und Nora Fröder. Frankfurt a.M.: Suhrkamp, 2006.

Roy, Oliver. *Der Islamische Weg nach Westen. Globalisierung, Entwurzelung und Radikalisierung*. Aus dem Englischen von Michael Bayer, Norbert Juraschitz, und Ursel Schäfer. Bonn: Pantheon, 2006.

Stosch (von), Klaus. “Offenbarung und Vernunft in Islam und Christentum.” In *Herausforderung Islam*, edited by Anja Bettenworth, Andreas Funke, Mirja Lecke, and Klaus von Stosch, 100–30. Paderborn u.a.: Schöningh, 2011.

Tatari, Muna. *Gott und Mensch im Spannungsverhältnis von Gerechtigkeit und Barmherzigkeit. Versuch einer islamisch begründeten Positionsbestimmung*. Münster: Waxmann, 2016 (Graduiertenkolleg Islamische Theologie; 4).

Vasalou, Sophia. *Moral Agents and Their Deserts: The Character of Mu‘tazilite Ethics*. Princeton, NJ: Princeton University Press, 2008.

Weber, Anne. "Religion im postsäkularen Diskurs. Bemerkungen aus interreligiöser Perspektive." In *Religion, Öffentlichkeit, Moderne. Transdisziplinäre Perspektiven*, edited by Judith Könemann und Saskia Wendel, 257–88. Bielefeld: Transcript, 2016.

Wittgenstein, Ludwig. *Über Gewissheit.* Frankfurt a.M.: Suhrkamp, 1984.

Chapter 9

The Hermeneutical Approach of Shāṭibī on the Basis of the *Maqāṣid* Definition of Reason

Fundamental Issues of a Modern Reinterpretation

Mohammed Nekroumi

FAITH AND THE SEARCH FOR MEANING

The term *islām*, in its universal meaning of humanity's devotion to God's will, reveals the monotheistic character common to all three "religions of the book," its historical manifestation being expressed in the meaning of the term *dīn*. What is noteworthy is the fact that, according to traditional Islamic faith doctrines, the semantic content of the word *īmān* (faith) has a certain kinship with the term *dīn*, so far as the original lexical meaning of both the terms within the semantic fields of "trust" and "debt" can still be found in their theological-terminological meaning.[1] The concrete historical manifestation of faith by means of the proclamation of *sharīʿah* as divine world order describes, albeit incompletely, the covenant between God and humanity as a prescriptive relationship between command and obedience, which inevitably provides limits to casuistic interpretation. The three monotheistic world religions of Judaism, Christianity, and Islam view obedience vis-à-vis the *ius divinum* as recognition of the meaning of life imparted through proclamation. The irrevocable ambiguity of the term *dīn* not the least provides an explanation for the conception of a "debt of meaning" connected to its lexical meaning, a concept that is evident in the ways all three "religions of the book" portray laws of creation.

Within the framework of the theology of creation, the term *shariʿī*, from which the word *sharīʿah* is derived, means legal authority or legislation. The historical manifestation of faith through the proclamation of the *sharīʿah* describes, albeit imperfectly, the covenant between God and humanity dating from preexistence as a prescriptive relationship between command and obedience, which in turn poses natural limitations to casuistic interpretation.[2] God's entering the world by means of laws and doctrines is aimed at revealing the way (*sharī'ah*)[3] to Him. The intermediary signpost between what is worldly and what is divine is the attempt at a correct understanding (*fiqh*).[4] The process of understanding adds the necessary moral judgment to the mere regulatory character of a command or prohibition. However, correct moral judgment requires a thorough scrutiny of God's will within human existence, always being mindful that insights obtained in the process of *fiqh* can only ever lead to relative certainty when reaching a verdict.[5] The judgment (*ḥukm*) attained at the end of this process of realization driven by faith is reinforced through making reference to the four foundations stemming from divine revelation (*uṣūl*), ultimately making it true and morally "valid."

The role of reason and intellect in deducing these doctrines was briefly alluded to within the context of the hierarchical order of legal evidence as well as humanity's position regarding revelation. Unlike rational theology (*kalām*), which dealt with the symmetry of the relationship between reason and revelation within epistemological processes, the *maqāṣid* theory highlighted the instrumental role of reason as a path to God's intentions and as an authority for assessing worldly virtues.[6] Henceforth, many legal scholars were of the opinion that the quality of moral actions within the context of their execution is identifiable through common sense regarding a worldly judgment.[7]

More than almost any other school of thought within Islam's *fiqh* tradition, the *maqāṣid* theory contributed to the development of an Islamic ethical concept which discussed fundamental theological questions at length against the backdrop of the life of believers, and which systematized these questions. The following passages will provide an overview of the hermeneutical potential contained in the *maqāṣid* theory within the context of its historical development.

ETHICAL PRINCIPLES OF *SHARĪ'AH* FROM A PERSPECTIVE OF HISTORICAL CHANGE

The Issue of Justifiability

According to Aḥmad Dīb,[8] one of the most important and earliest stages in the development of the theory of *maqāṣid* was the approach of Abū al-Ma'ālī' 'Abd al-Mālik Ibn Abd Allāh Juwaynī, known as Imām al-Ḥaramayn (d. 478/1085). For the legal scholars of the postclassical era, Juwaynī's main oeuvre *al-Burhān fī Uṣūl al-Fiqh* replaced the former principal legal source, al-Shāfiʿī's *al-Risālah*, in its function as a manual for future generations. Al-Ghazālī is of the opinion that the commentary on *al-Risālah*, written by Juwaynī's father, represented a turning point regarding this work's scope of influence on the future development of legal theory. The influence of *al-Burhān* on the later fundamental science of *uṣūl al-fiqh* was further pursued by one of his students—none other than al-Ghazālī. Legal scholars now consider it as given that the way al-Ghazālī uses the term *maqāṣid* can be attributed to Juwaynī. Juwaynī was one of the first scholars to consciously include and analogically apply the term *maqāṣid* (intentions) as well as some of its synonyms, such as *al-aghrāḍ* (motives/objectives), in his analyses. Within this context, he justifies the meaning and importance of *maqāṣid* within the context of deducing commands and prohibitions from the *Qurʾān* as follows, "Those who disregard the intentions and objectives [of legislation] when deducing commands and prohibitions have failed to grasp the meaning of *sharīʿa*."[9]

However, the significance of *al-Burhān*, within the context of the development of the theory of *maqāṣid* in later jurisprudence, lies in the fact that within the framework provided by the categorization of the *ʿilal* (rationales of the *sharīʿah*), based on supposed legislative objectives and using the concept of *maqāṣid*, it attempts to differentiate between legislation supported by rational evidence and legislation lacking worldly justification (*aḥkām*).[10] Taking a closer look at Juwaynī's categorization, it becomes evident that his view of the legislative intentions certainly served as a theoretical foundation for the threefold categorization of ethical principles of the *sharīʿah* in *al-ḍarūriyāt* (necessary principles), *al-ḥājiyāt* (needs-based principles), and *al-taḥsīniyāt* (supplementary principles) developed within later legal theories. It appears obvious that the term *al-ḍarūriyāt al-kubrā* (the main principle of ethical behavior) coined by him was at the source of the necessary ethical principles of the *sharīʿah* of late Islamic jurisprudence. Thanks to al-Ghazālī's *al-Mustaṣfā*, the principles referred to as *al-ḍarūriyāt al-khamsa* (the five necessary principles) have been considered as a main part, or even cornerstone, of jurisprudence among advocates of the rational approach ever since the standardization period of the theory of intentions. This refers to five ethical principles that must be considered when deducing legal doctrines from textual sources. It follows that any *sharīʿah* legislation must be compatible with the following principles: *al-dīn* (protection of faith), *al-nafs* (protection of soul/self), *al-ʿaql* (protection of intellectual abilities/intellect), *al-nasl* (protection of reproduction), and *al-māl* (protection of property).

Al-Ghazālī's *al-Mustaṣfā* marked a turning point in *maqāṣid* research in the sense that this was the first time within the tradition of the approach that a systematization of the term was provided. According to al-Ghazālī's reasoning, ethical principles (*maqāṣid*) are encompassed by worldly interests and goods (*maṣāliḥ*). This led to the development of a hierarchy of *maṣāliḥ* based on their position within the predefined threefold grading of priorities: *al-ḍarūrāt* (necessities), *al-ḥājiyāt* (needs), and *al-taḥsīniyāt* (supplements).[11] Al-Ghazālī's particular focus was on the delicate nuances between these categories, in which he continually indicated that the deduction and classification of binding legal regulations (*al-aḥkām al-sharīʿah*) are to be preferred to the independent reaching of a verdict (*ijtihād*) by individual scholars. What is remarkable about al-Ghazālī's approach is his attempt at breaking new ground by categorizing ethical principles as universal legal sources,[12] highlighting the significance of the context of actions when deducing legal aspects.

The Binding Character of Theology and Rational Hierarchy of Ethical Principles

Approximately a century after al-Ghazālī, Sayf al-Dīn al-Āmidī (d. 631/1255)[13] took up his teachings and noticed the issue of providing a hierarchy of principles in light of their binding legal nature.[14] By means of his method of weighting (*tarjīḥ*), al-Āmidī, in his book *al-Iḥkām fī Uṣūl al-Aḥkām*, supplied a hierarchy of ethical *sharīʿah* principles based on an action theory; in his hierarchy, necessary principles (*al-maqāṣid al-ḍarūriyya*) superseded needs-based (*al-maqāṣid al-ḥājiya*) and supplementary (*al-maqāṣid al-taḥsīniya*) ethical principles when deducing norms. Legislative objectives based on human needs (*al-maqāṣid al-ḥājiya*) and those referring to unnecessary supplements (*al-maqāṣid al-taḥsīniya*) are awarded, respectively, second and third rank by al-Āmidī within the process of deducing legal aspects. The book *al-Iḥkām fī Uṣūl al-Aḥkām* also systematized necessary principles (*al-ḍarūriyāt*) and provided them with rational hierarchical subcategories.[15] Following his reasoning, the protection of reproduction (*al-nasl*) along with the protection of the soul (*al-nafs*) should be prioritized above the protection of intellectual abilities (*al-ʿaql*) and that of property (*al-māl*) when deducing legal norms of *sharīʿah*, as he was of the opinion that without reproduction and life it would be superfluous to consider intellectual abilities or property. The protection of faith (*ḥifẓ al-dīn*), on the other hand, bests all other *maqāṣid* principles and ranks number one in the hierarchy of reaching verdicts based on ethics deduced from principles.[16]

The development of the *maqāṣid* theory (*uṣūl al-fiqh*) pursued a relatively clear objective after al-Āmidī's death (d. 631/1255); this was to more clearly define the five necessary principles of ethical judgments (*al-ḍarūriyāt al-khamsa*), which, in principle, form the basis of deducing legal aspects in *sharīʿah* with regard to the everyday lives of people and to conduct research on them as objects of ethical reflection.[17] Ibn al-Ḥājib (d. 646/1248), for example, defended al-Āmidī's order of *ḍarūriyāt* from the point of view of human well-being. According to Ibn al-Ḥājib, the fundamental principles of an ethical approach to reaching a verdict should be considered in the following order when drawing up legislation: protection of faith (*al-dīn*), of the self/of life (*al-nafs*), of reproduction (*al-nasl*), of intellectual ability (*al-ʿaql*), and lastly, of property (*al-māl*). Yet most remarkable is Ibn al-Ḥājib's suggestion to prioritize fundamental rights vital to human existence over ritualistic duties of divine right should they happen to clash, as "unlike God only a human person can be damaged." In this case, requirements and duties that derive from the principle of faith may be given lesser priority in favor of protecting the self (*al-nafs*).[18] This way of thinking went hand in hand with a theological-hermeneutical concept of divine order, which lends a comprehensive and profound ethical character to the term *sharīʿah.*

Unfortunately, up until now, *fiqh* research as a whole has failed to devote interest in Ibn al-Ḥājib's theory, contrary to what it deserves. In a similar way, Bayḍāwī[19] (d. approx. 685/1286) and Isnawī[20] (d. 772/1370) later interpreted the ethical concept elaborated by al-Āmidī and al-Ghazālī, including it in the discussion on divine rights and human rights. In this context, they greatly advanced the process of sacralizing ethical principles. Toward the mid-eighth century, Ibn al-Subkī (d. 771/1369) added a sixth principle to the five necessary principles, the "protection of morality." However, due to the overlap with the principle of "protection of reproduction," it did not have an impact on the development of the *maqāṣid* theory. Qarāfī (d. 684/1285) classified the principle of protection of morality (*al-ʿirḍ)* as a subcategory of the "reproduction principle."[21] However, among the late Islamic legal scholars a number of researchers can be found, known as *al-fuqahā' al-uṣūliyūn*, who were both legal theorists and legal practitioners and whose innovative spirit raised new questions in the development of the *maqāṣid* theory. These were ʿIzz al-Dīn al-Sulamī Ibn Abdessalām (d. 660/1262), Qarāfī (d. 684/1285), Ibn Taymīyya (d. 728/1328), and Ibn al-Qayyim who, in addition to Shāṭibī, played a vital role in completing and perfecting the *maqāṣid* theory.

Fundamental Principles of the *Maqāṣid* Approach in the Mālikī School of Law

Unlike the Ḥanafī, Shafiʿī, and Ḥanbalī schools of law, which, respectively, are named after their famous founders Abū Ḥanīfa al-Nuʿmān (d. 151/767), Muḥammad Ibn Idrīs al-Shāfiʿī (d. 204/820), and Aḥmad Ibn Ḥanbal (d. 270/855), the Mālikī school of law refers to the academic institution of Mālik Ibn Anas (d. 179/795), of which he was a part of and may have systematized, but which he by no means founded. By referring back to the Medina scholars, who were his predecessors, Mālik demonstrates the large extent to which he owes his innovations and developments in the field of reaching independent verdicts (*ijtihādāt*) to earlier Medina scholars.[22] Ibn Farḥūn's *Dībāj* contains a detailed passage about Mālik's comments on the sources of his jurisprudential approaches.[23] According to Qāḍī Iyād's monumental oeuvre *Tartīb al-madārik*, the scholars Mālik based his *fiqh* conclusions on were none other than Zayd Ibn Thābit, and ʿAbdullāh Ibn ʿUmar,[24] whose jurisprudential deductions, according to Ibn Taymīyya, were directly based on ʿUmar Ibn al-Khaṭṭāb's practice (May Allah be pleased with him).[25] With the aim of legitimizing the authoritative and tradition-steeped character of the *maqāṣid* approach, its origins are directly based on ʿUmar's legal deliberations. Ibn Taymīyya, for example, confirms that the students of the so-called seven scholars of Medina imparted ʿUmar's deliberations, which were innovative at the time, to Mālik Ibn Anas.[26]

ʿUmar's legal opinions, which have been passed down by traditional history books, influenced the fundamental theoretical principles of the so-called Medina school of law and had a significant influence on the development of the theological principles underlying Mālikī law.[27] Ibn Taymīyya's statements in this regard left no doubt that the Mālikī school of law derived its legal foundations from what would later be called *madhhab ahl al-madīna* (Medina Theory of Law). The fact that Ibn Taymīyya did not belong to the Mālikī school leaves no doubt as to his statements regarding the relationship between the Mālikī school and the Medinan legal approach.[28] Taking a closer look at the texts on Mālikī law—which were written just after Mālik's time, for example the very old fragment on the topic of pilgrimage (*hajj*) by Ibn al-Mājishūn (d. 164/780) which was found in Kairouan in 1985[29] or the legal compendia of Abū Muṣʿab al-Zuhrī (d. 242/856) and Ibn Abd al-Ḥakam (d. 214/829)—it becomes apparent that these texts are mainly comprised of abstract cases and rules with only rare references to the theoretical conclusions that could be drawn from them. On one hand, this phenomenon can be explained from a theological point of view by taking into consideration its historical closeness to the time of revelation. On the other hand, the lack of interest in conceptual work can be explained by the fact that the social reality of the time hardly raised any questions that would have required urgent reflection in order to formulate a comprehensive approach to social ethics.

Mālik Ibn Anas' and Mājishūn's texts contain references to the *Qurʾān* and the *sunna*, the difference being that Mālik evokes both *aḥadīth* [traditions (singular: *ḥadīth*)] of the Prophet and the tradition of the Prophet's companions. This led the late *fuqahā'* to consider his legal tracts a continuation of the so-called *fiqh al-madīna* (Medinan legal tradition) or even *al-fiqh al-ʿumarī* (ʿUmar's legal deliberations). Fully aware that the oral tradition of the Prophet (peace and blessings be upon him) is the most credible from a theological point of view and the most relevant Qur'anic exegesis for the day-to-day life of believers at the time, Mālik includes almost no direct references to the *Qur'ān* itself in his legal interpretations. What he does include is his own opinion on the prophetic interpretation of the *Qur'ān*. Ibn Mājishūn, one of the scholars transmitting *aḥadīth*, considered himself obliged to provide evidence by means of Qur'anic quotes, followed by Prophetic *aḥadīṯh*, in his legal tracts. He was convinced of a certain sacred nature of tradition and hence often referred back to a number of authorities when justifying his own legal doctrines.[30] In the Mālikī legal tradition, the development of the *maqāṣid* theory cannot be traced back systematically and diachronically because no linear development can be established for Mālikī legal writings, concerning well-known legal theories.

The further development of the *maqāṣid* approach based on the justification principle of *ta'līl* (the effective cause of rulings) in the intellectual history and evolution of Malikism, questions the theory of some modern scholars.[31]According to this concept, Islamic law was not characterized by a straightforward evolution in the direction of the well-known *uṣūl al fiqh*, that is, *Qur'ān, sunna, ijmā'*, and *qiyās*. This fact, once again, highlights the assumption this chapter is based on; any process of theorization in Islamic legal history was developed in the process of socio-ethical, context-bound issues. This highlights the necessity of working out fundamental key concepts related to the *maqāṣid* approach, for example tracing the theory of justifiability *(naẓariyyat al-ta'līl)* back to a non-Mālikī source with regards to possible parallel genealogies, employing a trans-scholastic approach.[32]

The development stages of the *maqāṣid* approach in Islamic legal history presented in this brief historical overview clearly indicate the dynamic nature of Islamic theology and also highlight the particular significance of reconsidering tradition within a process of ethical approaches to reaching verdicts regarding social change. Shāṭibī's work *al-Muwāfaqāt* highlights the issue of a socio-ethical reconsideration of Islamic law more than almost any other classical Islamic oeuvre. The following passage aims to work out prospects and outlooks of a hermeneutical reconsideration of the term *maqāṣid* in contemporary *sharī'ah* discourse by putting Islamic ethics within its creation theology-based context.

SHARĪ'AH'S PLACE WITHIN *MAQĀṢID* ETHICS

Sharī'ah's World Order Based on Creation Theology

Al-Sharī'ah represents a divine legal order. Legal opinion considers judicial sources handed down, not devised by reason, but in the case of the *Qur'ān*, revealed to Muslims, and in the case of the *ḥadīṯh* tradition, collected and passed on. According to legal scholars, the clear support for divine revelation taking priority over reason stems from the fact that human beings require reliable information in order to assess moral behavior, with its complex involvement in human actions.[33] The very fact that it can only see what derives from its own approach means that *a priori* reason cannot produce *fiqh* knowledge. This leads to a kind of dialectical relationship between revelation and reason, which appears to be subject to a double principle of determination, meaning the interpretative process links *fiqh* to the hermeneutical understanding of a discourse by means of the interdependency of a part and the whole. Human beings can only understand the part of the divine legal order which God has endowed an understanding of upon him or her via his or her "disposition" (*fiṭra*). However, when it comes to the relationship between disposition and duty, this can only be considered by indicating the reciprocate interconnection of human moral responsibility and the meaningfulness of a human's existence. The idea of "being created for something" (fiṭra) as a key concept of an ethical focus suspends the dichotomy or "division" of revelation and reason.

Unlike the interpretation provided by determinist rational theology, according to which being created for something represents an antithesis to predetermination, Ibn ʿAshūr,[34] following Shāṭibī's concept of *maqāṣid*, highlights God's statement that indicates created inherent innocence as God's "blueprint" for creation:

> So set thou thy face steadily and truly to the faith: (Establish) Allah's handiwork according to the pattern on which He has made mankind: No change (let there be) in the work (wrought) by Allah: that is the standard religion: But most among mankind understand not.[35]

Caught Between Creation for Something and Duty

From the point of view of the *maqāṣid* approach, humanity's "pre-created nature" stems from an intentional act of God, which takes place according to the covenant (*mīthāq*) concluded between God and his creation in preexistence and which is expressed in the Ḥanafī concept of "original monotheism."[36] In combination with the context of living conditions, *sharīʿah* sources represent clues for interpretation, which form the backdrop of the process of rediscovering one's *fiṭra*. By considering *fiṭra* an order to act, intentionalist legal methodology rejected the conflict between advocates of predestination and advocates of free will, purported by rational theology.[37] The paradox according to which being created for something is to represent an objective as such, while continuing to pursue a different objective as point of departure of the act of creation, would be resolved by the logic of understanding the path of a believer, not necessarily as a forward movement (toward a human being's unknown future), which he or she has no power over anyway, but as a backward movement toward the origin of his or her state of faith.[38] Both aspects can be clearly identified in the definition of being created for something, as put forward by the early theologian Ghailān al-Dimashqī. According to him, *fiṭra,* as primary inherent knowledge of God, is distinct from the *created innocence* imparted by revelation.[39] According to Ghailān al-Dimashqī's theological deliberations, intellect plays a major role in the context of discovering the precreated knowledge of God, a position later upheld by Mu'tazilite theology.[40]

By putting *fiṭra* on one level with intellect as a means of discovering the divine order of creation, intentionalist approaches to legal interpretation appear fairly close to Mu'tazilite concepts. However, later jurisprudence was vehemently opposed to the Mu'tazilite concept of rational theology and natural ethics, as intellect as such was awarded a highly nuanced function in legal theory, making the notional world of the Holy Scripture its main field of application.[41]

Divine Right between Revelation and Reason

According to Shāṭibī's concept of ethics, intellect is in itself obedient to God in the sense that it is this that directs human beings to God, and in the sense that intellect alone allows human beings to perceive God's message directed at them.[42] The limits of human intellect, with respect to the transcendental world of revelation, stem from the obligations of mortal and worldly disposition that the reality of human actions is subject to, *kullukum min ādam wa-ādam min turāb* (You people all descend from Adam and Adam originates from the earth).[43] Human beings only disobey divine laws because, following their own emotions, they misunderstand God's intention behind His creation and lose sight of the divine order of things. Yet, with the realization that the *sharī'ah* law of action corresponds to God's point of view, the burden connected to implementing this law diminishes and human beings once again "live based on their inherent own creation focused on God." To their knowledge, human beings are obliged to follow divine moral stipulations and therefore must adopt a position regarding this fact, either by complying with the obligation or by disregarding it: "Whoever works righteousness benefits his own soul; whoever works evil, it is against his own soul: Nor is thy Lord ever unjust (in the least) to His servants."[44] Here, the issue of moral behavior seems directly connected to appreciating the unequal relationship between *disposition* and *obligation.* While all four schools of law share the opinion that, according to the covenant between God and the descendants of Adam, respecting the divine legal order is solely a human trait, the relationship between being created for something and being obliged to something in the process of the implementation of religious-ethical guidelines and the ideals of public welfare for the entire human existence contained in them is far from uncontroversial in the context of rational-theological interpretation.[45]

This discursive interpretation of obligation (*taklīf*), maintained by legal theorists, opens up a hermeneutical perspective, which allows for a transition of the allegedly finalized status of being created for something, to a dynamic process of responsibility. The intentionalist theory of legal order corresponds with a theory of ethics that primarily focuses on the notion of responsibility, referring to people being created for something to complement the theory.[46]

THEOLOGICAL IDEALS OF PUBLIC WELFARE IN RELATION TO RATIONAL VALUE JUDGMENTS

The Practical Focus of Islamic Ethics

Based on the discursive relationship between intellect and the Holy Scripture implied by the notion of intent, Shāṭibī not only developed a theory of ethics which was capable of legally categorizing social and worldly reality, he also formulated a theosophical concept which, based on the fruitful discussions between mystics, theologians, and legal scholars, pursued an ethical reform based on a reciprocal relationship between the image of humanity in the *Qur'ān* and social welfare. However, the fact that Shāṭibī determines the reasons for the existence of the *sharī'ah* by means of the three legal categories *al-ḍarūriyāt, al-ḥajiyāt,*[47] and *al-taḥsīniyāt* by no means implies that he considered the development of a worldly ethical approach in a contemporary sense,[48] as his approach was intended to guarantee that the interests of believers are upheld in the here and now and in the hereafter and that God acts in the best interest of His subjects.

The *ḥājiyāt* imply those legal aspects that are necessary in order to alleviate the hardships of the law, meaning the law can be obeyed without grief or difficulties. Shāṭibī names the particulars of trade law as an example. The *taḥsīniyāt* (improvements/complimentary principles) in turn are subordinate to the *ḥājiyāt*. As they are not connected to necessities, the functioning of the law is guaranteed without their influence. Prime examples in this context are the freeing of slaves, generosity toward the poor or conduct in public locations, as is outlined in a remarkable fashion in the last part of the Luqmān testament *waṣiyyat Luqmān* in the Holy *Qur'ān*:

> O my son! Establish regular prayer, enjoin what is just, and forbid what is wrong; and bear with patient constancy whatever betide thee; for this is firmness (or purpose) in (the conduct of) affairs (17). And swell not thy cheek (for

> pride) at men, nor walk in insolence through the earth: for Allah loveth not any arrogant boaster (18). And be moderate in thy pace, and lower thy voice; for the harshest of sounds without doubt is the braying of the ass (19).[49]

In general, these three categories form the *raison d'être* of law, and therefore their hierarchical order in terms of influencing practical life is to remain unaffected.

Transcending the Worldly

As opposed to the Aristotelian worldly concept of norms, theological legal scholarship must always take into consideration the notion of actions and their consequences on people's fate in the hereafter. Reflecting on "true" divine intentions can help to achieve a better assessment of the consequences of an action on the fate of the person in the hereafter and therefore indicate the appropriate way to repentance and atonement in the here and now. The fact that the aspect of legal objectives focused on the hereafter plays a key role in Shāṭibī's argument clearly shows that his *maqāṣid* theory is not one of the ethical approaches based on the dichotomy of "good vs. evil," so popular with theologians. Shāṭibī's legal tracts are more characterized by an Ashʿarite view, which ascribes *relational* status to predicates such as "good" and "evil," depriving them of any characteristic of entities.[50] The *ḍarūriyāt*, which aim to protect faith, life, reproduction, property, and intellectual abilities, refer to those ethical aspects which, within the framework of a relational dynamic, are essentially necessary for the regulation of all worldly aspects of existence, with the aim of achieving happiness in the here and now and (to be noted) the hereafter.[51] Here, the notion of a happiness transcending worldly existence, first, represents the duality between body and soul, faith and reason, finite and eternal, as a continuum, which comes close to the true notion of religion as the unity of what is divine and what is human.[52]

Sharīʿah as an Expression of Righteousness and Care

In his rational-theological approach, al-Rāzī determines that God, thanks to His character trait of wisdom (*ḥakīm*), which is recognized by all Muslims, acts solely to bring about a specific interest. Anything other than this would mean that God acts arbitrarily (*ʿābith*). However, holy scriptures, consensus, and reason contradict this assertion.[53] As far as the rational justification of the *sharīʿah* (*ta'līl* procedure) is concerned, the Ashʿarite al-Rāzī clearly advocates a Muʿtazilite opinion, which is vehemently opposed to ascribing arbitrariness and fault to God's actions. As far as textual proof explicitly advocating the *ta'līl* principle is concerned, al-Rāzī quotes a number of Qur'anic verses which describe the revelation of the divine message as *raḥma*[54] (God's mercy), *yusr* (alleviation), or *taskhīr*[55] (disposition of creation in support of humanity).

The link between *maqāṣid* (intentions) and *aḥkām* (legal doctrines) based on God's mercy, which al-Rāzī and Shāṭibī developed, poses a methodological and a theological challenge to modern theology. Only a hermeneutically and theologically sound reflection on the links between deontology (character of obligation) and teleology (objective) in Islamic ethics would make this challenge comprehensible. The foundation of such an approach is a concept of Islamic ethics that encompasses both the focus of God's divine plan for humanity and the conditions under which it becomes reality. The key question of such an approach should be how God's mercy and God's justice can be compatible with a coherent system of morality and which role terms such as care, God's compassion and causality play in the connection between *maqāṣid* and *aḥkām*. By raising this issue, Shāṭibī highlighted the role of theological public utility (*maṣlaḥa)* as the ultimate objective and end point of a theological-ethical approach.

Following this system of classification, the theological-ethical focus of the *sharīʿah* could be determined in two ways: on the one hand, based on the transcendental faith-oriented pursuit of the eschatological salvation, which it is primarily in aid of, and, on the other, its moral requirements which offer practical guidance for life and actions to the community of believers. Shāṭibī's *maqāṣid* approach clearly shows that transcendence and immanence here and now and in the hereafter are essential factors of, and linked to, the legislator's intentions.

CONCLUSION

The five ethical principles of the *sharīʿah* represent the theological framework for moral behavior, and adhering to them follows a faith-oriented reflection of what is best for the community. The *sharīʿah* can ultimately be considered to be a mission which is not limited to *managing* mortality. The ethical principles of the *sharīʿah* are essentially concerned with actively organizing our lives as believers and about viewing ourselves based on the Qur'anic message, which guides us toward a certain end to history. *Sharīʿah* hermeneutics' main duty must be to influence individual and public life against the backdrop of faith-oriented reflection, which balances out reason and revelation, divine and human. This once again raises the issue of the changeability of *sharīʿah* norms. In order to highlight the ethical focus of the *sharīʿah* within the context of a contemporary epistemological framework, we require an interpretation of sources which places ethical principles within the context of a current understanding of the realities of life and actions (*fiqh al-wāqiʿ*).

This chapter has outlined and discussed the main features of the *maqāṣid* theory with reference to different influences over the course of several centuries. The remaining concluding passage is intended to focus in more detail on the relationship between abstract legal-theoretical discourse and worldly reality, which has strongly influenced form, substance, and focus of the intentionalist approach.

Shāṭibī's legal theory should be considered from the point of view of the interplay of theory and practical implementation not only because it presents a clue to understanding this important relationship, but also because this theory represents the intellectual culmination of a development which was evident as early as the fourth/tenth century. Back then, legal theory had gained such a high level of substance that a new focus was possible, while at the same time maintaining its traditional function—the identification and continuous renewal of legislation. The unique character of Shāṭibī's theory stems from the fact that legislation in place up until the eighth/fourteenth century could not match that century's socioeconomic changes in Andalusia, which led to the aspiration for this legal theory to provide answers to the problems of the time and thus to adapt legislation to new social conditions. In this context, it is worth highlighting that the success of Shāṭibī's theory cannot be seen as linked to a desire for flexibility and adaptability of positive legislation. On the contrary, Shāṭibī's theory with all its "insincerity" and its new character was aimed at reestablishing "true legislation," a legislation which had been neglected by some legal scholars on the one hand and abused excessively by some Sufis, including some legal scholars, on the other.

The subject of discussion of this publication, that is, the relationship between theory and practical implementation in the Islamic discipline of *fiqh*, makes the theory of the objectives of the *sharīʿah* the focal point of theological interest by highlighting its epistemological and methodological potential for the modern debate about a renewal of Islamic thought.

NOTES

1. See the definition of *dīn* in: *The Encyclopaedia of Islam*, fascs. 27–29, Volume II, 293, Leiden, 1963.

2. According to F. W. Graf, fundamental interfaith similarities can be found examining the process of understanding divine creational law. "Particularly as in the three monotheistic 'world religions' of Judaism, Christianity and Islam symbol memory reservoirs dating back thousands of years contain concepts of an *ius divinum* which closely link two religious patterns of imagination by means of metaphors of high suggestive power still bearing significance for the present: God as creator and God as legislator." (cf. Friedrich Wilhelm Graf, *Moses Vermächtnis (Moses' Legacy)*, Munich 2006, 22f.) In Rabbinic Judaism, Ḥalakha, just like *sharīʿah*, is understood as guidance "leading human beings in their actions by means of divine revelation,"

cf. Thomas Amberg, *Auf dem Weg zu neuen Prinzipien islamischer Ethik* (*Discovering New Principles of Islamic Ethics*), Würzburg 2010, 29–32; and Stefan Schreiner, *Die jüdische Bibel in islamischer Auslegung* (*The Jewish Bible In Its Islamic Interpretation*), Tübingen 2012.

3. The word's original meaning, that is, "path to the trough," is still contained in its terminological meaning, insofar as some scholars still understand *al-sharīʿah* in the sense of a path to salvation.

4. Cf. A. Kevin Reinhart, *Islamic Law as Islamic Ethics*, *Journal of Religious Ethics*, 11, no. 2 (1983): 186–203. As a reminder, *fiqh* is either translated as "Islamic Jurisprudence" or as "Positive Law." This usually refers to the process of bringing about understanding and insight with regards to a decision and which draws on the four legislative sources mentioned earlier, when reaching a verdict. The deduction of legal doctrines from textual sources is the subject matter of the field of *uṣūl al-fiqh* (legal methodology), also referred to as Legal Theory or Fundamental Science.

5. Absolute certainty in what is hidden within things is a solely divine privilege, according to al-Shāfiʿī.

6. The question of to what extent a connection is created between reason, on the one hand, and revelation, on the other, in order to prevent divine order from becoming nothing more than a matter of individual faith is a fundamental issue of theology, cf. e.g. George Makdisi, *Religion, Law and Learning in Classical Islam*, Hampshire 1991, IV, 62.

7. In the fourth Islamic century, Islamic intellectuals split into advocates of sufficient knowledge for assessing moral actions existing and those wanting to refocus on original Islamic sources, that is, the sources of Islamic Jurisprudence listed above.

8. This is the editor of Juwaynī's *'al-Burhān.'*

9. Cf. ʻAbd al-Mālik ibn ʻAbd Allāh al-Juwaynī, *Al-Burhān fī ʾuṣūl al-fiqh*, Cairo 1980, II, 294f.

10. This analysis was included in the chapter dedicated to analogy (*al-qiyās*). The distinction between *maqāṣid* and *ʿilal* aims to assess the practicability of analogy in legislation, cf. ibid., 923–64.

11. Abū Ḥāmid Muḥammad al-Ghazālī, *Kitāb al-Mustaṣfā min ʿilm al-uṣūl, s.l., s.a.*, I, 286–93.

12. Ibid., I, 325.

13. Toward the end of the fifth century, Fakhr al-Dīn Rāzī's (d. 606/1209) *al-Maḥsūl* provided new justification for *sharīʿa* and thus fresh impetus for the *maqāṣid* theory, protecting it from *ta'līl* opponents, cf. Jamāl al-Dīn al-Isnawī, *Nihāyat as-sūl fī sharḥ min hāj al-wūṣūl*, Cairo 1943, I, 4.

14. Cf. Bernard G. Weiss, *The Search for God's Law. Islamic Jurisprudence in the Writings of Sayf al-Dīn al-Āmidī*, Salt Lake City 1992.

15. Sayf al-Dīn al-Āmidī, *al-Iḥkām fī Uṣūl al-Aḥkām*, Beirut, 1983, IV, 380.

16. Cf. ibid., 377; also cf. Bernard G. Weiss, ed., *Studies in Islamic Legal Theory*, Leiden 2002.

17. This is based on the assumption that we are able to discover the intention behind divine legislation. The connection between divine intention and the experience of believers in everyday life goes back to al-Ghazālī (d. 505/1111), who evaluated

the analogy of *qiyās* as a positive method of legal deduction by putting forward the argument that achieving public well-being represents a necessity (*ḍarūra*). According to him, the objectives of the *sharī'a* can be classified into three categories: (1). *al-ḍarūrāt* (necessities), (2). *al-ḥājiyyāt* (needs), and (3). *al-taḥsīnyāt* (improvements/embellishments).

18. Cf. Abū 'Amr 'Uthmān Ibn al-Ḥājib, *Muntahā al-wuṣūl wa l-'amal fī 'ilm ay al-'uṣūl wa l-jadal*, Beirut 1985, 182f.

19. Cf. Nāṣir al-Dīn 'Abdullāh Ibn 'Umar al-Bayḍāwī, *Minhāj al-wuṣūl 'ilā 'ilm al-uṣūl*, Khartoum 1980, IV, 75.

20. Cf. Jamāl al-Dīn al-Isnawī, *Nihāyat as-sūl fī sharḥ min hāj al-wūṣūl*, Cairo 1943, IV, 82ff.

21. Cf. Shihāb ad-Dīn al-Qarāfī, *Sharḥ tanqīḥ al-fuṣūl fī ikhtiṣār al-maḥṣūl fī l-uṣūl*, Cairo 1973, 391.

22. Cf. Mālik Ibn Anas, *al-Muwaṭṭa'*, 70.

23. Cf. Burhān ad-Dīn Abū al-Fidā' Ibrāhīm Ibn Muḥammad Ibn Farḥūn, *Al-Dībāj al-mudhahhab fīma 'rifata'yān 'ulamā' al-madhab*, Beirut s.a., 25ff.

24. Cf. al-Qāḍī 'Iyāḍ, *Tartīb al-madārik wa-taqrīb al-masālik li-ma'rifat'a'lā maḏhab mālik,* Rabat, s.a., I, 77.

25. Following Ibn Taymīyya's assumption, Omar's legal deductions were first passed on to the so-called seven legal scholars of Medina: Sa'īd Ibn al-Musayyab, 'Urwa Ibn az-Zubair, al-Qāsim Ibn Moḥammad Ibn Abī Bakr as-Ṣiddīq, 'Ubaid Allāh Ibn 'Abd Allāh Ibn 'Utbah, Ḫārija Ibn Zayd, Sulaymān Ibn Yassār, and, lastly, Sālim Ibn 'Abd Allāh Ibn'Umar Ibn al-Khaṭṭāb, cf. Ibn Taymīyya, *Majmū' al-fatāwī*, XX, 312–13.

26. His statement in this regard is unambiguous:
"ويقال: إن مالكا أخذ جل الموطأ عن ربيعة، وربيعة عن سعيد بن المسيب، وسعيد بن المسيب عن عمر، وعمر محدث." This article is published for the first time in English.

27. Cf. Ibn Taymīyya, *Majmū' al-fatāwī*, XX, 294–396.

28. On the Arabic quotations earlier on cf. ibid., XX, 312–28.

29. Cf. M. Muranyi, *Ein altes Fragment medinensischer Jurisprudenz aus Qairawān* (*An Old Fragment of Medinan Jurisprudence from Qairawān*), Stuttgart 1985, 46.

30. Cf. M. Muranyis Edition (1985: 47–75).

31. Cf. Jonathan E. Brockopp, *Competing Theories of Authority in Early Maliki Texts*, Leiden 2002, 3–22.

32. The trans-scholastic, epistemological relations that can be established in this context point to a dialectical process between sources which are based on *Qur'ān* and *sunna* as legitimization and others which seek different forms of legitimization, for example by way of the personality of a great scholar. In this context, adherence to a specific theological school plays a key role. J. Brockopp assumes the existence of further parallel concepts in addition to the linear concept of "authoritative ideas," which he calls "Salvation History Theory," further highlighting the need for a reconsideration in light of this rich tradition, cf. Bernard G. Weiss, ed., *Studies in Islamic Legal Theory*, Leiden 2002, 34; Mohammed Nekroumi, *Qur'āninterpretation im Kontext intentionalistischer Rechtstheorien* (*Qur'ānic Interpretation in the Context of Intentionalist Legal Theories*), Hamburg 2009, 153–96.

33. Legal scholars' clear vote for revelation taking priority over reason is often linked to skepticism and distrust regarding pure human reasoning, which was characteristic of the late phase of oral transmission, the latter being based on a fear of speculative thinking, which in turn was based on weak transmission links.

34. Cf. Ibn ʿAshūr, *Maqāṣid al-sharīʿah al-islāmiyya*, new edition, Dār as-salām, Cairo, 2005, 54.

35. *Qurʾān* 30:30. In his Qurʾānic exegesis (*al-Kashāf*), al-Zamakhsharī interprets the term *fiṭra* as an inherent ability to surrender oneself to God's will (*Islām*) as well as a predisposition to monotheistic belief, something which was proclaimed as early as in the early stages of the Abrahamic religions. This is illustrated by the Qurʾānic verse 42: 13, "*The same religion has He established for you as that which He enjoined on Noah—that which We have sent by inspiration to thee—and that which We enjoined on Abraham, Moses, and Jesus: Namely, that ye should remain steadfast in religion, and make no divisions therein: To those who worship other things than Allah, hard is the (way) to which thou callest them. Allah chooses to Himself those whom He pleases, and guides to Himself those who turn (to Him).*"

36. Van Ess points out (1975: 106) that the theologian al-Ḥasan al-Baṣrī (d. 124/742) was one of the first advocates of free will who likened the term *fiṭra* to original monotheism in order to put an end to the predeterministic interpretation of the verse (30:30), as it appears difficult to reconcile free will of human beings with a predetermined created "good" nature (cf. Van Ess, *Zwischen Ḥadīṯ und Theologie. Studien zum Entstehen prädestinatianischer Überlieferung* (Between Ḥadīṯ and Theology. Studies on the Development of Pre-Deterministic Transmission), Berlin 1975).

37. In order to avoid the question of how nonbelief can be predetermined if human beings are inherently faithful and good, some predeterminist theologians felt forced to limit *fiṭra* to a specific point in time (intellectual maturity) or a specific group (the time of the Prophet's companions), cf. Shaibānī 189/805 or Ibn al-Mubārak 181/797 cf. Josef van Ess, Zwischen Ḥadīṯ und Theologie. Studien zum Entstehen prädestinatianischer Überlieferung (Between Ḥadīṯ and Theology. Studies on the Development of Pre-Deterministic Transmission), Berlin 1975, 107–8.

38. In this context, Islamic exegesis, for example, emphasizes that the prophetic biographies and stories contained in the *Qurʾān* are only to be understood retrospectively in a particular way. The stories contained in the *Qurʾān* transmitted as "narrative quasi-past" include concepts, expectations, and anticipations by means of which the people portrayed in the narration focus on their mortal future by making use of the so-called *ʿibar* (maxims for life). This notion of a future anticipation of the past is common in Muslim (e.g., with al-Zamakhsharī, up to Sayyid Quṭb) as well as Christian tradition, yet showing differences between both traditions, the extensive nature of which means they cannot be covered as part of this chapter.

39. This would mean that the *fiṭra*'s ambiguity as postulated in *Tahḏīb Tāʾrīkh Dimashq*, III. 177 excludes a paraphrasist relationship between the Qurʾānic verse (30:30) and the famous *fiṭra* hadith *"Every child is created in a state of pre-created innocence; it is only its parents which make it a Jew, a Christian or a magician"* (Bukhārī collection no. 3) from the very start; cf. Van Ess (1975: 106).

40. cf. al-Qāḍī ʿAbd al-Jabbār, *Tanzīh al-qurʾān*, 153, 12 ff., al-Zamaḫšarī, *al-Minhāj fī ʿulūm al-dīn*.

41. On Shāṭibī's concept of reason, cf. MU, DK, I, 61 and MU, Kairo, II, 31. The following analytical section will address this in more detail.

42. This sometimes means that *sharīʿa* does not simply require an act of declaration by the believer or is only valid for him by means of faith. It follows that the path to God must be directly and indirectly embedded in intellect, cf. among others Tillman Nagel, *Das islamische Recht* (*Islamic Law*), Westhofen 2001, 13–15.

43. The original philosophical approaches to this notion go as far back as Aristotle's definition of human actions as *mimèsis*, imitation, subject to the constraint of our being embedded in the world (cf. Aristote, *La Poétique*, French transl. Charles Batteux, VI, 1450 a 7, 15–19, Paris 1874).

44. *Qurʾān* 41:46.

45. Tradition saw the emergence of two fundamental tendencies. The first one is based on the assumption that human beings must act morally because of an inherent *disposition* and ability in their nature, while the second hypothesis presumes that human beings must act morally based on an external *order*, or in other words based on an external *obligation* (*taklīf*).

46. On the notion of responsibility cf. Georg Picht, *Wahrheit, Vernunft, Verantwortung. Philosophische Studien* (*Truth, Reason, Responsibility. Philosophical Studies*), Stuttgart 1969, 318.

47. Cf. MU, II, 5, Cairo as well as MU, II, 7, Cairo.

48. According to a certain philosophical convention, we are inclined to reserve the term "ethics" to a focus on a fulfilled life, modeled after the Aristotelian definition of the so-called *eupraxis* (right action). It follows that *eupraxis* is "an aim in itself" (NE, VI, 1140b 6), while *poièsis* and its corresponding poetic science "has an aim outside of itself," Aristoteles, N. E., I, 1, 1094a, 1–3. The essays by Wolfhart Pannenberg (1967), *Grundfragen systematischer Theologie* (*Fundamental Issues of Systematic Theology*), illustrate the influence of the Aristotelian heritage on Christian theology in an excellent way. M. Fakhry's (1991): *Ethical Theories in Islam* on the other hand does not address the comparison between Islamic and Western sources in detail.

49. *Qurʾān* 31: 17–19.

50. The term "*relational* status," as used in this chapter, is based on the causal-theoretical hypothesis of the so-called *accidents*. Accident (*al-ʿaraḍ*) refers to any alterable characteristic of an otherwise stable medium (substance or essence, Arab.: *al-jawhar*). According to the Asharite concept, God acts based on a momentary state of the world (*occasio*) in order to create the next state, cf. D. Perler & U. Rudolph, *Occasionalismus* (*Occasionalism*), Göttingen 2000, 116. It should be added to the view upheld by D. Perler & U. Rudolph that with the notion of *accidents* the Asharites aimed to underpin their assumption that God's omnipotence does not interfere with human causality inherent in actions, responsible for evoking characteristics, such as good and bad inclinations, because of their interconnection with interactive actions.

51. MU, II, 9–10, Cairo.

52. This refers to a characteristic which, according to Hegel, stems from the *un-polemic notion* of religion, cf. M. Häussler: *Der Religionsbegriff in Hegels,*

"Phänomenologie des Geistes" (*The Notion of Religion in Hegel's "Phenomenology of Spirit"*), Munich 2008, 116–17.

53. Islamic philosophy as well as Islamic jurisprudence rejected the idea of ascribing arbitrariness to God's actions. The philosophical approach has adopted an extratextual concept of causality and jurisprudence adopted discursive analogy.

54. *Qur'ān* 16, 89/2, 29 etc.

55. *Qur'ān* 22, 65/22, 78 etc.

BIBLIOGRAPHY

Abū Zayd, Hamid. *Mafhūm an-naṣṣ*. Dirāsa fī 'ulūm al-Qur'ān. Casablanca: n.p., 1990.

Al-Āmidī, Sayf al-Dīn. *Al-Iḥkām fī uṣūl al-aḥkām*. Beirut: Dār al-Kutub al-'Ilmīyah, 1983.

al-'Asadabādī, 'Abd al-Jabbār. *Al-Mughnī fī abwāb al-tawḥīd wa al-'adl*. Cairo, s.a.

Al-Bayḍāwī, Nāṣir al-Dīn 'Abd Allāh Ibn 'Umar. *Minhāj al-wuṣūl 'ilā 'ilm al-uṣūl*. Khartoum: 1980.

———. *Al-Mankhūl min ta'līqāt al-uṣūl*. Damascus: n.p., 1980.

Al-Isnawī, Jamāl al-Dīn. *Nihāyat al-sūl fī sharḥ minhāj al-wūṣūl*. Cairo: al-Maktabah al-Azharīyah lil-Turāth, 1943.

Al-Juwaynī, 'Abd al-Malik ibn 'Abd Allāh Imām al-Ḥaramayn. *Al-Burhān fī uṣūl al-fiqh*. Cairo: n.p., 1980.

Al-Qarāfī, Shihāb ad-Dīn. *Sharḥ tanqīḥ al-fuṣūl fī 'khtiṣār al-maḥṣūl fī l-uṣūl*. Edited by 'Abdar-Ra'ūf Sa'd Ṭaha. Cairo: Maktabat al-Kullīyāt al-Azharīyah, 1973.

Al-Shāfi'ī, Abū 'Abdallāh Muḥammad Ibn Idrīs. *Al-Risālah*. Edited by Sayyid Kilānī. Cairo: n.p., 1969.

Al-Shāṭibī, Abū Isḥāq Ibrāhīm Ibn Mūsā. *Al-'Itiṣām*. Maktabat al-Riyāḍ al-Ḥadīṭah, s.l., s.a.

———. *Al-Mūwāfaqāt fī uṣūl al-shari'ah*. Edited by 'Abd'Allāh Darrāz, Muḥammad and A. Abd al-shāfī, Muḥammad. Beirut: Dār al-Kutub al-Ilmiyah, 2003.

———. *Al-Mūwāfaqāt fī uṣūl al-sharī'ah*, 'Abd al-Ḥamīd, Moḥammad Muḥyī al-dīn (Ed.), Cairo, s.a.

Amberg, Thomas. *Auf dem Weg zu neuen Prinzipien islamischer Ethik* (*Discovering New Principles of Islamic Ethics*). Wurzburg: n.p., 2010, 29–32 u.

———. "Pour une histoire réflexive de la pensée islamique. Sharī'a, Fiqhet critique de la Raison Juridique." Review and Commentary by Bernard G. Weiss, ed., *Studies in Islamic Legal Theory*, Arabica LI (fascicule 3, 2004). Leiden: Brill, 2004.

Aristote. *La Poétique*. Translation by Charles Batteux, Delalin, Paris, 1874.

Arkoun, Mohammed. *Pour une critique de la raison islamique*. Paris: Maisonneuve et Larose, 1984.

Brockopp, Jonathan E. "Competing Theories of Authority in Early Maliki Texts". In *Studies in Islamic Legal Theory*, edited by Bernard G. Weiss, 3–22, Leiden: Brill, 2002.

Brunschvig, Robert. "Herméneutique normative dans le judaisme et dans l'Islam." In *Études sur l'Islam classique et l'Afrique du Nord Turki*, edited by Abdel-Magid Turki. London: Ashgate Publishing, 1986.

Calder, N. "Ikhtilāf and Ijmā' in Shāfi'is's Risāla." *Studia Islamica* 63 (1983): 55–81.

Fakhry Majid. *Ethical Theories in Islam*. Leiden: Brill, 1991.

Ghazālī, Abū Ḥāmid. *Al-Mustaṣafā min 'ilm al-ušūl*. S.l., s.a.

Goldziher, Ignaz. "The Principles of Law in Islam. In The Historian's History of the Word." In *The Historians' History of the World: VIII The History of Parthia, the Arabs, and the Crusades*, edited by Henry Smith Williams. Newcastle: Cambridge Scholars Publishing, 1904.

Graf, Friedrich Wilhelm. *Moses Vermächtnis (Moses' Legacy)*. Munich: n.p., 2006, 22f.

———. *Die Ẓahiriten*. Hildesheim: Georg Olms Verlag, 1967 (Reprint of the Leipzig 1884 edition).

Hallaq, Wael B. "Considerations on the Function and Character of Sunni Legal Theory." *Journal of the American Oriental Society* 104 (1984): 679–89.

———. "The Primacy of the Qur'ān in Shāṭibi's Legal Theory." In *Islamic Studies Presented to Charles J. Adams*, edited by Wael B. Hallaq and Donald P. Little, 69–90. Leiden: Brill, 1991.

———. *A History of Islamic Legal Theories: An Introduction to Sunnī Uṣūl Al-Fiqh*. Cambridge: Cambridge University Press, 1997.

Häussler, Matthias. *Der Religionsbegriff in Hegels „Phänomenologie des Geistes*. Freiburg: Karl Alber, 2008.

Hildebrandt, Thomas. "Waren Jamal al-Dīn al-Afghānī und Muḥammad 'Abdu Neo-Mu'taziliten?" *Die Welt des Islams* Vol. 42, no. 2 (2002): 205–262.

Ibn al-Ḥājib, Abū 'Amr 'Uthmān. *Muntahā al-wūṣūl wa-l-'amal fī 'ilmay al-uṣūl wa-l-jadal*. Beirut: n.p., 1985.

Ibn al-Qayyim, Muhammad Ibn Abu Bakr. *I'lām al-muwaqqi'īn 'an rabb al-'ālamīn* Beirut: s.a.

Ibn 'Ashūr, Muḥammad al-Tāhir. *Maqāṣid al-sharī'ah al-'islāmiyya*. New edition. Cairo: Dār as-Salām, 2005.

Ibn Farḥūn, Burhān ad-Dīn Abū al-Fidā'Ibrāhīm ibn Muḥammad. *Ad-Dībāj al-muḏahhab fī ma'rifa ta'yān 'ulamā' al-maḏhab*. Beirut: Dār al-Kutub al-'Ilmiyya., s.a.

Ibn Mūsa, al-Qāḍī Iyāḍ. *Tartīb al-madārikwa-taqrīb al-masālik li-ma'rifat 'a'lām maḏhab mālik*. 8 vols., second edition. Rabat: Al-Mamlakah al-Maghribīyah, Wizārat al-Awqāf wa-al-Shu'ūn al-Islāmīyah, 1981–1983.

Ihsan, Abdul Wajib. *Utility in Classical Islamic Law. The Concept of Maṣlaḥa in Uṣūl al-Fiqh*. PhD Thesis, University of Michigan, 1986.

Jackson, Sherman. *Islamic Law and the State: The Constitutional Jurisprudence of Shihāb al-Dīn al-Qarāfī*. Leiden: Brill, 1996.

Masud, Muhammed Khalid. *Islamic Legal Philosophy: A Study of Abū Isḥāq al-Shāṭibī's Life and Thought*. Delhi: International Islamic Publishers, 1995.

Motzki, Harald. *Die Anfänge der islamischen Jurisprudenz. Ihre Entwicklung in Mekka bis zur Mitte des 2./8. Jahrhundert*. Stuttgart: Franz Steiner, 1991.

Muranyi, Miklos. *Ein altes Fragment medinensischer Jurisprudenz aus Qairawān*. Stuttgart: Steiner-Wiesbaden, 1985.

Nagel, Tilman. *Die Festung des Glaubens: Triumph und Scheitern des islamischen Rationalismus im 11. Jahrhundert*. München: C. H. Beck Verlag, 1988.

Nekroumi, Mohammed. "Zur Rolle postklassischer Sufibruderschaften in der Entwicklung des Volksislam im Maghreb." In *Bonner Islamwissenschaftler/innen stellen sich vor*, edited by Stephan Conermann. Hamburg: EB-Verlag, 2006.

———. "Qur'āninterpretation im Kontext intentionalistischer Rechtstheorien." In *Modern Controversies in Qur'anic Studies*, edited by Mohammed Nekroumi and Jan Meise, 153–196. Hamburg: EB-Verlag, 2009.

———. *Modern Qur'ānic Debate*: *In Modern Controversies in Qur'anic Studies*, edited by Mohammed Nekroumi and Jan Meise, Bonn. Hamburg: EB-Verlag, 2009.

Nöldecke, Theodor. *Geschichte des Qorans*. Hildesheim: Olms, 1961.

———. "Zur Sprache des Qur'āns II. Stilistische und syntaktische Eigentümlichkeiten der Sprache des Qur'āns." In *Neue Beiträge zur semitischen Sprachwissenschaft*. Strasbourg: Verlag von Karl J. Trübner, 1910.

Pannenberg, Wolfhart. *Grundfragen systematischer Theologie*. Göttingen: Vandenhoeck & Ruprecht, 1967.

Paret, Rudi, *Der Qur'ān. Kommentar und Konkordanz*. Stuttgart: Kohlhammer, 1971.

Perler, Dominik, and Ulrich Rudolph. *Occasionalismus*. Göttingen: Vandenhoeck und Ruprecht Verlag, 2000.

Picht, Georg. *Wahrheit, Vernunft, Verantwortung. Philosophische Studien*. Stuttgart: Ernst Klett Verlag, 1969.

Reinhart, A. Kevin. "Islamic Law as Islamic Ethics." *Journal of Religious Ethics* Vol. 11, no. 2 (1983): 186–203.

Schacht, Joseph. *An Introduction to Islamic Law*. Oxford: Oxford University Press, 1964.

Schreiner, Stefan. *Die jüdische Bibel in islamischer Auslegung* (*The Jewish Bible In Its Islamic Interpretation*). Tubingen: n.p., 2012.

Van Ess, Josef. *Zwischen Ḥadīṯ und Theologie. Studien zum Entstehen prädestinatianischer Überlieferung*. Berlin: de Gruyter, 1975.

Weiss, Bernard G. "Language and Law: The Linguistic Premises of Islamic Legal Science." In *In Quest of an Islamic Humanism: Arabic and Islamic Studies*. In *Memory of Mohamed al-Nowaihi*, edited by Arnold H. Green, 15–21. Cairo: n.p., 1986.

———. *The Search for God's Law: Islamic Jurisprudence in the Writings of Sayf al-Dīn al-Āmidī*. Salt Lake City: University of Utah Press, 1992.

———, ed. *Studies in Islamic Legal Theory*. Leiden: Brill, 2002.

Chapter 10

The Challenge Facing Islamic Banking and Finance

Has It Moved Away From Its Core Objectives, With Special Reference to Maqāṣid?

Habib Ahmed

INTRODUCTION

The proponents of Islamic economics envisioned that an economy based on Islamic values and principles would strive to fulfill the goals of the *sharīʿah* (*maqāṣid al-sharīʿah*) and result in achieving a just, stable and vibrant economy. They argued that the realization of the *maqāṣid* would produce a moral economy with a financial system that would serve the needs of not only Muslims, but also humanity at large. Based on this worldview, the value propositions for the Islamic financial system was that it would entail risk-sharing features and serve all sections of the population, thereby bringing about equity, stability and growth. The implications of this vision were that other than fulfilling the legal requirements, an Islamic financial system would be ethical and cater to the social needs of a society.

The manifestation of Islamic economics ended up as sub-economies in the financial sector. Starting with a handful of Islamic banks in the 1970s, the industry has grown rapidly during its short history and has become a global phenomenon. While the quantitative growth of the industry has been impressive, there are questions raised on its quality. The practice of Islamic finance turned out to be predominantly a prohibition-driven industry, whereby the goal is to exclude *riba* and *gharar* from financial transactions. As a result, even with the high growth rates of the Islamic financial industry, there is a general feeling that Islamic finance has failed to fulfill the social goals of the *sharīʿah* and is not playing the anticipated positive role in the economy.

Given the above, the aim of this chapter is to examine the concept of *maqāṣid al-sharīʿah* and its implications for Islamic banking and finance, and how these are reflected in the practice of the Islamic financial sector. After identifying the key challenges that the Islamic financial industry face to incorporate *maqāṣid al-sharīʿah*, the chapter discusses ways in which these can be resolved at the conceptual and operational levels.

MAQĀṢID AL-SHARĪʿAH AND FINANCE: DIVERSE PERCEPTIONS

Maqāṣid al-sharīʿah constitutes the essential elements of a good life. Al-Ghazālī identifies the *maqāṣid* as safeguarding the faith (*dīn*), self (*nafs*), intellect (*ʻaql*), posterity (*nasl*), and wealth (*māl*).[1] An economy should strive to protect and enhance one or several of these goals. Specifically, contractual and commercial transactions are sanctified and encouraged as these preserve, support and enhance property and progeny.[2]

There are various views on the implications of the *maqāṣid* for the financial sector. One categorization of the *maqāṣid* would be to classify them at the macro/general level (*maqāṣid ammah*) and micro/specific level (*maqāṣid khassah*).[3] Whereas macro/general *maqāṣid* relates to the benefits and well-being of the overall society, micro/specific *maqāṣid* deals with issues related to individual transactions. The implications of the *maqāṣid* from these perspectives for the financial sector are presented below.

General/Macro *Maqāṣid*

The maqāṣid, at the broader level, would involve realizing human wellbeing by enhancing *maṣlaḥa* (benefit) on the one hand and preventing *mafsadah* (harm) on the other hand.[4] Enhancing *maṣlaḥa* at the macro level is linked to the overall vision and worldview of Islamic finance that is based on brotherhood and justice. At the broadest level, this vision would protect and preserve "public interests (*maṣlaḥa*) in all aspects and segments of life and produce an economic system that balances between growth (*tazkīyah*) and equity."[5] Two preventive principles of the *sharīʿah,* namely removal of hardship (*rafʿa al ḥaraj*) and prevention of harm (*dafʿa al ḍarar*) complement realization of essentials and enhance welfare.[6]

Whereas enhancing *maṣlaḥa* would mean protecting and preserving the five essential *maqāṣid* (religion, life, intellect, posterity and wealth), some authors emphasize focussing on wealth as being more relevant for economics and finance. For example, Laldin and Furqani identify the specific *maqāṣid* related to Islamic finance as preservation of wealth, which can be done through its acquisition, development, circulation and protecting its value by protecting ownership and preserving it from damage. Similarly, Ibn ʿĀshūr identifies specific *maqāṣid* related to economic transactions as preservation of wealth, equity, transparency, persistence and durability and circulation of wealth.[7] He asserts "one of the meanings of circulation intended by the *sharīʿah* is the transfer of wealth in the community among as many hands as possible without causing any harm to those who have acquired it lawfully."[8]

Specific/Micro *Maqāṣid*

The micro-*maqāṣid* relates to specific issues arising in the operations and transactions of the Islamic financial sector. Dusuki and Abdullah apply the three levels of *maṣlaḥa* [*ḍarūrīyyāt* (necessities), *ḥājīyyāt* (requirements) and *taḥsīnīyyāt* (supplements)] in the framework of corporate social responsibility at the firm level.[9] At the *ḍarūrīyyāt* level, the firms are expected to protect and preserve the essential needs (religion, life, intellect, posterity and wealth) of the stakeholders. This would include avoiding any activities that can cause disruption and chaos in peoples' lives and intellects. This can be achieved by, for example, providing a good work environment and protecting faith and health on the one hand, and avoiding harmful activities such as producing illicit drugs on the other. At the level of *ḥājīyyāt,* steps need to be taken to remove any difficulties and would include fair pay and enhancing workers intellectual wellbeing and skills by providing training. At the *taḥsīnīyyāt* level, firms should strive to contribute to improving the conditions of the poor and needy, provide scholarships and truthful information disclosure, etc.

Dusuki and Abdullah and Dusuki and Bouheraoua discuss the ways in which the operations of firms should also prevent harm.[10] Using various legal maxims, they conclude that prevention and minimizing harm should be a key objective of an Islamic firm. This would include not engaging in harmful activities such as selling products that harm the consumers, dumping toxic waste to harm the environment or residential areas and engaging in speculative ventures. One view of the *maqāṣid* at the micro or product level is to focus on *sharīʿah* compliance. For example, Kahf views the *maqāṣid* in transactions as fulfilling the objectives stipulated in contracts.[11] These include upholding property rights, respecting the consistency of entitlements with the rights of ownership, linking transaction to real life activity, the transfer of property rights in sales and prohibiting debt sale, etc. Dusuki and Abozaid equate achieving *maqāṣid* to fulfilling both the form and substance of Islamic contracts. They distinguish between the validity and permissibility of transactions. They assert that when the form of a contract is fulfilled, but not the substance, then the contract may be valid but will not be permissible. To be permissible, both the form and substance must be fulfilled. They conclude that whereas a permissible contract fulfils the *maqāṣid*, a valid contract does not.

MAQĀṢID AL-SHARĪʿAH AND ISLAMIC FINANCE: PRACTICE AND EVIDENCE

As indicated above, the implications of *maqāṣid* for Islamic finance can be viewed at macro and micro levels. A number of empirical studies investigate the role of Islamic finance in achieving ethical and social goals. These studies identify a list of activities that Islamic financial institutions should undertake, based on ethical and social values and principles, which can be broadly categorised into four types. The first element involves *sharīʿah* related issues that include matters relating to the *sharīʿah* compliance of products and the role of the *sharīʿah* supervisory boards in ensuring this compliance. The second feature deals with commitments to stakeholders, such as employees and debtors. The third aspect relates to charitable activities and includes *zakāt, qarḍ ḥassan* (interest-free loans) and other charities. The final component concerns broader social issues such as the impact on society, community development and environment. In terms of the categorization of *maqāṣid* as micro and macro, the first element identified above would fall under micro *maqāṣid* (the *sharīʿah* related issues) and the remaining three types can be considered macro *maqāṣid* (social and environmental impact). The practice of Islamic financial institutions in terms of macro and micro- *maqāṣid* are presented below.

Macro-*maqāṣid*

Kamla and Rammal studied the social reporting of nineteen Islamic banks to examine five variables: adherence to the *sharīʿah*, funding socially motivated investments and projects, access to credit and schemes for the financial inclusion of the poor and disadvantaged, community contribution, *zakāt*, charitable activities and donations and *qarḍ ḥasan*.[12] They found that while Islamic banks disclose their adherence to *sharīʿah* principles, their contribution to social development was not evident. The disclosure analysis shows that Islamic banks do not have "serious schemes targeting poverty elimination or enhancing equitable redistribution of wealth in society."[13] They conclude that "failure to make social justice the core value of their operations has contributed to the failure of Islamic banks to fulfil their ideological claims."[14]

Haniffa and Hudaib developed an ethical index for Islamic banks that includes eight indicators covering governance, *sharīʿah* compliance, charitable activities (such as *zakāt* and *qarḍ ḥasan*) and commitments towards employees, debtors and society.[15] A content analysis of the annual reports of seven Islamic banks over three years, reveal that information on the *sharīʿah* supervisory board and commitments to lenders scores the highest. Whereas commitment towards debtors and employees score high, the weakest elements of the operations of the banks in the sample include commitment towards society, which scores the lowest.

Mohammed and Razak prepared a *maqāṣid* index and studied its implementation in six Islamic banks globally.[16] The index constitutes seven variables that fulfil the objectives of education and welfare. While they found variations in the performance of banks, they conclude that none achieved high *maqāṣid* performance indicators. Maali et. al. (2006) studied social reporting for a sample of twenty nine Islamic banks globally by considering ten indicators. They foundd high disclosures for activities such as *sharīʿah* opinion and *zakāt* distribution, whereas charitable activities and employee related issues appear moderately, information provided on *qarḍ ḥasan* is low and none of the Islamic banks report anything related to environment.

Aribi and Arun conducted interviews with eighteen senior executives to gauge the corporate social responsibility practices in nine Islamic financial institutions in the Gulf Cooperation Council (GCC) region.[17] The study covers the following seven themes: *sharīʿah* compliance, *zakāt*, charity and donation, *qarḍ ḥasan* and the treatment of debtors, environment and employees. They found that the issue of CSR is not a major concern for Islamic banks. Whereas the focus of their operations is *sharīʿah* compliance, none of the banks report anything on environmental issues. They concluded that Islamic financial institutions are similar to conventional financial institutions with "the only difference being that the transactions and contracts of an IFI [Islamic financial institutions] must comply with Islamic law."[18] In a study of forty eight Islamic financial institutions from nineteen countries, Sairally (2007) finds that while they did some corporate philanthropy, social responsibility was not an integral part of their business policy. She concludes that their activities were "not thought to be [. . .] socially responsible."[19]

To sum up, the evidence shows that while the disclosures of the second and third types of social activities (charitable activities and commitments to direct stakeholders) are moderate to low, implementation of the broader social issues is either poor or non-existent.[20]

Micro-*maqāṣid*

The evidence from the empirical studies presented above show that Islamic financial institutions score high in disclosing *sharīʿah* related issues. While the studies indicate good disclosure of *sharīʿah* compliance related issues, there is a contention that the *sharīʿah* requirements are being diluted from the micro-*maqāṣid* perspective. The crux of the condemnation is that the products offered by Islamic financial institutions fulfil the legalistic forms of contracts but not the substance and spirit. This is apparent in some studies and also in a few court cases involving Islamic finance. For example, in a recent study Dusuki and Mokhtar found that only 11 out of a total of 560 *ṣukūk* (Islamic bond) issues (or around 2 per cent of the total) qualify to be asset-backed, as these fulfil the legal *sharīʿah* requirements of an actual sale of the underlying asset to the investors.[21] The remaining 98 per cent of the *ṣukūk* replicates conventional unsecured bonds with the sale of underlying asset not being actual, from both accounting and legal perspectives.

Similarly, some Islamic banks in the GCC region use *tawarruq* extensively, even though the Islamic Fiqh Academy issued a ruling declaring organized *tawarruq* illegal, as it entails elements of *riba*.[22] Some *sharīʿah* scholars also point out problems with the legalistic approaches of approving Islamic financial transactions. Usmani points out the majority of the *ṣukūk* (Islamic bonds) issues in the market replicate conventional bonds and are not in line with the spirit of Islamic law.[23] Similarly, Delorenzo is critical of total return swap and declares it to be unacceptable, even though the form is *sharīʿah* compatible. A few court cases involving Islamic finance also reveal that the contracts diluted the *sharīʿah* requirements.[24] For example, in the first case involving Islamic finance in the English court in 2002 (Investment Co. of Gulf vs. Symphony Gems), a *sharīʿah* expert opined the *murābaḥah* used did not fulfil pillars of sale and was not a valid contract from a *sharīʿah* point of view.[25]

As indicated, focusing on fulfilling the legal format of contracts would only make these valid but not permissible, implying that these contracts fail to fulfil the *maqāṣid* at the micro-level. The failure of Islamic finance to fulfil the legal requirements in both form and substance has generated criticisms from both detractors and proponents of the industry. For example, the Islamic financial industry has been denounced as "deception" and "charade."[26] Seniawski and Holden identify the current practice in the Islamic financial industry as "legal hypocrisy" and Hamoudi calls it "semantic fantasy" and "jurisprudential schizophrenia."[27]

MAQĀṢID AND ISLAMIC FINANCE: CHALLENGES AND THE WAY FORWARD

In order to discuss the social and environmental issues in some perspective, the contemporary developments on the role of finance on these need to be explored. There is an increasing awareness at different levels globally to include social and ethical issues in business operations and activities. SIIT views the development as a new paradigm in which entrepreneurship, capital and innovation are used for social improvement to solve the multitude of problems facing societies.[28] The initiatives under this paradigm have been termed variously as corporate social responsibility (CSR), socially responsible investment or social impact investments, corporate citizenship and corporate social performance.[29] Under these approaches, the environmental, social and governance (ESG) factors are also considered in the decision making process of organizations, along with financial returns. While environmental factors comprise pollution, biodiversity, climate change, deforestation, energy efficiency, hazardous materials, etc., social elements include equal opportunity, customer satisfaction, employee engagement, human rights, labour standards and product mis-selling, etc. Governance includes a variety of operational issues such as accounting standards, anti-competitive behaviour, bribery and corruption, compliance, executive remuneration and stakeholder dialogue.[30]

Although there is increasing awareness of the need to include ESG factors in investment decisions globally, the evidence on *maqāṣid* and Islamic finance reveal shortcomings and challenges at different levels. The challenges in implementing the *maqāṣid* in Islamic finance in light of contemporary developments can be broader categorised as conceptual and operational. Part of the problem of not realising the *maqāṣid* at the micro and macro levels lies in the understanding of the *maqāṣid* itself and lack of conceptualization of contemporary notions of ethical and social issues in the discussions of the *maqāṣid* related to financial transactions. Once the concept of the *maqāṣid* for contemporary times is clarified, the challenge is to operationalize these in the Islamic financial practices. The conceptual and operational challenges facing Islamic finance in implementing the micro and macro *maqāṣid* in Islamic finance are presented next.

Maqāṣid: Means vs. Goals

A key problem in incorporating social and environmental factors in the operations of Islamic finance is conceptual. The focus of micro perspectives on the *maqāṣid,* on the nature of contracts and transactions and ignoring the outcomes, limits the social impact of Islamic finance. The practice of the industry is to equate *maqāṣid* to fulfilling the *sharīʿah* principles at the contract levels only, and not consider the impact or outcomes of these contracts on the society or environment. This is apparent when one observes the screening criteria used for Islamic stocks and mutual funds. *Sharīʿah* compliant stocks are identified by using negative screening criteria involving prohibited sectors (such as companies dealing with gambling, alcohol and pornography, etc.) and some financial ratios. Unlike the conventional ethical and socially responsible funds, the Islamic investment screening process does not consider positive screening criteria emphasizing on the operations and impact, such as human rights, community investing and environmental protection.[31]

Some scholars, engaged with the Islamic financial industry, thus present a narrow perspective of the *maqāṣid,* whereby they consider fulfilling the legal stipulations of a contract as inherently fulfilling the *maqāṣid al-sharīʿah.*[32] Accordingly, as the *maqāṣid* is achieved when a contract is *sharīʿah* compliant, there is no need to examine other ethical and social implications resulting from it. They point out that, contractually, banks are required to maximize returns of the shareholders and investors and carrying out social activities may contradict the contractual stipulations. They maintain that the broader social objectives should be dealt with at some higher level, such as by the government or the regulators.

Moving forward, there is a need to distinguish between the goals and means of achieving the *maqāṣid.*[33] Whereas *sharīʿah* compliant financial contracts are the means of achieving *maṣlaḥa* and preventing *mafsadah,* the goals of the *maqāṣid* would require examining the impact of these transactions on social welfare environments. From a classical *fiqh* perspective, this implies that both the pre-contract and post-contract implications of any transaction have to be examined in order to achieve the *maqāṣid* in finance.

The post-contract impact or outcome of a transaction will also have implications on the validity of a contract and achieving the *maqāṣid.* Consequently, any legal contract that results in harmful effects will not only contradict the *maqāṣid* but affect the validity of a contract from a *sharīʿah* point of view. For example, whereas the Mālikīs and Hanbalīs consider selling grapes to the winemaker or weapons to highway robbers as invalid, the Hanafīs and Shafiʿīs view these sales to be reprehensible.[34] In other words, the outcome of the contracts should be an integral part of evaluating transactions from the *maqāṣid* viewpoint. This is particularly true for many ESG factors that are viewed as beneficial or harmful to society and the environment. At the bank level, it is the *sharīʿah* supervisory boards that should not only ensure that the *maqāṣid* are achieved at the contract level by ensuring that form and substance are fulfilled, but also review the impact and outcome of different products offered by Islamic banks.

THE CHALLENGE OF DEFINING *MAṢLAḤA* AND *MAFSADAH* IN MODERN TIMES

One of the problems of not including the contemporary ESG factors in the activities of Islamic financial institutions lies in the *sharīʿah* scholars' understanding of the *maqāṣid* framework. Anecdotal evidence from the conversations with some *sharīʿah* scholars involved with the Islamic financial industry suggests that they do not consider ESG factors to be relevant to the *maqāṣid,* as these do not exist in classical *fiqh.* When pressed with the lack of ESG considerations in Islamic financial practices, the response from the scholars is that these are western notions with no basis in Islamic jurisprudence.

The absence of the broader concept of *maqāṣid* in terms of ESG issues is also reflected in the Accounting and Auditing Organization for Islamic Financial Institutions (AAOIFI) disclosure standards.[35] Whereas the standard requires Islamic financial institutions to report sources and uses of funds related to *zakāt*, charity and *qarḍ ḥasan*, there is no mention of disclosing either environmental related issues or other aspects of social or community development.

As indicated, the outcome of the contract should be considered to evaluate the fulfilment of the goals or *maqāṣid*. However, the question arises as to what issues should be considered when examining impact. Whereas it is acceptable to include the matters already identified in *fiqh* literature, the question arises on how to treat the contemporary issues from a *maqāṣid* perspective. In other words, although there is broad agreement that activities that contribute to *maṣlaḥa* and prevent *mafsadah* would fulfil the goals of the *maqāṣid*, the question arises on whether to include the newer issues related to the ESG factors identified above. This brings us to the epistemological challenge of defining *maṣlaḥa* and *mafsadah* for contemporary concepts and notions.

Promoting the *maqāṣid* to include the broader ESG perspectives would require interpreting the *maqāṣid* by examining and endorsing these issues from a *sharīʿah* perspective. In other words, the ESG factors need to be studied and appropriately classified in the categories identified under the classification scheme of Islamic law (*al-aḥkām al-khamsa*). Accordingly, any act will fall under one of the following five types: obligatory (*wājib* or *farḍ*), recommended (*mandūb*), reprehensible (*makrūh*), permissible (*mubāḥ*) and forbidden (*ḥarām*).[36] Kamali contends that while the first and last types of activities (*wājib* and *ḥarām*) have legal force, the remaining three activities fall in the domain of morals that cannot be adjudicated in courts.[37] When *sharīʿah* proscribes usury or gambling, these become legal obligations. However, Islamic teachings encouraging people not to cause injury to animals reflect "the moral underpinnings of *shari'ah'*."[38]

Ullah et. al. uses *al-aḥkām al-khamsa* to categorize socially responsible investments (SRI) into three types. Firstly, *required* SRI would constitute the obligatory and the prohibited and would imply avoiding interest-bearing transactions, excessive uncertainty (*gharar*) and investments in prohibited sectors such as gambling, intoxicants and pornography.[39] Secondly, *expected* SRI includes the recommended and reprehensible and would include things such as fair dealings with stakeholders and not investing in sectors such as tobacco and arms. The final category is *desired* SRI that entails the permissible and include social impact projects, animal rights and environmental protection. Ullah et. al. note that the three categories correspond to the three levels of *maṣlaḥa* identified in Dusuki and Abdullah, whereby the required SRI would be considered *ḍarūrīyyāt*, the expected SRI would be categorized as *ḥājīyyāt* and the desired SRI as *taḥsīnīyyāt*.

From the Islamic legal theory (*uṣūl al-fiqh*) perspective, placing the ESG factors under the appropriate classifications would require evidence from the texts. Unless this link is established with the texts, it may be difficult to convince the *sharīʿah* scholars and Islamic financial institutions that ESG should be an integral part of the Islamic nature of banking operations. This would require conducting basic research on ESG related issues and their applications in economic transactions by exploring the fundamental concepts of *maqāṣid al- sharīʿah* for contemporary times. A resolution from an international *fiqh* body, such as OIC International Fiqh Academy, in this regard, can help guide the industry to go beyond negative screening and introduce positive screenings that would consider environmental, social and cultural aspects in Islamic financing and investments.[40]

Organizational Culture, Operations and *Maqāṣid*

One of the key questions that arise is what determines the involvement of firms in ESG. To understand this, there is a need to understand the nature and culture of a firm and how decisions are made in a corporate framework. At the firm level, Carroll and Schwartz and Carroll identify the responsibilities of an organization as *economic, legal, ethical* and *philanthropic/social*.[41] The economic responsibility is obvious, given that firms supply goods and services to earn profit. Firms have to comply with all the laws and regulations of a country in the pursuit of profit. Other than the economic and legal responsibilities, the society also expects firms to follow certain ethical norms. Finally, it may be desirable for firms to be philanthropic, though this is left to their choice and discretion. The extent to which an organization will fulfil the ethical and social objectives will depend on the nature and culture of an organization.

Hills and Jones define organizational culture as "the set of values, norms, and standards that control how employees work to achieve an organization's mission and goals."[42] Thus, an organization's values and norms would determine the extent it focuses on the economic factors relative to ethical and social factors. Maon *et al.* identify three cultural phases of firms in relation to corporate social responsibility (CSR).[43] Firstly, the CSR cultural reluctance phase signifies when there is no motivation for a firm to take on CSR and it ignores issues related to social and environmental impact. The organization would oppose any pressures from stakeholders to undertake CSR initiatives. In the second phase of CSR there is a cultural grasp; firms become more sensitive towards CSR issues and begin to accept them. While the organization becomes aware that a reduction in environmental and social burdens can protect its value in the long run, it takes a cautious approach. Finally, in the CSR cultural embedment phase, a corporation integrates CSR within the organization, decision making process and all its stakeholders. They move from viewing CSR as a value-protection concept to one that is value-creating.

Being a part of the moral economy and following the *sharīʿah* principles, the nature of the responsibilities of Islamic firms, including Islamic financial institutions, is expected to be imbued with the principles of the *maqāṣid*. In terms of Carroll's identification of a firm's responsibilities, Islamic firms, in pursuing economic goals, have to conform not only to the national laws and statutes, but also the form and substance of Islamic law at the transactions level, thereby fulfilling micro-*maqāṣid*.[44] In addition, being ethical is required of an Islamic firm, not just expected. The macro-perspective of the *maqāṣid* would require that the Islamic financial sector embrace the contemporary ESG factors in their operations. As discussed above, this would require integrating the ESG factors into the *maqāṣid*, so that the industry can contribute positively to social and environmental issues.

Whereas implementation of the social aspects of the firm would partly depend on how the *maqāṣid* are conceptualised, an Islamic financial institution would ideally belong to the CSR cultural embedment phase in terms of the organizational cultures discussed above. However, the evidence shows that the current practices of the Islamic financial sector appear to be in the CSR cultural reluctance phase. In order to move to the CSR cultural embedment phase, Islamic financial institutions would have to modify their organizational culture, which would include changing their values and norms to ones that embed the notion of *maqāṣid* in the broader sense. This change has to come from the top, starting from the board of directors and implemented by the senior management.

CONCLUSION

Being a part of an Islamic moral economy, the value proposition of the Islamic financial industry was the promotion of welfare and prevention of harm. The macro-perspective of *maqāṣid* includes an enhancement of broad socio-economic factors and the focus of the micro-perspective is the fulfilment of the form and substance of the contracts at the product level. The practice of the Islamic financial industry appears to be focussed primarily on avoiding legal prohibitions. Lack of contribution to broader social and environmental issues by Islamic banks raises concerns about its essence and foundational principles. Ignoring the foundational values and focussing only on legal compliance will strip the industry of its essence and spirit. To play a proactive positive role, there is a need to address the novel and contemporary ethical and social matters at two levels. Firstly, at the epistemological level, the impact of transactions need to be considered and the legal (*fiqhi*) opinions on these concepts need to be clearly specified. Secondly, at the operational level, these dimensions need to be incorporated in the practices of the Islamic financial industry to create a positive and healthy impact on the economy and society. If the industry fails to promote the foundational values, it will continue to being identified as a "prohibition-driven industry" and fail to claim its uniqueness as being a positive ethical and social force in the economy.

NOTES

1. Cf. Chapra, M. Umer, "The Maqasid Al-Shari'ah and the Role of the Financial System in their Realization," closing lecture delivered at the Eighth Harvard University Islamic Finance Forum on April 19–20, 2008.

2. Cf. Hallaq, Wael B., *A History of Islamic Legal Theories: An Introduction to Sunni Usul al-Fiqh* (Cambridge: Cambridge University Press, 2004).

3. Cf. Abozaid, Abdulazeem, "Contemporary Islamic Financing Modes Between Contract Technicalities and Shari'ah Objectives," *Islamic Economic Studies* 17, no. 2 (2010): 55–75; Dusuki, Asyraf Wajdi, *Challenges of Realizing Maqasid al Shari'ah (Objectives of Shari'ah) in the Capital Market: Special Focus on Equity-Based Sukuk Structures*, ISRA Research Paper No. 5/2009 (Kuala Lumpur: International Shari'ah Research Academy, 2009).

4. Cf. Landin, Mohamad Akram, and Hafas Furqani, *The Objective of the Shari'ah in Islamic Finance: Identifying the Ends (Maqasid) and the Means (Wasail)*, ISRA Research Paper No. 32/2012 (Kuala Lumpur: International Shari'ah Research Academy, 2012).

5. Cf. Abozaid, "Contemporary Islamic Financing Modes Between Contract Technicalities and Shari'ah Objectives," 67.

6. Cf. Kamali, Mohammad Hashim, *Shari'ah Law: An Introduction* (Oxford: Oneworld Publications, 2008), 35.

7. Though "*rawāj*" is translated as marketability of wealth in Ibn ʿĀshūr, the discussion on it implies circulation of wealth. See, for example, discussion Ibn Ashur, Muhammad Al-Tahir, *Treatise on Maqasid al-Shari'ah* (Herndon, VA: International Institute of Islamic Thought, 2006), 292.

8. Ibn Ashur, *Treatise on Maqasid al-Shari'ah*, 288.

9. According to al-Shāṭibī, *maṣlaḥa* is achieved by promoting the essentials (*ḍarūrīyyāt*), the complementary requirements (*ḥājīyyāt*) and the beautifications or embellishments (*taḥsīnīyyāt*). *Ḍarūrīyyāt* are elements that are necessary for proper functioning of an individual's life and society and their absence would lead to chaos and disruption of social order. *Ḥājīyyāt* are elements that complement the *ḍarūrīyyāt* by facilitating life. Their absence leads to hardship but not breakdown of the social order. *Taḥsīnīyyāt* are elements that enhance and refine the customs, culture and conduct of people and society, cf. Dusuki, Asyraf Wajdi and Nurdianawati Irwani Abdullah, "Maqasid al-Shari'ah, Maslahah, and Corporate Social Responsibility," *Islamic Journal of Islamic Social Sciences* 24, no. 1 (2007): 25–45.

10. Cf. Dusuki, Asyraf Wajdi, and Said Bouheraoua, *The Framework of Maqasid Al-Shari'ah (Objectives of Shari'ah) and its Implications for Islamic Finance*, ISRA Research Paper No. 22/2011 (Kuala Lumpur: International Shari'ah Research Academy, 2011).

11. Cf. Kahf, Monzer, "Maqasid al Shariah in the Prohibition of Riba and their Implications for Modern Islamic Finance," Paper presented at IIUM International Conference on Maqasid al Shari'ah, Malaysia, August 8–10, 2006.

12. Cf. Kamla, Rania, and Hussain G. Rammal, "Social Reporting by Islamic Banks: Does Social Justice Matter?" *Accounting, Auditing and Accountability Journal* 26, no. 6 (2013): 911–45.

13. Ibid., 933.

14. Ibid.

15. Cf. Haniffa, R., and Hudaib, M., "Exploring the Ethical Identity of Islamic Banks via Communication in Annual Reports," *Journal of Business Ethics* 76 (2007): 97–116.

16. Cf. Mohammed, Mustafa Omar, and Dzuljastri Abdul Razak, "The Performance Measures of Islamic Banking Based on the Maqasid Framework," paper presented at IIUM International Accounting Conference, Putra Jaya Marriot, June 25, 2008.

17. Cf. Aribi, Zakaria Ali, and Thankom Gopinath Arun, "Corporate Social Responsibility in Islamic Financial Institutions (IFI): A Management Insight" (May 6, 2012). Available at http://papers.ssrn.com/sol3/papers.cfm?abstract_id=2052635.

18. Ibid.

19. Sairally, Salma, "Evaluating the 'Social Responsibility' of Islamic Finance: Learning from the Experience of Socially Responsible Investment Funds," in M. Iqbal, S. S. Ali, and D. Muljawan, eds., *Advances in Islamic Economics and Finance* (Jeddah: Islamic Research and Training Institute, Islamic Development Bank Group, 2007), 299.

20. Cf. Maali, Bassam, Peter Casson, and Christopher Napier, "Social Reporting Islamic Banks," *ABACUS* 42, no. 2 (2006): 266–89.

21. Cf. Dusuki, Asyraf Wajdi, and Shabnam Mokhtar, *Critical Appraisal of Shari'ah Issues on Ownership in Asset-based Sukuk as Implemented in the Islamic Debt Market*, Research Paper No. 8/2010 (Kuala Lumpur: ISRA, 2010).

22. *Tawarruq* involves the buying of a commodity spot and selling it with a markup, with payment due at a future date. The buyer in turn sells the commodity spot and gets cash. The ruling was issued by the International Council of Fiqh Academy in its 19th session which was held in Sharjah, United Arab Emirates during April 26–30, 2009.

23. Cf. Usmani, M. Taqi, *An Introduction to Islamic Finance* (Karachi: Idaratul Maarif, 1999).

24. Cf. DeLorenzo, Yusuf Talal, "The Total Returns Swap and the '*Shari'ah* Conversion Technology' Stratagem" (New York: Mimeo, 2007).

25. Cf. Hasan, Zulkifli, and Asutay, Mehmet, "An Analysis of the Courts Decisions on Islamic Finance Disputes," *ISRA International Journal of Islamic Finance* 3, no. 2 (2011): 41–71; Moghul, Umar F., and Arsahd A. Ahmed, "Contractual Forms in

Islamic Finance Law and Islamic Investment Company of the Gulf (Bahamas) Ltd v Symphony Gems NV & Ors: A First Impression of Islamic Finance," *Fordham International Law Journal* 27 (2003–2004): 150–94.

26. Cf. Saleem, Muhammad, *Islamic Banking: A $300 Billion Deception* (Bloomington, IN: Xlibris Corporation, 2006); Saleem, Muhammad, *Islamic Banking: A Charade: Call for Enlightenment* (Charleston, SC: BookSurge Publishing, 2006).

27. Cf. Seniawski, Barbara L., "Riba Today: Social Equity, the Economy and Doing Business Under Islamic Law," *Columbia Journal of Transnational Law* 39 (2001): 700–28; Holden, Kelly, "Islamic Finance: 'Legal Hypocrisy' Moot Point, Problematic Future Bigger Concern," *Boston University International Law Journal* 25 (2007): 341–68; Hamoudi, Haider Ala, "Jurisprudential Schizophrenia: On Form and Function in Islamic Finance," *Chicago Journal of International Law* 7, no. 2 (2007): 605–22.

28. Cf. SIIT (Social Impact Investment Taskforce), "Impact Investment: The Invisible Heart of Markets, Report of the Social Impact Investment Taskforce," September 15, 2014.

29. Cf. Caplan, Lauren, John S. Griswold, William F. Jarvis, *From SRI to ESG: The Changing World of Responsible Investing* (Wilton, CT: Commonfund Institute, 2003); Silberhorn, D., and R. C. Warren, "Defining Corporate Social Responsibility: A View from Big Companies in Germany and the UK," *European Business Review* 112, no. 4 (2007): 533–52.

30. Cf. UNEP, "Integrating ESG in Private Equity" (Nairobi: UNEP, 2014), http://www.unpri.org/viewer/?file=wp-content/uploads/PRI_IntegratingESGinprivateequity_digital.pdf.

31. Cf. BinMahfouz, Saeed, and Habib Ahmed, "*Shari'ah* Investment Screening Criteria: A Critical Review," *Journal of King Abdul Aziz University, Islamic Economics* 27, no. 1 (2014): 111–45.

32. At different occasions (annual Harvard-LSE Workshops and ISRA-IRTI-Durham University Roundtables in Islamic Finance) I had the chance to interact with *sharīʿah* scholars who are involved with the Islamic financial industry. Several times, when the question of *maqāṣid* was raised, they assert that when a contract is *sharīʿah* compliant it automatically fulfills the *maqāṣid al-sharīʿah.*

33. Cf. Landin, Mohamad Akram, and Hafas Furqani, *The Objective of the Shari'ah in Islamic Finance: Identifying the Ends (Maqasid) and the Means (Wasail)*, ISRA Research Paper No. 32/2012 (Kuala Lumpur: International Shari'ah Research Academy, 2012).

34. CF. Al-Zuhayli, Wahbah, *Financial Transactions in Islamic Jurisprudence, Volume 1*, trans. Mahmoud A. ElGamal (Beirut: Dar al-Fikr al-Mouaser, 2003), 117.

35. AAOIFI Financial Accounting Standard No. 1 (FAS1), *General Presentation and Disclosure in the Financial Statements of Islamic Banks and Financial Institution.*

36. Cf. Reinhart, A. Kevin, "Islamic Law as Islamic Ethics," *The Journal of Religious Ethics* 11, no. 2 (1983): 186–203, 195.

37. Cf. Kamali, *Shari'ah Law: An Introduction*, 47.

38. Ibid., 49.

39. Cf. Ullah, Shakir, Dima Jamali, and Ian A. Harwood, "Socially Responsible Investment: Insights from Shari'a Departments in Islamic Financial Institutions," *Business Ethics: A European Review* 23, no. 2 (2014): 210–33.

40. Cf. BinMahfouz, Saeed, and Habib Ahmed, "*Shari'ah* Investment Screening Criteria: A Critical Review," *Journal of King Abdul Aziz University, Islamic Economics* 27, no. 1 (2014): 111–45.

41. Cf. Carroll, Archie B., "A Three-Dimensional Conceptual Model of Corporate Performance," *Academy of Management Review* 4, no. 4 (1979): 497–505; Schwartz, Mark S., and Archie B. Carroll, "Corporate Social Responsibility: A Three-Domain Approach," *Business Ethics Quarterly* 13, no. 4 (2003): 503–30.

42. Cf. Hill, Charles W. L., and Gareth R. Jones, *Essentials of Strategic Management*, 2nd edition (South-Western, Mason, OH, 2008), 30.

43. Cf. Maon, Francois, Adam Lindgreen, and Valerie Swaen, "Organizational Stages and Cultural Phases: A Critical Review and a Consolidative Model of Corporate Social Responsibility Development," *International Journal of Management Reviews* 12, no. 1 (2010): 20–38.

44. Cf. Carroll, Archie B., "A Three-Dimensional Conceptual Model of Corporate Performance," *Academy of Management Review* 4, no. 4 (1979): 497–505.

BIBLIOGRAPHY

Abozaid, Abdulazeem. "Contemporary Islamic Financing Modes Between Contract Technicalities and Shari'ah Objectives." *Islamic Economic Studies* 17, no. 2 (2010): 55–75.

Al-Zuhayli, Wahbah. *Financial Transactions in Islamic Jurisprudence*, Volume 1, translated by Mahmoud A. El-Gamal. Beirut: Dār al-Fikr al-Muʿāsir, 2003.

Aribi, Zakaria Ali, and Thankom Gopinath Arun. *Corporate Social Responsibility in Islamic Financial Institutions (IFI): A Management Insight* (May 6, 2012). http://papers.ssrn.com/sol3/papers.cfm?abstract_id=2052635.

Bin Mahfouz, Saeed, and Habib Ahmed. "Shari'ah Investment Screening Criteria: A Critical Review." *Journal of King Abdul Aziz University, Islamic Economics* 27, no. 1 (2014): 111–145.

Caplan, Lauren, Griswold, John S., Jarvis. William F. *From SRI to ESG: The Changing World of Responsible Investing*. Wilton, CT: Commonfund Institute, 2013.

Carroll, Archie B. "A Three-Dimensional Conceptual Model of Corporate Performance." *Academy of Management Review* 4, no. 4 (1979): 497–505.

Chapra, M. Umer. *The Maqasid Al-Shari'ah and the Role of the Financial System in their Realization.* Closing lecture delivered at the Eighth Harvard University Islamic Finance Forum on 19–20 April, 2008.

DeLorenzo, Yusuf Talal. *The Total Returns Swap and the 'Shari'ah Conversion Technology' Stratagem.* New York: Mimeo, 2007.

Dusuki, Asyraf Wajdi. *Challenges of Realizing Maqasid al Shari'ah (Objectives of Shari'ah) in the Capital Market: Special Focus on Equity-Based Sukuk Structures.* ISRA Research Paper no. 5. Kuala Lumpur: International Shari'ah Research Academy, 2009.

Dusuki, Asyraf Wajdi, and Abdullah, Nurdianawati Irwani, "Maqasid al-Shari'ah, Maslahah, and Corporate Social Responsibility." *Islamic Journal of Islamic Social Sciences* 24, no 1 (2007): 25–45.

Dusuki, Asyraf Wajdi, and Bouheraoua, Said. *The Framework of Maqasid Al-Shari'ah (Objectives of Shari'ah) and its Implications for Islamic Finance.* ISRA Research Paper No. 22. Kuala Lumpur: International Shari'ah Research Academy, 2011.

Dusuki, Asyraf Wajdi, and Mokhtar, Shabnam. *Critical Appraisal of Shari'ah Issues on Ownership in Asset-Based Sukuk as Implemented in the Islamic Debt Market.* Research Paper no. 8. Kuala Lumpur: ISRA, 2010. http://www.iefpedia.com/english/wp-content/uploads/2011/02/B108.pdf.

GSIA (Global Sustainable Investment Alliance). *Global Sustainable Investment Review 2012* http://gsiareview2012.gsi-alliance.org/pubData/source/Global%20Sustainable%20Investement%20Alliance.pdf.

Hallaq, Wael B. *A History of Islamic Legal Theories: An Introduction to Sunni Usul al-Fiqh.* Cambridge: Cambridge University Press, 2004.

Hamoudi, Haider Ala. "Jurisprudential Schizophrenia: On Form and Function in Islamic Finance." *Chicago Journal of International Law* 7, no. 2 (2007): 605–22.

Haniffa, R., and Hudaib, M. "Exploring the Ethical Identity of Islamic Banks via Communication in Annual Reports." *Journal of Business Ethics* 76 (2007): 97–116.

Hasan, Zulkifli, and Asutay, Mehmet. "An Analysis of the Courts Decisions on Islamic Finance Disputes." *ISRA International Journal of Islamic Finance* 3, no. 2 (2011): 41–71.

Hill, Charles W. L., and Gareth R. Jones. *Essentials of Strategic Management*, 2nd edition. Mason, OH: South-Western College Pub., 2008.

Holden, Kelly. "Islamic Finance: 'Legal Hypocrisy' Moot Point, Problematic Future Bigger Concern." *Boston University International Law Journal* 25 (2007): 341–68.

Ibn Ashur, Muhammad Al-Tahir. *Treatise on Maqasid al-Shari'ah.* Herndon, VA: The International Institute of Islamic Thought, 2006.

IFC (International Finance Corporation). (2012), IFC Performance Standards on Environmental and Social Sustainability. Washington, DC: World Bank Group, 2012. http://www.ifc.org/wps/wcm/connect/c8f524004a73daeca09afdf998895a12/IFC_Performance_Standards.pdf?MOD=AJPERES.

Kahf, Monzer. *Maqasid al Shariah in the Prohibition of Riba and their Implications for Modern Islamic Finance.* Paper presented at IIUM International Conference on Maqasid al Shari'ah, Malaysia, August 8–10, 2006.

Kamali, Mohammad Hashim. *Shari'ah Law: An Introduction.* Oxford: Oneworld Publications, 2008.

Kamla, Rania, and Hussain G. Rammal. "Social Reporting by Islamic Banks: Does Social Justice Matter?" *Accounting, Auditing and Accountability Journal* 26, no. 6 (2013): 911–945.

Landin, Mohamad Akram, and Hafas Furqani. *The Objective of the Shari'ah in Islamic Finance: Identifying the Ends (Maqasid) and the Means (Wasail).* ISRA Research Paper no. 32. Kuala Lumpur: International Shari'ah Research Academy, 2012.

Maali, Bassam, Peter Casson, and Christopher Napier. "Social Reporting by Islamic Banks." *ABACUS* 42, no. 2 (2006): 266–289.

Maon, Francois, Adam Lindgreen, and Valerie Swaen. "Organizational Stages and Cultural Phases: A Critical Review and a Consolidative Model of Corporate Social Responsibility Development." *International Journal of Management Reviews* 12, no.1 (2010): 20–38.

Moghul, Umar F., and Arsahd A. Ahmed. "Contractual Forms in Islamic Finance Law and Islamic Investment Company of the Gulf (Bahamas) Ltd v Symphony Gems NV & Ors: A First Impression of Islamic Finance." *Fordham International Law Journal* 27 (2003–2004): 150–194.

Mohammed, Mustafa Omar, and Abdul Razak, Dzuljastri. *The Performance Measures of Islamic Banking Based on the Maqasid Framework*. Paper presented at IIUM International Accounting Conference, Putra Jaya Marriot, June 25, 2008.

Reinhart, A. Kevin. "Islamic Law as Islamic Ethics." *The Journal of Religious Ethics* 11, no. 2 (1983): 186–203.

Sairally, Salma. "Evaluating the 'Social Responsibility' of Islamic Finance: Learning from the Experience of Socially Responsible Investment Funds." In *Advances in Islamic Economics and Finance*, edited by M. Iqbal, S. S. Ali, and D. Muljawan, 419–458. Jeddah: Islamic Research and Training Institute, Islamic Development Bank Group, 2007.

Saleem, Muhammad. *Islamic Banking: A $300 Billion Deception. Observations and Arguments on Riba (Interest or Usury), Islamic Banking Practices, Venture Capital and Enlightenment*. Bloomington, IN: Xlibris Corporation, 2006a.

———. *Islamic Banking: A Charade: Call for Enlightenment*. North Charleston, SC: BookSurge Publishing. 2006b.

Schwartz, Mark S., and Archie B. Carroll. "Corporate Social Responsibility: A Three-Domain Approach." *Business Ethics Quarterly* 13, no. 4, (2003): 503–30.

Seniawski, Barbara L. "Riba Today: Social Equity, the Economy and Doing Business Under Islamic Law." *Columbia Journal of Transnational Law* 39 (2001): 700–728.

Siddidi, M. Nejatullah. *Riba, Bank Interest and the Rationale of its Prohibition*. Visiting Scholars' Research Series no. 2. Jeddah: Islamic Research and Training Institute, Islamic Development Bank, 2004.

SIIT (Social Impact Investment Taskforce). "Impact Investment: The Invisible Heart of Markets," Report of the Social Impact Investment Taskforce, September 15, 2014. https://www.csi.uni-heidelberg.de/downloads/Impact%20Investment%20Report%20FINAL.pdf.

Silberhorn, D., and R. C. Warren. "Defining Corporate Social Responsibility: A View from Big Companies in Germany and the UK." *European Business Review* 112, no. 4 (2007): 533–552.

Ullah, Shakir, Dima Jamali, and Ian A. Harwood. "Socially Responsible Investment: Insights from Shari'a Departments in Islamic Financial Institutions." *Business Ethics: A European Review* 23, no. 2 (2014): 210–233.

UNEP. *Integrating ESG in Private Equity*. Nairobi: UNEP, 2014. http://www.unpri.org/viewer/?file=wp-content/uploads/PRI_IntegratingESGinprivateequity_digital.pdf.

Usmani, M. Taqi. *An Introduction to Islamic Finance*. Karachi: Idaratul Maarif, 1999.

Chapter 11

The Relationship between *Maqāṣid al-Sharī'ah* and *Uṣūl al-Fiqh*

Cefli Ademi

The *maqāṣid al-sharī'ah* (the higher objectives of Islamic law), which *inter alia* deal with the "why" behind Islamic legal rulings, show obvious parallels to the Philosophy of Law. However, a clear distinction between *maqāṣid* theory and traditional *uṣūl al-fiqh* (principles of Islamic jurisprudence) appears as promising as the unsuccessful attempt to strictly distinguish between the Philosophy of Law and Legal Theory, as well as other fundamental legal disciplines. Everything is characterized by constant overlap, which is why this chapter will propose a humble attempt to provide a schematic overview of the relationship between the aforementioned fundamental Islamic disciplines, mostly based on legal history.

THEOLOGICAL BACKGROUND OF ISLAMIC JURISPRUDENCE

Arguably, the biggest challenge Islamic scholars have faced throughout the ages has been understanding God's word (the *Qur'ān*), specifically taking into consideration the prophetic tradition (*sunnah*) and gaining an understanding of individual, as well as collective, codes of conduct from it; both ritual and worship related (*'ibādāt*) and religious-legal (*mu'āmalāt*). Law is unquestionably deeply rooted in the Islamic-monotheistic outlook on life, which is closely linked to (systematic) theology (*kalām*). In a number of legal theoretical *uṣūl* writings, Muslim scholars not only postulated God's existence, but also attempted to prove it through philosophical-theological means, partially using authentic and remarkable argumentative patterns that cannot be explained in detail in this essay.[1] This revealed God's all-encompassing sovereignty. As God is the creator of everything that exists,

Muslim legal scholars take it as part of their very identity to determine what is "right" based on His word, both from a textual point of view (in the *Qur'ān*) and from the point of view of meaning (mainly drawing from the prophetic tradition). God's role as creator is what gives rise to His legal sovereignty. In this context, all of God's creation is endowed with a positive worth, as the *Qur'ān* declares not only its "verses," but also the entire universe, as signs of God (*āyāt*). Here, we are considering two revelations.[2] It is this Quranic identity from which the following statement, which can likely be attributed to al-Ghazālī, stems from, *al-quranu kawnūn nāṭiqun wa-l-kawnu quranun ṣāmitun* (the *Qur'ān* is a talking universe; the universe is a silent *Qur'ān*). According to this doctrine of oneness, the entire creation is in God's *possession*. Human beings, representing the part of creation which is endowed with reason, have a responsible and just duty of care and are trustees (*khilāfa*) following God's guidance, or at least intention, in the *Qur'ān* and *sunnah*, a trusteeship which should be understood and employed for the welfare (*maṣlaḥa*) of creation. In this context, *sharī'ah* in a normative sense is a means to an end.[3]

EPISTEMOLOGICAL BACKGROUND OF *FURŪ' AL-FIQH*

Literally, *sharī'ah* means "a path to the inexhaustible source." While Islamic Jurisprudence is generally known for precise definitions of terms, it often remains descriptive when it comes to *sharī'ah*. From these descriptions, which cannot be listed separately here, a normative definition of *sharī'ah* as divine judgment (*ḥukm shar'ī*) of human behavior in a comprehensive sense can be concluded.[4] However, only God has the absolute knowledge of the *sharī'ah*. Human beings are limited when it comes to our epistemological capacities, as we are aware that the infinite cannot reliably be perceived by finite means. *Sharī'ah* primarily encompasses faith in God, righteousness, ethics, and morals. Compared to these elements, its normative-legal component is marginal. The Book of Samuel, as well as *ṣaḥīḥ* Muslim, provides early accounts of human beings having limited epistemological capacities. Human beings see what is in front of their eyes. God's "vision," on the other hand, is all encompassing.[5]

"So did you open up his heart and look into it?" the Prophet Muhammad angrily and repeatedly asked his companion Usāma bin Zaid, who had taken the creed of faith by one of his opponents on the battlefield as a mere self-serving declaration and so killed him.[6] The second caliph 'Umar reacted very angrily when someone commented on his verdict, "this is the opinion of 'Umar and Allah." Enraged by this comment, 'Umar insisted it was only the legal opinion of 'Umar.[7] The companions of the Prophet, as well as early legal scholars, all emphasized their relative and therefore diverse understanding of absolute *sharīʿah*. Impressively, yet albeit unsuccessfully, ʿAlī—the fourth caliph and the Prophet's cousin—highlighted this implicitness critical of epistemology to the *khawārij*.[8] They accused him of not complying with God's verdict and dominance (*ḥākimiyya*), as he assigned the issue of the position of caliph to a human arbitrator in the conflict with Muʿāwiyā instead of following "God's law" and upholding and continuing his caliphate by force. ʿAlī had people gather and took a copy of the *Qur'ān*. He touched the *Qur'ān* and ordered it to talk to the people and to inform them about "God's law." One of the audience cried out, "What are you doing? The *Qur'ān* can't speak, it's not a human being!" This is precisely what ʿAlī wished to make clear. The *Qur'ān* (in its printed version), said ʿAlī, "is merely ink and paper, it takes effect through people, in line with their limited personal ability to judge."[9]

Against this simple but convincing epistemological backdrop, Muslim legal scholars (*fuqahā'*) have undertaken the endeavor (*ijtihād*) to get as close to the divine judgment of human *actions,* which can be perceived objectively and which may be judged, as possible. What is remarkable is that they named this very discipline, which leads to nothing more than a relative, action-oriented image of absolute *sharīʿah*, *fiqh* (comprehension) and divided it into several branches of law (*furūʿ*). God is not bound by human inadequacies. Ibn al-Qayyim, based on an authentic account of the prophetic tradition, phrased it as follows, "*An-nabī . . . nahā an yusammā ḥukmu-l-mujtahidīn hukma-llāh*"[10] (the Prophet . . . has forbidden to call the legal verdicts of an important scholar (deduced by human reasoning) God's legal verdict). At the same time, differences of opinion and various, sometimes-diverging, expert understandings (*ikhtilāf al-fuqahā'*) are inherent in the discipline.[11]

This reserve, rooted in epistemology, is also reflected in the Islamic legal scale of assessment (*al-aḥkām al-khamsa*)[12] with its "genuinely Islamic process of conceptualisation"[13] and parallels to the concept of supererogation.[14] In this context, only the categories of *farḍ* (obligatory) and *ḥarām* (forbidden) have justiciability status, but not the categories of *mustaḥabb* (recommended), *makrūh* (disapproved), and *mubāḥ* (indifferent). It follows, for example, that the *qāḍī* generally only bases his decisions on what he can perceive with his senses (*aẓ-ẓāhir ʿinda-l-ḥākim*),[15] as well as musts and must-nots in connection with human actions. What people should do, what is indifferent and what is disapproved of from a moral point of view does not inform his decision-making authority, although he may highlight moral aspects. Baseline in this context is the indifference and, therefore, the permissibility of issues (*al-aṣlu fi-l-ashyā' al-ibāḥa*).[16] Carelessly postulating commands and prohibitions would be akin to playing with (otherworldly) fire. The companions of the Prophet were among the first to avoid administering justice by saying *hādhā ḥalāl wa hādhā ḥarām* (this is allowed and that is forbidden). They attempted to restrict themselves to statements such as *nakrahu kadhā wa narā hādhā ḥasan* (we do not approve of this and we welcome that).[17] After all, it would be presumptuous and pretentious to put a command or prohibition, which is ultimately deduced by human standards, into "God's mouth."

This reservation, rooted in epistemology, and the diversity of opinions aimed at probabilities, is characteristic of Islamic jurisprudence. Legal codifications of only specific *sharīʿah* approaches are alien to Islamic legal tradition, in particular as it acknowledges a large number of methodology-based legal opinions. However, this should not lead us to assume a lack of legal certainty; *fiqh*, as a "highly complex texture" with its ultimate reference point in *sharīʿah*, has been successfully ordering the legal position in societies characterized by Islam for centuries.[18] Thomas Bauer claims, "There is much evidence that a balance between acceptance of a plurality of legal opinions on one hand and the need for a functioning, largely consistent legal order on the other was achieved which was highly functional on all levels."[19,20]

THE LEGAL FACTUAL BACKGROUND OF *UṢŪL AL-FIQH*

While the companions of the Prophet and the subsequent generation (*at-tābiʿūn*) could refer directly to the Prophet when it came to identifying, interpreting, and implementing legal Quranic verses—their methodology hence being based on citing the Prophet or relatively simple conclusions drawn by analogy as they lived in the same times and environment—circumstances changed over time. The constant expansion of the Islamic territory and the resulting geographical and temporal distances complicated the process of determination based on the *Qur'ān* and *sunnah* previously mentioned. The heritage of the highly complex Roman-Byzantine and Persian-Sassanid civilizations also raised new legal challenges that needed to be faced in line with Islam and the situation. People were confronted with more and more complex situations for which neither the *Qur'ān* nor the prophetic tradition provided explicit instructions. This fact by no means justified stagnation in the sense that all new, not explicitly regulated issues would radically be superseded by explicit source texts, making anything "new" *de facto* inconceivable. On the contrary, following the Prophet, legal scholars interpreted the *Qur'ān's* "silence" regarding a vast number of issues as a sign of divine mercy, allowing for a dynamic process. Legal scholars regarded a pragmatic, well-balanced response governed by mercy to new challenges as a timeless prophetic stipulation and, therefore, as a natural element of Islam. A statement by Muʿādh ibn Jabal is often invoked in this context. The Prophet had sent him to Yemen as a *qāḍī* (judge) and asked him on what basis he was to administer "justice." The Prophet was pleased to hear the answer that he would first consult the *Qur'ān*, should he not find an explicit solution there he would then regard the prophetic *sunnah*, should this source also "remain silent" with regards to the issue at hand, he would tirelessly strive to form his own opinion (*ijtahid ar-raʾy*).[21]

The increasing temporal and geographical distance from the original site where the Prophet was active, as well as the differing contextual circumstances, inevitably led to a wide range of opinions, but also to concerns among the scholars who feared the essence of the message was in danger of being neglected. Free legal opinions became inflationary and eventually culminated in an increasing fundamental scepticism toward the *raʾy*, which had had a positive connotation to begin with, particularly in the *hijāz* (Mecca and Medina). Soon thereafter, during the reign of the Umayyad Caliphate, the so-called people of the traditions (*ahl al-ḥadīth*) faced the so-called people of free legal reasoning (*ahl ar-raʾy*). The former criticized free legal reasoning, particularly widespread among Iraqi scholars, which they considered excessive; unlike them, they referred more strictly to prophetic tradition, which had been handed down and practised in Medina.[22]

With the foundation for judging human actions in principle and method laid down during the Prophet's lifetime,[23] the Islamic-legal core discipline now began to take shape and had its heyday during the Abbasid Dynasty. Scholars felt particularly obliged to nip the allegation of arbitrariness in the bud. The theorization of fundamental and methodological research on systematic and calculable determination of religious-legal, as well as ritual/worship-based norms, dubbed *uṣūl al-fiqh*, was the inevitable result.

The debate surrounding the status of *maqāṣid al- sharīʿah* and its scope must be considered against the backdrop of this feared judicial and legal-ethical arbitrariness. The classical approach to *uṣūl al-fiqh* focused on textual sources was to avoid this and successfully did so for centuries.

Before attempting to work out some modest, unfinished approaches to determining the status of *maqāṣid al- sharīʿah*, a basic overview of the classic disciplines and methodological approaches of *uṣūl al-fiqh* will be given.[24]

THE CLASSIC DISCIPLINES OF *UṢŪL AL-FIQH* AND ITS APPROACHES

Traditionally, the discipline of *uṣūl* is divided into four sections:

1. Identifying, categorizing, and determining the status and relations of the *adillatu-l-aḥkām*, often translated as primary and secondary legal sources, such as the *Qur'ān, sunnah*, *ijmāʿ* (scholarly consensus), *qiyās*

(legal-logical deductions, for example analogy), *istiḥsān* (legal preference), *istiṣlāḥ* (taking into consideration public welfare / interests), *ʿurf* (custom), and *sadd adh-dharāi*ʿ (obstructing hazards).
2. A linguistic-legal analysis of the source texts, which contain indications giving rise to regulations (*dalālāt al-alfāẓ*), follows. In this context, grammatical factors, as well as factors pertaining to legal terminology and linguistic philosophy, are of particular importance. Establishing and distinguishing terminological categories and the linguistic-legal methodology of deducing norms (*istinbāṭ al-aḥkām*) fall in this category.
3. Moreover, the *al-aḥkām al-sharʿiyya* (legislative regulations and assessments) are researched and sorted into categories. For example, the legal scale for assessment mentioned earlier, according to which actions can be obligatory, recommended, indifferent, not approved of or forbidden, falls under this heading.
4. Another section concerns *ijtihād* (finding verdicts) and *taqlīd* (imitation) and their respective requirements.

Approaches to all of the branches are characterized by various specific *uṣūl* methods (*manāhij*), which are in turn traditionally divided into four categories. One such approach is the approach of theologians (*mutakallimūn)*, which is characterized by deduction. This means that established legal theory is essential for specific legal teachings. Advocates of this approach include the Shafi'ites, Mālikīs, and Hanbilites, each having their own genuine emphasis. On the other hand, the so-called legal scholars (*fuqahā*ʾ) employ an inductive method in their approach, using specific established norms to reach an abstract *uṣūl* theory. Another approach is the *uṣūl* approach attempting to combine these two methods. Lastly, the *maqāṣid* approach must be named as an additional *uṣūl* method, placing specific emphasis on the objectives and intentions of the *sharīʿah*. Modern-day research mainly links this approach to the fourteenth-century Andalusian scholar al-Shāṭibī.[25]

The scope of the *maqāṣid* approach has been controversially discussed. One of the stumbling blocks to interpretation based on *maqāṣid* are the clear instructions in the *Qur'ān*, such as numbers concerning inheritance. The classical *uṣūl* methodology, in general, does not allow for any reinterpretation of such a clear text. According to *uṣūl* methods, such texts must be followed literally, regardless of changes in time, place and circumstance. This creates a seemingly unsolvable problem; if the interpretative endeavor is to accommodate *maqāṣid*, the ruling related to the clear instruction may have to be modified in line with the *maqāṣid* of that ruling. But the necessity of following the text seems to negate such a modification. *Maqāṣid* is thus often reduced to a form of empty rhetoric as far as ethical-legal texts are concerned. Thus, the main questions are whether the discipline of *maqāṣid al-sharīʿah* can be considered to be strictly related to the traditional *uṣūl* methodology or, at least, as a modification of it or even as an independent legal approach.

Maqāṣid from a Theological and Legal Point of View

The linguistic meaning of *maqṣid* (plural: *maqāṣid*) is "destination," "meaning," "intention," "objective," or "purpose." From a normative point of view, Islamic legal scholars discussed the question of whether or not *maqāṣid*, which in turn form the basis of normative provisions (*furūʿ al-fiqh*), are inherent in the *sharīʿah*.[26]

From a theological point of view,[27] the question of causality behind divine action has always been discussed. Do God's actions have a cause, a reason (*taʿlīl afʿāl allah*)?[28] Was there a divine intention behind revelation (of norms and norm indicators)? The highly differentiated theological positions in Islam on this question can only be touched upon in this essay, by no means providing a complete account. The Muʿtazilies were of the opinion that divine actions *must* have an intention. Actions can be rationally universally categorized *and* judged as "good" or "bad" (*at-taḥsīn wa-t-taqbīḥ*), indeed for both human beings and God. The majority of Muʾtazila operated from the assumption that either of these attributes is inherent in any action, regardless of varying circumstances (*dhātī*). Based on the "Concept of Justice" proposed by the Muʾtazila, "good" actions are obligatory while "evil" actions are prohibited. With regards to God, good actions are such which He *must* do, while bad actions are such actions which are impossible for Him. In addition, actions without intention (*gharaḍ*) are pointless (*ʿabat*) and therefore bad. The conclusion was that any divine action must necessarily be based on an intention.[29] The Ash'arites vehemently opposed these theological hypotheses.[30] According to them, God is free of any human attribution and causalities. Rationally, God is not obliged to do anything, not even to fulfill a purpose claimed to be "good" with His actions. He is not bound by human standards, which at any rate lack an *absolute* definition of good and bad, and therefore of "(un) just" and "(un) merciful." As such, God does not need to do what human beings consider good or refrain from doing the opposite. A rational functionality phrased in relative terms[31] is of no relevance for God, the Sublime, and His actions. According to the important Ottoman scholar *Muṣṭafā Ṣabrī*, this understanding also defies the faulty conclusion drawn by analogy of a "divine arbitrariness," one of the reproaches put forward by the Mu'taliza who draw conclusions from human conditions and dependences and transfer them onto God (. . . *khaṭaʾuhum fī hāḍa-l-qiyās*). Human actions are based on thoughts and reflections about consequences of actions. It follows that if an action has no objective or purpose, it is arbitrary and pointless (*ʿabatan*). These human mechanisms and dependences cannot provide analogical conclusions for

God, who does not have to reflect and ponder consequences, as human beings appropriately must.[32] Someone whose action is based on purpose is dependent on this purpose. However, God is not tied down by any dependence.[33] This does not contradict the fact that God's actions contain wisdom and benefit, without the action being based on aiming to achieve this wisdom or benefit. This wisdom or benefit is simply not termed "functional," especially as the utility of an action implies a prior need to think and reflect, which is precisely something God is not bound by. God's actions, therefore, do not follow a wisdom or purpose; it is rather that wisdom follows the divine action.[34] The Maturidis provided an intermediary position in assuming that divine actions follow a purpose that is rooted in divine mercy, without being possible to oblige God to do anything. According to them, God is indeed not dependent on intentions, while human beings are dependent on purpose and benefit. Reason is not endowed with the authority to judge what is good and what is bad. On the contrary, reason is a tool granted by God simply allowing us to know what is good and what is bad.[35]

All these philosophical-theological discrepancies put aside, theological and legal scholars were largely in agreement that *the normative standard* for what is morally good (*taḥsīn*) and bad (*taqbīḥ*) is ultimately set by God. Reason, at least following a divine intervention by means of *waḥy* (revelation), merely allows human beings to gain an understanding of norms, not to set them. The Mu'tazila law school, the theological rationalists, also shared this understanding. Contrary to what is often assumed, their conviction, according to which reason is also able to realize what is morally good or bad *and* to legally assess it from a legal point of view, was generally directed at the philosophical-theological "pre-revelation hypothesis," which is of hardly any relevance when it comes to concrete legal standards because of divine intervention by means of *waḥy*.[36] Even in the source methodology of *uṣūl al-fiqh*, a general trend of different theological schools approaching each other can be witnessed.[37] One typical example is the trans-scholastic agreement concerning reaching legal verdicts based on the four judicial sources: *Qur'ān*, *sunnah*, *ijmā'*, and legal-logical conclusions like *qiyās*.[38] While some schools rejected the latter judicial sources in their terminology, we can still witness substantial parallels in their argumentative patterns. It goes without saying that individual schools had their own genuine approaches when it comes to legal methodology. However, there was a general effort to develop objective methods for determining divine norms. Scholars were largely in agreement that the normative standards of the *sharī'ah* have the following three main functions:

1. Purification of the individual by means of *'ibādāt* (service to God/worship)
2. Bringing about (social) justice [*'adāla (ijtimā'iyya)*] and peace (*salām*)

3. Promoting value and general welfare (*maṣlaḥa*) as well as preventing harm (*mafsadah*)[39]

It was upheld that the *Qur'ān* and *sunnah* contain virtually no normative issues, which are not tied to some purpose or benefit,[40] regardless of, theologically speaking, whether revelation comes before purpose or vice versa.

Maqāṣid al-Sharīʿah in *Uṣūl al-Fiqh*

A substantial dedication to understanding the purposes underlying the *sharīʿah* goes as far back as the Prophet and the Prophet's companions. One example of this is the authentic account,[41] which reveals that the Prophet sent some of his companions to Banū Qurayẓa instructing them to recite the afternoon prayer (*al-ʿaṣr*) there (. . . *lā yuṣalliyanna aḥadun al-aṣra illā fī banī qurayẓa* . . .).[42] However, the group risked missing the time in which the recital of *al-aṣr* prayer would have still been valid before reaching Banū Qurayẓa. This led to arguments among the companions about how to deal with the situation and the Prophet's instructions. While one group advocated waiting until they reached Banū Qurayẓah before praying, thus literally following the Prophet's instructions, another group preferred praying along the way before the appropriate time span for the afternoon prayer had elapsed. According to the latter group, the intention behind the prophetic instruction had been to hurry to Banū Qurayẓa and not to imperatively pray or make up for *al-aṣr* prayer in a strict grammatical sense. When the Prophet was informed about this difference in opinion afterwards, he opposed neither of them (. . . *fa lam yuʿannif wāḥidan minhum*).[43] Legal scholars deduced from this prophetic endorsement (*sunnah taqrīriyya*) that both opinions were correct.[44]

Among the early caliphs, ʿUmar in particular appears representative of a *maqāṣid*-oriented approach, with a number of instances showing him reaching verdicts based on teleological rather than grammatical grounds, thus also making a clear distinction between *ibādāt* and *muʿāmalāt*. Other people have provided instructive accounts of his goal and purpose-oriented legal verdicts on interpersonal issues,[45] making a repetition here redundant. The focus should rather be drawn to the fact that he showed legal restraint when it came to a teleological judgment of worship-related issues compared to interpersonal issues. Al-Bukhārī, for example, provides an authentic account[46] of this. ʿUmar is said to have seen no reason in exposing the right shoulder when walking round the Kaʿaba (*ar-ramal*) other than demonstrating physical strength and health toward some Meccan hypocrites when some unfavorable rumors were circulating regarding the ill-health of the Prophet's and that of his companions as a result of their long stay in Medina. In order to put an end to these speculations, the Prophet instructed his companions to walk round the Ka'aba at a quick pace and with the shoulder exposed. Confronted with the question of whether such behavior had not become obsolete with Islam having been established in Mecca, 'Umar answered *shay'un ṣana'ahu an-nabiyyu ṣallā-llahu 'alayhi wa sallam falā nuḥibbu an natrakahu* (this was practised by the Prophet, peace and blessing be upon him, and we will not break with it).[47] This differentiated approach to worship-related issues on one hand and interpersonal affairs on the other when it comes to legal methodology, was later adopted and upheld by all *uṣūl* schools.

Despite these clear indications for justice being administered based on objectives and purpose in the early Islamic period, a theoretical footing for *maqāṣid al-sharī'ah* had by no means been established. At any rate, the legal schools (*madhāhib*) later approached the issue of *maṣlaḥa* with substantially genuine emphases and their individual *uṣūl* methods, for example, within the framework of *qiyās* (e.g., the Shafi'ite legal scholars), *istiḥsān* (here, mainly the Hanafī legal scholars), and taking into consideration general well-being *istiṣlāh* (in particular, Mālikī and Hanbalī scholars).[48] From the eleventh-century onwards in particular, Muslim legal scholars came to regard *maṣlaḥa* as the embodiment of the objectives of the *sharī'ah*. The theorization of *maṣlaḥa* and their interconnection and consolidation with induced purposes of *al-sharī'ah* became more and more concrete.[49]

What needed to be taken into consideration was that neither *ijmā'* nor *qiyās* could disregard textual norm indicators. Any deviation from established and accepted norms considered necessary, or any new regulations for complex new social developments, saw legal scholars referring back to subsidiary sources, such as *istiḥsān* ("considering something better"/legal preference) or *'urf*. However, at least the Ash'arite legal scholars voiced doubts on the latter. In connection with *istiḥsān*, a danger of arbitrariness was often raised. With regards to *'urf*, it was argued that the direct connection to the "revealed norm" was missing. In order to be able to deal with new issues of legal relevance despite these obstacles, the concept of *maṣlaḥa* gained greater importance, which has remained controversial to this day for epistemological reasons. One controversy concerns the question of whether or not human intellect is actually capable of recognizing *maṣlaḥa* without specific textual indications (*maṣlaḥa mursala*).[50] If this were possible, then the question would need to be raised *how* legally valid *maṣlaḥa* can be identified and determined without contradicting or opposing God's will.[51]

Theoretically, two legal-epistemological approaches lend themselves to the task of achieving legal certainty, that is, a procedural, formal legal rationality making epistemology logically accessible or a material legal rationality through a teleological approach.[52] Both forms of legal rationality can be found, albeit differently emphasized, in traditional *uṣūl al-fiqh*.

Formal-procedural legal rationality means that the validity of a norm that has been deduced depends on a strict procedural-logical analysis, as it was traditionally used in *qiyās* to determine the *ʿilla* (*ratio legis*). A logical analysis first establishes criteria, which can be used to determine the *ʿilla* of the textually indicated fundamental norm (*aṣl*). If the new, unregulated case (*farʿ*) is based on the same *ratio legis*, then the same *ḥukm* (legal evaluation) is applied as for the regulated case. The conclusiveness of the formal procedure of determining the correct *ʿilla*, which represents the focus of this means of reaching legal verdicts, makes the new regulations valid.

The material-teleological method of reaching legal verdicts, on the other hand, uses congruence between deduced norms and their underlying ethical purpose (*maqṣad*) as the key element for achieving legal certainty. A determined norm can only then be valid when it matches the ethical normative objectives and purposes, which are mainly established as abstract principles. Naturally, such teleological interpretations cannot be based directly on the will of God as "legislator." For example, in the sense of a subjective interpretation, particularly as God normally has not communicated the objective behind His norm *expressis verbis*, given such an objective can even be theologically assumed. It is more the purpose, which is objectively expressed in the determined norm, which deliberations are based on (*manhaj al-istiqrāʾ*).[53] One representative example for material legal rationality is the Mālikī and Hanbalī principle of *sadd adh-dharāʾiʿ* (averting danger by blocking means). If an action, which is *per se* allowed, could violate the objective behind the norm, then the action as such is prohibited. Similar substantial deliberations can be witnessed with the Hanafī school in the context of *istiḥsān* or *ʿurf*, as well as with the Shafiʿī school in the context of *qiyās*.[54]

The above-mentioned differing mechanisms of reaching legal verdicts within the framework of traditional *uṣūl al-fiqh* are also evident in the debates surrounding *maqāṣid al-sharīʿah* and *maṣlaḥa*. Depending on the preferred legal rationality, a legal scholar will consider *maṣlaḥa* either within the context of a formal process determining legal verdicts providing logical access to epistemology, for example regarding *qiyās*, or based on an independent principle of corrective guidelines rooted in finding legal verdicts based on objectives and purpose.[55] While traditional legal schools *(madhāhib)* focused on formal legal rationality, some of their scholars either put greater emphasis on *maṣlaḥa* and *maqāṣid* within the framework of this legal logical approach typical for the schools or even attempted to develop an independent corrective principle for establishing norms based on teleological reasoning. The following section will present some of the most influential approaches in this context.

MAQĀṢID AS A SUBSECTION OF *UṢŪL AL-FIQH*

Imām al-Juwaynī (d. 1047) is generally regarded as the first systematist of *maqāṣid al-sharīʿah*. He considers them within the framework of *qiyās* and distinguishes five categories: necessities (*ḍārūriyyāt*), public needs (*al-ḥāja al-ʿāma*), moral behavior (*mukarramāt*), what is recommended (*mandhūbāt*), as well as the *maṣlaḥa* whose *maʿnā* (rational meaning) is unclear, for example the merely physical *ʿibādāt*.[56] His approaches were refined and complemented by his student Abū Ḥāmid al-Ghazālī (d. 1111). Despite being somewhat critical of *maṣlaḥa* (*al-mursala*)[57] as a legal source, he nevertheless integrated it into *qiyās* as long as it fulfilled the purposes of the *sharīʿah*.[58] Unlike his teacher, he classified *maṣlaḥa* in three categories of subsidiary order: *al-ḍarūrāt* (necessities), *al-ḥājāt* (requirements), and *al-taḥsīnāt* (supplements). According to him, the concrete objective of setting up norms (*maqṣūd sharʿi*) is, to put it in contemporary terms, the protection (*ḥifẓ*) of necessary legal interests, such as worldview (*dīn*), life (*nafs*), intellect (*ʿaql*), ancestry and posterity (*nasl*), as well as property and wealth (*māl*).[59] Upholding these legal assets is essential for the welfare and order of any society. Anything that protects these legal interests can be classified as *maṣlaḥa*, anything that is harmful to them can be classified as the opposite *mafsadah* and anything that can prevent the latter is in turn *maṣlaḥa*.[60] Following the Ash'ari- Shafiʿī tradition, al-Ghazālī conceded no independent legitimacy to induced *maqāṣid*, but took them into consideration within the framework of *qiyās* and *istiṣlāḥ*, that is, clearly within a formal-procedural approach to *uṣūl al-fiqh*. Nevertheless, al-Ghazālī put forward some interesting conclusions based on analogy, for example using an induced *maqṣad* by way of the criterion of appropriateness (*munāsaba*)[61] as ratio legis, despite fundamental Shafiʿī criticism of a lack of accuracy (*ghair munḍabiṭa*).[62] He elaborates, *ḥukmunā anna kulla mā askara—min mrūbin aw maʾkūlin—fayaḥrumu; qiyāsan ʿala-l-khamr; li-annahā ḥurrimat li-ḥifẓ al-ʿaq* [63] [(for example) our legal verdict according to which anything which causes intoxication—liquid and solid—is prohibited; based on the analogy to "alcohol," in particular as alcohol was banned in order to protect intellect and consciousness].[64] However, this teleological aspect of al-Ghazālī's argumentation does not represent a rejection of his general formal-procedural approach to finding legal verdicts, particularly as even *this* teleological aspect must be in line with the spirit of the textually indicated norms and, therefore, ultimately with the divine text.[65] Al-Ghazālī's influence on jurisprudence, as well as later *maqāṣid* theories, is of such great significance that many researchers regard his work as a watershed ("pre and post al-Ghazali periods").[66]

A number of important personalities, such as ar-Rāzī, al-Qarāfī, as-Subkī, ʿIzz ad-Dīn Abdassalām, Ibn Taymiyya, and Ibn Qayyim al-Jawziyya to name but a few, picked up on this *maqāṣid* heritage. Some of them rejected al-Ghazālī's concept of *maṣlaḥa*, others only criticized some aspects of it. Others confirmed it or developed it further[67] and incorporated aspects beyond penal law, the discipline whose regulations had hitherto often (although not exclusively) provided the legal assets worth protection, to a much greater extent than before.[68]

The aforementioned "teachers of the law" were—at least tacitly—in agreement that the *maqāṣid* doctrine is a subordinate discipline of *uṣūl al-fiqh*. According to them, the crucial basis for *ijtihād* (establishing legal verdicts) is the *nuṣūṣ* (text) -based, grammatical-procedural determination and interpretation of norms, allowing at best for legal-logical conclusions, such as analogy, using strictly textually based indications in order to determine the *ratio legis*. More reason-based principles, such as *istiḥsān* and *istiṣlāḥ*, which were also linked to *maqāṣid* theory, were merely considered subsidiary sources of law. For these legal scholars, it was critical to obtain legal certainty by means of formal-procedural, that is, strongly text-oriented legal rationality.

Maqāsid as an Essential Part of *Uṣūl al-Fiqh*

The *maṣlaḥa* approach of the Hanbalī legal scholar Najm ad-Dīn aṭ-Ṭūfī (d. 1316) differed from the traditional emphasis on a formal-procedural establishment of legal verdicts advocated by the previously named teachers. The crucial foundation of his argumentation was the prophetic statement *lā ḍarara wa lā ḍirār* (neither do harm nor react in a harmful way). He did not incorporate *maṣlaḥa* in a formal procedural approach to establishing legal verdicts, as had been customary up until then. On the contrary, he used it as a substantial-teleological tool for the determination of legal verdicts. To him, *maṣlaḥa* stood for the purpose behind legal order and thus represented fundamental and independent criteria for deducing norms. After all, he saw *maṣlaḥa* as the most reliable indicator (*dalīl*), due to it having been established by means of an inductive interpretation of source texts and being accessible by human intellect. Anything that promotes *maṣlaḥa* and prevents *mafsadah* corresponds to the objective and *maqṣad* of the *sharīʿah*. However, as far as *ʿibādāt* was concerned, aṭ-Ṭūfī ruled out any predominance of rationally accessible *maṣlaḥa* in determining law. In addition, he maintained that deliberations in connection with *maṣlaḥa* can neither supersede explicit textual norm provisions (*muqaddarāt*), nor specific norm indicators (*dalīl khāṣṣ*) in the *Qur'ān*, *sunnah* and consensus.[69] This shows that despite divergent interpretations regarding the actual scope of his *maṣlaḥa* concept, as well as his clearly strong affinity for a material-teleological approach to finding legal verdicts, aṭ-Ṭūfī's approach did not question traditional *uṣūl* methodology as such. In fact, he seems to have only invoked *maṣlaḥa* in cases where traditional sources (the *Qur'ān*, *sunnah*, *ijmāʿ*, and *qiyās*) provided no clues.[70]

The Andalusian legal scholar Abū Isḥāq Ibrāhīm b. Mūsā al-Shāṭibī (c. 1388), in his oeuvre *al-Muwāfaqāt*,[71] was a scholar who particularly focused on objectives and purpose when establishing legal verdicts. What is very obvious is his emphasis on early Quranic chapters (plural: *suwur*; singular: *sūrah*) as the embodiment of universal principles of Islamic jurisprudence with, on the other hand, Medinan *suwur* and the *sunnah* indicating particular norms, explaining, specifying, qualifying, and complementing Meccan *suwur*.[72] The superior objectives of the *sharīʿah* have been induced from a comprehensive analysis of particular provisions (*manhaj al-istiqrāʾ*) and, therefore, provide legal certainty (*qaṭʿī*), while being unalterable. The particular provisions, on the other hand, are of a speculative nature (*ẓannī*) and might be alterable under specific circumstances.[73] Promoting *maṣlaḥa* and preventing *mafsadah* with a view to the categories of necessity (*ḍārūriyyāt, ḥājiyyāt, taḥṣīniyyāt*) established as early as with al-Ghazālī, represented a universal source of reaching legal verdicts for al-Shāṭibī.[74] However, despite this clearly teleological emphasis, scholars were literally of "different minds" when it came to al-Shāṭibī's *maqāṣid* theory. While some enlisted them as the foundation of *uṣūl* reformation, interpreting al-Shāṭibī in the sense of him giving priority to universal principles over (even explicit) particular provisions in case of conflict, other more traditional *uṣūl* scholars considered al-Shāṭibī's *ijtihād maqāṣidī* as nothing more than an additional reference for an inductive textual interpretation. According to them, it was the very function of particular provisions to protect the objective and purpose of the *sharīʿah*. In order to back up their reasoning, they invoked al-Shāṭibī's statement according to which the good of the *sharīʿah* is absolute and comprehensive (*kullī*). This means that particular provisions are encompassed as the interpretation of particular norms constitutes a comprehensive regard of the good of the *sharīʿah*. *Maṣlaḥa* is said to be that which corresponds to God's orders, which in turn echoes the Ash'ari position according to which an understanding of *maṣlaḥa* can only be gained from particular textual provisions, true *maṣlaḥa* being congruent with God's orders.[75] One of the possible reasons for the many contradictory interpretations of al-Shāṭibī's *maqāṣid* theory could be that his book *al-Muwāfaqāt* was not published until 1884 and remained largely unknown until that point. Consequently, the oeuvre seems to be missing the traditional Islamic *ijāzāt* and *salāsil* roots, with texts being studied by authorized experts in direct lineage back to the author himself.[76]

Despite conflicting opinions on how to correctly interpret al-Shāṭibī's *maqāṣid* theory, we can establish, in regard to the topic of this chapter, that his theory, whether or not it represented reformation, is to be included in *uṣūl al-fiqh*, albeit with a specific affinity toward a material-teleological approach to legal rationality.

Modern-Day Legacy

The nineteenth-century modernist "reformation" movement, which often, against the backdrop of colonialism and the challenges posed by modernity, represented nothing more than apologetics, gave rise to a revival of *maṣlaḥa-maqāṣid* theory which has lasted to this day. Specifically, the genuinely modern debates surrounding national states, democracy, liberalism, human rights, and secularization have seen it invoked. In this context, modern-day legal scholars consulted previous *maṣlaḥa-maqāṣid* concepts in Islamic jurisprudence, providing their own particular emphasis depending on socialization and challenges, something that cannot be discussed in detail here. What appears significant is that early so-called Muslim reformers, such as Muḥammad ʿAbdūḥ (d. 1905) and his pupil Muḥammad Rashīd Riḍā (d. 1935), invoked al-Shāṭibī's and, particularly, aṭ-Ṭūfī's *maṣlaḥa* concepts,[77] especially as they considered them to provide the greatest potential for facing modern challenges. According to them, against the backdrop of a new rationalist worldview, it could be best demonstrated that "Islam is the solution" (*al-islām huwa al-ḥāl*) by echoeing at-Ṭūfī's *maṣlaḥa* concept. As nearly all Islamic scholars considered *maṣlaḥa* the purpose of the *sharīʿah*, as well as the wisdom (*ḥikmah*) behind Islamic norms, aṭ-Ṭūfī's particular *maṣlaḥa* emphasis provided the opportunity to draw parallels between rational benefit-oriented decisions and the spirit of Islamic law.[78] This seemed to promise a particularly credible return to "true Islam" without disturbing traditional opinions. Aṭ-Ṭūfī's assumption that *maṣlaḥa* is accessible to human intellect could also be made productive in light of the colonialist allegation of an incompatibility of Islamic law and reason.[79] For the so-called Muslim modernists, the shift in emphasis toward a more teleological approach to reaching legal verdicts and, therefore, the partial departure from the traditional logic of aṭ-Ṭūfī's school, set a precedent for a possible break with *taqlīd* of a school of law if necessary. At the same time, aṭ-Ṭūfī did not question traditional *uṣūl al-fiqh* as such, allowing his successors to fancy themselves representatives of tradition.[80]

While Islamic jurisprudence was limited to identifying the most likely solution, meaning that differences in opinion were inherent as only God is aware of the absolute truth, Muslim reformers saw themselves confronted with a colonialist "obsession with the truth" and the need to define themselves by way of absolute norms and values.[81] Against this backdrop, aṭ-Ṭūfī's *maṣlaḥa* concept was considered a bridge in order to overcome the diverging opinions of different schools of law and, therefore, the split among Muslims.[82] At any rate, reformist movements were influenced by Eurocentric-ideological calls for a reform of Islamic jurisprudence, if possible following the European example. In European intellectual history, the term "reform" stands for a radical break with tradition, for a leap toward civilization.

It is embedded in Universalist Historicism "in which the history of the Other merges into the major and defining currents of the European (read: universal) civilizational march."[83] Among other things, this Universalist Historicism failed to recognize that Islamic legal tradition acknowledged various different legal-theoretical and philosophical concepts put forward by Muslim legal scholars—even if criticized—as additional aspects among many others, without this structurally representing a break with a dogmatized tradition, that is, representing reform. As a matter of fact, Islamic tradition could only be understood as an open process because "dogmas" in the strict sense of the word, which would have necessitated "reforms" in a European sense, are alien to it. From the point of view of civil society, Muslim mainstream opinion has been established by way of discourse based on recognized (privately organized) scholarship, plausibility of methods and arguments, plausibility of statements, as well as the credibility of those handing down opinions and of scholars. Churchlike hierarchically structured institutions defining dogmas did not exist but rather "with its professional legal guilds now in place, Sunni Islam professionalized an individualistic and autonomous system . . . that led to the determination of orthodoxy."[84]

It did not take long for traditional legal scholars focusing on schools of law to react to this advance by Muslim reformers, whom they considered modernist, by implementing formal-procedural *maṣlaḥa* concepts, for example echoing al-Ghazālī or ar-Razī. One representative example, which should be named in this context, is the impressive *maṣlaḥa* research "critical of modernism" provided by the Syrian scholar Muḥammad Sa'īd Ramadān al-Būṭī (d. 2013) in his book *Ḍawābiṭ al-maṣlaḥa fī-sh-sharī'ah al-islāmiyya*.[85] Well-known scholars of Islamic studies, such as Wael Hallaq, consider the reformist *maqāṣid* approaches of, for example, Riḍā—which in their eyes can only be understood in the context of modernity—as religious utilitarianism influenced by natural law, not able to compete when it comes to methodology.[86] Malcolm Kerr also understands Riḍā's equalization of *maṣlaḥa* with *ḍarūra* (necessity) and his subordination of source texts as mere natural law.[87] David Johnston regards the "hermeneutical turning point" away from the literal wording toward the spirit of the text, as proclaimed by Muslim reformers, as ethical objectivism.[88] In fact, Riḍā's genuine attempt to establish rationally postulated *maṣlaḥa* as a crucial legal source seems to factually bring about a negation of traditional *uṣūl al-fiqh*.[89] At least, rhetorically, his *maṣlaḥa* approach forms part of *uṣūl al-fiqh*.

Maqāṣid as an Independent Science Discipline

The Tunisian scholar Muḥammad Aṭ-Ṭāhir Ibn 'Āshūr (d. 1973) provides a seemingly more courageous and methodically more mature approach. While the *uṣūl*-based understanding of *maṣlaḥa* was characterized by the interplay of both formal-logical and material-teleological legal rationality, distinguished only by varying individual emphasis, Ibn ʿĀshūr's approach seems to represent a complete emancipation of the teleological legal approach from *uṣūl al-fiqh*. His criticism of the traditional *uṣūl* method, accusing it of being characterized by loyalties toward specific schools of law, largely neglecting the objectives and purposes of the *sharīʿah*, led him to call for the establishment of *maqāṣid al-sharīʿah* as an independent discipline. According to him, this would help to further develop *maqāṣid*, independent of the narrow scope of *uṣūl*. He states:

> if we want to lay down definitive and categorical principles for the understanding of the *sharīʿah*, we need to return to the traditionally accepted propositions of *uṣūl al-fiqh* and reformulate them. We should critically evaluate them, rid them of the alien elements that crept into them and supplement them with the results of thorough comprehension and careful thought. Then, we need to reformulate the whole and classify it as an independent discipline called "*ʿilm maqāṣid al-sharīʿah*." In other words, we should leave the discipline of *uṣūl al-fiqh* as it is, a source from which the methods of formulating legal argumentation could be derived.[90]

Regardless of the undisputed position of Ibn ʿĀshūr as an academic and religious authority, he failed to enforce his unprecedented claim. This may not come as a surprise, given the close interdependence of *maqāṣid al-sharīʿah* and *uṣūl al-fiqh* in Islamic legal tradition. As emerges from the previous illustrations, they serve as two corrective authorities, which back each other up epistemologically. The contemporary scholar ʿAbdullah b. Bayyah, therefore, compares the relationship between *maqāṣid al-sharīʿah* and *uṣul al-fiqh* to that of the soul and body.[91]

CONCLUSION

This humble presentation has intended to show that the relationship between *uṣul al-fiqh* and *maqāṣid al-sharīʿah* depends on the preferred legal rationality Islamic jurists use to avoid arbitrariness in achieving legal certainty. Accordingly, the theory of *maqāṣid al-sharīʿah* can be considered to be a secondary or fundamental part in the *uṣul*-based law-finding process, or even as an independent discipline. This depends on the emphasis legal scholars put on teleological legal rationality. The more emphasis they put on a teleological-substantive legal rationality, the more important *maqāṣid al-sharīʿah* becomes in their law-finding process.

NOTES

1. On the link between theology and law in Islamic Jurisprudence, cf.: Umar F. Abd-Allah, "Theological Dimensions of Islamic Law," 237ff., in *The Cambridge Companion to Classical Islamic Theology*, ed. Tim Winter (Cambridge: Cambridge University Press, 2008).

2. Revelation, in a Quranic context, is not at all to be understood in the sense that God became "word" in the *Qur'ān* as a kind of equivalent to the widespread Christian concept of God having become human through Jesus. According to an Islamic concept of God, any anthropomorphic tendencies should preferably be avoided. As for the Islamic understanding of God, similar to the Jewish, God is Himself unutterable as removed from our perception. The "mistake" in our concept of God or invoked through it which forms the a priori basis for the act of conception must be minimized through utmost abstraction. The more concrete the image of God, the bigger is the mistake. Against this backdrop, revelation can simply be understood as signs of His existence brought about by God, without God Himself taking shape in these signs.

3. On this section, cf.: "Çefli Ademi, Lehrstühle für 'Islamisches Recht'? Eine kritische Begriffsanalyse bzw. die Frage nach einer substanzadäquaten Lehrstuhlbezeichnung" (Professorships for 'Islamic Law'? A Critical Analysis of the Term and the Question of a Substantially Adequate Name), in *Jahrbuch für Islamische Theologie und Religionspädagogik* (Yearbook for Islamic Theology and Religious Education), ed. Milad Karimi and Mouhanad Khorchide, (2012), 172ff.

4. This chapter consciously only refers to the normative definition of *sharīʿah*, while at the same time acknowledging that, depending on professional outlook, a large number of definitions exist. This is something else, which is regularly neglected when discussing *sharīʿah*. The *sharīʿah* debate is also firmly controlled by the mainly modernist desire to find dogmatic consistency.

5. Cf. 1 Samuel—Chapter 16:7; Ṣaḥīḥ Muslim reads: " . . . *Inna Allāha lā yanẓuru ilā ajsādikum wa lā ilā ṣuwarikum wa lakin yanẓuru ilā qulūbikum* . . . " (Truly, Allah sees not your bodies nor your faces but your hearts).

6. Saḥīḥ Muslim, ed. *Maktabat al-Īmān* (n.d.), 65 (Ḥadīth 41:159).

7. Ibn Qayyim al-Jawziyya, *Iʿlām al-Muwaqqiʿīn ʿan Rabbi l-ʿālamīn* (Beirut: Lebanon Edition, 2013), 35.

8. Roughly translated as "those who are removed from tradition."

9. Ibn Hājar al-Asqalānī, Shihāb ad-Dīn, *Fatḥ al-bārī bi sharḥ Saḥīḥ al-Bukhārī* (Beirut: Dār al-Fikr, 1993), 14:303; Khaled Abou El Fadl, "The Human Rights Commitment in Modern Islam," (online PDF), 133. Last accessed January 7, 2015.

10. Ibn Qayyim al-Jawziyya, *Iʿlām al-Muwaqqiʿīn ʿan Rabbi l-ʿalamīn* (Beirut: Lebanon Edition, 2013), 35.

11. However, without a doubt and for obvious reasons, legal scholars, in their race for "what is most probable" in deducing divine *sharīʿah* judgments (*aḥkām sharʿiyya*), invoked God's word (the *Qur'ān*) as well as the authentic prophetic tradition (*sunnah*) as divine legitimate indicative reference, both fundamentally and linguistically (*adillat al-aḥkām* sowie *dalālāt al-alfāẓ*).

12. Cf., for example, Wahbah Az-Zuḥailī, *al-wajīz fī uṣūl al-fiqh* (Damascus: Daru'l-Fikr, 2012), 119 ff; Abū Isḥāk al-Shāṭibī, *al-Muwāfaqāt fī uṣūl al-sharīʿah*, ed. ʿAbdullah Darrāz (Lebanon: Dar al-Kutub al-Ilmiyah, 2009), 63 ff.

13. Irene Schneider, "Die Terminologie der aḥkām al-ḥamsa und das Problem ihrer Entstehung, dargestellt am Beispiel der šafiʿītischen adab al-qaḍī-Literatur" (The Terminology of the aḥkām al-ḥamsa and the Issue of How They Developed Portrayed Using the Example of the Shafi'ite adab al-qaḍī Literature), in Werner Diem and Abdoldjawad Falaturi, ed., *ZDMG*, Suppl. VIII, XXIV. Deutscher Orientalistentag vom 26. bis 30. Sep. 1988 in Köln (German Orientalist Meeting From 26 to 30 Sep 1988 in Cologne) (Stuttgart: Steiner, 1990), 223.

14. Jan C. Joerden, "Logik im Recht. Grundlagen und Anwendungsbeispiele" (The Logic Behind Law, Foundations and Practical Examples) (Berlin: Springer, 2010), 227 ff.

15. Muḥammad bin Idrīs al-Shāfiʿī, *Kitāb al-Umm*, 2001, 487.

16. Çefli Ademi, "Säkularitätsmomente im Rechtsdenken As-Saraḫsīs" (Secularist Elements in As-Saraḫsī's Legal Tradition), in *Jahrbuch für Islamische Theologie und Religionspädagogik* (Yearbook for Islamic Theology and Religious Education), ed. Milad Karimi and Mouhanad Khorchide (Freiburg: Verlag Herder, 2014).

17. Ibn Qayyim al-Jawziyya, *Iʿlām al-Muwaqqiʿīn ʿan Rabbi l-ʿalamīn* (Beirut: Lebanon Edition, 2013), 35.

18. Rüdiger Lohlker, *Islamisches Recht* (Islamic Law), 2012, 16; Wael B. Hallaq, *Sharīʿa. Theory. Practice. Transformations*, 2009, 2.

19. Thomas Bauer, *Kultur der Ambiguität. Eine andere Geschichte des Islam* (Culture of Ambiguity. A Different History of Islam), 2011, 180.

20. On the following passage, cf.: Çefli Ademi, "Säkularitätsmomente im Rechtsdenken As-Saraḫsīs" (Secularist Elements in As-Saraḫsī's Legal Tradition), in *Jahrbuch für Islamische Theologie und Religionspädagogik* (Yearbook for Islamic Theology and Religious Education), ed. Milad Karimi and Mouhanad Khorchide (Freiburg: Verlag Herder, 2014).

21. Jāmīʿ at-Tirmidī, Book 15, Hadith No. 7.

22. It would be incorrect to picture these two opposing parties as two geographically monolithic camps. The so-called "traditionalists" also existed in Iraq, and advocates of free legal reasoning also existed in the Hijāz. In addition, both camps were equally "traditional" insofar as both methods—unlike suggested by a few modern-day scholars, such as Nasr Hamid Abu Zaid—were text- and tradition based; they only differed when it came to interpreting sources, with either a stronger focus on literal wording or on meaning and intention.

23. Cf. Rüdiger Lohlker, *Islamisches Recht* (Islamic Law), 2012, 67ff.

24. On this passage, cf., for example: Muḥammad abū Zahra, *Tārikh al-madhāhib al-islamiyya* (Cairo: dār al-fikr al-ʿarabiyy, 2009), 241ff; Çefli Ademi, "Lehrstühle für 'Islamisches Recht'? Eine kritische Begriffsanalyse bzw. die Frage nach einer substanzadäquaten Lehrstuhlbezeichnung" (Professorships for "Islamic Law"? A Critical Analysis of the Term and the Question of a Substantially Adequate Name), in *Jahrbuch für Islamische Theologie und Religionspädagogik* (Yearbook for Islamic Theology and Religious Education), ed. Milad Karimi and Mouhanad Khorchide (Freiburg: Verlag Herder, 2012), 172ff.

25. Ibrāhīm b. Mūsā al-Shāṭibī, *al-muwāfaqāt fī uṣūl al-sharīʿah*, 4 vols. (Cairo: Dār al-Fikr al-ʿArabī, n.d.).

26. Cf. Yusūf al-Qaraḍāwī, *madkhal li-dirāsāt al-sharīʿah al-islamiyyah* (Beirut: Muʾassasāt ar-Risālah, 1993), 53; Birgit Krawietz, *Hierarchie der Rechtsquellen im tradierten sunnitischen Islam* (Hierarchy of Legal Sources in Sunni Islam) (Berlin: Duncker & Humblot, 2002), 223f.

27. A more detailed account of the theological positions in Islam can be found in: Muḥammad Abū Zahra, *tārīkh al-mathāhib al-islāmiyya fī assiyāsa wa-l-ʿaqāʾid wa tārīkh al-madhāhib al-fiqhiyya* (Cairo: dār al-fikr al-ʿarabiyya, 2009), 143ff.; a concise account of the theological issue of purpose behind divine actions can be found in: Jasser Auda, *Maqasid al-Shariah as Philosophy of Islamic Law. A Systems Approach* (London: IIIT, 2008), 52ff.

28. On this issue and the following section cf.: Jasser Auda, *Maqasid al-Shariah as Philosophy of Islamic Law. A Systems Approach* (London: IIIT, 2008), 52.

29. Muḥammad at-Ṭayyib al-Baṣrī, *al-muʿtamad fī ʿuṣūl al-fiqh*, 1st edition. Khalil al-Mees, Band 2 (Beirut 1983), 184.

30. On the following, cf.: Ali Ghandour, "Die Freiheit Gottes und des Menschen. Zur Theorie des *kasb* in der ašʿarītischen Theologie" (On the Freedom of God and Human Beings. The Theory of *kasb* in Ash'arite Theology), in *Jahrbuch für Islamische Theologie und Religionspädagogik* (Yearbook for Islamic Theology and Religious Education), ed. Milad Karimi and Mouhanad Khorchide, Hrsg. (Freiburg: Verlag Herden, 2013), 86 ff., with further references.

31. On divine action not being bound by purpose, cf.: al-Āmidī, *Sayf ad-Dīn: abkār al-afkār fī ʿilm al-kalām*. Vol. II (Cairo: Lağnat Iḥyā' at-Turāt al-Islāmī, 2004). 152f.

32. Ṣabrī, Muṣṭafā, *mawqifu-l-ʿaqli wa-l-ʿilm wa-l-ʿālam min rabbi-l-ʿālamīn*, 3. Vol. III (Beirut 1981), 16.

33. Ṣabrī, Muṣṭafā, *mawqifu-l-ʿaqli wa-l-ʿilm wa-l-ʿālam min rabbi-l-ʿāin ra*, 3. Vol. III (Beirut 1981), 16; Taha Jabir al-Alwani, *Maqāṣid al-Shariʿah*, 1st edition, (Beirut: IIIT and Dār al-Hādī, 2001), 75.

34. Ṣabrī, Muṣṭafā, *mawqifu-l-ʿaqli wa-l-ʿilm wa-l-ʿālam min rabbi-l-ʿālamīn*, 3. Vol. III (Beirut 1981), 16.

35. Shihāb ad-Dīn al-Alūsī, *rūḥ al-maʿānī fī tafsīr al-qurʾān al-ʿaẓīm* Vol. 15 (Beirut: Dār al-iḥyāʾ, n.d.), 39.

36. Jasser Auda, *Maqasid al-Shariah as Philosophy of Islamic Law* (2008), 79; Kevin Reinhart, *Before Revelation. The Boundaries of Muslim Moral Thought* (Albany: SUNY Press, 1995); on the influence of theology in a more narrow sense of the term (*kalām*) on Islamic Jurisprudence, cf.: Umar F. Abd-Allah, *Theological dimensions of Islamic Law*, 237ff., in *The Cambridge Companion to Classical Islamic Theology*, ed. Tim Winter (Cambridge: Cambridge University Press, 2008).

37. On the following cf.: Felicitas Opwis, "Maṣlaḥa in Contemporary Islamic Legal Theory," in *Islamic Law and Society* 12, no. 2 (2005): 182 (190 ff.). (Also available online as PDF). Last accessed March 18, 2015.

38. Legal analogy is only one type of *qiyās*. Others include, for example, the *lega e contrario* or *argumentum a minore ad maius*.

39. Cf., for example, Birgit Krawietz, *Hierarchie der Rechtsquellen im tradierten sunnitischen Islam* (Hierarchy of Legal Sources in Sunni Islam) (Berlin: Duncker & Humblot, 2002), 223f.

40. Cf. Muḥammad Abū Zahra, uṣūl al-fiqh, Dār al-Fikr al-ʿarabiyya o.J. o.O., 277; Felicitas Opwis, "Islamic Law and Legal Change: The Concept of Maṣlaḥa in Islamic Law in Classical and Contemporary Islamic Legal Theory," in *Islamic Law in the Contemporary Context. Shari'a*, ed. Abbas Amanat and Frank Griffel. (Palo Alto, CA: Stanford University Press, 2007), 62ff; Jasser Auda, *Maqasid al-Shariah as Philosophy of Islamic Law* (2008), 66.

41. Jasser Auda, *Maqasid al-Shariah as Philosophy of Islamic Law* (2008), 9.

42. Ṣaḥīḥ al-Bukhārī, Book 64, Ḥadīth no. 163.

43. al-Bukhārī, Book 64, Ḥadīth no. 163.

44. The only renowned legal scholars who rejected the group who prayed along the way was the Zāhirīte, Ibn Ḥazm. According to him, the *aṣr* prayer—as per literal wording of the Prophet—should not have been recited before reaching Banū Qurayẓah, even if it had been after midnight, cf. Jasser Auda, *Maqasid al-Shariah as Philosophy of Islamic Law* (2008), 9, with further references.

45. Muḥammad aḍ-Ḍawābilī, *al-madkhal ilā ʿilm uṣūl al-fiqh*, 4th edition (Damascus: Verlag, 1963), 303ff; concise examples can, among others, be found in Jasser Auda, *Maqasid al-Shariah as Philosophy of Islamic Law* (2008), 10f., 11.

46. Authentic based on the science of Ḥadīth.

47. Ṣaḥīḥ al-Bukhārī, Book 25, Ḥadīth no. 91.

48. Cf. Muḥammad az-Zuḥaylī, *uṣūl al-fiqh al-islāmī* (Damascus: Dār al-Fikr, 1986), 766ff; Muḥammad aḍ-Ḍawābilī, *al-madkhal ilā ʿilm uṣūl al-fiqh*, 4th edition (Damascus: Verlag, 1963), 287ff.

49. Felicitas Opwis, "Islamic Law and Legal Change: The Concept of *Maṣlaḥa* in Classical and Contemporary Islamic Legal Theory", in *The Cambridge Companion to Classical Islamic Theology*, ed. Tim Winter (Cambridge: Cambridge University Press, 2008), 62ff; Jasser Auda, *Maqasid al-Shariah as Philosophy of Islamic Law* (2008), 16ff.

50. An overview of varying opinions on *maṣlaḥa al-mursala* is provided by Birgit Krawietz, *Hierarchie der Rechtsquellen im tradierten sunnitischen Islam* (Hierarchy of Legal Sources in Sunni Islam) (Berlin 2002), 242ff.

51. On this point and the following section, cf.: Felicitas Opwis, "Maṣlaḥa in Contemporary Islamic Legal Theory," in *Islamic Law and Society* 12, no. 2 (2005): 182 (191) (Also available online as PDF). Last accessed March 18, 2015.

52. Inspired by Max Weber's Typology of Rationalisation, indicating no congruence with regards to Islamic Jurisprudence, as early as Felicitas Opwis, "Maṣlaḥa in Contemporary Islamic Legal Theory," in *Islamic Law and Society* 12, no. 2 (2005): 182 (191), Fn. 33 (Also available online as PDF). Last accessed March 18, 2015.

53. It is not just Islamic jurisprudence that partially criticizes this methodology for reaching legal verdicts, but also Western legal tradition. An objection that is often put forward is that whoever implements a norm can only interpret it within the framework of a teleological approach to reaching legal verdicts based on the purpose he himself attributed to it in the first place. It follows that the implementer more or less arbitrarily establishes the purpose.

54. Mohammad Hashim Kamali, *Principles of Islamic Jurisprudence* (Cambridge: The Islamic Texts Society, 2011), 397ff, 401; Felicitas Opwis, "Maṣlaḥa in Contemporary Islamic Legal Theory," in *Islamic Law and Society* 12, no. 2 (2005): 182 (191). (Also available online as PDF). Last accessed March 18, 2015.

55. Cf. Ḥuseyn Ḥāmid Ḥassān, *naẓariyyat al-maṣlaḥa fī-l-fiqh al-islamī* (Cairo: Maktabat al-Mutanabbī, 1981).

56. Abū al-Maʿālī al-Juwaynī, *al-burhān fī uṣūl al-fiqh*, ed. ʿAbd al-ʿAẓīm ad-Dīb (1399 n.H.), Vol. 2, 923ff.

57. With this, he means such interests which are neither explicitly condoned nor rejected in divine sources, Abū Ḥāmid al-Ghazālī, *al-mustṣfā min ʿilm al-uṣūl*, Vol. 1, ed. Muḥammad Tāmir (Cairo: al-Maktaba al-Tawfīqiyya, 2011), 536.

58. Abū Ḥāmid al-Ghazālī, *al-mustṣfā min ʿilm al-uṣūl*, Vol. 1, ed. Muḥammad Tāmir (Cairo: al-Maktaba al-Tawfīqiyya, 2011), 538.

59. Ibid.

60. Ibid.

61. A summary of the issue of *munāsaba* in al-Ghazālī's work can be found in: Wael B. Hallaq, *A History of Islamic Legal Theories: An Introduction to Sunni uṣūl al-fiqh* (Cambridge: Cambridge University Press, 2005), 88ff.

62. Jasser Auda, *Maqasid al-Shariah as Philosophy of Islamic Law* (2008), 18.

63. Abū Ḥāmid al-Ghazālī, *al-mustṣfā min ʿilm al-uṣūl*, Vol. 1, ed. Muḥammad Tāmir (Cairo: al-Maktaba al-Tawfīqiyya, 2011), 536.

64. Ibid.

65. Wael B. Hallaq, *A History of Islamic Legal Theories. An Introduction to Sunni uṣūl al-fiqh* (Cambridge: Cambridge University Press, 2005), 90.

66. Hayatullah Laluddin, "An Analysis of Maslaha´s Development Through al-Ghazali. Pre and Post al-Ghazali Periods," in *International Business Management* 6, no. 2 (2012): 187–93.

67. Overviews can be found in: Muhammad Khalid Masud, *Shatibi's Philosophy of Islamic Law* (Islamabad: The Islamic Research Institute, 1995), 142ff., Felicitas Opwis, "Islamic Law and Legal Change: The Concept of *Maṣlaḥa* in Classical and Contemporary Islamic Legal Theory," in *The Cambridge Companion to Classical Islamic Theology*, ed. Tim Winter (Cambridge: Cambridge University Press, 2008), 62ff; Jasser Auda, *Maqasid al-Shariah as Philosophy of Islamic Law* (2008), 16ff; Muhammad Khalid Masud, *Shatibi´s Philosophy of Islamic Law* (Islamabad: The Islamic Research Institute, 1995), 135ff.

68. One representative example being Abū Ḥāmid al-Ghazālī, *al-mustṣfā min ʿilm al-uṣūl*, Vol. 1, ed. Muḥammad Tāmir (Cairo: al-Maktaba al-Tawfīqiyya, 2011), 536ff.

69. Cf. Muṣṭafā Zayd, *al-maṣlaḥa fī-l-tashrīʿ al-islāmī wa Najm ad-Dīn aṭ-Ṭūfī*, Vol. 2 (Cairo: Dār al-Fikr al-ʿArabī, 1964), 206ff, 231ff.

70. Cf. Felicitas Opwis, "Maṣlaḥa in Contemporary Islamic Legal Theory," in *Islamic Law and Society* 12, no. 2 (2005): 199. (Also accessible online as PDF). Last accessed March 18, 2015; also—albeit critically—Muhammad Khalid Masud, *Shatibi's Philosophy of Islamic Law* (Islamabad: The Islamic Research Institute, 1995), 150.

71. Wael B. Hallaq, *A History of Islamic Legal Theories, Provides an Accomplished Overview of al-Shāṭibī's Theory: An Introduction to Sunni uṣūl al-fiqh* (Cambridge: Cambridge University Press, 2005), 162ff; also cf. Felicitas Opwis, "Maṣlaḥa in Contemporary Islamic Legal Theory," in *Islamic Law and Society* 12, no. 2 (2005): 196; a more in-depth analysis is provided by Muhammad Khalid Masud, *Shatibi´s Philosophy of Islamic Law* (Islamabad: The Islamic Research Institute, 1995).

72. Ibrāhīm b. Mūsā al-Shāṭibī, *al-muwāfaqāt fī uṣūl al-sharī'ah*, 4 vols. (Cairo: Dār al-Fikr al-'Arabī, n.d.), vol. 3, 366ff., vol. 4, 20ff.

73. Ibrāhīm b. Mūsā al-Shāṭibī, *al-muwāfaqāt fī uṣūl al-sharī'ah*, 4 vols. (Cairo: Dār al-Fikr al-'Arabī, n.d.), vol. 1, 34ff.

74. Ibrāhīm b. Mūsā al-Shāṭibī, *al-muwāfaqāt fī uṣūl al-sharī'ah*, 4 vols. (Cairo: Dār al-Fikr al-'Arabī, n.d.), vol. 1, 29ff.; vol. 3, 15ff.

75. Rosabel Martin-Ross provides an interesting investigation into the various different interpretations of al-Shāṭibī's maqāṣid theory, Trends in modernist approaches to the study of *maqāṣid al-sharī'ah* with special reference to al-Shāṭibī's *al-Muwāfaqāt fī Uṣūl al-Sharī'a.* Neo-Mu'tazilism in the writings of Aḥmad al-Raysūnī and others, 14ff. (online as PDF). Last accessed April 7, 2014.

76. Rosabel Martin-Ross, "Trends in Modernist Approaches to the Study of *maqāṣid al-sharī'ah*," with special reference to al-Shāṭibī's *"al-Muwāfaqāt fī Uṣūl al-Sharī'ah.* Neo-Mu'tazilism in the writings of Aḥmad al-Raysūnī and others," 42 (online as PDF). Last accessed April 7, 2014.

77. Wael B. Hallaq, *A History of Islamic Legal Theories. An Introduction to Sunni uṣūl al-fiqh* (Cambridge: Cambridge University Press, 2005), 214ff.; Felicitas Opwis, "Maṣlaḥa in Contemporary Islamic Legal Theory," in *Islamic Law and Society* 12, no. 2 (2005): 198ff.

78. Mazheruddin Siddiqi, *Modern Reformist Thought* (Islamabad: Islamic Research Institute, 1982), 74ff; Felicitas Opwis, "Maṣlaḥa in Contemporary Islamic Legal Theory," in *Islamic Law and Society* 12, no. 2 (2005): 198, 199.

79. Malcolm H. Kerr, *Islamic Reform: The Political and Legal Theories of Muḥammad 'Abdūh and Rashid Riḍā* (Princeton, NJ: Princeton University Press, 1966), 107, 157; Felicitas Opwis, "Maṣlaḥa in Contemporary Islamic Legal Theory," in *Islamic Law and Society* 12, no. 2 (2005): 199.

80. Felicitas Opwis, "Maṣlaḥa in Contemporary Islamic Legal Theory," in *Islamic Law and Society* 12, no. 2 (2005): 199, with further references.

81. Cf. the excellent analysis provided by Thomas Bauer, *Die Kultur der Ambiguität. Eine andere Geschichte des Islams* (Culture of Ambiguity. A Different History of Islam) (Berlin: Verlag der Weltreligionen im Insel Verlag, 2011).

82. Cf. Wolfhart Heinrichs, *Ǧadal bei Aṭ-Ṭūfī: Eine Interpretation seiner Beispielsammlung* (Ǧadal bei Aṭ-Ṭūfī: An Interpretation of His Collection of Examples), in: Zeitschrift der Deutschen Morgenländischen Gesellschaft (Magazine of the German Orientalist Association). Supplement III. 19. Deutscher Orientalistentag (German Orientalist Meeting) 1975. Speeches, ed. Wolfgang Voigt, Wiesbaden: Franz Steiner 1977, vol. 1, 463ff.; Felicitas Opwis, "Maṣlaḥa in Contemporary Islamic Legal Theory," in *Islamic Law and Society* 12, no. 2 (2005): 200.

83. Wael B. Hallaq, *Sharī'a. Theory—Practice—Transformations* (Cambridge: Cambridge University Press, 2012), 5f.

84. George Makdisi, "Scholasticism and Humanism in Classical Islam and The Christian West," *Journal of the American Oriental Society* 109, no. 2 (April–June 1989): 175, (176).

85. Edition: Beirut Mu'assassat ar-Risāla 1982.

86. Wael B. Hallaq, *A History of Islamic Legal Theories: An Introduction to Sunni uṣūl al-fiqh* (Cambridge: Cambridge University Press, 2005), 214ff, 219f.

87. Malcolm H. Kerr, *Islamic Reform: The Political and Legal Theories of Muḥammad ʿAbdūh and Rashid Riḍā* (Princeton, NJ: Princeton University Press, 1966), 107, 157; Felicitas Opwis, "Maṣlaḥa in Contemporary Islamic Legal Theory," in *Islamic Law and Society* 12, no. 2 (2005): 201f.

88. David Johnston, "Turn in Epistemology and Hermeneutics of Twentieth Century Uṣūl," in *Islamic Law and Society* 11, no. 2 (2004): 233ff, (257).

89. Wael B. Hallaq, *A History of Islamic Legal Theories. An Introduction to Sunni uṣūl al-fiqh* (Cambridge: Cambridge University Press, 2005), 219.

90. Muḥammad aṭ-Ṭāhir Ibn ʿĀshūr, *maqāṣid al-sharīʿah al-islāmiyyah*, ed. Mohamed El-Tāhir el-Mesawi and Jordan Dār an-Nafāʾis (2001), 172. The translation is taken from Ibn ʿĀshūr treatise on maqāṣid al-Sharīʿah, xxii.

91. ʿAbdullah b. Bayyah, *ʿalāqat maqāṣid al-sharīʿa bi uṣūl al-fiqh* (2006), 134.

BIBLIOGRAPHY

Abd-Allah, Umar F. "Theological Dimensions of Islamic Law." In *The Cambridge Companion to Classical Islamic Theology*, edited by Tim Winter, 237–339. Cambridge: Cambridge University Press, 2008.

Abou El Fadl, Khaled. "The Human Rights Commitment in Modern Islam." In *Human Rights and Responsibilities in the World Religions*, edited by Joseph Runzo, Nancy M. Martin, and Arvind Sharma. Oxford: Oneworld Publications, 2002.

Abū Zahra, Muḥammad. *Uṣūl al-fiqh*. Cairo: Dār al-Fikr al- ʿArabī, 1958.

———. *Tārikh al-madhāhib al-islamiyya fī assiyāsa wa-l-ʿaqāʾid wa tārīkh al-madhāhib al-fiqhiyya*. Cairo: Dār al-Fikr al-ʿArabi, 2009.

Ademi, Çefli. "Lehrstühle für 'Islamisches Recht'? Eine kritische Begriffsanalyse bzw. die Frage nach einer substanzadäquaten Lehrstuhlbezeichnung." In *Jahrbuch für Islamische Theologie und Religionspädagogik*, edited by Khorchide Mouhanad and Karimi Milad. Freiburg: Verlag Herder, 2014.

Aḍ-Ḍawābilī, Muḥammad. *Al-Madkhal ilā ʿilm uṣūl al-fiqh*. 4th edition. Damascus: Verlag, 1963.

———"Säkularitätsmomente im Rechtsdenken As-Saraḫsīs." In *Jahrbuch für Islamische Theologie und Religionspädagogik*, edited by Khorchide Mouhanad and Karimi Milad. Freiburg: Verlag Herder, 2014.

Al-Alūsī, Shihāb ad-Dīn. *Rūḥ al-maʿānī fī tafsīr al-qurʾān al-ʿaẓīm*. Beirut: Dār al-Iḥyāʾ, n.d.

Al-Alwani, Taha Jabir. *Maqāṣid al-Shariʿah*. 1st edition. Beirut: IIIT and Dār al-Hādī, 2001.

Al-Āmidī, Sayf ad-Dīn. *Abkār al-afkār fī ʿilm al-kalām*. Cairo: Lağnat Iḥyā' at-Turāt al-Islāmī, 2004.

Al-Asqalānī, Shihāb ad-Dīn Ibn Hājar. *Fatḥ al-bārī bi sharḥ saḥīḥ al-bukhārī*. Beirut: Dār al-Fikr, 1993.

Al-Ghazālī, Abū Ḥāmid. *Al-Mustṣfā min ʿilm al-uṣūl*. Edited by Muḥammad Tāmir. Cairo: al-Maktaba al-Tawfīqiyya, 2011.

Al-Jawziyya, Ibn Qayyim. *Iʿlām al-muwaqqiʿīn ʿan rabbi l-ʿālamīn*. Beirut: Lebanon Edition, 2013.

Al-Juwaynī, Abū al-Maʿālī. *Al-Burhān fī uṣūl al-fiqh*. Edited by ʿAbd al-ʿAẓīm ad-Dīb (1399 n.H.), 2 vols. Cairo: Dār al-Anṣār, 1980.
Al-Qaraḍāwī, Yusūf. *Madkhal li-dirāsāt al-sharīʿah al-islamiyyah*. Beirut: Muʾassasāt ar-Risālah, 1993.
Al-Shāfiʿī, Muḥammad bin Idrīs. *Kitāb al-Umm*. Ort: Verlag, 2001.
Al-Shāṭibī, Abū Isḥāq. *Al-Muwāfaqāt fī uṣūl al-sharīʿah*. Edited by ʿAbdullah Darrāz. Lebanon: Dar al-Kutub al-Ilmiyah, 2009.
Al-Shāṭibī, Ibrāhīm b. Mūsā. *Al-Muwāfaqāt fī uṣūl al-sharīʿah*. 4 vols. Cairo: Dār al-Fikr al-ʿArabī, n.d.
Al-Zuḥaylī, Muḥammad. *Uṣūl al-fiqh al-islāmī*. Damascus: Dār al-Fikr, 1986.
At-Ṭayyib al-Baṣrī, Muḥammad. *Al-Muʿtamad fī uṣūl al-fiqh*. Beirut: n.p., 1983.
Auda, Jasser. *Maqasid al-Shariah as Philosophy of Islamic Law: A Systems Approach*. London: IIIT, 2008.
Az-Zuḥailī, Wahbah. *Al-wajīz fī uṣūl al-fiqh*. Damascus: Daru'l-Fikr, 2012.
Bauer, Thomas. *Kultur der Ambiguität. Eine andere Geschichte des Islam* (Culture of Ambiguity: A Different History of Islam). Berlin: Verlag der Weltreligionen im Insel Verlag, 2011.
Bin Bayyah, ʿAbdullah. *ʿAlāqat maqāṣid al-sharīʿah bi uṣūl al-fiqh*. London: Markaz Dirāsāt Maqāṣid al-Sharī'ah al-Islāmīyah, 2006.
Ghandour, Ali. "Die Freiheit Gottes und des Menschen. Zur Theorie des kasb in der ašʿarītischen Theologie (On the Freedom of God and Human Beings: The Theory of kasb in Ash'arite Theology)." *Jahrbuch für Islamische Theologie und Religionspädagogik*, edited by Khorchide Mouhanad and Karimi Milad. Freiburg: Verlag Herder, 2013.
Hallaq, Wael B. *A History of Islamic Legal Theories: An Introduction to Sunni uṣūl al-fiqh*. Cambridge: Cambridge University Press, 2005.
———. *Sharīʿa. Theory—Practice—Transformations*. Cambridge: Cambridge University Press, 2012.
Ḥassān, Ḥuseyn Ḥāmid. *Naẓariyyat al-maṣlaḥa fī-l-fiqh al-islamī*. Cairo: Maktabat al-Mutanabbī, 1981.
Heinrichs, Wolfhart. "Ǧadal bei Aṭ-Ṭūfī: Eine Interpretation seiner Beispielsammlung (Ǧadal bei Aṭ-Ṭūfī: An Interpretation of His Collection of Examples)." *Zeitschrift der Deutschen Morgenländischen Gesellschaft* (Magazine of the German Orientalist Association). Supplement III. 19. Deutscher Orientalistentag (German Orientalist Meeting) 1975. Speeches 1, 463 (1977), 463–473.
Ibn ʿĀshūr, Muḥammad aṭ-Ṭāhir. *Maqāṣid al-sharīʿah al-islāmiyyah*. Edited by Mohamed El-Tāhir el-Mesawi. Jordan: Dār an-Nafāʾis, 2001.
ibn al-Ḥajjāj, Muslim. *Saḥīḥ Muslim*. Rabat: Maktabat al-Īmān, n.d.
ibn Ismā'īl Bukhārī, Muḥammad. *Ṣaḥīḥ al-Bukhārī*. Beirut: Dār al-Fikr, 1997.
Joerden, Jan C. *Logik im Recht. Grundlagen und Anwendungsbeispiele* (The Logic Behind Law: Foundations and Practical Examples). Berlin: Springer, 2010.
Johnston, David. "Turn in Epistemology and Hermeneutics of Twentieth Century Uṣūl." *Islamic Law and Society* 11, no. 2 (2004): 233–282.
Kamali, Mohammad Hashim. *Principles of Islamic Jurisprudence* 3. Revised and enlarged edition. Cambridge: The Islamic Texts Society, 2011.

Kerr, Malcolm H. *Islamic Reform: The Political and Legal Theories of Muḥammad ʿAbdūh and Rashid Riḍā*. Berkeley: University of California Press, 1966.

Krawietz, Birgit. *Hierarchie der Rechtsquellen im tradierten sunnitischen Islam* (Hierarchy of Legal Sources in Sunni Islam). Berlin: Duncker & Humblot, 2002.

Laluddin, Hayatullah. "An Analysis of Maslaha's Development Through al-Ghazali: Pre and Post al-Ghazali Periods." *International Business Management* 6, no. 2 (1, 2012): 87–93.

Lohlker, Rüdiger. *Islamisches Recht* (Islamic Law). Wien: facultas wuv, 2012.

Makdisi, George. "Scholasticism and Humanism in Classical Islam and the Christian West." *Journal of the American Oriental Society* 109, no. 2 (April–June 1989): 175–182.

Martin-Ross, Rosabel. *Trends in Modernist Approaches to the Study of Maqāṣid al-Sharīʿah with Special Reference to al-Shāṭibī's al-Muwāfaqāt fī Uṣūl al-Sharīʿah: Neo-Muʿtazilism in the Writings of Aḥmad al-Raysūnī and Others*. Dissertation, Cambridge 2012. https://pdfs.semanticscholar.org/c72c/c85767ecb5aff0b74a551f-c028a2ea4529d8.pdf.

Masud, Muhammad Khalid. *Shatibi's Philosophy of Islamic Law*. Islamabad: The Islamic Research Institute, 1995.

Opwis, Felicitas. "Islamic Law and Legal Change: The Concept of Maṣlaḥa in Islamic Law in Classical and Contemporary Islamic Legal Theory." In *Islamic Law in the Contemporary Context. Shari'a*, edited by Abbas Amanat and Frank Griffel, 62–82. Palo Alto, CA: Stanford University Press, 2007.

———. "Maṣlaḥa in Contemporary Islamic Legal Theory." In *Islamic Law and Society* 12, no. 2 (2005): 182–223.

Reinhart, Kevin. *Before Revelation. The Boundaries of Muslim Moral Thought.* Albany: State University of New York Press, 1995.

Ṣabrī, Muṣṭafā. *Mawqifu-l-ʿaqli wa-l-ʿilm wa-l-ʿālam min rabbi-l-ʿālamīn*. 3 vols. Beirut: n.p., 1981.

Schneider, Irene. "Die Terminologie der aḥkām al-ḥamsa und das Problem ihrer Entstehung, dargestellt am Beispiel der šafiʿītischen adab al-qaḍī-Literatur." In *ZDMG, Suppl. VIII, XXIV. Deutscher Orientalistentag vom 26. bis 30. Sep. 1988 in Köln*. Edited by Werner Diem und Abdoldjawad Falaturi. Stuttgart: Steiner Verlag, 1990.

Siddiqi, Mazheruddin. *Modern Reformist Thought in the Muslim World*. Islamabad: Islamic Research Institute, 1982.

Zayd, Muṣṭafā. *Al-Maṣlaḥa fī-l-tashrīʿ al-islāmī wa Najm ad-Dīn aṭ-Ṭūfī*. Vol. 2. Cairo: Dār al-Fikr al-ʿArabī, 1964.

Chapter 12

Which Comes First, the *Maqāṣid* or the *Sharīʿa*?

Rumee Ahmed

It is now well known, at least in academic circles, that precolonial jurists who wrote books on normative Islamic law (*fiqh*) were not composing official legal documents like today's state-based criminal and civil codes. Rather, they were using legal language to reflect on an ideal law that had a tenuous relationship to actual court-based litigation and adjudication. Jurists wrote *fiqh* books not as codes, but as arguments about the way that humans ought to relate to God. As arguments, they were speculative and theoretical, exhibiting a high level of abstraction, and contemplating cases that might never occur in everyday life. These books regularly promoted injunctions related to criminal and civil law that would, if actually implemented in a legal code, result in inefficiencies and outright injustices. That wasn't an immediate problem, because those injunctions were not designed for practical implementation, but rather for buttressing their authors' larger theoretical arguments; and theoretical arguments often value internal coherence over practicality.

In the postcolonial era, however, these theoretical texts have become problematic, as many of their injunctions are now being adopted directly into the civil and criminal codes of many Muslim-majority nation-states. Whereas precolonial jurists used their *fiqh* books to argue for wide-ranging and vastly different injunctions in the service of larger theoretical arguments, nation-states have taken to choosing single injunctions from these books divorced from their argumentative contexts, labeling them "Islamic law," and applying them uniformly to all citizens in official legal codes.[1] This modern drive for codification finds roots in precolonial history, but it got a huge boost from colonial powers seeking legal uniformity in their colonized lands, and from Muslim anticolonialists seeking self-determination.[2]

In their attempts to codify Islamic law, both colonists and anticolonialists, for different reasons, looked to the precolonial past to define authentic expressions of Islamic law. Both presumed that modern laws were inherently corrupt, and that the truest articulations of Islamic law were made long ago, as though a law's authenticity is directly proportional to its age. Many colonial-era Muslim jurists, for example, argued that Islamic law's authenticity lay in its ancient past, and that they, as Islamic legal scholars, were uniquely capable of identifying those ancient laws. These jurists warned that modern laws, being inherently corrupt, were only legitimate if and when they agreed with precolonial laws. Their rhetoric was adopted on the state level, and several Muslim-majority states, to demonstrate the authority and legitimacy of their laws, tried to incorporate at least some historical, precolonial Islamic laws into their legal codes.[3]

Having done so, however, these Muslim-majority states now find themselves in a difficult position. Putting precolonial Islamic laws into their legal codes was easy, but the practical results have proved less than ideal. The inefficiencies and injustices that were heretofore theoretical in precolonial legal texts have now become actualized in the context of nation-states.[4] Many of the historical Islamic laws that nation-states chose to adopt run counter to popular movements that promote human rights, gender egalitarianism, religious liberty, modern finance, and pluralistic governance, among other concerns. This would not normally be a problem; ideally, a nation-state would simply adapt and change its laws to reflect the changing beliefs of its citizens and the needs of the state. But these nation-states find themselves in a bind because of their laws' "Islamic" appellative. That is, Islamic laws are only presumed to be authentic when they are linked to an ancient past, yet nation-states need those same laws to somehow address modern concerns. Thus, nation-states are faced with the daunting prospect of coming up with Islamic laws that are rooted in the precolonial Islamic legal past, yet speak to citizens' contemporary beliefs. In effect, they must have laws that are both ancient and contemporary at the same time.

In this context, *maqāṣid al-sharīʿa* (the objectives of Islamic law) gives us a tantalizing prospect: an ancient legal method that can deliver new and modern laws. The *maqāṣid* (singular: *maqṣad*) promise the ancient part of the law, not by reproducing historical injunctions, but by appealing to a methodology sanctioned by precolonial Islamic legal scholars. Once that ancient method is used, the resulting laws, even if they are unprecedented, will carry with them vestiges of an ancient legacy. Thus, new laws can be ancient, appearing legitimate to scholars and laypersons alike.

The *maqāṣid* methodology—promoted by towering precolonial figures like al-Ghazālī (d. 1111) and al-Shāṭibī (d. 1388), and described in detail in other chapters in this volume—works by (1) identifying the fundamental objectives of the *sharīʿa* and (2) testing existing laws that claim to be "Islamic" against those objectives. By identifying the objectives of the *sharīʿa*, modern scholars can test all existing Islamic laws, whether promoted by the state or not, to see whether they should be retained, modified, or replaced. Any laws found to be in violation of the objectives can be thereby replaced without compromising the historical nature of Islamic law as a whole. New laws can be called "Islamic" based on the fact that they better achieve the original objectives of the *sharīʿa*. Even if those laws are new, the objectives that they achieve are old.

Proponents of the *maqāṣid* methodology describe it as a way to reform Islamic law from "within the tradition," so that reforms are not imposed from the outside and without religious justification. Rather, they say, when you look at the legal tradition through the lens of the *maqāṣid*, it becomes clear that renewal is actually part and parcel of the tradition itself. That is, the Islamic legal tradition demands that laws be constantly renewed to ensure that they continue to achieve their underlying objectives. This is a truly exciting prospect for Islamic legal reform, and numerous studies have been commissioned and hundreds of works written to explore the *maqāṣid* methodology's ability to serve as a foundation from which to derive new, authoritative Islamic laws that accord with contemporary values and notions of justice.

Yet, despite the theoretical soundness of and widespread interest in this approach, the *maqāṣid* have thus far been unable to institute widespread and meaningful reforms.[5] While they have found limited success in creating new laws related to Islamic finance and minority jurisprudence (*fiqh aqaliyyāt*),[6] on most other issues they have failed to gain traction in Muslim communities. Proponents of the *maqāṣid* say that this is because Muslims are still unaware that the *maqāṣid* method of reform is truly a part of the Islamic legal tradition. Proponents suggest that when Muslims are properly educated about the history and the methodology of the *maqāṣid*, they will fully embrace them, and the *maqāṣid* will be highly effective for instituting Islamic legal reforms.[7]

It may indeed be the case that with more education the *maqāṣid* will become more appealing to Muslims and will be widely adopted as a method for legal reform. In recent years, however, several academic scholars of Islam have argued that resistance to the *maqāṣid* is not due to lack of education, but rather because the *maqāṣid* themselves are ill-suited to the reform project. They argue that the *maqāṣid*, by their very nature, cannot institute meaningful reform, and that, in fact, they were never intended to do so. Quite the opposite, they say that the *maqāṣid* were devised to restrict the use of reason and to curtail the development of new laws, that Muslim scholars almost always used them for that end in the past, and that they continue to do so today.

HISTORICAL AND PHILOSOPHICAL CRITIQUES

Felicitas Opwis, for instance, has written extensively on how the *maqāṣid* were developed in the medieval period as a means to defend Islamic laws, not to change them.[8] She carefully describes how the most vocal champions of the *maqāṣid* had no interest in using them to change substantive jurisprudence. Rather, the five *maqāṣid* of intellect, life, lineage, property, and religion were articulated in order to explain and defend five related *ḥudūd* (singular: *ḥadd*) punishments mentioned in the *Qur'ān* and *sunnah*, for drunkenness, murder, adultery, theft, and apostasy, respectively.

What this means is that the *maqāṣid* were not conceived as purely theoretical objectives that underpin the law, but that they were themselves derived from existing laws, or, more accurately, corporal punishments for perceived crimes. Starting with the laws on corporal punishments, some jurists abstracted about the reasoning behind those laws, not to question them, but to justify them. These jurists reasoned that since corporal punishment is so serious, there must have been some reason why God prescribed it. Thus, starting from the punishments themselves, they theorized about the divine wisdom behind those punishments. The conclusion that they came to, according to Opwis, is that God prescribed the five punishments to protect five inalienable rights that are violated by certain crimes. That is, the crimes for which the five corporal punishments were prescribed were thought to rob humans of inalienable rights, and the corporal *ḥudūd* punishments were intended to protect those rights.

Murder, for instance, is a crime that many jurists thought, based on their readings of foundational sources, warrants corporal punishment. Some of these jurists presumed that since murder results in corporal punishment, murder must rob humans of some inalienable right. Abstracting from that presumption, they figured that since murder robs people of their lives, "life" must be an inalienable right and the objective of the corporal punishment for murder is to protect that right. These jurists then followed the same abstraction process for the other four crimes that they thought warranted corporal punishment. The punishment for drunkenness was seen as a protection of intellect, theft as a protection of property, adultery as a protection of lineage, apostasy as a protection of religion, and murder as a protection of life. Jurists came up with these *maqāṣid* by moving from the law to the *maqṣad*, not from *maqṣad* to law; in other words, the *maqāṣid* were derived to defend and explain existing criminal laws, not to derive new ones.

In Opwis' historical account, the *maqāṣid* were postulated as second-order reflections on the law. The question, then, is whether or not that was their only function; that is, could the *maqāṣid*, despite having been postulated to explain existing laws, nevertheless be used to derive new ones? Opwis suggests that most precolonial jurists would answer, "no."[9] She describes them as hesitant in giving any law-deriving power to the *maqāṣid*, because that would also give them dangerous theological power. Jurists were worried that if they were to clearly identify the legal objectives, then they would effectively be saying that they had thereby captured the underlying, divine intention behind God's laws. That was to be avoided at all costs; most jurists insisted that God's logic is beyond all human comprehension, and so no one can ever definitively know the true intent behind God's laws. God prescribes laws for reasons known only to God, and though we can guess at those reasons, we can never know them for sure. For that theological reason, jurists were adamant that the *maqāṣid* should never be thought of as objectives that explained the *intention* behind God's laws, but rather as explanations for the *existence* of certain laws.

Arguing along similar lines, Anver Emon has shown that scholars used terms like *maṣlaḥa* and *maqāṣid* to limit the use of reason when deriving law.[10] In his reading, scholars who championed the *maqāṣid* were primarily interested in promoting and defending their schools' legal positions, not in reforming them. He, like Opwis, links the *maqāṣid* to a defense of the five *ḥudūd* punishments, but goes further to say that the *maqāṣid* were used to defend not only the five *ḥudūd*, but most of the *fiqh* of one's legal school. Emon describes precolonial legal scholars as being highly skeptical of human reason, and hesitant to abandon historical legal opinions. This, again, was largely for theological reasons. Humans, many precolonial jurists thought, possess limited and highly fallible intellects, and so it's better to follow historical opinions than to strike out on one's own. The primary function of the *maqāṣid*, in that context, is to defend existing Islamic laws from rational inquiry, and to help explain why believers should continue following existing laws rather than come up with new ones. This leads Emon to doubt the efficacy of the *maqāṣid* for any future legal reform, since they were not intended to reform *fiqh*, but to justify it.[11]

Emon's conclusion leaves us with an important question: since the *maqāṣid* were never intended for deriving new Islamic laws, does that mean that they cannot be used for that purpose in the future? Legal terms certainly change their meanings and resonances all the time; that is part of the miracle of language. But is the logic of the *maqāṣid* irremediable; can it only be used to defend and not derive law? To answer this question, we should focus on the theological findings of Opwis and Emon. They both point out that jurists hesitated to use human reason when deriving law for fear of imputing human rationality on the Lawgiver, and for fear of corrupting existing laws through faulty reasoning. In this respect, precolonial jurists exhibited an anxiety about law that is similar to contemporary jurists, the latter of whom are consumed with keeping Islamic law free from the taint of modern corruptions and colonial ideas.

Emon, Opwis, and others[12] draw our attention to something very important about how Islamic law and legal reform functioned in the precolonial period, and about how it continues to function today. Muslim jurists exhibit a persistent fear of corrupting Islamic law by introducing outside influences, whether human logic, colonial values, or something else. For a variety of reasons, jurists are hesitant to derive any new laws, especially when they challenge existing ones. What jurists tend to do instead is assume the authority of historical Islamic laws, even when those laws do not make sense, since sense-making is a function of the human intellect, which is itself subject to corruption. It is better to follow historical laws, jurists believed, because that way one is less likely to introduce their own corruptions into the process of law-making. If, as an intellectual exercise, people want to theorize about *maqāṣid* that would justify those historical laws, then they are free to do so, but if they were then to derive laws based on those *maqāṣid*, those laws would be highly suspect for containing corrupt reasoning.

THE DEFENSIVE POWER OF THE *MAQĀṢID*

At this point, we must confront the question that if the *maqāṣid* cannot be used to derive laws, then why do prominent jurists consistently discuss and promote them? It might seem an awful waste of time and energy to repeatedly examine these five objectives if they have no positive function. Put another way, if we accept that the *maqāṣid* were designed to defend existing laws, then we should ask what jurists are defending when they appeal to the *maqāṣid*, who is it being defended against, and why?

In fact, there are many groups in Muslim history that do not agree with the laws that the *maqāṣid* justify, including many prominent jurists. Ḥanafīs, for instance, were famously divided about whether or not drunkenness and apostasy should elicit corporal punishment.[13] Similarly, many Ottoman jurists believed that adultery should be punished with a fine, rather than with physical chastisement.[14] These jurists disagreed with the very laws and punishments that the *maqāṣid* justify, and so they would have no reason to promote the *maqāṣid* theory. These dissenters pointed out that the *maqāṣid* are highly speculative and are in no way inevitable; even if one agreed that drunkenness should elicit corporal punishment, who is to say that the punishment is intended to preserve the right of intellect as opposed to, say, a healthy liver, or coherent speech?

In the face of such criticism, proponents of the *maqāṣid* use the language of objectives to portray their view of Islamic law as normative and to discredit others. That is, they use the "objectives" theory to argue that the particular Islamic laws that they promote are objective. So, proponents of the *maqāṣid* can argue that those who interpret Islamic law to say, for example, that adultery does not elicit corporal punishment, are not only incorrect, but are going against the very objective core of the *sharīʿa.*

This suggests that the *maqāṣid* do, in fact, serve a positive function: they sanctify particular views of Islam and Islamic law as normative and objectively true. Proponents of the *maqāṣid* can say that their critics are not only disagreeing with a specific law or punishment, but that they are disagreeing with the objective foundations of the *sharīʿa* itself. By extension, they can say that their critics are not only wrong, but are demonstrably un-Islamic. The *maqāṣid* are, therefore, a very potent tool for promoting one view of Islam as objectively true while discrediting others, and promoting some Muslims as following "true" Islam while impugning others for following a corrupted version. Historically, we see that whenever the *maqāṣid* gained prominence, they were used for precisely this purpose. Recently, we have seen them used in this way, and to great effect, with respect to the *maqṣad* of property.

PROPERTY, THE *MAQĀṢID*, AND ISLAMIC SOCIALISM

Those who promote the *maqṣad* of property believe that Islamic law prescribes corporal punishment for the crime of theft, which is the act of stealing someone else's property. Since they believe that stealing property elicits corporal punishment, they further reason that property must be a fundamental right protected by the law, and must be an objective of the *sharīʿa*. This presumption stems from their reading of Q. 5:38, which they translate as, "The thief, male and female, cut off their hands as recompense for what they did, an exemplary punishment from God. God is Exalted and Wise!" Working backward from the corporal punishment for theft, they argue that property must be a *maqṣad*, and therefore that *maqṣad* should be used to define the limits of Islamic law. One can say, for instance, that since property is a God-given right, every believer has the right to acquire and dispose of private property. By extension, the *sharīʿa* cannot abide any interpretation of Islamic law that does not recognize the right to own private property, and any laws that try to do away with private property are inherently un-Islamic.

There have been, however, many Muslim scholars who interpreted Islamic law such that it does not endorse owning private property, relying upon different readings of Q. 5:38 mentioned above. They read the verse in a metaphorical sense, focusing on the phrase "an exemplary punishment" to argue that the prescribed punishment in the verse is not to be read literally.[15] They point out that the word in Q. 5:38 used for "their hands" (*aydiyahum*) is also used in the *Qur'ān* as a metaphor for power, and so the verse is referring not to cutting off physical hands, but to cutting off the means for people to engage in theft. In this reading, the verse is warning people about the dangers of private property, in that it leads people toward acquisitiveness, jealousy, and thievery, and so believers should create a society in which those behaviors are not only discouraged, but are impossible. This would be a society in which all resources were shared, and in which no one owned private property, thus making thievery impossible. The *Qur'ān*, in this reading, is not faulting people for theft, but impugning the institution of private property for enticing people to steal.

Muslims intermittently held such ideas about private property throughout Islamic history, and the late nineteenth and early twentieth centuries saw a number of movements arguing that Islam demands the abolition of private property. The most prominent of these groups were the Islamic Socialists, who rooted their thought in the teachings of Muslim scholars like Jamāl al-Dīn al-Afghānī (d. 1897), 'Ubayd Allāh Sindhī (d. 1944),[16] and Salāma Mūsā (d. 1958), and who traced their intellectual lineage to Ibn Ḥazm (d. 1064) and Shāh Walīullāh (d. 1762).[17] These Islamic Socialists held that the Prophet Muhammad's mission was to level class barriers and to destroy the concept of private property. To them, this was evident in Muhammad's practice, most notably in the vaunted *ukhuwwa* of Medina.

The *ukhuwwa* describes the period immediately following Muhammad's migration from Mecca to Medina, at which point Muhammad ordered all Muslims in the new city-state to be like siblings, which many residents reportedly understood as a command to share property. In the *ukhūuwwa*, and in other practices like dividing spoils of war, freeing slaves, and establishing a shared treasury, Islamic Socialists saw Muhammad and his companions making regular and progressive efforts toward socializing property. Islamic Socialists suggest that, even if Muhammad did not explicitly abolish private property in his lifetime, he intended to set into motion a series of events that would eventually, much like slavery, end the practice altogether. According to Asghar Ali Engineer, the Prophet's community represented "the first organized socialist movement in the world."[18]

Islamic Socialists buttressed their view of Muhammad's practice with interpretations of the *Qur'ān*. In particular, they cited Q. 7:128 ("the earth is God's to give"), Q. 21:105 ("the earth shall be an inheritance for my righteous servants"), and Q. 53:31 ("to God belongs all that is in the heavens and the earth") to argue that believers are meant to share the earth, rather than to own any part of it. The overall Qur'anic and prophetic message was, in the words of Ali Shariati, to create a "monotheistic classless society."[19] Islamic Socialists held *ishtirāk*, or, the belief that all property should be shared, to be the very foundation of Islamic social and economic thought.[20]

Islamic Socialism enjoyed widespread popularity throughout the twentieth century. Some polls from the middle of the century suggest that roughly one-third of Muslim professionals believed that Islamic Socialism best captured the spirit of Islam.[21] Groups like the Wäisi in Russia and the Majlis-e-Aḥrār in India argued that socialism was the fulfillment of the Islamic concept of *musāwa*, or, radical equality among humanity.[22] Islamic Socialism caught fire with Arab nationalist movements of the mid twentieth century, and took various forms in official state documents like Gamal Abdel-Nasser's National Charter and Muammar Qaddafi's Green Book.[23] Islamic scholars from all over the Muslim world began to extol socialism as the truest, most just embodiment of the Prophetic and Qur'anic message. Some scholars moderated their socialist views to allow for some measure of private property, but many held a sincere belief that Islam was economically Marxist at its core and did not condone ownership of private property. The poet-philosopher Muhammad Iqbal went so far as to say that Karl Marx was "Moses without Divine epiphany, the Christ without the Cross. He is not a prophet, but he has brought a book."[24]

In this Islamic Socialist perspective, theft loses its meaning. If everything is shared, then nothing can really be stolen, only borrowed, or appropriated. And if theft does not exist, then how can it be punished? Based on their readings of the *Qur'ān*—Q. 5:38 in particular—their interpretation of the life of the Prophet and his companions, and articulation of principles like *musāwa* and *ishtirāk*, Islamic Socialists were convinced that theft was never meant to be a punishable offence in Islam. But if we assume that theft is not punished, then the *maqṣad* of property loses it reason for being. Since the *maqṣad* is predicated on the punishment, once the punishment disappears, so does the *maqṣad*. Essentially, Islamic Socialism and the *maqṣad* of property cannot coexist.

Islamic Socialists' view of shared wealth and radical class equality is rooted in a careful study of Islamic history and foundational sources, and is a coherent interpretation of Islamic law. Yet, the *maqāṣid* model affords their reading no space, since it enshrines private property as an indispensible part of the *sharīʿa*. According to the *maqāṣid* model, Islamic Socialism is anathema to the very foundations of the *sharīʿa*, which cannot abide the abolition of private property. The *maqāṣid* model cannot countenance Islamic Socialism or change historical Islamic laws to accommodate it because it is not designed for that purpose. Rather, it is designed to defend the institution of private property, and to promote some level of capitalism as divinely sanctioned.

It is no coincidence that, in the wake of colonialism, Muslim-majority nation-states that embraced capitalism were the most fervent champions of the *maqāṣid*. As Islamic Socialists were expanding their influence across the Muslim-majority world, scholars in capitalist regimes used the *maqāṣid* to undermine Islamic Socialism as antithetical to the *sharīʿa*. Relying on the *maqāṣid*, these thinkers asserted that socialism was not only a non-Islamic doctrine, but an un-Islamic doctrine, and that Islamic Socialists were themselves disbelievers.[25] For example, the great champion of the *maqāṣid* in the twentieth century, Muḥammad al-Ṭāhir ibn ʻĀshūr (d. 1973), is thought to have composed his magnum opus on the topic for the purpose of safeguarding private property and denouncing socialism, which to him was "un-Islamic in theory, and would be catastrophic in practice."[26] Similarly, Taqi Usmani, a Pakistani federal judge and board member of at least ten Islamic banking institutions, declared Islamic Socialism an oxymoron; since the *maqāṣid* sanctify private property, he believes that one cannot be both a Muslim and socialist at the same time.[27] One of the leaders of the modern Islamic banking movement and prominent advocate of the *maqāṣid* model, Yusuf al-Qaradawi, argues that, since socialism is un-Islamic, Muslim socialists should not receive Islamic burials, and their marriages should be annulled.[28]

Each of these thinkers is foundational to modern Islamic banking conversations; each used the *maqāṣid* to promote their own versions of capitalism, and to denounce Islamic Socialism. It is surely no accident that each of these thinkers also held official positions in staunchly capitalist and antisocialist regimes. Ibn ʻĀshūr was the chief justice and *Shaykh al-Islām* in Tunisia when the greatest threat to the ruling regime was Habib Bourguiba's Socialist Destourian Party.[29] Taqi Usmani was appointed to a federal judgeship by the strident anticommunist Zia ul-Haq, who waged a protracted campaign against land reforms that would redistribute property. Usmani famously reversed a high court decision that would allow for land reform, arguing instead that any "quantitative limits" on landownership are repugnant to Islam.[30] Yusuf al-Qaradawi, based in Qatar, advises both the state-run Qatar National Bank and the Qatar International Islamic Bank,[31] along with a host of state-run banking institutions across the Middle East and South Asia, and serves as the "chairman of the supreme expert panel and supervisory board of the International Association of Islamic Banks."[32] All of these thinkers had the backing of capitalist regimes and institutions, and all used their positions and the *maqāṣid* to repel Islamic Socialism.

Here, we see that the *maqāṣid*, once again, serve a particular interest, in this case capitalist financial enterprises. The *maqāṣid* not only give such enterprises an Islamic veneer, they also delegitimize all other conceptions of Islam, as though the only "Islamic" economic system is some version of capitalism. It is no wonder that banks and capitalist regimes have funneled millions of dollars into supporting scholars, think tanks, and foundations that promote the *maqāṣid*. That is because the *maqāṣid* function to validate their status quo, and to invalidate all challengers. This, again, is how the *maqāṣid* were intended to work: to give exclusive theoretical backing to a particular conception of the *sharīʿa* and historical Islamic laws against all others.

The *maqāṣid* are regularly used in this way to promote certain historical Islamic laws in a way that shuts down debate and stifles reform, especially concerning religious freedom, women's rights, and sexual activity. Malaysian courts used the *maqṣad* of religion to argue that non-Muslims cannot utter the word "Allah";[33] the UAE cited the *maqāṣid* to explain why a wife owes her husband obedience;[34] and Saudi Arabia notoriously uses the *maqāṣid* discourse to restrict women's mobility. There are many other such examples, all of which tend to serve those in power, rather than empower those without.

Of course, many have tried to use the *maqāṣid* for more progressive ends, like, for example, arguing that women's rights and religious freedom are enshrined in the *maqāṣid*. But those arguments, unfortunately, tend not to be taken up and adopted by state actors. Rather, the *maqāṣid* seem to be embraced by the powerful only when they serve their interests and maintain the status quo. That is because the *maqāṣid* were designed to limit the use of the intellect and the scope for legal change. The *maqāṣid* work when they support following historical laws, and they fail whenever they try to change historical laws against the will of the powerful.

ISLAMIC LEGAL CHANGE

This all begs the question, if the *maqāṣid* only function to justify historical laws, then how *do* historical laws get changed, and how are new laws derived, especially given the rhetoric that all new laws are inherently suspect? The answer, in short, is that Islamic legal change starts not in the discourse of objectives, but in the discourse of *fiqh*. From its inception, Islamic law and legal change moved from practice to theory, not the other way around. This might seem counterintuitive; shouldn't laws be derived according to their objectives? That is a reasonable proposition, but it presumes that laws are created *ex nihilo*, without a prevailing context of practice to ground them. All legal systems, in fact, start by assuming that certain practices and existing laws are given, and from there, legal scholars abstract objectives. Islamic law is no exception.

Muslim jurists always start from practice, and then compose books of jurisprudence and legal theory to justify those practices. The Ḥanafī school was unabashed about this, and the Mālikī school staked its reputation on adherence to practice rather than on abstract objectives.[35] Even the Shāfiʿī school, from which the *maqāṣid* language stems, has been shown time and again to rely on inherited practice, and to have used objectives only to limit the use of reason in determining law, not to expand it. Al-Shāfiʿī and his followers were deeply suspicious of any application of reason, rationality, and objectives to

Islamic law, preferring even a weak transmission about historical Muslim practice to applied rationality.[36]

None of these schools started from objectives when coming up with law, and, other than the short-lived Ẓāhirī school, no major school even claimed that they were trying to do so. They all stated quite openly that they were following inherited practice; objectives were only used to check, modify, or critique existing laws, not to derive them. In fact, Muslim jurists seeking authority, especially those in the Sunni tradition, need to say that they are not using objectives to derive new laws, especially given how the schools of law mentioned above are structured. These schools arose in the early centuries of Islam, and by the fifth/eleventh century were recognized as authoritative sources of legal knowledge. Followers of one school might claim that theirs is better than others, but would at the same time acknowledge that following any of the schools guarantees one salvation. Since these legal schools enjoy hegemony in the Sunni Muslim community, authority is only gained by working within the schools, and lost by renouncing them.

In this framework, virtue is found not in deriving laws anew through objectives, but by following the historical legal opinions of one's school as closely as possible. A sentiment regularly attributed to the Prophet and found throughout Muslim legal thought reads, "The best thing is to imitate, and the worst thing is to innovate." It is considered dangerous to innovate for fear of introducing corruptions into legal thought, and it is considered much safer to simply follow laws that have already been laid down. At the very least, one can claim authority within a legal school by claiming to follow its early luminaries.

However, we should not think that just because authority is gained by appealing to the historical legal tradition that Muslim jurists blindly follow and reproduce historical laws. Quite the contrary, jurists regularly change laws and deviate from historical precedent. Muslim jurists are highly adept at changing historical Islamic laws, including those as foundational to the legal tradition as slavery and finance, to respond to changing times and circumstances. However, in order to maintain authority within a legal school, jurists have to work *within* the Islamic legal tradition, not *around* it. That is why Sherman Jackson refers to the Islamic legal tradition as "legal scaffolding" that jurists work within, as opposed to a list of unchangeable rules that they are condemned to reproduce.

This legal scaffolding gives jurists cover, so that whenever they propose new laws, those laws are seen as part of an historical legacy. New laws are therefore not really "new," they are simply the best and most relevant manifestations of historical laws. Jurists would propose new laws from within the scaffolding in a variety of ways, but the most prominent and best studied of them is the commentary tradition. By commenting on historical *fiqh* texts, jurists came up with new, and sometimes radically different, laws that nonetheless expressed fidelity to the legal tradition. Commentators would essentially use an historical religious text as a canvas upon which to illustrate new readings of Islam and Islamic law.

COMMENTARIES AS SITES OF LEGAL REFORM

Muslim scholars composed commentaries on a variety of Islamic topics, from the *Qur'ān* to Sufism to law. It is perhaps easiest to see how a foundational text can serve as scaffolding for new readings in the case of *Qur'ān* commentaries. By commenting upon the *Qur'ān*, one can construct a story of Islam that might look very different from others, depending on how one reads the text. However, to ensure authenticity, one would have to stick closely to the original wording of the text, thereby reassuring the reader that the commentary is explaining, rather than deviating from the *Qur'ān* and its plain-sense meaning. *Qur'ān* commentators were thereby able to use the words of the *Qur'ān* as scaffolding to construct their own, unique Islamic narratives, even when that meant running completely counter to the denotation of the *Qur'ān* and its words.

Take, for example, Q. 2:45–46, " . . . and seek help in patience and in prayer. Indeed, that is difficult except for the humble (*khashiʿīn*); those who suspect (*yaẓunnūn*) that they will meet their Lord and that they will be returned to God." At first glance, these verses might seem entirely unproblematic, describing true believers as those who have humbled themselves fully before God and who seek God's help through patience and prayer. But there is one phrase that might be surprising: true believers "suspect that they will meet their Lord." True believers, one might think, would more than suspect that they will meet their Lord. Rather, one would think that they would be certain of such a meeting, which would explain why they were true believers in the first place.

This seems like an odd construction that requires addressing foundational theological issues, such as why true believers only suspect that they will meet their Lord, and does suspicion count as faith? However, *Qur'ān* commentators rarely felt the need to probe these questions. Instead, they often simply said that the term "those who suspect" (*yaẓunnūn*) in the verse actually means "those who know" (*yaʿlamūn*), or, even more commonly, "those who are certain" (*yastayqinūn*), so that the verse ought to be read as follows: "those who are certain that they will meet their Lord and that they will be returned to God."[37] This reading requires defining the word "suspect" as the exact opposite of its denotation; one who suspects, by definition, is not certain. Yet this did not disturb *Qur'ān* commentators. Rather than wrestle with the text, they usually said, "what is meant here is" (*yaʿnī*), and then provided a reading that made sense to them, even despite going against the grain of the text.

Islamic studies scholars have demonstrated that this linguistic move is pervasive in *Qur'ān* commentaries. Ayesha S. Chaudhry, for example, notes that many *Qur'ān* commentators interpreted the command in Q. 4:34 to "abandon [wives] in bed" to mean "call [wives] to bed," its exact opposite.[38] Walid Saleh similarly points out that certain commentators interpreted the term "misguided" in Q. 93:7 to mean "guided."[39] Whenever *Qur'ān* commentators would make these interpretations, they would not argue with the text of the *Qur'ān* or provide elaborate justifications for their readings. Rather, they would simply say, "what is meant here is," and provide their own interpretations. These interpretations served to buttress larger arguments that commentators were making about Islam, but rather than overtly state their positions, they worked within the scaffolding provided by the text of the *Qur'ān*.

Similarly, jurists produced commentaries on historical legal texts, parsing them word for word, and explaining what the original author "really" meant. In doing so, they demonstrated that they were working within the legal tradition; they were not changing the rulings found in texts so much as elaborating upon them and clarifying their intended meanings. These legal commentaries were produced in service to larger arguments about Islamic law that might have been unprecedented, and the interpretations found therein might have been in complete opposition to the plain-sense meaning of the original text. Yet, they would nevertheless be viewed as part and parcel of the legal tradition, rather than as foreign impositions.

For example, the great Ḥanafī jurist, al-Marghinānī (d. 1197), produced a legal commentary titled *al-Hidāya* that was premised on an earlier, foundational Ḥanafī legal text. *Al-Hidāya* is commonly viewed as an authoritative Ḥanafī *fiqh* book, even though it often explicitly diverts from the plain-sense meaning of the original text upon which it is commenting. Though al-Marghinānī regularly departed from the original text, whenever he did so, he would say that he was merely explaining its true meaning. Take, for instance, a section from his chapter on ritual purity. The original text has a passage on *ʿawra*, or, parts of the body that must be covered in public and during prayers. The original text states, "a male's *ʿawra* includes whatever is below the navel up to (*ilā*) the knees." This seems quite innocuous, but by al-Marghinānī's time, most Ḥanafīs believed that a male's *ʿawra* not only extended up to the knees, but included the knees as well. Ḥanafīs were proud of this law, and they chastised their legal counterparts in the Shāfiʿī and Mālikī schools—who did not include the knees in a male's *ʿawra*—for their loose morals. Here, al-Marghinānī was challenged with reconciling the dominant Ḥanafī opinion of his time, namely that the male *ʿawra* includes the knees, and the original historical text upon which he was commenting, which clearly states that a male's *ʿawra* only includes the area below the navel and "up to (*ilā*) the knees."

Rather than try to wrestle with these two positions, or disagree with the original text, al-Marghinānī simply explained what the text "really meant." He said, "The phrase 'up to' (*ilā*) should be understood as 'including' (*maʿa*), just like the word 'until' (*ḥattā*) [can be understood as meaning 'up to and including']."[40] In his commentary, al-Marghinānī simply states that "up to" really means "including." This is, linguistically, a very difficult argument to make, because "up to," by definition, does not mean "including." Yet, by stating that "up to" really means "including," al-Marghinānī was able to reconcile the original text with a new law, making it seem like the new law was actually rooted in the historical Ḥanafī tradition. He effectively changed the law without appearing to change anything; now the *ʿawra* included the knees, whereas before it did not.

The commentary tradition is a tried and true site of legal reform for jurists throughout Muslim history, for reforms both large and small. Muslim legal scholars produced commentaries that outlaw slavery, empower women, criminalize domestic violence, promote the use of contraceptives, and much more. They have used commentaries to justify socialism, capitalism, democracy, human rights, and any number of other ideas and ideologies. When doing so, they would not say that they were changing laws or endorsing ideologies; instead, they simply said that they were explaining the "real meaning" of the original text. Thus, they were able to promote new laws while maintaining allegiance to the historical tradition, freeing them from the perceived taint of human reason and modern innovation.

Being thus freed from suspicion, jurists are given broad creative license to articulate new laws in their commentaries. The laws thus promoted can look completely different from historical laws, even promoting their exact opposite. This is in direct contrast to the limited nature of reform that can be realized through the *maqāṣid*. In commentaries, jurists can advocate for absolute religious freedom, sanction broader notions of sexuality, and promote more diverse economic theories than would be possible under the *maqāṣid*. The *maqāṣid*, by their very nature, limit the extent to which human reason can determine law, and narrow the imaginative horizons available to jurists.

The *maqṣad* of intellect provides yet another example of this dynamic. Many Muslim-majority countries cite the *maqṣad* of intellect as justification for their drug policies. Based on a reading of Islamic texts in which corporal punishment is prescribed for consuming alcohol, this *maqṣad* has been used to criminalize alcohol and drug sale and use in these countries, and according to the *maqāṣid* model, it is inconceivable that the recreational use of drugs, especially alcohol, might be licit under Islamic law. The *maqṣad* limits the scope of the law.

Using the commentary method, however, Pakistan's Federal Shariat Court recently argued that, technically, alcohol consumption does not elicit a *ḥadd* punishment according to Islam's foundational texts.[41] Certainly, alcohol consumption is strongly discouraged in religious sources, but the court cited Islamic legal texts to demonstrate that, even if it is frowned upon, it does not necessarily warrant corporal punishment. They worked within the logic of historical texts to reconceive the law, and to demand that amendments be made to existing laws prescribing whipping for those who consume alcohol.

The Federal Shariat Court, not known for its liberal interpretations, was able to lend authority to their reading of the *Qur'ān* and practice of Muhammad by citing Islamic legal texts and commenting upon them. Had the court started with the *maqāṣid* instead, then they would have had to presume that alcohol consumption is a corporally punishable offence, and their reinterpretation of Islamic law would not have been possible. In fact, critics of the court ruling are already using the *maqṣad* of intellect to delegitimize the Court's ruling as un-Islamic.

My intention here is not to extol the virtues of socialism or to debate the legality of alcohol consumption in Islam. Nor is it to say that the commentary tradition is inherently progressive; indeed, this same court reinterpreted the Ḥanafī legal tradition to institute Pakistan's notorious blasphemy laws. Rather, my intent is to illustrate that the *maqāṣid* are not used to open up interpretations of Islamic law, nor were they intended to. Instead, they are always used to maintain historical articulations of Islamic law and to delegitimize all other interpretations. The *maqāṣid* are not neutral, objective facts; they are ideological tools that are used and deployed to buttress one version of *sharīʿa* against others.

These visions of *sharīʿa* might be either restrictive or emancipatory; they might embrace individual rights or constrict them, depending on who is doing the interpreting. However, we should recognize that the *maqāṣid* discourse has sharply defined limits, and that they are designed to maintain such limits, not to expand them. That helps explain why ruling regimes are so keen to promote the *maqāṣid*, and why they are so readily deployed when they serve the interests of the powerful. They are designed to maintain the status quo, and to delegitimize attempts at structural legal reform. As exciting and as promising as the *maqāṣid* might seem, they are designed to only allow incremental, limited changes that do not threaten the power structures that Islamic laws currently serve.

The alternative to the *maqāṣid*—namely, the commentary tradition—is far less glamorous, and lacks the conceptual clarity of having five principles that underlie Islamic law. Engaging with commentaries requires patience and attention to nuance, as well as familiarity with their structure and composition. However, what the commentary tradition lacks in conceptual clarity and ease of use, it makes up for in scope and authority. Those looking to effect authoritative, structural Islamic legal reform should ascertain whether the change they seek serves the interests of the powerful. If not, then the commentary tradition would prove a more effective, if more labor intensive, site for making their proposed reforms. If the change they seek does, in fact, serve the interests of the powerful, then perhaps that would be work best left to state functionaries, who will happily deploy the *maqāṣid* to achieve their ends, and are already hard at work doing so.

NOTES

1. For a concise description of this process, see Nandini Chatterjee, "Law, Culture and History: Amir Ali's Interpretation of Islamic Law" in *Legal Histories of the British Empire: Law, Engagements and Legacies*, ed. S. Dorseet and J. McLaren (New York: Routledge, 2014), 46–48.
2. Ziba Mir-Hosseini, "Classical Fiqh, Modern Ethics, and Gender Justice" in *Changeable and Unchangeable: New Directions in Islamic Thought and Practice*, ed. K. Vogt, L. Larsen, and C. Moe (London: I. B. Tauris, 2009), 77–79; also see Iza Hussin, *The Politics of Islamic Law* (Cambridge: Cambridge University Press, 2017).
3. Rudolph Peters, "From Jurists' Law to Statute Law or What Happens When the Shari'a is Codified," *Mediterranean Politics* 7 (2002): 82–95. Many nations adopted constitutional clauses known as "*sharīʿa* source laws" or "repugnancy laws" that established parallel religious institutions to develop Islamic laws and to deem 'un-Islamic' laws unconstitutional; see Clark Lombardi, "Constitutional Provisions Making *Sharīʿa* 'A' or 'The' Chief Source of Legislation: Where Did They Come From? What Do They Mean? Do They Matter?" *Am. U. Intl'l Rev.* 28, no. 3 (2013): 733–74.
4. These are most acutely felt in the realm of family law and *ḥudūd* ordinances; see Lynn Welchman, *Women and Muslim Family Laws in Arab States: A Comparative Overview of Textual Development and Advocacy* (Amsterdam: University of Amsterdam Press, 2007), 157ff; and Rudolph Peters, "The Islamization of Criminal Law: A Comparative Analysis," *Die Welt des Islams* 34, no. 2 (November 1994), 246–74.
5. Muhammad Hashim Kamali, "Law and Ethics in Islam: The Role of the *Maqāṣid*," in *New Directions in Islamic Thought: Exploring Reform and Muslim Tradition*, ed. K. Vogt, L. Larsen, and C. Moe (London: I. B. Tauris, 2008), 45.
6. Younes Soualhi, "Application of *Sharīʿah* Contracts in Contemporary Islamic Finance: A *Maqāṣid* Perspective," *Intellectual Discourse* 23 (2015): 333–54; Alexandre Caeiro, "Theorizing Islam without the State: Discourses on the Minority Status of Muslims in the West," in *Islam, Law and Identity*, ed. M. Diamantides and A. Gearey (New York: Routledge, 2012), 209–35.
7. Mufsir bin Ali al-Qahtani, *Understanding Maqāṣid al-Sharīʿah: A Contemporary Perspective* (Herndon, VA: IIIT, 2015), 92; Halim Rane, *Islam and Contemporary Civilisation: Evolving Ideas, Transforming Relations* (Melbourne: Melbourne University Press, 2010), 140ff.

8. See Felicitas Opwis, *Maṣlaḥa and the Purposes of the Law: Islamic Discourse on Legal Change from the 4th/10th to 8th/14th Century* (Leiden: Brill, 2010). Opwis suggests that even al-Shāṭibī, often presumed to be a great champion of legal reform, used the *maqāṣid* to maintain the substantive jurisprudence of his school; Ibid., 329.

9. Ibid., 41 and 87. Both Opwis and Emon note that Najm al-Dīn al-Ṭūfī (d. 1316) was a possible exception to this rule.

10. Anver Emon, *Islamic Natural Law Theories* (Oxford: Oxford University Press, 2010).

11. Ibid., especially 195ff; Anver Emon, "Response to David Novak's 'Natural Law and Judaism'," in *Natural Law: A Jewish, Christian, and Islamic Trialogue*, ed. A. Emon, M. Levering, and D. Novak (Oxford: Oxford University Press, 2014), 52ff.

12. For example, Aydogan Kars, "*Maqāṣid* or *Sharīʿa*? Secularism, Islamic Reform, and Ethics in Modern Turkey," in *Maqāṣid al-Sharīʿa and Contemporary Reformist Muslim Thought*, ed. A. Duderija (New York: Palgrave MacMillan, 2014), 127–50; Ebrahim Moosa, "The Poetics and Politics of Law After Empire: Reading Women's Rights in the Contestations of Law," *UCLA Journal of Islamic and Near Eastern Law* 1, no. 1 (Fall 2001/Winter 2002), 44ff; Meryem F. Zaman, "Islamic Movements, Women, and Social Reform: Who Speaks of the *Sharīʿa* in Pakistan?" in *Sharīʿa Dynamics*, ed. T. Daniels (New York: Palgrave Macmillan, 2017), 239ff.

13. Colin Imber, *Ebu's-Su'ud: The Islamic Tradition* (Palo Alto, CA: Stanford University Press, 2009), 89–93; Irene Schneider, "Imprisonment in Pre-Classical and Classical Islamic Law" *Islamic Law and Society* 2, no. 2 (1995): 161.

14. Elyse Semerdijan, *Off the Straight Path: Illicit Sex, Law, and Community in Ottoman Aleppo* (Syracuse, NY: Syracuse University Press, 2008), 31–32.

15. Khaled Abou El Fadl, "Islam and the Challenge of Democracy," *Journal of Scholarly Perspectives* 1, no. 1 (2005): 13–14 (3–17); Asghar Ali Engineer, *Rethinking Issues in Islam* (Mumbai: Orient Longman, 1998), 97; The Monotheist Group, *The Qur'an: A Monotheist Translation* (n.p.: Brainbow Press, 2011), xiv–xv.

16. Sindhi's support for socialism is much debated, but at the very least he supported strong restrictions on private property, arguing that, among other things, "private ownership of movable and immovable property was to be restricted and property exceeding a prescribed limit was also to be taken over by the state"; Tanvir Anjum, "A Voice from the Margins: An Appraisal of Ubaid-Allah Sindhi's Mahabharat Sarvrajia Party and its Constitution," *Journal of Political Studies* 20, no. 1 (2013): 166. This type of thinking was roundly denounced as both socialist and un-Islamic by Taqi Usmani in his ruling on land reforms, mentioned below.

17. For more on Islamic Socialists, see Lina T. Darling, *A History of Social Justice and Political Power in the Middle East: The Circle of Justice From Mesopotamia to Globalization* (New York: Routledge, 2013), 193–97; Humeira Iqtidar, *Secularizing Islamists? Jama'at-e-Islami and Jama'at-ud-Da'wa in Urban Pakistan* (Chicago: University of Chicago Press, 2011), 55–83; Nasim A. Jawed, "Islamic Socialism: An Ideological Trend in Pakistan in the 1960s," *The Muslim World* 65, no. 3 (July 1975): 196–215; Sami A. Hanna and George H. Gardner, ed., *Arab Socialism: A Documentary Survey* (Leiden: Brill, 1969); Yudi Latif, *Indonesian Muslim Intelligentsia and Power* (Singapore: Institute for Southeast Asian Studies, 2008), 199ff.

18. Asghar Ali Engineer, "Is Islam Compatible With Socialism?" *The Radical Humanist*, 74, no. 1 (August 2011): 12. Engineer attributed this to a "left-leaning Christian priest" and "noted scholar of Islam," but not as a direct quote, in the context of endorsement.

19. Farhad Nomani and Sohrab Behdad, *Class and Labor in Iran: Did the Revolution Matter?* (Syracuse, NY: Syracuse University Press, 2006), 2.

20. Sami A. Hanna and George H. Gardner, *Arab Socialism: A Documentary Survey* (Leiden: Brill, 1969), 52 and 269.

21. Nasim A. Jawed, *Islam's Political Culture: Religion and Politics in Pre-divided Pakistan* (Austin: University of Texas Press, 1999).

22. Bidanda M. Chengappa, "Pakistan: Impact of Islamic Socialism," *Strategic Analysis* 26, no. 1 (2002): 27–47; Tahir Kamran, "Majlis-i-Ahrar-i-Islam: Religion, Socialism, and Agitation in Action," *South Asian History and Culture* 4, no. 4 (2013): 465–82.

23. For Nasser's view of Islamic Socialism, see Yvonne Y. Haddad, *Contemporary Islam and the Challenge of History* (Albany: SUNY Press, 1982), 25–41; for Qaddafi's, see Mahmoud M. Ayoub, *Islam and the Third Universal Theory: The Religious Thought of Mu'ammar al-Qadhdhafi* (New York: Routledge, 2016).

24. Quoted in Annemarie Schimmel, *Gabriel's Wing: A Study Into the Religious Ideas of Sir Muhammad Iqbal* (Leiden: Brill, 1963), 327.

25. In an interesting inversion of this, Tamara Sonn notes that Bandali al-Jawzī used the term "socialist" as a pejorative when denouncing historical groups he thought heretical like the Khurramīs, Isma'īlīs, and Qarāmaṭīs; Tamara Sonn, *Interpreting Islam: Bandali Jawzi's Islamic Intellectual History* (Oxford: Oxford University Press, 1996), 48–51.

26. Robert D. Crane, "Human Rights in Traditionalist Islam: Legal, Political, Economic, and Spiritual Perspectives," *The American Journal of the Islamic Social Sciences* 25, no. 1 (Winter 2008): 98; see also Gemal Eldin Attia, *Towards Realization of the Higher Intents of Islamic Law*, trans. Nancy Roberts (London: IIIT, 2007), 88.

27. Muhammad Qasim Zaman, *Modern Islamic Thought in a Radical Age: Religious Authority and Internal Criticism* (Cambridge: Cambridge University Press), 254.

28. Sami E. Baroudi, "Sheikh Yusuf Qaradawi on International Relations: The Discourse of a Leading Islamist Scholar (1926-)," *Middle Eastern Studies* 50, no. 1: 23. (2–26). Al-Qaradawi is not alone in this belief, as many Islamic scholars have denounced marriages in which one of the partners is a socialist. See, for example, https://islamqa.info/en/21380. (Accessed February 28, 2017).

29. On the famous tension between Ibn 'Āshūr and Bourguiba, especially with respect to social order and the *maqāṣid*, see Basheer M. Nafi, "Ṭāhir ibn 'Āshūr: The Career and Thought of a Modern Reformist 'ālim, with Special Reference to His Work of tafsīr," *Journal of Qur'anic Studies* 7, no. 1 (2005): 1–32.

30. *Qazalbash Waqf v. Chief Land Commissioner*, PLD 1990 Supreme Court 99.

31. Qaradawi's ownership stake in these ventures is unclear, though a 1999 FBI investigation found that he was the fourth-largest shareholder in al-Taqwa bank, which at the time has assets of $220 million. According to a wikileaks cable, the US ambassador to Qatar stated "Qaradawi has been granted other favors by the

Qatari government; in particular, he was given substantial properties including villas, which he rents, and the building which houses the Ruling Family Council, an organization of the Al Thani family. We have no figures on Qaradawi's income, but it is substantial." Embassy Qatar, "Qaradawi Viewed Locally as a Moderate." Wikileaks Cable: 05DOHA1268_a. Dated July 12, 2005. https://www.wikileaks.org/plusd/cables/05DOHA1268_a.html.

32. Christine Schirrmacher, *"Let There Be No Compulsion in Religion" (Sura 2:256): Apostasy From Islam as Judged by Contemporary Islamic Theologians* (Eugene, OR: Wipf & Stock, 2016), 165.

33. Wan Naim Wan Mansor, "Protecting the Religion (*Maqṣad Ḥifẓ al-Dīn*) in Malaysian Political Islam: A Preliminary Analysis," *Islam and Civilizational Renewal* 7, no. 3: 379–98.

34. See the Federal Supreme Court notes (no. 321/2002, dated December 22, 2002) to Personal Status Code Article 56; http://www.elaws.gov.ae/EnLegislations.aspx. (Accessed February 28, 2017). FSC notes are at this time only available in Arabic.

35. Yasin Dutton, *The Origins of Islamic Law: The Qur'an, the Muwatta, and Madinan 'Amal* (London: Curzon Press, 1999), 21.

36. Kecia Ali, *Imam Shafi'i: Scholar and Saint* (Oxford: Oneworld, 2011), especially Chapter 4.

37. See for example, al-Bayḍāwī, *Anwār al-Tanzīl wa Asrār al-Tanzīl* (Beirut: Dar Ihya al-Turath al-Arabi, 1997), 1:78; Abū al-Layth al-Samarqandī, *Tafsīr al-Samarqandī* (Beirut: Dar al-Kutub al-Ilmiyya, 1993), 1:116; Jalāl al-Dīn al-Suyūṭī, *al-Durr al-Manthūr* (Cairo: Markaz Hijr lil-Buhuth wa-l-Dirasat al-Arabiyya wa-l-Islamiyya, 2003) 1:261–62; or for a text with a few lines of justification, see Ibn 'Atiyya, *al-Muharrar al-Wajīz* (Beirut: Dar al-Khayr, 2007), 1:201–202.

38. Ayesha S. Chaudhry, *Domestic Violence and the Islamic Tradition: Ethics, Law, and the Muslim Discourse on Gender* (Oxford: Oxford University Press, 2013), 78.

39. Walid Saleh, *The Formation of the Classical Tafsīr Tradition: The Qur'ān Commentary of al-Tha'labī* (d. 427/1035) (Leiden: Brill, 2004), 139.

40. Al-Marghinānī, *al-Hidāya: Sharḥ Bidāyat al-Mubtadi'* (Karachi: Idarat al-Qur'an wa Ulum al-Islamiyya, 1996), 1:289. Al-Marghinānī did cite part of the *ḥadīth*, which is itself ambiguous, "the knees are from the *ʿawra*." There was strong disagreement among legal scholars on whether "from" in the *ḥadīth* means "apart from" or "within." Though the debate between the Shāfi'īs and the Ḥanafīs was intense, al-Marghinānī did not find the need to engage in it. For more on the debate, see al-ʿAynī, *al-Bināya fī Sharḥ al-Hidāya* (Beirut: Dar al-Fikr, 1990), 2:135–37; Ibn al-Humām, *Sharḥ Fatḥ al-Qadīr* (Beirut: Dar al-Kutub al-Ilmiyya, 2003), 1:265.

41. PLD 2010 Federal Shariat Court 191. See especially FSC 210–13.

BIBLIOGRAPHY

Abou El Fadl, Khaled. "Islam and the Challenge of Democracy." *Journal of Scholarly Perspectives* 1, no. 1 (2005): 3–17.

Ali, Kecia. *Imam Shafi'i: Scholar and Saint*. Oxford: Oneworld, 2011.
Al-ʿAynī, Maḥmūd b. Aḥmad. *al-Bināya fī Sharḥ al-Hidāya*. Beirut: Dar al-Fikr, 1990.
Al-Bayḍāwī, 'Abd Allah b. 'Umar. *Anwār al-Tanzīl wa Asrār al-Tanzīl*. Beirut: Dar Ihya al-Turath al-Arabi, 1997.
Al-Marghinānī, 'Alī b. Abī Bakr. *al-Hidāya: Sharḥ Bidāyat al-Mubtadi'*. Karachi: Idarat al-Qur'an wa Ulum al-Islamiyya, 1996.
al-Qahtani, Mufsir bin Ali. *Understanding Maqāṣid al-Sharī'ah: A Contemporary Perspective*. Herndon, VA: IIIT, 2015.
Al-Samarqandī, Abū al-Layth. *Tafsīr al-Samarqandī*. Beirut: Dar al-Kutub al-Ilmiyya, 1993.
al-Suyūṭī, Jalāl al-Dīn. *al-Durr al-Manthūr*. Cairo: Markaz Hijr lil-Buhuth wa-l-Dirasat al-Arabiyya wa-l-Islamiyya, 2003.
Anjum, Tanvir. "A Voice from the Margins: An Appraisal of Ubaid-Allah Sindhi's Mahabharat Sarvrajia Party and its Constitution." *Journal of Political Studies* 20, no. 1 (2013): 159–77.
Attia, Gemal Eldin. *Towards Realization of the Higher Intents of Islamic Law*. Translated by Nancy Roberts. London: IIIT, 2007.
Ayoub, Mahmoud M. *Islam and the Third Universal Theory: The Religious Thought of Mu'ammar al-Qadhdhafi*. New York: Routledge, 2016.
Baroudi, Sami E. "Sheikh Yusuf Qaradawi on International Relations: The Discourse of a Leading Islamist Scholar (1926-)." *Middle Eastern Studies* 50, no. 1 (2014): 23, 2–26.
Caeiro, Alexandre. "Theorizing Islam without the State: Discourses on the Minority Status of Muslims in the West." In *Islam, Law and Identity*, 209–35. New York: Routledge, 2012.
Chatterjee, Nandini "Law, Culture and History: Amir Ali's Interpretation of Islamic Law." In *Legal Histories of the British Empire: Law, Engagements and Legacies*, 45–59. New York: Routledge, 2014.
Chaudhry, Ayesha S. *Domestic Violence and the Islamic Tradition: Ethics, Law, and the Muslim Discourse on Gender*. Oxford: Oxford University Press, 2013.
Chengappa, Bidanda M. "Pakistan: Impact of Islamic Socialism." *Strategic Analysis* 26, no. 1 (2002): 27–47.
Crane, Robert D. "Human Rights in Traditionalist Islam: Legal, Political, Economic, and Spiritual Perspectives." *The American Journal of the Islamic Social Sciences* 25, no. 1 (Winter 2008): 82–105.
Darling, Lina T. *A History of Social Justice and Political Power in the Middle East: The Circle of Justice from Mesopotamia to Globalization*. New York: Routledge, 2013.
Dutton, Yasin. *The Origins of Islamic Law: The Qur'an, the Muwatta, and Madinan 'Amal*. London: Curzon Press, 1999.
Emon, Anver. *Islamic Natural Law Theories*. Oxford: Oxford University Press, 2010.
———. "Response to David Novak's 'Natural Law and Judaism'." In *Natural Law: A Jewish, Christian, and Islamic Trialogue*. Oxford: Oxford University Press, 2014.

Engineer, Asghar Ali. *Rethinking Issues in Islam*. Mumbai: Orient Longman, 1998.
———. "Is Islam Compatible With Socialism?" *The Radical Humanist* 74, no. 1 (August 2011): 12.
Haddad, Yvonne Y. *Contemporary Islam and the Challenge of History*. Albany: SUNY Press, 1982.
Hanna, Sami A., and George H. Gardner, ed. *Arab Socialism: A Documentary Survey*. Leiden: Brill, 1969.
Hussin, Iza. *The Politics of Islamic Law*. Cambridge: Cambridge University Press, 2017.
Ibn al-Humām, Muḥammad b. 'Abd al-Waḥīd. *Sharḥ Fatḥ al-Qadīr*. Beirut: Dar al-Kutub al-Ilmiyya, 2003.
Ibn 'Atiyya, 'Abd al-Ḥaqq. *al-Muharrar al-Wajīz*. Beirut: Dar al-Khayr, 2007.
Imber, Colin. *Ebu's-Su'ud: The Islamic Tradition*. Palo Alto, CA: Stanford University Press, 2009.
Iqtidar, Humeira. *Secularizing Islamists? Jama'at-e-Islami and Jama'at-ud-Da'wa in Urban Pakistan*. Chicago: University of Chicago Press, 2011.
Jawed, Nasim A. "Islamic Socialism: An Ideological Trend in Pakistan in the 1960s." *The Muslim World* 65, no. 3 (July 1975): 196–215.
———. *Islam's Political Culture: Religion and Politics in Pre-divided Pakistan*. Austin: University of Texas Press, 1999.
Kamali, Muhammad Hashim. "Law and Ethics in Islam: The Role of the *maqāṣid*." In *New Directions in Islamic Thought: Exploring Reform and Muslim Tradition*, 23–46. London: I. B. Tauris, 2008.
Kamran, Tahir. "Majlis-i-Ahrar-i-Islam: Religion, Socialism, and Agitation in Action." *South Asian History and Culture* 4, no. 4 (2013): 465–82.
Kars, Aydogan. "Maqāṣid or Sharī'a? Secularism, Islamic Reform, and Ethics in Modern Turkey." In *Maqāṣid al-Sharī'a and Contemporary Reformist Muslim Thought*. New York: Palgrave Macmillan, 2014.
Latif, Yudi. *Indonesian Muslim Intelligentsia and Power*. Singapore: Institute for Southeast Asian Studies, 2008.
Lombardi, Clark. "Constitutional Provisions Making *Sharī'a* 'A' or 'The' Chief Source of Legislation: Where Did They Come From? What Do They Mean? Do They Matter?" *Am. U. Intl'l Rev.* 28, no. 3 (2013): 733–74.
Mansor, Wan Naim Wan. "Protecting the Religion (*Maqṣad Ḥifẓ al-Dīn*) in Malaysian Political Islam: A Preliminary Analysis." *Islam and Civilisational Renewal* 7, no. 3 (April 2016): 379–98.
Mir-Hosseini, Ziba. "Classical Fiqh, Modern Ethics, and Gender Justice." In *Changeable and Unchangeable: New Directions in Islamic Thought and Practice*, 77–88. London: I. B. Tauris, 2009.
Moosa, Ebrahim. "The Poetics and Politics of Law after Empire: Reading Women's Rights in the Contestations of Law." *UCLA Journal of Islamic and Near Eastern Law* 1, no. 1 (Fall 2001/Winter 2002): 1–28.
Muhammad Aslam Khaki v. Federation of Pakistan. PLD 2010 Federal Shariat Court 191.

Nafi, Basheer M. "Ṭāhir ibn ʻĀshūr: The Career and Thought of a Modern Reformist ʻālim, with Special Reference to His Work of tafsīr." *Journal of Qur'anic Studies* 7, no. 1 (2005): 1–32.

Nomani, Farhad, and Sohrab Behdad. *Class and Labor in Iran: Did the Revolution Matter?* Syracuse, NY: Syracuse University Press, 2006.

Opwis, Felicitas. *Maṣlaḥa and the Purposes of the Law: Islamic Discourse on Legal Change from the 4th/10th to 8th/14th Century*. Leiden: Brill, 2010.

Peters, Rudolph. "From Jurists' Law to Statute Law or What Happens When the Shari'a is Codified." *Mediterranean Politics* 7 (2002): 82–95.

———. "The Islamization of Criminal Law: A Comparative Analysis." *Die Welt des Islams* 34, no. 2 (November 1994): 246–74.

Qazalbash Waqf v. Chief Land Commissioner, PLD 1990 Supreme Court 99.

Rane, Halim. *Islam and Contemporary Civilisation: Evolving Ideas, Transforming Relations*. Melbourne: Melbourne University Press, 2010.

Saleh, Walid. *The Formation of the Classical Tafsīr Tradition: The Qur'ān Commentary of al-Thaʻlabī* (d. 427/1035). Leiden: Brill, 2004.

Schimmel, Annmarie. *Gabriel's Wing: A Study Into the Religious Ideas of Sir Muhammad Iqbal*. Leiden: Brill, 1963.

Schirrmacher, Christine. *"Let There Be No Compulsion in Religion" (Sura 2:256): Apostasy From Islam as Judged by Contemporary Islamic Theologians*. Eugene, OR: Wipf & Stock, 2016.

Schneider, Irene. "Imprisonment in Pre-Classical and Classical Islamic Law." *Islamic Law and Society* 2, no. 2 (1995): 157–73.

Semerdijan, Elyse. *Off the Straight Path: Illicit Sex, Law, and Community in Ottoman Aleppo*. Syracuse, NY: Syracuse University Press, 2008.

Sonn, Tamara. *Interpreting Islam: Bandali Jawzi's Islamic Intellectual History*. Oxford: Oxford University Press, 1996.

Soualhi, Younes. "Application of *Sharīʻah* Contracts in Contemporary Islamic Finance: A *Maqāṣid* Perspective." *Intellectual Discourse* 23 (2015): 333–54.

The Monotheist Group, *The Qur'an: A Monotheist Translation*. N.p.: Brainbow Press, 2011.

Welchman, Lynn. *Women and Muslim Family Laws in Arab States: A Comparative Overview of Textual Development and Advocacy*. Amsterdam: University of Amsterdam Press, 2007.

Zaman, Meryem F. "Islamic Movements, Women, and Social Reform: Who Speaks of the *Sharīʻa* in Pakistan?" In *Sharīʻa Dynamics*. New York: Palgrave Macmillan, 2017.

Zaman, Muhammad Qasim. *Modern Islamic Thought in a Radical Age: Religious Authority and Internal Criticism*. Cambridge: Cambridge University Press, 2012.

Chapter 13

How Objective Are the Objectives (*Maqāṣid*)?

Examining Evolving Notions of the Sharīʿah *through the Lens of Lineage* (Nasl)

Ayesha S. Chaudhry

THE EGALITARIAN DILEMMA

Muslim history is full of men viewed as revivalists and reformists, men who took on the challenges of reinterpreting and rethinking Islamic law in order to make it relevant and meet the needs of ever-changing Muslim communities. In the twentieth and twenty-first centuries, the need to reform Islamic law to meet the needs of postcolonial Muslim communities and nation-states has persisted, but the postcolonial context has introduced a new challenge for Muslims. For the first time in Muslim history, millions of Muslims believe in gender equality as an intrinsic good and in a just God whose law guarantees human equality by eliminating social, racial, economic, and *gender* discrimination. I call this new way of thinking an "egalitarian idealized cosmology."[1] An idealized cosmology is the imagination of how the world ought to work, ideally, as God intends it. In this postcolonial way of thinking, Muslims imagine a universe very much influenced by the human rights discourse of the twentieth century in which God endows humans with intrinsic dignity and worth, regardless of social markers like class or gender. This new egalitarian idealized cosmology creates a tricky problem for the project of reforming Islamic law. The problem stems from the irreconcilable and mutually exclusive relationship between the egalitarian idealized cosmology espoused by Muslims today, and the pre-colonial Islamic tradition, which was essentially, unambiguously and ubiquitously patriarchal.[2] Precolonial Muslim scholars and jurists across the board upheld a "patriarchal idealized cosmology," wherein they imagined an ideal universe in which God privileged men over women and this was reflected throughout their writings on every subject matter. [3]

The emergence of an egalitarian idealized cosmology that challenges a patriarchal idealized cosmology creates a dilemma for the Muslim reformer; I call this problem the "egalitarian-authoritative dilemma." Modern Muslim scholars who seek gender egalitarian readings of Islamic texts confront a serious and unprecedented difficulty: given the ubiquitous patriarchy of precolonial Muslim scholarship, how can one interpret these texts to promote gender-egalitarianism without fundamentally subverting these texts or rejecting them altogether? Since authority in religious communities is derived in large part from adherence to their traditions, breaking from tradition results in a loss of authority in the eyes of the community. The flipside of this dilemma is that if scholars rely on the patriarchal tradition in order to maintain authority and legitimacy, then they must compromise their commitment to gender-egalitarianism. When seen in this light, the gender problem in Muslim discourse has cosmological implications. Scholars who advocate for an egalitarian vision of Islam are seen not as merely offering a new interpretation of a particular text or legal ruling, but rather as threatening the stability of the entire patriarchal cosmological order. The very serious theological and cosmological implications of discussions about gender make this topic an especially important and dangerous one for Muslim scholars. The implications of this study are far reaching and can endanger one's life, as seen in the 2015 assassination of Professor Muhammad Shakeel Auj in Pakistan for his "liberal" views on gender-related issues.

MAQĀṢID, PATRIARCHY, AND *NASL*

As Islamic law has come under increased pressure to reform in order to reflect the gender egalitarian beliefs of Muslims, many Muslim scholars have championed the *maqāṣid al-sharīʿa* approach as especially well suited to meet the challenges of reforming Islamic law in the modern period. Since perhaps the greatest challenge facing Muslim reformers is the reformation of Islamic law so that it no longer discriminates against women, it makes sense to think about what the *maqāṣid* approach has to offer the gender debate in Islam. In its most widespread form, the *maqāṣid* purport to preserve five principles: intellect, life, lineage, property, and religion. When thinking about the *maqāṣid* in terms of the gender debate, it is important to note at the outset that the *maqāṣid* themselves are deeply patriarchal, both in their inception and application. To examine this claim, let us look more closely at the principle of *nasl*, commonly translated as "lineage" or "progeny." In precolonial Islamic law, the preservation of lineage was linked to two key patriarchal concepts. First, the purpose of the preservation of lineage was to verify paternity, thereby protecting the reproductive rights of men. Second, lineage was preserved through laws that restrained women's sexuality; the main law that is justified by *nasl* is the prohibition against *zinā* which is punishable by flogging or stoning. Accompanying laws that support this sexual regulation include laws about the false accusation of adultery (*qadfh*) and sworn allegation for adultery (*li'ān*).

In her book, *Maslaḥah and the Purposes of the Law*, Felicitas Opwis traces the development of the concept of *nasl* in classical Islamic law. She tells us, for instance, that initially in his *al-Shifā'* al-Ghazālī (d. 1111) conceived of four *maqāṣid:* intellect, life, lineage, and property—leaving out religion. And rather than the word *nasl*, he literally used the word *buḍ'*, or "vulva." So, in al-Ghazālī's conception, one of the principles of law was control of a woman's sexual organ, the vulva. Controlling entry into the vulva ensured the preservation of lineage, since lineage was preserved through the determination of paternity. The fact that al-Ghazālī used the word "vulva" as a stand-in for "lineage" is significant because using the term "vulva" ties control of women's sexuality to the concept of lineage. And the specific lineage the law is concerned with, according to al-Ghazālī, is paternal, rather than maternal. Pregnancy and childbirth ensure knowledge of maternal lineage. But this is insufficient, and perhaps even irrelevant, for lineage as conceived by al-Ghazālī. In his mind, paternal lineage determines the "real" lineage of a person, but it is more difficult to ascertain, and requires the strict control of a woman's body. The four *maqāṣid* for al-Ghazālī, then, were intellect, life, property, and vulva.[4]

Al-Rāzī (d. 1209) further established the strong connection between controlling women's sexuality and lineage when he wrote that *nasl* is protected by the prohibition against *zinā*, which is punishable by the *ḥadd* penalty of lashing or stoning. Al-Razi explained the patriarchal and very gendered reasoning that underpins the connection between controlling women's sexuality and lineage, stating that if *zinā* were permissible, not prohibited, then this would lead to social chaos. Such chaos might include the following: men would compete over women for sex; there would be confusion over paternity; men would abandon the support of children; and they would display aggressive and domineering behavior toward women, causing corruption and fighting among people.[5]

Al-Qarāfī (d. 1285) discussed the debates among jurists about the relevance of honor (*'irḍ*) to the *maqāṣid* as a whole, mentioning that while others substitute *'irḍ* for religion, he preferred to list it as an additional *maqṣad* alongside the five principles. Either way, he emphasized that there was agreement that "the law protects honour (*'irḍ*), as is manifest in God's ruling to prohibit slander (*qadhf*)."[6] In his *al-Muwāfaqāt*, al-Shāṭibī (d. 1388) subsumed preservation of honor under the value of life, and mentioned that other jurists consider male honor as one of the principles. These jurists saw the impulse for protecting male honor as rooted in the *Qur'ān* and *sunnah*, in discussions of the sworn allegation for adultery (*li'ān*) and the false accusation of fornication (*qadhf*). Together, the discussion of *nasl* and its surrounding web of laws reflect and reinstantiate discriminatory gender binaries, in which women are at once sexualized, reduced to their sexual organs, and turned into representations of male honor.

REFORMING THE *MAQĀṢID*

Having very briefly explored the patriarchal conceptions of *nasl*, we can see that when approaching the *maqāṣid* with an eye to reforming Islamic law to be gender egalitarian, before we can think about reforming specific Islamic laws, we must first reform the *maqāṣid* themselves. At the moment, the *maqāṣid* are part of the problem; they reinforce a social construction of gender that privileges men and disempowers women. The patriarchal nature of the *maqāṣid* should not be surprising. After all, the very jurists that created gender discriminatory laws also came up with the idea of the *maqāṣid.* The very aspect of the *maqāṣid* approach that gives this methodology authority and legitimacy ensures its patriarchal nature; the *maqāṣid* are rooted in the precolonial Islamic tradition. This means that when using the *maqāṣid* approach, Muslim reformists must engage in a "double reformation," reforming our understanding of the *maqāṣid* themselves alongside Islamic laws.

The abstract idea of the egalitarian-authoritative dilemma and this unprecedented clash of egalitarian and patriarchal idealized cosmologies might sound compelling, but what does this clash look like in tangible terms, in relation to particular legal problems? In order to answer this question, let us keep our lens focused on the *maqṣad* of *nasl* and its attendant *ḥadd* punishment of *zinā*. From the perspective of a patriarchal idealized cosmology, men always have the right to access multiple sexual partners, while women are always restricted to one sexual partner at a time. According to patriarchal Islamic law, a man has sexual rights over his wives (up to four) and unlimited concubines, whom he can force into sexual submission. Women may only have sex with their husbands or masters. In this scheme, the paternal lineage of any resulting children is safeguarded. While a man may have sex with multiple female partners, his female partners must remain exclusively loyal to him. If either gender breaks from their designated sexual partners, they ought to be punished. This punishment is either 100 lashes or stoning to death.

From the perspective of an egalitarian idealized cosmology, assumptions about a gender equal Islam turn this entire legal structure on its head. What is legally permissible in the patriarchal legal structure becomes criminalized in the egalitarian worldview, and what is criminal becomes legal. Let me explain: in an egalitarian Islam, where an egalitarian idealized cosmology is operative, slavery, polygamy, and marital rape are criminalized because they are considered to be inherently oppressive practices. Instead, sex between consenting individuals becomes a moral good. Protecting this right becomes virtuous. Furthermore, the very fact of punishing consenting individuals for their sexual choices becomes abhorrent, and the idea of punishing them corporally with either lashing or stoning is barbaric and immoral.

The moment of this confrontation, between two irreconcilable idealized cosmologies, is a frightening one; it can be imagined as the moment one realizes one is standing on a precipice and must either jump into the unknown or retreat to safety to a position that is known even if it has become oppressive and tyrannical. For the sake of adventure, and perhaps even a commitment of justice, let's see what happens if we take the plunge. What might the *maqṣad* of *nasl* look like if we reimagine it through the lens of an egalitarian idealized cosmology? Can we free the concept from its patriarchal roots to serve the needs of present-day Muslims committed to gender equality? The fact is that the precolonial intent for the preservation of *nasl* as a means to determine paternity is no longer relevant. Scientific advancements, particularly DNA testing, have made the determination of paternity a nonissue. Now that paternity can be determined with certainty, we are even less likely to see the sort of social chaos of which al-Rāzī warned. Paternity can be settled with a test, women's entrance into labor markets—despite persistent unequal pay around the globe—means that women often are the breadwinners in their families so that they no longer rely on men to provide for their children, and we know that "free sex" in liberal democracies has not led to any more aggressive and domineering male behavior toward women than in patriarchal societies.

Taking into account the changed social and historical circumstances of Muslim communities, what should *nasl* protect if it no longer needed to determine paternity, ensure men's dominance in the family, or protect women from predation? One way to reimagine the purpose of *nasl* is to shift its focus away from protecting the sexual and reproductive rights of men over and against women to protecting the sexual and reproductive rights of women for themselves. Thinking of *nasl* in this light allows us to consider the persistent link between *nasl* and its accompanying prohibition of *zinā* as an opportunity to rethink gender discriminatory laws around sexual regulation from an egalitarian perspective. In this light, women (and men) ought to have the right to consensual sex, meaning that a sexual encounter's moral worth is considered through the lens of consent. All nonconsensual sex, including marital rape, thereafter becomes immoral and criminal. In this conception, punishing sex between consenting adults becomes irrelevant and even abhorrent. This gives *nasl* immediate relevance to the lives of contemporary Muslims, especially given the proliferation of reliable contraception, which means that women and men can choose to not procreate, to not have a lineage. And further, safer procedures for abortions allow women to make the choice to procreate or not, even after pregnancy. In contrast to the patriarchal framework where the preservation of lineage protected men's right to lineage, the egalitarian worldview can envision the *maqṣad* of *nasl* so that it protects women's sexual rights in such a way that grants them the right to produce lineage or not.

Interestingly, this line of reasoning was anticipated by Muslim scholars in the twentieth century who were less than enthused by the *maqāṣid* as a means for legal reform. These scholars worried precisely about the *maqāṣid* becoming a slippery slope, and pointed out the necessary cultural and moral relativism involved in the use of human reason, upon which the *maqāṣid* approach must rely. One of these scholars was the South Asian scholar Ashraf Ali Thanvi (d. 1943). He warned:

> If [reasons are always sought for the law], then *ḥalāl* will no longer remain *ḥalāl* and *ḥarām* no longer *ḥarām*, because every person will extract a reason to suit him, be it *ḥalāl* or *ḥarām*. If, for example, someone says that the reason for the prohibition of adultery is confusion in lineage, meaning that if many men fornicate with one woman and she conceives, then it will be possible that every one of those men will lay claim to the child. There is a real fear of arguments and fighting. It is also possible that each of them refutes fatherhood, then all this will result in great difficulty and strife for the woman and child. And now I ask you, what if someone devises a plan for the woman not to conceive. Or a person seeks a woman who is barren, or he finds such a group of women from whom there is no fear of fighting and arguments regarding parenthood of the possible offspring. Then in all these cases, fornication will be (God forbid!) permissible, because the reason is no longer present. What confusion will reign thereafter! Will such reasoning ever make fornication *ḥalāl*? Never![7]

Thanvi was clearly disturbed by the precolonial justifications for the *ḥadd* penalty for *zinā* in light of the emergence of an egalitarian idealized cosmology. He was able to foresee the line of reasoning in which Muslims might engage, and in order to prevent Muslims from rethinking *zinā* and the *ḥadd* penalty, he was willing to sever it from the *maqṣad* of *nasl*, and instead uphold the prohibition and punishment for *zinā* as a standalone divine rule, beyond reason, that had to be uncritically obeyed, without the corrupting influence of human reason, let alone Western values. Thanvi's nightmare scenario is one where *zinā* is no longer criminalized; he is distraught at the prospect and worried that it might lead to "confusion." Though he uses the same term "confusion" as with al-Rāzī, the word signifies a separate concern for him; al-Rāzī was worried about confusion of paternity and the ensuing social chaos, and Thanvi is worried about confusion in Islamic law more generally if Muslims decided to decriminalize *zinā*, if they stopped seeing it as a social crime. He was afraid of an Islam that was not patriarchal, an Islam that was egalitarian. Muslims today find themselves living Thanvi's nightmare scenario, and it turns out that it's not so bad, especially for women.

CONCLUSION

There is confusion today about how best to reform Islamic law and what the limits of reform might be, but these questions are an opportunity for us to think anew our relationship to the Islamic legal system, so that it can once again become a framework that delivers justice, rather than a discriminatory system that institutionalizes gender inequalities. My question for us is that when we confront the reconception of *nasl* as a principle that protects the sexual and reproductive rights of women and men, rather than simply a determination of paternal lineage, do we think that this reimagination of *nasl* is viable? Would such a law still be "Islamic"? Why or why not? The answers to these questions are profoundly important, because they get us to the root of what we think about the *maqāṣid*. They also force us to confront our own limits in terms of how far we are willing to go when reforming Islamic law. In answering these questions, we must think carefully about what we believe about each of the following terms: "reform," "Islamic," and "law." Of course, reimagining *nasl* as protecting the sexual and reproductive rights of women and severing the link between *nasl* and the *ḥadd* penalty for *zinā* does not solve the moral problems that arise from other patriarchal laws around marriage, polyandry and slavery. But it does get us started on a path of honest, self-critical engagement with the Islamic "tradition," forging a path between uncritical submission and outright rejection, a path that permits us to see the shape and contours and beauty of an Islam fashioned in the light of an egalitarian idealized cosmology.

NOTES

1. Ayesha S. Chaudhry, *Domestic Violence and the Islamic Tradition: Ethics, Law and the Muslim Discourse on Gender* (Oxford: Oxford University Press, 2014), 11.
2. Ibid., 12.
3. Ibid., 12–13.
4. Felicitas Opwis, *Maṣlaḥa and the Purpose of the Law: Islamic Discourse on Legal Change from the 4th/10th to the 8th/14th Century* (Leiden: Brill, 2010), 68.
5. Ibid., 100. This trend continues into the contemporary period, where Al-Fāsī (d. 1974) and al-Ṭawīla connect the restriction of women's sexuality to the preservation of lineage, by shifting the emphasis of preserving lineage away from the protection of

women and children to the protection of male honor (*ʿirḍ*). They view the prohibition of *zinā* and the accompanying *ḥadd* penalty as protecting male honor. ʻAllāl al-Fāsī, *Maqāṣid al-sharīʿa al-islāmiyya wa-makṛīmuhā* (Rabat: Maṭba'at al-Risāla, 1979), 138; ʻAbd al-Wahhāb Ṭawīla, *Fiqh al-ashriba wa-ḥadduhā* (Cairo: Dār al-Salām, 1986), 10.

6. Ibid., 157–58 and 259.

7. Ashraf Ali Thanvi, *The Principles and Codes of Law in Ḥanafī Fiqh*, trans. Afzal Hossen Elias (Karachi: Zamzam Publishers, 2010), 35.

BIBLIOGRAPHY

ʻAbd al-Wahhāb, Ṭawīla. *Fiqh al-ashriba wa-ḥadduhā*. Cairo: Dār al-Salām, 1986.

Al-Fāsī, ʻAllāl. *Maqāṣid al-sharīʿa al-islāmiyya wa-makṛīmuhā*. Rabat: Maṭba'at al-Risāla, 1979.

Chaudhry, Ayesha S. *Domestic Violence and the Islamic Tradition: Ethics, Law and the Muslim Discourse on Gender*. Oxford: Oxford University Press, 2014.

Opwis, Felicitas. *Maṣlaḥa and the Purpose of the Law: Islamic Discourse on Legal Change from the 4th/10th to the 8th/14th Century*. Leiden: Brill, 2010.

Thanvi, Ashraf Ali. *The Principles and Codes of Law in Ḥanafī Fiqh*. Translated by Afzal Hossen Elias. Karachi: Zamzam Publishers, 2010.

Chapter 14

Maqāṣid al-Sharī'ah as a Legitimization for the Muslim Minorities Law

Mouez Khalfaoui

THE CONCEPT OF ISLAMIC MINORITIES LAW

"*Fiqh al-aqalliyāt* is a special law that takes into consideration the relationship between legal decisions and the situation and context of a community."[1]

The Muslim minorities law, as perceived by contemporary Muslim scholars, is different from the "right of minorities" as understood in modern democratic and pluralistic societies. The legislations supporting minorities in modern pluralistic societies are meant to preserve their respective cultural and religious specificities. This takes place in contexts where states are supposed to treat all religious groups regardless of the number of their adherents and level of power equally. This was not the case in the classical Islamic conception for the treatment of minorities. Regarding the legal treatment of the life of Muslims (minorities or individuals), who prefer to live outside of the Muslim territories, Muslim legal scholars have developed different approaches and strategies. As far as the history of the minorities law in the Islamic culture is concerned, Khaled Abu El Fadl has shown that since the very beginning of Islamic history Muslim groups lived under non-Muslim rule outside *dar al-islām*.[2] The spread of Islam and the subsequent changes that occurred in the geopolitical situation of the Muslim communities resulted in several Muslim minorities living under non-Muslim rule. The main challenge was therefore to deal with the question whether Muslims were/are allowed to live under a non-Muslim rule. This question has been answered from different legal perspectives. Those differences in legal opinions depended on the religious and social context in which they were developed.[3] This presents a theoretical framework for dealing with the same questions when they are posed nowadays. The Muslim minorities law that is currently debated is therefore not an *ex-nihilo* creation. Instead, it is rather a new development within an already-established discipline in the Islamic legal literature.

Before dealing with the methodology of the contemporary Muslim minorities law, it is worth précising its subject and distinguishing it from other disciplines that deal with religious minorities. The contemporary Muslim minorities law consists mainly of legal opinions (singular: *Fatwa*; plural: *fatāwa*) regarding the difficulties Muslims face in non-Muslim societies in modern era; it does not deal with subjects such as those relevant to the life of non-Muslim minorities under Muslim rule. This later discipline was called the law of dhimma (relevant to/applied for the people of the book who were allowed to live as minorities under Muslim rule). Furthermore, the contemporary Muslim minorities law is different from the classical legal treatment of the life of Muslims under non-Muslim rule.

Based on the assumption that life under a Muslim ruler is the best guarantee for a life in accordance with Islamic norms and values,[4] premodern Muslim legal scholars have developed different and sometimes contrasting attitudes regarding the implementation of Islamic law outside of *dar al-islām*. This paradigm still represents the main framework for the debate on the life of Muslim minorities outside of the Muslim majority societies. This debate is mainly focused on two issues:

1. The religious status of Muslims who live in non-Muslim territories, and the question of whether life in non-Muslim territories threatens the religiosity and piety of Muslim minorities; and
2. The status of territories that experience shifts from Muslim to non-Muslim rule and vice versa.

The status of Muslims living in non-Muslim territories is related to conceptions of the Muslim community (*ummah*) and that of *ʿismah* (inviolability of the life of Muslims). Scholars of Islamic law unanimously think that every Muslim belongs to the *ummah*, regardless of where he or she lives.[5] When it comes to the question of inviolable Muslim rights, two conceptions dominate the debate. On the one hand, the Hanafī doctrine sees the protection of Muslims as ensured through their choice of residence, that is, the range of Islamic law is therefore limited to Muslim countries. The *ʿismah* is hence made dependent on aspects of space, and Muslims are requested to stay in Muslim territories. Shafiʿī theory, on the other hand, argues that Islamic law guarantees the inviolability of Muslim rights, regardless of their place of residence. Consequently, if a Muslim were to commit a crime in a non-Muslim country, he or she would be punished according to Islamic law. Hanafī scholars, on the contrary, think that crimes committed by Muslims might be forgiven in the case that they were committed outside of Muslim territories, where Muslim law is invalid.[6] The issue of how to deal with crimes committed by Muslims in non-Muslim territories has been debated regardless of the validity of the local legal norms of the hosting territory. In case of the application of Muslim norms, those Muslims who committed a crime outside of *dar al-islām* were to be exposed to a double punishment. Nevertheless, there is no historical evidence that such a punishment took place, although several Muslims used to live in non-Muslim territories even for short terms. Regarding the status of territories, Abou El-Fadl remarks that multiple opinions exist on this issue. While the *fuqahā'* (scholars of Islamic jurisprudence) of the Muslim formative period emphasized the difference between Muslim and non-Muslim territories, scholars of later eras (twelfth–sixteenth centuries) developed a new concept that corresponded with their respective historical and political contexts.[7] The most important argument in discussions on the status of territories was that those areas that were once conquered and brought under Muslim rule never lose their Muslim status even if falling under non-Muslim rule.[8] This premodern position is not in use anymore.

A review of the literature on Muslim and non-Muslim territories reveals that there are at least two main reasons that make this area of research relevant to contemporary modern societies. The first results from the growth of the number of Muslims outside of Muslim territories. About one-third of the entire Muslim population currently lives as minority.[9] Therefore, the debate about Muslim minorities law cannot be limited to some sporadic opinions that doctors of Islamic law issue on the margin of their daily work. The problems faced by these Muslims are proliferating, necessitating an expanding body of Muslim legal literature. Muslim minorities have to be dealt with by scholars who have obtained specialized training.[10] The second reason focuses on the fact that Muslim scholars can no longer speak of "special solutions" for a few Muslims who temporarily live outside *dar al-islām*. The permanent existence of Muslims in non-Muslim states such as India and South Africa and in the so-called West has led to a change of paradigms. That shift is best summarized as follows: while legal questions about Muslim minorities in premodern times were focused on whether or not life in non-Muslim territories is legally permitted and, and, if so, for how long, a large number of Muslims currently living in the West and other parts of the world have no intention to move [back] to *dar al-islām*. They often want to live as a minority outside of Muslim majority societies because they feel part of the host countries they live in. While questions related to Muslims outside of *dar al-islām* in the premodern era were mostly dealt with by scholars who lived in Muslim societies, scholars living in non-Muslim societies nowadays address the same set of questions.[11] To do so, they try to introduce a new set of methods which is mainly based on *Maqāṣid*. Evidences of this subject can be found in the *fatāwa* developed in modern era to answer the questions frequently asked by Muslims living permanently outside the Muslim world.

Summing up, the theoretical debate on the Muslim minorities law, the Muslim classical legal literature has developed two disciplines. The first one addresses the legal status of non-Muslim minorities living in Muslim territories. This discipline was called the law of dhimma, referring to the dhimmis, that is, non-Muslims, who were either Jews or Christians or other religious groups, subsumed under the category of dhimmis, such as the Zoroastrians. Generally speaking, the discipline (the law of dhimma) deals with the conditions that those non-Muslim minorities should fulfill in order to be permitted to live in the territories ruled by Muslims. The second branch of the classical Muslim minorities law is the one that deals with the life of Muslims who live in non-Muslim territories. In classical Muslim literature, this discipline was part and parcel of the chapters reserved to war and peace; they were addressed under the question whether, and if so, under which conditions Muslims are allowed to live outside of *dar al-islām*. This classical discipline differs from the modern Muslim minorities law by the fact that the classical *fiqh al aqalliyat* was based on the paradigm of return to the Muslim territories, that is, the legal scholars conceived this law within the framework of the premise of living in *dar al islam*. The new Muslim minorities law claims that living permanently in Muslim territories is how it is meant to be. This is due to the fact that these Muslim groups faced (are facing) challenges that were/are different from the everyday problems they were confronted with in the Muslim world.[12] For this reason, it seems that the birth of a modern Muslim minorities law needs further clarification. It is legitimate to ask why the field seems more necessary nowadays than in previous periods of time? And how *maqāṣid al-sharīʿah* could be useful for its development?

FIQH AL-AQALLIYĀT AND *MAQĀṢID AL-SHARĪʿAH*

In his book *Muslim Minorities Law: The Life of Muslims Within Other Societies*,[13] Yusuf al-Qaradawi suggests a theoretical framework of *fiqh al-aqalliyāt*. He appreciates that Muslims live in the West, arguing that representative parts of the Muslim community should move to establish themselves in Western non-Muslim countries.[14] According to him, the West has become the global center of wealth and the existence of representative Muslim minorities would help Muslims worldwide to gain access to power and wealth.[15] In explaining his approach, Qaradawi uses the concept of *maqāṣid al-sharīʿah* to argue that nowadays the *fiqh al-aqalliyāt* has shifted from being a marginal issue of Islamic legal thought to being a central topic in Muslim legal debates. Qaradawi's approach toward questions of Muslim minorities is based on the notion of common good (*maṣlaḥa*), which he uses as a synonym for *maqāṣid*. Within this framework, Qaradawi refers to several key concepts when formulating his stance on a Muslim minorities law, such as "the flexibility of *fiqh*," "fatwas change along with time and circumstance," and "the priority of living context vis-a-vis the Islamic texts."[16] These norms, Qaradawi argues, should constitute the theoretical and methodological framework for *fatāwa* in the field of Muslim minorities law.[17]

When it comes to the specificity of the Islamic minorities law, Jaber Al-Alwani emphasizes that the Muslim minorities law is "special" and considers the specificities of the life of Muslims in non-Muslim societies.[18] He argues further that this law wouldn't be suitable for every Muslim. Regarding the issue of *maqāṣid*, al-Alwani argues that the norms of Islamic law can be changed, always being the product of time and place. He claims that the legal decisions of premodern Muslim lawyers should thus be read in the light of their historical context. As a case in point, al-Alwani lists several legal decisions that have been changed, that is, abrogated by the companions of the Prophet Muhammad after his death. He points out that the first *khalīfah* (successor), Abu Bakr (d. 634), refused to share the spoils of war with non-Muslims who had sympathized with Muslims during the very first period of Islamic history (*muʾallafati qulūbuhum*). The Qur'an states:

> Zakah expenditures are only for the poor and for the needy and for those employed to collect [zakah] and for bringing hearts together [for Islam] and for freeing captives [or slaves] and for those in debt and for the cause of Allah and for the [stranded] traveler—an obligation [imposed] by Allah. And Allah is Knowing and Wise.[19]

Abu Bakr modified the understanding of the *Qur'ānic* recommendation regarding the way the spoils of war should be shared, although it was mentioned as a religious obligation in the *Qur'ān*. Another precedent was set by the second *khalīfah*, Omar (d. 644), who stopped applying Islamic punishments (*ḥudūd*) during natural catastrophes.[20] Al-Alwani emphasizes that it is not only the companions of the Prophet who have changed (i.e., abrogated) the ways of application of several notions of Islamic law. In later eras of Islamic history, many cases occurred in which legal norms were changed in order to meet the latest sociopolitical and technical developments. According to al-Alwani, all the innovations and changes that took place in the field of Islamic law were justified by the concept of *maqāṣid*. Accordingly, *maqāṣid* appear to have long acted as a general framework for the development and reform of legal decisions. Al-Alwani not only claims that the creation of a new minorities law should be preceded by methodological work, he also argues that in order "to build the fundaments of innovation (*ijtihād*), we need to re-evoke some important norms, to understand it [*ijtihād*] and testify to its efficiency in the area of minorities law."[21] Al-Alwani thinks that the first step in the course of the development of a Muslim minorities law should be the reconsideration of two main sources in Islamic law, or as al-Alwani calls them, "the two scriptures" (*Al-kitābayn*). In the process, al-Alwani argues that values contained in these two scriptures can be discovered. These values are as follows:

1. *Tawḥīd* (unity of God)
2. *Tazkīyah* (introspection and self-purification of human beings who act as the successors of God on earth)
3. *Al-ʿumran* (civilization), which refers to the assumption that the world is used by human beings for their own purposes

These three key values constitute the concept of *maqāṣid* that, according to al-Alwani, should be a reference in judging human behavior. Generally, al-Alwani argues the acts of people are best qualified by a dual system of values including a positive one for those acts that should be supported, and a negative one for those acts that are not accepted and should be avoided.

Following this epistemological introduction, al-Alwani lists several cases in which Islamic norms are applicable to Muslim communities in non-Muslim societies. These examples refer mainly to the relation of Muslims to non-Muslims and the relation of Muslims to secular states in the West. Al-Alwani seems to try and convince his readers of the fact that a Muslim minorities law should adapt to local laws and customs. Muslims are expected to integrate and subordinate themselves to the legal systems in their chosen place of residence. The norms and values mentioned above are thought to help them reach this goal.[22]

Overall, it seems that a scholarly consensus exists among Muslim academics who support the formulation of a Muslim minorities law on the basis that changing contexts require legal reforms. They underline the differences between Muslims living in Muslim majority societies and those living in the West. Scholars in support of a discrete Muslim minorities law view *maqāṣid* as the appropriate theoretical framework for this law.[23] Furthermore, they argue that the distinct problems of Muslims in non-Muslim societies cannot be solved by reference to the classical norms of Islamic law, which were developed by jurists living in the Muslim world. Al-Qaradawi insists that a Muslim minorities law should be developed and applied by scholars living in non-Muslim environments, who know the local Muslim living conditions.

Summing up, it appears that *maqāṣid al-sharīʿah*, a key concept in the reformulation of Islamic law, has become a milestone in debates on Muslim minorities law. Analysis of the literature shows that the debate remains concentrated on the theoretical framework of *maqāṣid*, while practical issues and results remain absent. In spite of their novel character, responses and *fatāwa*, which are produced in the framework of the *fiqh al-aqalliyāt*, using *maqāṣid* methodology, do not appear to be very innovative.[24] Therefore, it is legitimate to ask whether Muslim minorities law is really needed and whether it will solve the problems of Muslims living in non-Muslim majority societies.

IS MUSLIM MINORITIES LAW A DISCRETE LEGAL AREA?

As shown above, the primary argument in favor of a "new" Muslim minorities law is related to the contextual difference between Muslim and non-Muslim territories. Daily contact with non-Muslim communities and a non-Muslim legal system poses a challenge to Muslims and Muslim legal theory alike. The ultimate purpose of developing an Islamic minorities law is to facilitate the development of solutions that take into consideration both the special context and the specificity of problems Muslim minorities face. Both Qaradawi and al-Alwani point out examples for the application of *fiqh al-aqalliyāt* in Western Europe and the United States.[25] A closer look at these case studies suggests that the classical geographical and theological distinction between the Muslim world and the West continues to be a main argument in debates about a Muslim minorities law. Although scholars like Qaradawi and al-Alwani oppose the classical enmity between *dar al-islām* and *dar al-ḥarb*, it seems that this classical dualism still impacts the writings of leading Muslim scholars.[26] While ongoing globalization trends rendered the geographical distinction less important, the moral and conceptual differentiations between *dar al-islām* and non-Muslim territories has become a crucial point in the literature on minorities laws. The moral distinction is usually expressed through the image of a Muslim "self" and a non-Muslim "other." The complexity of these images is the key to the understanding of current debates on Islamic minorities law. Both are explicitly related to the conception of *maqāṣid*.

THE SELF AND OTHER IN MUSLIM MINORITIES LAW

The majority of contemporary Muslim scholars specialized in Muslim minorities law refuse the classical distinction between Muslim and non-Muslim territories, which was originally based on the religious and political enmity between both areas. Yet, this premodern doctrine continues to affect the work of those scholars in the field. As a case in point, the *fatāwa* issued by *the European Council for Fatwa and Research* are usually based on the assumption that the Muslim world is (still) a harmonic place, governed by the norms of Islamic law.[27] Non-Muslim countries are portrayed as spaces in which many Islamic values are contradicted in spite of a range of positive norms and values, such as democracy and the respect for religious and cultural differences. Starting from the assumption that living in non-Muslim environments will automatically lead to violations of Islamic norms, the majority of classical scholars argued that Muslims should not live there permanently and that moving outside the Muslim world should be a "last option." They even limited the residence of Muslims in non-Muslim territories to two purposes, namely trade and war.[28] This juxtaposition of Muslim versus non-Muslim territories and the thesis of the existence of a Muslim world that lives in accordance with Islamic norms are simplified and surreal. Neither are the current legislations in Muslim states purely Islamic, nor are the problems of diaspora Muslims very different from those who live in the Muslim world. Furthermore, the legal values of life and human rights of modern Western states could be seen as being in line with the genuine Islamic conception of Human existence and human dignity. The historical, political, and social reality of the contemporary world invalidates this alleged (and constructed) opposition of these two territories. In spite of a limited number of Muslim countries in which Islamic law constitutes the sole official legal reference, most Muslim states limit the application of Islamic law to a few areas, such as family law. Furthermore, the reformation and codification of Islamic law in several Muslim countries during the twentieth century have led to new legal interpretations that are more Western than Islamic. At the same time, the daily life and social organization in Muslim societies is often less Islamic than assumed.

A brief overview of the contemporary life of Muslim communities in the West shows more similarities than differences between Muslims and non-Muslims. Despite religious life, which is guaranteed by western legislations, Muslims and non-Muslims are facing the same difficulties of daily life. As far as Muslim communities of the Islamic world are concerned, Muslims in both non-Muslim and Muslim societies face almost the same challenges of modernity, globalization, etc. As a case in point, factory workers in Muslim states and the West are equally debating the issues of praying during working hours; likewise, Muslim women in both non-Muslim and Muslim contexts are challenged by combining their role as housewives and working mums. The issue of female employment is no longer an exclusively Western concern. The similarities of Muslim lifes inside and outside *dar al-islām* question the legal distinction between Muslim and non-Muslim territories, and the necessity of a special Muslim law exclusively reserved to the solution of the problems of this group would become counterproductive.

A second argument put forward by the supporters of *fiqh al-aqalliyāt* is related to the experts of Islamic law. Qaradawi complains about the weak cultural and contextual competences of the *fuqaha* who work in the West.[29] In his opinion, legal scholars working on minorities law should live in the same context as the minorities under study and have a Muslim background. But again, it seems that the problem is not limited to the West or to Muslim minorities law. Good *fuqaha* are not only required for European or American Muslims; deep knowledge of the local context has always been one of the main requirements to be appointed as Mufti, Qadi, or Imam in classical Islamic legal history. Well-trained scholars, who understand local specificities everywhere and can understand legal texts as well as apply them according to the requirements of new contexts, are needed in all fields of Islamic law regardless of the factors of place and time. In the past, scholars like al-Shafi' ī (d.820) moved to various places where they were appointed judges. They were able to modify their legal opinions according to the circumstances of their new living environment. While traveling the Muslim world, Ibn Battouta (d.1377), a North African scholar, was an appointed *qadi* (judge) in different places, even in South and South-East Asia, where he lacked any knowledge on the local environment. Ibn Battouta speaks about his issuing of *fatāwa*, explaining how he combined his knowledge of the law and the traditions of the regions he lived in. These examples suggest that regardless of the place where the Muslim imam, scholar, or judge works, they need to prove that they understand the context-dependent problems of Muslims in their various living environments. Furthermore, it seems that even in the Muslim world, imams who can adequately address the vast variety of complex contemporary challenges are missing. The dominating scholastic training of Imams and Muftis has led to their increasing detachment from real life. In his call for a *maqāṣid*-based reform of Islamic legal thought, Ibn 'Ashūr (d. 1973) accused the classical scholars of their lacking understanding of modernity. He emphasizes that their lack of awareness and incompetence leads to the treatment of very particular and irrelevant issues of Islamic law instead of insisting on the general framework, which presents Islamic legal theory as a solution for global problems rather than being a small register of solutions for particular problems.[30]

The last points that should be addressed in the debate on the Muslim minorities law are the social and cultural changes that are currently occurring in Western societies and elsewhere. It seems that the difficulties and problems faced by Muslim minorities in the West are in many cases similar to those of other minorities and are not always of a religious origin. It is thus difficult sometimes to speak of discrete "Muslim problems." While the legal systems in Western democratic societies guarantee minorities a broad range of rights, they often contradict the classical legal norms of the Islamic faith. In cases of marriage, divorce, conversion, or political participation, for example, Muslims are required to adapt to and live by Western legal standards. If Muslims were to try to implement their own Islamic rulings, they would inevitably complicate and intensify their isolation. In fact, thinking that the application of Islamic law may solve some of the problems of Muslim minorities may have counterproductive results; it would make the differences between Islamic and secular law more visible and lead to greater alienation among Muslims living there. Therefore, it would be most opportune for Muslims to initiate public debates within their host and home societies and cooperate with other minorities in an attempt to develop common solutions for similar problems. Muslim and Jewish minorities in Western Europe, for example, have cooperated in the last years to legitimize the circumcision of boys and the private slaughter of animals during religious festivities. The similarities of their concerns contradict the particularism underlying the concept of a Muslim minorities law. Thus, the problems of Muslim minorities should not be dealt with as "special problems," for dealing with them as a global interdisciplinary challenge is more likely to solve them. The examples of bioethics, work ethics, communication, globalization, etc. shed light on the importance of legal Islamic research that transcends disciplinary boundaries. Furthermore, dealing with the problems of Muslims in a global context might help to address challenges in non-Muslim societies, too. The issue of Islamic banking, which is becoming very important in global economics nowadays, shows that Muslim concepts can be beneficial to non-Muslims as well. The intensive debate about Islamic banking in the West is not meant to find solutions for Muslims who want to establish Islamic monetary institutions in the West; it is rather a debate about Muslims' potential to help correct in-built flaws of the global banking system. In this regard, it is worth pointing out that Islamic law has always been conceived as a universal law. Reducing it to a sectarian law would contradict its own purposes. To my mind, Muslims living in the West have the opportunity to develop their law in a new context, without the same public and political pressure that similar reform projects would face in the Muslim world. They could help reconnect Islamic legal thought with the universal aims of the *sharīʿah*, which have long been marginalized.

Summing up, let us ask again if the Muslim minorities law is a new and necessary area of law for contemporary Muslims. Does this law contribute to solving their legal and social problems? And what would be the future of this discipline?

Fiqh al-aqalliyāt is not a new branch in the field of Islamic legal thought. Early on, Islamic scholars emphasized the difference between living contexts within and outside the Muslim world, relying on regional and customary law (*ʿurf and ʿada*) to explain alterations in their decisions. At that time, the concept of *maqāṣid* was already being used. The increasing importance of *fiqh al-aqalliyāt* in Islamic legal thought is primarily caused by changing conceptions of life outside of *dar al-islām* and the relationship between Muslim and non-Muslim territories. As shown above, the concept of *maqāṣid al-sharīʿah*, the higher objectives of Islamic law, has been used to develop a special law for "special Muslims." The same argument can also be applied in refuting the need for a Muslim minorities law. In my opinion, Muslims would be better off working together with other religious minorities and social groups who face similar challenges. Working together with other minorities and civil society institutions in an attempt to overcome everyday challenges of integration would help Muslims in non-Muslim environments. According to Islamic legal norms, Muslims are asked to integrate and submit themselves to existing local laws. They are invited to strive for improvement within their societies and seek to increase their prosperity.

Given the current global context, which brings Muslims in permanent contact with other communities, it seems that the justification of a minorities law has lost its validity, if it ever had any. Due to ongoing globalization trends, sociopolitical challenges are increasingly interconnected and transcend state and religious boundaries. Muslims, regardless of the place they live in, are asked to contribute to the solution of modern-day challenges, rather than to focus solely on "Muslim problems." Therefore, the Muslim minorities law should be opened up to include global problems and all human beings. Accordingly, the Islamic minorities law would change into a general minorities law, applicable to minorities of different religious affiliations across the globe. This would give back the long-lost universal dimension to Islamic legal thought. This is due to the fact that the concept of *maqāṣid al-sharīʿah*, which is used nowadays to justify the existence and the need for a new concept of *fiqh al-aqalliyāt* (jurisprudence of minorities), can also be used to demonstrate that the concept of a "Muslim minorities law" can have counterproductive effects on the life and integration of Muslim minorities in the West. This leads to the assumption that developing a specific law, designated for the needs of Muslim minorities in the West, would intensify their isolation rather than solve their problems. Rather than developing a new discipline that develops a special law for Muslims in non-Muslim states which would intensify the isolation of these minorities, there are several reasons for intensifying their cooperation with other minorities and the whole society: This would give Muslims more opportunities to strengthen their own rights and the relation to the whole society. This issue needs a deep understanding of the conceptions of pluralism and plurality which build up the framework for the life and development of minorities in the West. To achieve this task, Muslim scholars in Muslim societies and in the West need to develop innovative legal concepts instead of trying to modify classical legal norms to make them fit to the modern context. It goes without saying that many premodern thoughts, such as the opposition between *dar al-islām* and *dar al-ḥarb* (lands not ruled by Islamic law), the restrictive relationship of Muslims to other religious communities, or the conception of *dhimma* (non-Muslim citizens in an Islamic state) have been revisited, but this revision alone does not lead to a change in situation. As long as Muslim scholars are promoting the Muslim minorities law as a special law for "special Muslim communities"[31] living in diaspora, the problems of these communities will never be solved. Contemporary scholars of Islamic law should view the problems of Muslim minorities in the framework of Western legislation and deal with them alongside and in accordance with leading paradigms of Western social and political thought, such as human rights and pluralism. The ethical values of Islamic law would be considered as a source of guidance together and in interaction with other values. This would reopen the Islamic law to a global dimension, which accords with its original intention.

NOTES

1. Al-Alwani, *muqaddima*, 3.
2. Khalid Abu El Fadl, "Islamic Law and Muslim Minorities: The Juristic Discourse on Muslim Minorities from 8th to 17th Century," in *Islamic Law and Society*, vol. 1 (Leiden: Brill, 1994), 141–87.
3. Khaled Abou El Fadl, "Muslim Minorities and Self-Restraint in Liberal Democracies," *Loyola of Los Angeles Law Review* 6, no.1 (1996): 1524–42.
4. Abou El Fadl, *Islamic Law*.
5. Ibid.
6. Ibid.
7. Ibid.
8. Ibid., 160f.
9. Salah Din Sultan, methodological criteria of the Muslim minorites law, azzawabit al manhajiyya li fiqh al Aqalliyat al Muslima in: http://www.onislam.net/arabic/fiqh-a-tazkia/fiqh-papers/134401–2011–09–15–12–16–36.html. (February 27, 2015).
10. Yusuf Qaradawi, *fiqh al aqalliyat al muslima (The Life of Muslims within Non-Muslim Societies)* (Cairo: *Dar Ash Shourouq*, 2001), 24ff.
11. Many of these scholars come from the Muslim world, and their experience in the West is limited to short moments of residence, or academic journeys. They were not born in Western societies, which sometimes render their knowledge of the West superficial.
12. Abou El Fadl, *Islamic Law*.
13. This is the second part of the title of the book of Yusuf al-Qaradawi: The Life of Muslims within Non-Muslim Societies. Yusuf al-Qaradawi, *fiqh al aqalliyat al muslima (The Life of Muslims within Non-Muslim Societies)* (Cairo: *Dar Ash Shourouq*, 2001).
14. Qaradawi, 2001, 24ff.
15. Ibid.
16. Ibid.
17. Ibid.
18. Al-Alwani, *muqaddima*.

19. Quran 9:60.

20. Al-Alwani (1994) lists those cases in his *Introduction to the Minorities Law*: Alwani, *muqaddima*, 4.

21. Al-Alwani, *muqaddima*.

22. Ibid.

23. Ibid.

24. See the website of the European Council for Fatwa and Research: http://e-cfr.org/new/fatwa/%D8%AA%D8%B9%D8%B1%D9%81%D8%AA-%D8%B9%D9%84%D9%89-%D8%A7%D9%85%D8%B1%D8%A3%D8%A9-%D8%BA%D8%B1%D8%A8%D9%8A%D8%A9-%D8%A7%D8%B9%D8%AA%D9%86%D9%82%D8%AA-%D8%A7%D9%84%D8%A5%D8%B3%D9%84%D8%A7%D9%85%D8%8C-3/. (February 23, 2015).

25. Qaradawi, 2001; Al-Alwani, *muqaddima*.

26. This dualism is frequently reflected in the legal argumentation of the European Council for Fatwa and Research.

27. Sultan, Salah-Din, "Methodological Maxims of the Muslim Minorities' Law," in: http://www.google.de/url?sa=t&rct=j&q=&esrc=s&source=web&cd=6&ved=0CEcQFjAFahUKEwjw7NDe04nGAhVQWdsKHbD5ADk&url=http%3A%2F%2Fwww.saaid.net%2FPowerPoint%2F562.pps&ei=Ho16VfDlNNCy7Qaw84PIAw&usg=AFQjCNFLhPGOoRJtJWZW-ZWynAn2nTyqaw&bvm=bv.95515949,d.bGg. (February 23, 2015).

28. Learning or searching for knowledge was not mentioned in this issue, since Muslim theologians conceived *dār al-islām* as the place of the true knowledge. This issue will change categorically in modern time.

29. Qaradawi, 2001, 24ff.

30. Muhammad at-Tahir Ibn Ashour, *Maqasid ash-Sharia al-Islamiyya (Islamic Maqasid ash-Sharia)* (Amman: Dar an-Nafais, 2001), 197ff.

31. Al-Alwani, *muqaddima*.

BIBLIOGRAPHY

Abou El Fadl, Khaled. "Islamic Law and Muslim Minorities: The Juristic Discourse on Muslim Minorities from 8th to 17th Century." *Islamic Law and Society* 1 (1994): 141–87.

———. "Muslim Minorities and Self-Restraint in Liberal Democracies." *Loyola of Los Angeles Law Review* 6, no. 1 (1996): 1524–42.

Al-Alwani, Taher Jaber. *Muqaddima fi fiqh al-aqalliyāt*. http://www.onislam.net/arabic/madarik/politics/89614–2001–02–11%2014–50–15.html.

al-Tahir Ibn Ashour, Muhammad. *Maqasid ash-Sharia al-Islamiyya (Islamic Maqasid ash-Sharia)*. Amman: Dar an-Nafais, 2001.

Qaradawi, Yusuf. *Fiqh al aqalliyat al Muslima*. Cairo: Dar Ash Shourouq, 2001.

Schlabach, Jörg. *Scharia im Westen*. Berlin: Lit-Verlag, 2009.

Sultan, Salah-Din. *Azzawabit al manhajiyya li fiqh al Aqalliyat al Muslima*. http://www.onislam.net/arabic/fiqh-a-tazkia/fiqh-papers/134401–2011–09–15–12–16–36.html.

———. *Methodological Maximes of the Muslim Minorites Law*. http://www.google.de/url?sa=t&rct=j&q=&esrc=s&source=web&cd=6&ved=0CEcQFjAFahUKEwjw7NDe04nGAhVQWdsKHbD5ADk&url=http%3A%2F%2Fwww.saaid.net%2FPowerPoint%2F562.pps&ei=Ho16VfDlNNCy7Qaw84PIAw&usg=AFQjCNFLhPGOoRJtJWZW-ZWynAn2nTyqaw&bvm=bv.95515949,d.bGg. (February 23, 2015).

Website of the European Council for Fatwa and Research. In: http://e-cfr.org/new/fatwa/%D8%AA%D8%B9%D8%B1%D9%81%D8%AA-%D8%B9%D9%84%D9%89-%D8%A7%D9%85%D8%B1%D8%A3%D8%A9-%D8%BA%D8%B1%D8%A8%D9%8A%D8%A9-%D8%A7%D8%B9%D8%AA%D9%86%D9%82%D8%AA-%D8%A7%D9%84%D8%A5%D8%B3%D9%84%D8%A7%D9%85%D8%8C-3/.

Epilogue

Anver Emon

This collection of chapters on *maqāṣid al-sharīʿa* presents a conversation that has long been overdue. For much of the Muslim-majority world, the twentieth century was a period of reimagining. European colonization, the collapse of the Ottoman Empire, and the various modes of imperial subordination forced the Muslim intellectual elite to rethink the conditions of power, sovereignty, and supremacy in a world in which the glories of an Islamic empire were a painfully distant memory. Whether we call it angst, resentment, or nostalgia, this epilogue attends to the epistemic implications of imagining the content of the "Islamic" in a politically affirming and normative fashion. How does the history of the twentieth and the twenty-first century, with its colonization, and later economic dependency, inform the way the "Islamic" takes shape, by whom, and to what end? When applied to the chapters in this book, that question might be reformulated as: How might we better appreciate the politics that inform and are informed by the technical, legal discussions about *maqāṣid al-sharīʿa*?

In this epilogue, in which I reflect on the chapters in this volume, I suggest that the aspirational accounts of *maqāṣid* reflect a politics of hope. But this hope is itself a product of the elite positionality of those who espouse the virtues of *maqāṣid.* Thinking counterfactually about *maqāṣid* debates from the vantage point of the vulnerable or precariously positioned—as Guy Standing labels them, the "precariate"—it becomes plain to see that the failure of the *maqāṣid* legal technology to produce its long-promised reforms reflects an elitism that has hitherto been unaccounted for. That elitism makes possible an unacknowledged epistemic gap in the chapters of this volume that espouse the possibility, if not the virtue, of the *maqāṣid* approach. The chapters that uphold the promise of *maqāṣid* underappreciate both the *epistemic* and the *material* gap between redressing the law of the state, with its effects on the bodies of its most vulnerable subjects, and espousing the grandiose, if not overly pious, notions of justice intellectuals invest in their *maqāṣid* endorsements. Methodologically, we might characterize the gap as the difference between thinking about "law from the heavenly above" and "law from the earthly below." Politically, we might describe the gap as the difference between the elite and the underclass, where the discourse of *maqāṣid*, far from being a reformative device, is actually an elite discourse that ensures the compliance and conciliation of an underclass to the conditions of their precarity.

HOPE

Among the chapters promoting *maqāṣid* in this volume, the sentiment of hope is supremely at play. Advocates of *maqāṣid* remain convinced that *maqāṣid al-sharīʿa* offers a method of reform that can redress the calamities of the Muslim-majority world, respond to changing conditions, and speak *back to* and *with* dominant discourses in a distinctively Islamic lexicon. For instance, Mohammad Hashim Kamali writes in his contribution: "*Maqāṣid* are inherently dynamic . . . and open to growth in tandem with changing conditions, just as they are also seen to strike a closer note with the contemporary rights discourse."[1] Jasser Auda starts his chapter by claiming that the *maqāṣid* "could contribute to the application of *sharīʿah* in today's Muslim societies and to making the appropriate related juridical policies."[2] Kamali's insistence on the *maqāṣid* as "inherently dynamic," "open," and correlated with contemporary rights discourses betrays his hope that the *maqāṣid* provide a way of engaging the challenges of modernity without the heavy baggage of an Islamic tradition often considered antiquated, inflexible, and anything but dynamic. Auda's qualified hesitation, evinced by his use of "could," reveals the mere hope that underlies his long-standing scholarly commitment to *maqāṣid* as an affirmative, normative methodology. *Maqāṣid* may or could change things, but history has shown that it hasn't (though Auda might retort that it hasn't . . . *yet*).

Habib Ahmed, criticizing Islamic banking and finance for failing to fulfill the *maqāṣid* of the *sharīʿa*, nonetheless expresses a pious hope that a more macro-oriented *maqāṣid* approach would ensure a more systemic implementation of, what economists might call welfare-state economics. This macro-*maqāṣid* approach would chart new ground away from the current microeconomic, private contract, and firm orientations of Islamic banking and finance. Advocating for *maqāṣid*-informed environmental, social, and governance factors (ESG factors, in the technical discourse on ethics and firm management), Ahmed assumes (better yet, hopes) that by being part of the "moral economy and following the *sharīʿah* principles, the nature of the responsibilities of Islamic firms, including Islamic financial institutions, is expected to be imbued with the principles of the *maqāṣid*."[3] Importantly, Ahmed's use of the passive tense, "is expected to be imbued," raises poignant questions of who expects, who polices, who ensures compliance, and why. If the answer is little more than the metaphorical invisible hand of Adam Smith, then it is hard to see his hope for the *maqāṣid* as little more than the pious, neoclassical faith in the profit-maximizing firm of microeconomics, which is politically correct about issues like the environment when profitable. But why consumers would care about the environment more than the competitive prices of goods has little to do with either microeconomics or *maqāṣid* analysis, and instead rests in his hope that international nongovernmental organizations (NGOs), like the Organization of Islamic Cooperation (OIC), will dictate a *maqāṣid* foundation for consumer preferences. For him, such a dictate, clothed with the technical legal discourse of the International Fiqh Academy, "can help guide the industry to go beyond negative screening and introduce positive screenings that would consider environmental, social and cultural aspects in Islamic financing and investments."[4] The requirement for a dictate from the OIC, however clothed in the technicalities of *fiqh*, reveal the poverty of *maqāṣid* as a universal, reason-based mode of legal reform.

To characterize this advocacy of *maqāṣid* as premised upon the effect of hope, allows us to highlight the work, both political and epistemic, that hope does in promoting and sustaining the *maqāṣid* discourse. Hope allows advocates to gloss over the fact that the often-detailed method of *maqāṣid* reasoning has yielded little fruit. Such failures are instead described as the result of failing to implement the *maqāṣid* technique correctly. This hope is expressed in the subjunctive mood, through phrases that imply hope in the midst of failure: *if only* we understood the *maqāṣid* model or formula, then the objectives of the *sharīʿa* would be realized. *If only* is the counterfactual that makes hope in *maqāṣid* possible. But in making that hope possible, it precludes a more fundamental question about whether the *maqāṣid* are able to deliver on the promises of its ardent advocates.

Arguably, the *maqāṣid* cannot deliver on their promises because of what the rhetoric of hope hides, namely the elitism and privileged status of those who have the luxury to espouse hope in *maqāṣid*. In other words, to examine the *maqāṣid* debates from the perspective of *hope* allows us to ask, who has the luxury to hope? In his exceptional study of Iranian youth, Shahram Khosravi deploys an affective analysis of hope to understand the politics of domination implicit in it.[5] Writing about the widening gap between the rich and poor in Iran, and between the younger postrevolutionary generations and those who came before, Khosravi eloquently articulates how hope can become an instrument to secure the compliance of otherwise vulnerable subjects.

> A popular quote used by Iranians comes from Franz Kafka—"there is hope, but not for us"—cynical words from a German-speaking Jew living in Prague, who embodied the continuum of exclusion in early twentieth-century Europe. . . . Young Iranians do not feel hopeless because there is no hope (there is for others) but simply because they lack the entitlement to hope.[6]

Referring to scholars such as Ghassan Hage, Khosravi describes Iranian youth culture to showcase how hope informs an affective politics in the service of the already-elite structures of power and privilege. Australian scholar Ghassan Hage turns to the affective politics of hope in the context of the Australian state and the neoconservative turn away from a compassionate and inclusive politics toward, for instance, refugees. In doing so, Hage argues that the state's capacity to "distribute hope in the midst of massive social inequality has been the secret of the nation-state's enduring ability to sustain capitalist accumulation."[7] Indeed, preserving the nation-state and the capitalist system it makes possible depends upon an effective distribution of hope, despite the overt inequality that foments social discontent. He writes:

> Societal hope, which is . . . about one's sense of the possibilities that life can offer, is not necessarily related to an income level. Its enemy is a sense of entrapment, of having nowhere to go, not a sense of poverty. As the state withdraws from society and the existing configuration of hope begins shrinking, many people . . . have begun suffering various forms of hope scarcity.[8]

Hope offers a provocative standpoint from which to examine the advocacy of *maqāṣid* because of how the implicit (and often explicit) discourse of "hope" in *maqāṣid* debates allows *maqāṣid* advocates to overcome critiques, gloss over details, and render history as exceptional rather than a predictive. Hope, which can include fantasy or an aspirational sense of the future, allows advocates of *maqāṣid* to ignore inconvenient facts, the elitism of their own positionality, and the implications of that elite positionality on the capacity to hope at all, given how the capacity to hope may be unequally distributed.[9] The organizing principle of hope puts into stark relief the difference between the elite and the underclass, in part by allowing us to ask who has the greatest reserves of hope, who has the least reserves of it, and who is doing the giving? Most *maqāṣid* advocates take aim at the state, with the implication that the state does not give hope, but rather takes it away. In the context of *maqāṣid* debates, the hope-givers are those who promise to deliver on Islamic ideals of justice when the evidence suggests that the problem of justice is more complicated than ever. But to hope and to give hope is the stuff of an elite positionality that remains elite by virtue of a range of systemic factors (e.g., access to capital, education, and gendered study circles) that rarely constitute targets of *maqāṣid* debates. An elite positionality gives advocates of *maqāṣid* a surplus of hope to disperse to the less hopeful in order to convince them that there remain reasons to hope, wish, and anticipate an alternative (better) future. But to continue to wish or hope while experiencing deprivation in the details of mundanity is actually to wait. But, waiting is not the same as hoping. Rather, to wait is to enact one's compliance. Drawing upon Pierre Bourdieu, Khosravi suggests as much when he states, "To keep people waiting and enduring hardship without ruining their hope is an exercise of power over their time."[10] To identify hope with an exercise of power is to beg the question of how that power gets deployed or implemented.

MAQĀṢID AS TECHNIQUE, TECHNIQUE AS DISCIPLINARY

The language of hope is explicit in some of the chapters in this volume. Importantly, it is also implicit in the way others focus on *maqāṣid* as a technical method, whose proclaimed objectivity is the site of hope for the promise of change. But that objectivity, however technically articulated, serves as a smokescreen for the already-elite status of those who offer *maqāsid* as a hope to those who have reason to be hopeless. How often have elite scholars of Islam chided Muslims for not studying the tradition, not knowing their history, and not understanding the techniques of Islamic legal reasoning? It is fair, of course, to raise questions about the provincial nature of higher education and the politics of canonization that preclude meaningful study of Islam today. But it is also fair to suggest that the rhetoric elite scholars of Islam have historically used to describe the general, non-specialist Muslims (in Arabic, often pejoratively called the *ʿāmma*) is designed to preserve the elite status of those very scholars, in part by devaluing the voices of those who do not enjoy such elite status. This is not unique to Islam or Muslim elites.

Method and technique are the characteristic foci of those who advocate for *maqāṣid*. In this volume, the contributions by Kamali and Auda are almost entirely focused on defining terms and explaining techniques. This focus on method and technique is premised upon the subjunctive mood of hope, namely that *if only* one understood the technique or method of *maqāṣid*, the ultimate objectives of the law (whatever they may be) would be achieved. As Auda states at the outset of his chapter, "[c]ontemporary applications of the *sharīʿah* in any given Muslim society or juridical polity require a methodology that represents the universality and flexibility of the *sharīʿah* with changing circumstances."[11] The claim to universality as the hallmark of *shariʿah*, of course, goes against more recent scholarship that highlights the pragmatism that characterizes the practice of legal judgment in Islamic adjudications.[12] But it promises, or more poignantly, offers the hope of objectivity in the search for the law. To emphasize technique and technicality is to indulge in the presumption of objectivity, which when viewed from the perspective of an affective politics, casts the *maqāṣid* as prepolitical. When Mohammad Nekroumi pursues a positivist historical search of *maqāṣid* as a premodern method of analysis, the positivism in his historical inquiry serves the objectivity, and hope, of *maqāṣid's* promise. Despite attempting to contextualize the *maqāṣid* in a manner that avoids the politics of hope, he nonetheless provides, as he states, an "overview of the hermeneutical potential contained in the *maqāṣid* theory."[13] Between technique and hermeneutics, *maqāṣid* is cast as if it were both a scientific technique and lever of change. Focusing on objectivity and technicality covers the distributional politics of hope; advocating *maqāṣid*'s hermeneutic potential preserves the hope that might otherwise dissipate if the historicist enterprise takes the *maqāṣid* to its most particularist, if not deconstructed, extreme.

The distributional implications of hope in *maqāṣid* can be both profound and painful, as Ayesha S. Chaudhry shows. Examining the possibilities of *maqāṣid* reasoning takes her to positions on *nasl* (lineage) that she also shows are utterly disavowed by more conservative voices, suggesting that one cannot disentangle a patriarchal cosmology of Islam from the aspirational characterization of *maqāṣid.* Of course, this does not mean the *maqāṣid* are always and at all times captured by an implicit conservatism or paternalism. Adis Duderija's contribution shows how a progressive politics, coupled with a thematic approach to Qur'anic reasoning, can expand the scope of *maqāṣid's* reach. But his chapter perpetuates the fantasy or hope of *maqāṣid* by indulging in, again in a subjunctive mood, a technical discussion of method. Duderija, whose progressive commitments are part of his intellectual self-definition, turns to technique and method to generate universal values. Yet, in his chapter, he remains silent on the political vision that will, no matter what one's starting point, inform which values are deemed universal and particular, and which applications are considered acceptable and unacceptable. As Cefli Ademi's chapter suggests, abstracting the *maqāṣid* from the larger context of *uṣūl al-fiqh* (principles of Islamic jurisprudence) has a distorting effect, which plays into the affective politics of hope and its implications of waiting-compliance for those who might otherwise not have the resources to wait much longer.

PRECARITY

This section begins with a term that has increasingly informed much academic debate about the disenfranchized, the marginal, and the vulnerable in our society. While the academy is notorious at times for its "highfalutin" jargon, behind those terms are perspectives, angles, and approaches that warrant consideration and reflection. Indeed, in the field of Islamic legal studies, whose disciplinary formation lies in the historically positivist field of philology, such consideration is not only long past due, but has the potential of stifling novelty, innovation, and creativity.[14]

Of course, what we might call "creativity" or "innovation" in academic parlance might sound like *bid'a* (innovation) to a Sunni Muslim committed to a theological orthodoxy that proclaims Truth by policing boundaries through castigations such as *bid'a* and *ilḥād* (deviation). Ironically, one approach of theological policing in this field happens to adopt the scientific focus on methodology that parallels, if not draws upon, the historical positive approach of philology. The chapters that focus on method and technique draw upon a lexicon of terms, definitions, and juristic explanations, as if the claim of justice is self-evident from such texts and terms of art. One cannot escape the implication that such an approach to justice, with its focus on technique and method, both avoid the history of *maqāṣid*'s failures and police Muslims into a state of orthodox compliance by reference to a method that those with access to education claim to know and represent. Policing, in this fashion, is very much an enterprise of defining Islam or Islamic law from the top-down. Many disciplines adopt such an approach. Political scientists often reflect on the state, whether in terms of sovereignty (see, Carl Schmidt) or bureaucracy (see, Max Weber and, more recently, Theda Skocpol), or political economy and rational choice theory. In doing so, they render citizens and legal subjects as constants who are devalued in terms of the salience of their voice in the construction of the state to which they are subject.

As anthropologists of Islam have suggested, however, an "Islam from below" approach can yield a range of important insights about how Muslims make meaning for themselves in the complex, but also very ordinary, day-to-day ways in which life takes place and shape. Charles Hirschkind and Noah Salomon have examined the "soundscapes" of Egypt and Sudan to reflect on the experience and meaning of Islam in the cafes, taxis, and alleyways of Muslim majority states.[15] The voices in these spaces articulate an image of the "Islamic" that is not often present (let alone valued) in the more top-down studies of Islam. This is not to suggest that philology or the study of classical texts is irrelevant; rather it means that such approaches to Islamic legal studies are partial at best and potentially overdeterminative of what counts as "Islamic." Moreover, they are frequently subject to capture by those pursuing coercive, if not outright oppressive, policies that work on the bodies of the already vulnerable who, like zombies in today's popular media, seem to lack a voice to be heard and a will to be respected.

Muna Tatari's intervention in this volume is an important reminder of the need to remain vigilant toward the starting assumptions that inform what is and is not "Islamic."[16] Her turn to the history of Islamic theology and her juxtaposition of it with developments in political theory offers an important example of revisiting the borders of orthodoxy, the police powers granted to some, and the vulnerability of others to such policing. Felicitas Opwis' historical reading of Ibn ʿAshūr recognizes the importance of the modern state as conditioning what he meant by *maqāṣid,* or in other words, who could utilize it within one substantive law area as opposed to others.[17] Mouez Khalfaoui takes aim at *maqāṣid* when applied to Muslims living as minorities. The reality of the modern state, with its porous borders and immigration flows, raises fundamental questions about whether and to what extent attention to the *maqāṣid* actually orientalizes, and thereby marginalizes, Muslim communities in the West. Perhaps advocates of *maqāṣid* do not fully appreciate how such focused attention on that mode of reasoning may also have insulating implications that actually prevent Muslim communities in the West from being more actively engaged citizens.[18] And finally, Rumee Ahmed's elegant but poignant chapter is a painful illustration of the fruit such critical reexamination can yield if we remain vigilant toward the vulnerable and marginal, whose bodies and minds get policed into compliance with a system of capitalism that will never deliver them from the margins. In this case, *maqāṣid* not only preserves this economic status quo, but it also demands that those already on the margins remain compliant or on the "right" side of the policed border, which in the parlance of Islamic economics is located wherever a capital investor places the *halāl* (permissible) label on a product for consumption. Opwis and Khalfaoui "bring the state back in"[19] to provide a contextual approach that locates the operation of the *maqāṣid*; Ahmed and Tatari exercise a vigilance on the margins to appreciate the impact of *maqāṣid* in a complex institutional environment as it enacts itself on the bodies and minds of Muslims who might want something different, but are policed into silence. This sort of contextualization and critique make no appearance, for instance, when Younes Soualhi casts Islamic contract law as committed to the free market capitalist principle of the free flow of money,[20] a principle that has informed free market capitalism since Adam Smith's critique of mercantilism.[21]

This brings me back to the academic jargon that heads this section: precarity, and its related terms such as "precarious" and the "precariat."[22] The value of this particular constellation of terms lies in their demand upon us to account for those on the margins, those who are vulnerable. Khosravi helpfully explains the academic salience of the term:

> Originally the term *precarity* was used to depict a work condition without predictability or security in post-Fordist capitalism. It has been used to summarize contemporary neoliberal labor relations in postindustrial societies, irregular employment, vulnerability and "flexploitation."[23]

In the context of the Gulf countries, as well as European ones, "precarity" would be an apt term to apply to the plight of migrant laborers. In the Gulf, these laborers come from India, Pakistan, Bangladesh, and the Philippines, and work in conditions where they have few rights (political, civil, and otherwise) and limited mobility.[24] In Europe, Muslim migrants likewise struggle under a legal regime that has waffled on the scope of their political rights.[25] Precarity in these contexts demands that we take seriously the systemic ways in which the conditions of such vulnerability are enabled and normalized. When *maqāṣid* is viewed through the lens of precarity, the impetus will arguably shift to examine not only the limits of the *maqāṣid* enterprise, but also (and most importantly) who bears the costs of those limits. Indeed, R. Ahmed's critique resonates so poignantly because it identifies the already marginalized as those who *also* bear the costs of the politics of hope that inform *maqāṣid* analyses. While one can appreciate Yusuf al-Qaradawi's contribution to the discourse on *maqāṣid*, so too can we be curious about his ability to indulge the hope of such a discourse when he enjoys both the status of an *ʿālim* (scholar) and the wealth that comes from enabling joint venturers, private equity fund managers, and shareholders to profit where they can. Likewise, Ayesha S. Chaudhry's examination of *nasl* showcases the patriarchy that polices the limits of *maqāṣid*, with the powerful implication that women in particular bear the brunt of such policing and coercion. These implications, which can be captured disciplinarily through inquiries broadly dispersed through the humanities and social sciences, call for a consideration of *maqāṣid* that does not idolize remarkable jurists such as al-Ghazālī or al-Shāṭibī, or indulge with lexical glee the nuances of various Arabic terms of art, as much of *maqāṣid* discourse has done to date.

THINKING COUNTERFACTUALLY

One way to pierce the veil of hope that informs the current state of *maqāṣid* advocacy is to consider how one might inquire into the purpose and aims of the law, as if *maqāṣid* were not part of the tradition. In other words, rather than simply assuming *maqāṣid* as a given or a constant that must simply be understood better, what if *maqāṣid* were the variable? As a variable, we can then ask what happens when it changes or even disappears. To render *maqāṣid* as a variable is to think counterfactually, which in turn promises greater appreciation of the work (legal, political, and otherwise) that the *maqāṣīd* methodological architecture does. To think counterfactually is to appreciate the salience of the historical tradition, and from that standpoint to wonder and ponder what sorts of conversational space we might reside in were it not the case that al-Shāṭibī or al-Ghazālī presented the methodological architecture of *maqāṣid*. In other words, to think counterfactually is to adopt, akin to advocates of *maqāṣid* but in a different register, the subjunctive mood of hope while at all times attending to the reality against which we think subjunctively.

Thinking counterfactually will immediately raise the hackles of those who see in the *maqāṣid* method a manner of disciplining or policing the boundaries of orthodoxy and acceptability. That immediate reaction is itself a revelation of the politics of *maqāṣid* discourse, and by implication the positionality of those who seek to normalize that policing function. Their presumed reaction reveals *maqāṣid* as a disciplinary mechanism to forestall reflection, in an unchecked manner, on the purposes of the law. That disciplinary, policing orientation, as I have shown elsewhere, existed in the initial formulation of the *maqāṣid* approach. Al-Ghazālī, when articulating the rationale for adopting the *maqāṣid* model, argued that it prevented abiding Ashʿarī Sunnis from taking the path of heterodoxy through Muʿtazila rationality.[26] The possibility of a policing backlash only emphasizes the importance of bringing into play any subjunctive, counterfactual space of analysis. To play openly and effectively implies that we set down the intellectual batons used to police the boundaries of what counts as "Islamic" or "orthodox." It is not an invitation to anti-intellectualism, or a rejection of the historical tradition, literary or otherwise. Quite the contrary, it is a license to hope.

NOTES

1. Mohammad Hashim Kamali, "Goals and Purposes *Maqāṣid al-Sharīʿa* [*sic*]: Methodological Perspectives," in this volume.
2. Jasser Auda, "Realising *Maqāṣid* in the *Sharīʿah*," in this volume.
3. Habib Ahmed, "The Challenge Facing Islamic Banking and Finance: Has It Moved Away From Its Core Objectives, With Special Reference to *Maqāṣid*?," in this volume.
4. Ibid.
5. The Iranian example is useful here in part to reveal the implicit sectarian politics of *maqāṣid* debates, where the Shīʿa and their Jaʿfarī jurisprudence are excluded from consideration, parallel analysis, or commentary.
6. Shahram Khosravi, *Precarious Lives: Waiting and Hope in Iran* (Philadelphia: University of Pennsylvania Press, 2017), 13.
7. Ghassan Hage, *Against Paranoid Nationalism: Searching for Hope in a Shrinking Society* (London: Merlin Press, 2003), 14.
8. Hage, *Against Paranoid Nationalism,* 20.
9. Ibid., 12.
10. Khosravi, *Precarious Lives*, 14.
11. Auda, "Realising *Maqāṣid* in the *Sharīʿah*," in this volume.

12. See, for instance, Ahmed Fekry Ibrahim, *Pragmatism in Islamic Law: A Social and Intellectual History* (Syracuse, NY: Syracuse University Press, 2015).

13. Mohammed Nekroumi, "The Hermeneutical Approach of Shāṭibī on the Basis of the *Maqāṣid* Definition of Reason," in this volume.

14. On the limits of philology in the study of Islamic law, see Anver M. Emon, "Fiqh," in *Oxford Handbook of Islamic Law*, eds. Rumee Ahmed and Anver M. Emon (Oxford: Oxford University Press, 2017)

15. Charles Hirschkind, *The Ethical Soundscape: Cassette Sermons and Islamic Counterpublics* (New York: Columbia University Press, 2009); Noah Salomon, *For Love of the Prophet: An Ethnography of Sudan's Islamic State* (Princeton, NJ: Princeton University Press, 2016).

16. Muna Tatari, "Reason and Revelation: A Meaningful Contribution to Contemporary Ethical Debates in a Secular Context," in this volume.

17. Felicitas Opwis, "Ibn ʿĀshūr's Interpretation of the Purposes of the Law (*Maqāṣid al-Sharīʿa*): An Islamic Modernist Approach to Legal Change," in this volume.

18. Mouez Khalfaoui, "*Maqāṣid al-Sharīʿah* as a Legitimization for the Muslim Minorities Law," in this volume.

19. Peter B. Evans, Dietrich Rueschemeyer, and Theda Skocpol, eds., *Bringing the State Back In* (Cambridge: Cambridge University Press, 1985).

20. Younes Soualhi, "*Maqāṣid al-Sharīʿah* in Islamic Contracts: A Study of Current Practices of Islamic Finance in Light of Islamic Legal Maxims," in this volume.

21. Adam Smith, *The Wealth of Nations* (New York: Bantam Classics, 2003).

22. Guy Standing, "The Precariat," *Contexts* 13, no. 4 (Fall 2014): 10–12.

23. Khosravi, *Precarious Lives*, 4.

24. See for instance, the special issue on labor and migration in the Middle East, *Middle East Law and Governance* 5, no. 1–2 (2013).

25. On Germany, for instance, see Sandra Bucerius, *Unwanted: Muslim Immigrants, Dignity and Drug Dealing* (Oxford: Oxford University Press, 2014).

26. See, Anver M. Emon, *Islamic Natural Law Theories* (Oxford: Oxford University Press, 2010).

BIBLIOGRAPHY

Bucerius, Sandra. *Unwanted: Muslim Immigrants, Dignity and Drug Dealing*. Oxford: Oxford University Press, 2014.

Emon, Anver M. "Fiqh." In *Oxford Handbook of Islamic Law*, edited by Rumee Ahmed and Anver M. Emon. Oxford: Oxford University Press, 2017.

———. *Islamic Natural Law Theories*. Oxford: Oxford University Press, 2010.

Evans, Peter B., Rueschemeyer, Dietrich, Skocpol, Theda, eds. *Bringing the State Back In*. Cambridge: Cambridge University Press, 1985.

Fekry Ibrahim, Ahmed. *Pragmatism in Islamic Law: A Social and Intellectual History*. Syracuse, NY: Syracuse University Press, 2015.

Guy Standing. "The Precariat." *Contexts* 13, no. 4 (2014): 10–12.

Hage, Ghassan. *Against Paranoid Nationalism: Searching For Hope in a Shrinking Society*. London: Merlin Press, 2003.
Hirschkind, Charles. *The Ethical Soundscape: Cassette Sermons and Islamic Counterpublics*. New York: Columbia University Press, 2009.
Khosravi, Shahram. *Precarious Lives: Waiting and Hope in Iran*. Philadelphia: University of Pennsylvania Press, 2017.
Middle East Law and Governance 5, no. 1–2 (2013).
Salomon, Noah. *For Love of the Prophet: An Ethnography of Sudan's Islamic State*. Princeton, NJ: Princeton University Press, 2016.
Smith, Adam. *The Wealth of Nations*. New York: Bantam Classics, 2003.

Index

About the Contributors

Cefli Ademi is a postdoctoral fellow in the Center of Islamic Theology at the University of Münster, Germany. His research interests include Islamic jurisprudence in the German context, pluralism in Islamic jurisprudence, and Islamic theories of law, philosophy, and epistemology.

Habib Ahmed is professor of Islamic law and Sharjah Chair in Islamic Law and Finance at the Durham University Business School, United Kingdom. His research interests include Islamic economics and finance, contemporary applications of Islamic commercial law, nonprofit organizations, and endowments (awqāf).

Rumee Ahmed is associate dean of arts and associate professor of Islamic law at the University of British Columbia, Canada. His research interests include law and legal theory, Qur'anic studies, Islamic theology, and scriptural reasoning.

Jasser Auda is Distinguished Professor of Islamic law at the Universiti Brunei, Darussalam. His scholarship examines the relationship between the *maqāṣid al-sharī'ah* and the Qur'an and Sunnah.

Ayesha S. Chaudhry is the Canada Research Chair in Religion, Law, and Social Justice and Associate Professor of Islamic and gender studies at the University of British Columbia, Canada, where she sits on the Board of Governors. Her research interests include religion, Islamic law, social justice, religious feminisms, classical Islam, reformist Islamic thought, and gender studies.

Adis Duderija is lecturer of Islam and society in the School of Humanities, Languages, and Social Science at Griffith University, Australia. His research interests include progressive Islam, western Muslims' identity construction, contemporary Islamic hermeneutics, and interfaith dialogue and interreligious hermeneutics.

Anver Emon is the Canada Research Chair in religion, pluralism, and the Rule of Law, and professor of Islamic law in the Faculty of Law at the University of Toronto, Canada. His research interests include critical legal theory, Islamic law, judicial decision-making, law and religion, legal history, and legal theory.

Mohammad Hashim Kamali is professor of Islamic law and founding CEO of the International Institute of Advanced Islamic Studies in Malaysia. His research interests include Islamic legal studies, ḥadīth studies, and sharīʿah law.

Mouez Khalfaoui is professor and chair of Islamic law in the Centre for Islamic Theology at the Eberhard Karls University of Tübingen, Germany. His research interests include Islamic theology, Islamic law and history, minority rights, Arabic and Islamic writing, Islamic religious education, and social, economic, and practical ethics.

Muhammad Khalid Masud was professor of Islamic law and ad hoc member of the Shariat Appellate Bench of the Supreme Court of Pakistan, and former director general of the Islamic Research Institute at the International Islamic University, Islamabad, Pakistan. His research interests include Islamic law and Islamic legal philosophy.

Idris Nassery is a postdoctoral fellow in the Institute of Islamic Theology at Paderborn University, Germany. His research interests include comparative law, legal history and philosophy, *uṣūl al-fiqh*, *qawā'id fiqhiyya*, and *maqāṣid al-sharī'ah.*

Mohammed Nekroumi is professor and chair of text analysis and jurisprudence at the University of Tübingen, Germany, with emphasis on textual studies and standard sciences. His research interests include hermeneutics of the Qur´ān and *ḥadīth*, Islamic law, Islamic jurisprudence, and theological ethics.

Felicitas Opwis is associate professor and chair of Arabic and Islamic studies in the Department of Arabic and Islamic Studies at Georgetown University.

Her research interests include Islamic jurisprudence, and the relationship between Islamic legal theory and intellectual discourse in fields like politics and society.

Younes Soualhi is a Professor and Senior Researcher at the International Shariah Research Academy for Islamic Finance (ISRA) and a lecturer at the Global University of Islamic Finance(INCEIF), Malaysia. His research interests include *maqāṣid al-sharīʿah*, *uṣūl al-fiqh*, and Islamic banking and finance.

Muna Tatari is assistant professor of Islamic systematic theology in the Institute of Islamic Theology at the University of Paderborn, Germany. Her research interests include classical and modern Islamic theology (kalām), the relationship between faith and practice, epistemology, and comparative theology.

Lightning Source UK Ltd.
Milton Keynes UK
UKHW011846250320
360855UK00003B/319

9 781498 549936